ASSESSMENT
AND **ESL**

BARBARA LAW • MARY ECKES

ASSESSMENT
AND ESL

AN ALTERNATIVE APPROACH

SECOND EDITION

PORTAGE & MAIN PRESS

© 2007 by Barbara Law and Mary Eckes

Portage and Main Press acknowledges the financial support of the Government of Canada through the Book Publishing Industry Development Program (BPIDP) for our publishing activities.

Cover and text design: Relish Design Studio LTD.

Printed and bound in Canada by Kromar

LIBRARY AND ARCHIVES CANADA CATALOGUING IN PUBLICATION

Law, Barbara, 1950-
    Assessment and ESL : an alternative approach / Barbara Law, Mary Eckes.

Includes bibliographical references and index.
ISBN 978-1-55379-093-8

    1. English language – Study and teaching as a second language – Evaluation.
I. Eckes, Mary, 1954- II. Title.

PE1128.A2L37 2007   428.007   C2006-906175-0

PORTAGE & MAIN PRESS

100 – 318 McDermot Ave.
Winnipeg, MB Canada R3A 0A2
Email: books@portageandmainpress.com
Tel: 204-987-3500
Toll-free: 1-800-667-9673
Toll-free fax: 1-866-734-8477

Printed on 30% PCW paper.

CONTENTS

PREFACE **TO THE SECOND EDITION** (2007)

It was January, the start of an endless, miserable slog through winter. The excitement and anticipation of Christmas was over, and it was a long way until spring. The first week back was study-for-finals week. The material that the state curriculum framework had deemed important had to be reviewed. The second week was devoted to exams. Other middle schools across the city administered the exams in the mornings and students went home for the afternoons. But this was a K-8 building; the principal informed the middle-school team that they were considered an elementary school, and kids had to stay at school. The students were resentful. Most of the afternoons were wasted.

Two weeks later, all seventh and eighth graders across the state took the mandated standardized test by which students, schools, districts and, ultimately, the state, were judged. Tension ran at an all-time high. Everything rode on those scores. Schools were required to have a 95% attendance rate. Teachers at this school were not allowed to test on Mondays or Fridays. They could only test in the mornings. All teachers were given yogurt and string cheese to make sure students received proper nutrition and would not fade out during the exams.

what if they are lactose intorelent 😣, this isn't considering all the needs of the students.

On that first Tuesday, part one of a three-day segment began. Students were given the entire morning to read a selection of prose, answer some questions, and formulate a rough draft of an essay response. Most finished in forty-five minutes, some even less. Now what? No teaching was supposed to happen during testing days.

On Wednesday, schools were closed due to heavy snow. On Thursday, the principal had a hurried meeting with the middle-school teachers. They could not decide whether to continue with the test or wait until the following Tuesday. Barb said they should just get it over with.

Ten lashes with a soggy score sheet for being politically incorrect. "Get it over with" was not the right attitude to have with these tests. With so much riding on their outcome, they were serious business. The stakes were too high.

So, the middle-level team had to fill up the following Thursday, Friday and Monday with other "stuff," struggling to go on in this disjointed way, to attempt to continue with the curriculum until they could begin testing again the following Tuesday. It did not work: school essentially stopped; no learning happened. Days were filled by playing games, corralling students, and keeping them from running rampant. No matter how many times students were told to relax and just do their best, the strain got to them, manifesting itself in abominable antics.

Five weeks of learning lost—wasted—at the most productive time of year. No amount of yogurt and string cheese was going to make up for lost time in the classroom. And the future of the school and the students was hinging on their scores on this test.

The worst part was that they did not have a prayer. This was a poor, inner-city school made up mostly of African American and Hispanic kids. The highest score on the Gates MacGinitie Reading Test the year before had been a 67.

This meant the school would be punished. By engineering mergers with two other inner-city schools, the principal had managed to sidestep the baseline scores needed to establish where the school was to begin tracking progress and put off documenting adequate yearly progress (AYP) for two more years. But sooner or later it would be time to pay the piper, because it was doubtful that, without serious fudging and padding of scores, they would ever meet AYP.

It was not that teachers did not do their darndest to make school interesting and filled with enriching experiences. It was not because students did not try their hearts out. It was not because of the classic, parents-do-not-care excuse trotted out by people living in the suburbs who have never set foot in an inner-city school.

It was because the school was poor. Students did not have easy access to museums and zoos, trips to other states and abroad, the wealth of books in the home that most of us take for granted. It was because classroom books had been amassed from libraries that had closed, many of them too musty to open. It was because the only computer in the classroom belonged to the teacher, and students were forbidden to use it (unless the doors were locked, the window covered, and the vice-principal known to be out of the building). It was because students missed school when they moved from place to place because they were evicted or because they had returned to their home countries for the holidays. It was because many of the parents did not speak English and did not know how to help their children. Or, because they worked long hours and were too tired when they got home.

These are what Mary Myers (2003) calls "rigged outcomes" for English language learners (ELLs). The tests are an "expensive charade, racist in effect," which end up marginalizing students. This is not the "soft bigotry of low expectations" George W. Bush trumpeted during his 2000 and 2004 Presidential campaigns. It is the hard racism of punishing the victim, of narrowing the curriculum, and of driving creative teachers out of the very classrooms in which they are needed most.

At the same time, across the state, fifth graders were taking the science portion of the state test. When you read some of their answers to the questions, you can immediately

[handwritten margin note, left:] This sounds a lot like my students, not the all innercity school, but my kids.

[handwritten margin note, right:] ← sounds like the article "Is it real for all kids" from week #1.

see what was wrong with the test. In those answers, you can see logic ("If the earth didn't have water, everyone would dehijrate."), creativity ("The force working on the box is worker C. One way to reduce the force is to tell worker C to take a lunch break or something."), thoughtfulness ("The earth and sun give us light, heat and peace on earth."), common sense ("If people lived on the sun they would get blind and very hot! The sun would burn us up really bad."), humor ("The earth have life and making more."), and clear voices ("If the earth didn't have clothes I don't know what I'd do!"). But none of that mattered. If the student wrote "similarity" when he clearly meant "difference," the answer was wrong. Complete sentences did not matter, while three correct words could receive a score of three points.

Knowing how the students labored over these exams makes it even harder to bear. Thinking about them all writing neatly, reaching out to an unknown reader ("Wow!" wrote one, "Trees sure are valuable resources!" and "Try to stay focused on what I'll be telling you," admonished another), revealing little glimpses of their personalities is, in its own way, heartbreaking. Danielle, for instance, did well. She scored 3s on all her answers. She was one of an average of 1 in 100 kids across the state of Michigan who scored all 3s—a whopping .001%. Antonio scored a couple of 2s and two 0s. Melissa got three 0s and a 1. What do those scores mean? Does it mean Danielle had a good teacher and Melissa had a bad one? Does it mean the teachers ignored the curriculum for the year? Does it mean the teachers should lose their jobs? *H - No*

The scores scrutinized by the government on tests such as these do not take into account any of the reasons students might not have achieved the right answers. They are simply scores, hard and fast. Schools can stand or fall based on them. And, in some states, individual scores matter such that some students cannot graduate based on the score they achieved on the state test.

When we first wrote *Assessment and ESL*, alternative assessment was riding a wave of enthusiasm and positive potential. We were optimistic that we could use information gained on-site to make important decisions about the lives and futures of our students.

Since then, alternative assessment has been all but thrust into the back of the broom closet by a steamroller of mandated standardized testing and the agendas of politicos who have little or no experience with learners and what actually goes on in the classroom. And, although the purposes of testing have not changed, their reach, their uses, and their power have.

In spite of the challenges educators face since the first edition of this book, we still insist on more accurate, fair and reasonable ways of determining what students know and can do, as well as more effective methods both for placement of students into programs that suit their individual learning needs and for timely exit from those programs, back into the mainstream classroom.

This is why we have revised our book. It is, admittedly, angrier, more defiant, and filled with more stories of frustration and heavyheartedness. But it is also filled with great stories of success, of students who began with baby steps, progressed in leaps and bounds toward proficiency, and eventually, learned to fly on their own.

This book is about the adrenaline rush of seeing a kid finally get it. It is about being able to say, "I know what his test scores say, but let me show you what he *really* can do." It is about

Not everything that can be counted counts. —Albert Einstein

NCLB

hence the two prefaces

point to be heard

Yeah, I love that genre. Now I have a reason to go start a fight.

precisely !!

having all the realities of competency right there before you, not as a couple of numbers or lines on a graph, but in page after page of brilliant, funny, and glorious detail.

We have many people to thank for their help with this second edition of *Assessment and ESL*. We thank all the teachers who willingly and generously shared their expertise, their students' work, and their stories: Susie Beverstein, Jackie Deeb, Ellen Fetu, Judy Fritz, Suzanne Gut, Il Han, Marlene Hess, Cheri Mornard, Mark Rowland, Cathy Tegen, Keith Wakeman, and Sara Vander Woude. We thank all the students who have passed through our lives, who made us laugh, who enriched us, and who made the struggle to write this book and fight for the betterment of their lives worth the effort. We thank our editors at Portage & Main Press, Catherine Gerbasi, Annalee Greenberg, and Leslie Malkin for their endurance and careful attention to detail.

And, as always, we thank our loving families for their patience, their tolerance, and their continued support throughout these long years of struggle. When we began this book, our children were very small and they played under our kitchen tables while we hunched over student work, asking, "What are we looking at? What does this show?" again and again, trying to make sense of what we were seeing. Now, they have grown up and gone off to college—and we are still asking those same questions.

Lastly, we want to remember those, whom we loved deeply, who died during the years between this edition and the last: Gene Eckes, Austin Lamberts, Vangie Lamberts, and Ken Law.

About Our Chapter Titles

Each chapter title in this new edition of *Assessment & ESL* incorporates one of the many charming miscues we have encountered during our careers, while also conveying the theme of the chapter. Although many of these are self-explanatory, such as "we're working hardly," others take some thought to understand the meaning that the writer or speaker intended to convey. Still others need explanation. For instance, Mary was stumped when two students repeatedly came over to her desk and said "kiss me, teacher," all the while giggling shyly, only to return to their desks when she did not know how to respond. After much puzzlement and embarrassment, Mary finally realized they were saying, "excuse me, teacher."

We have no clue what "determining the navel assigned to the factor" means, which is the miscue we attached to chapter 3. But it seemed to be a natural for that chapter, since placement of ESL students can be challenging and confusing and the issues vary from student to student. Converting Fahrenheit to Cellulose" speaks to the government's attempts to reduce and quantify, by means of numbers, something as all-encompassing, complex, ephemeral, and personal as learning.

Although this is a modest book, we feel that attention to this issue is vital to the task of educating all children. The consequences of not watching and listening, collecting, and documenting, or of simply allowing someone else (who does not know you or your students) make sweeping judgments on the basis of one test, are extensive and potentially disastrous.

There is no margin for error.

PREFACE **TO THE FIRST EDITION** (1995)

"Mom, can I have a snack?" asked Barb's seven-year-old one night

"You can have an apple."

"I can't eat apples."

"Why not?"

"I don't have any front teeth, remember?"

"Ummmm." Long pause. "What have you been doing with all the apples I've been putting in your lunch?"

"Giving them to my friends."

Barb was stunned, not to mention outraged, over the thought of all those apples she had been buying and dutifully packing during the last three months that had been slipping, unbeknownst to her, into the hands and tummies of Kate's friends.

We have come to the conclusion that education and assessment are much like packing school lunches for your children. You put in everything that you think your child needs, all the necessary food groups, making it attractive and palatable. Then you send it off, hoping it will get eaten. The lunch box comes back empty, but you can't assume that the child has actually eaten what you packed. He may have traded those cookies for a candy bar, taken one bite of the apple and thrown it away, or chucked the entire contents of the box in the trash. There are three main ways for you to check to see if your child has actually eaten the lunch: ask him (monitoring closely for truth); see if he's ravenous when he comes home, if he's growing (or getting seriously skinny); or simply volunteer for lunch duty and watch him eat. The first one is only partially revealing of what happens: he may tell you, he may not. The second method is far removed from the actual fact: by the time you see your child losing weight, the lack of lunches has gone on for quite some time. The third—if not entirely feasible or practical—is of course the most effective. You can intervene when necessary, negotiate, and change the menu if it's not meeting the child's tastes and needs (or number of teeth).

The comparison to assessment is easy. Standardized testing, like weighing and measuring a child against the bathroom door every New Year's Eve, is a natural and logical part of quantifying growth. Parents want to know whether their child is growing, learning and achieving at a rate that is considered normal for his age. But it often occurs after the fact. It's the day-to-day watching of your child growing, of listening to what he says, of monitoring his eating habits, who he plays with and how much television he watches that tells you who your child is and what he's all about. This kind of assessment is ongoing. It is the observation of development as it happens, rather than the final product. Parents and teachers are masters of this art—it's what they do. Ask any good teacher and she can go on and on about what any one particular student can or can't do.

[margin note: same as teaching]

This fine art, this mastery of the craft of child-watching, has been invalidated in recent years and relegated to a less-than-important status, to be supplanted by impersonal, easy-to-read-and-quantify standardized tests.

The assessment of non-English-speaking students is not clear-cut. The regular standards and criteria that are used to assess English-speaking children cannot be used as reliable yardsticks. When a student does not speak the language of the test, it is difficult to gauge whether he knows the material and just doesn't have the English to display the knowledge, or whether he truly doesn't know the material.

There are many variables that come into play with students who do not speak English as their native language. Many of the things we take for granted with our regular students—an understanding of American culture, a basic background in government, science, math and reading—cannot be assumed with newcomers. We cannot even take it for granted that they understand that print has meaning. Giving a fair grade to a student who can barely read, who has just arrived from a foreign country, is a tangled issue that needs serious thought to resolve.

[margin note: I grade mostly on effort at this point until I can figure out what they do/do not know/get]

There are also many wild cards: students who arrive in senior high school with no previous schooling and have to learn such simple things as sitting in a desk; students who do not adhere to the time-line we impose on them, who learn at much slower rates than we consider normal because they have so much to learn in knowledge and concepts, on top of the materials presented in class; students who come to us with moderate to severe disabilities, whose problems are beyond our abilities to understand, diagnose and help correct. How can we assess them, and measure the knowledge they have and the gains they are making?

Those who do not understand these issues (unfortunately, many of our policymakers fall into this category) try to impose time limits to ESL schooling, advocate buying software instead of paying teachers, worse still, relegate students to remedial status, and, worst of all, advocate eliminating services altogether. And, those who do not understand try to use the same yardsticks on our ESL students without allowing them the time, the attention, and the input they need to achieve on a comparable level with mainstream students.

This is a modest book. We do not pretend to have all the answers to alternative assessment. In the past several years there has been a great deal of interest in and a burgeoning amount of research on this topic. But little attention has been paid to how this can relate to non-English speakers. As with our previous book, *The More-Than-Just-Surviving Handbook*, we have tried to make sense of the literature and the theories and apply them in a clear and usable way for the teacher in the trenches.

We have filled the book with examples drawn from our own experiences and the experiences of others.

We have many people to thank for their help in writing this book. To the teachers who so willingly and generously shared their expertise, their stories, and their students' work: Cathy Tegen, Bong Hee Lis, Dan Jones, Judy Lewis, Mary Miller, Corri Gossen, Heidi Meissner, Mary Delie, Debby Moon, Caitlin Cogburn, Dolores Duncan, John Patterson, Teresa Greer, Mary Marcus, Cherie Mornard, Andrea Davis, Ellen Kallio, Jackie Deeb, Miss Huong. We thank them for their input and their critiques. We'd especially like to thank all the students who have passed through our lives, made us laugh, enriched us, and made the struggle to write this book and fight for the betterment of their lives worth the effort. We'd like to thank our editor Annalee Greenberg for her patience and her careful attention to detail.

And, as always, we thank our loving families for their patience, their tolerance, and their continued support throughout these long years of struggle.

About our title: This book has been through many incarnations and had many titles (*Barb and Mary Have an Adventure; Mary and Barb Screw Up Again; But Officer, We Were Lost!; Why Isn't Chest Plural?*). Finally, the dilemma answered itself. The theme of this book is being able to look *through* the errors to the meaning intended, and so it was natural that we choose a title that incorporates one of the many delightful miscues we have encountered during our careers. Taken from one student's story retelling of the *Wizard of Oz*, it seems to sum up the idea that learning is a continuum, and that assessment must follow the same path. The titles of chapters are the same; each one conveys the theme of the chapter and takes some thought to understand the meaning that the writer or speaker intended to convey. Some are self-explanatory, such as "Flying without an Earplan." Some need an explanation. Mary was stumped when two students repeatedly came to her desk and said, "Kiss me, teacher," all the while giggling shyly, to return to their desks when she didn't know how to respond. After much puzzlement and embarrassment, she finally realized they were saying, "Excuse me, teacher." Then she could respond appropriately. We have no clue to the meaning of one title, "Determining the Navel Assigned to the Factor." But it seemed to be a natural for that chapter, since so many people argue for standardized testing and use the results without any idea as to what has been measured and what the results really mean.

[handwritten marginal note: "my job as a reading teacher"]

Editor's Note

One of the dilemmas facing today's editor is that of retaining writing clarity while ensuring gender balance. This relates specifically to the use of the personal pronouns *he/she, him/her, himself/herself*, and so on. Using both forms in all cases makes for particularly awkward reading. In this book, we have chosen to use masculine pronouns when referring to generic students and feminine pronouns when referring to generic teachers. We assure the reader that no affront is intended.

INTRODUCTION

For the first four months Hiro was in the United States, he ordered nothing but hotdogs at the school cafeteria. He did not know any other words for food, and could not read the menu. He just pointed and said, "Hotdog." Three years later, he told his teacher, "I don't eat hotdogs anymore."

+ + + + + +

Jenny arrived at the middle school speaking no English. At eleven, she had been in sixth grade in her home country, but here, her parents insisted on enrolling her in the seventh grade. Their rationale: the education system in their own country was so far advanced from the American system that when they returned to their country, Jenny would be held back a year. Although very shy, Jenny proved to be an exceptional language learner and, within three months, was speaking colloquial English without an accent. By year's end, she was competing with her peers.

Jenny got to play the role of the heroine when the sixth-, seventh-, and eighth-grade ESL students put on the play *Cinderella*. It was a success and, performing for the entire school, the students received a standing ovation. Jenny and her family never returned to their home country. Now a successful dentist, whenever Jenny sees Barb she says, "Remember when we did *Cinderella*? Wasn't that fun?"

These incidents in the lives of Hiro and Jenny were steps in their ongoing learning continuum toward competence in English and in school. One of the great joys of working with second-language learners is watching that magical unfolding as each one grows and gains competency in a new language. The challenge is to capture that growth and record it. Because growth is dynamic and ongoing, assessment should be, too.

Teacher's manuals now include, as a matter of course, discussions of ESL students and accommodations to be made for them to the curriculum. While many of the ideas, teaching methods, and solutions are the same, non-English-proficient students pose a special challenge for the teacher who wants to grade fairly and give credit for work done, progress gained, and concepts mastered. Trying to grade or chart the progress of a student who speaks little or no English, cannot communicate what he knows, does minimal work in class, and hands in no homework continues to be a perplexing dilemma.

This book has been written for those of you who are working with English-language learners—elementary and secondary, mainstream and ESL—to help you recognize the progress ESL students make, which may not always be apparent at first glance, and to identify ways of documenting that growth. As Gullickson (2003), writes, "Sound evaluations presume the need for substantial assessment skills on the part of the evaluator to deal effectively with a wide range of issues that arise."

In this book, we have undertaken to

- distill the latest research on effective assessment, literacy development, and second-language acquisition

- apply this research to the unique issues of learning to speak, read, and write in English as a new and additional language

- suggest activities to foster proficiency and competency in both oral and written language

THE FOUR THEMES

In our first book, *The More-Than-Just Surviving Handbook*, we discussed the process of learning another language effectively around four basic themes:

1. Real language

2. Integrated and whole language

3. A facilitating environment

4. Learning is a continuum, in which errors have a place and role

We can also discuss assessment within the framework of these four themes.

Real Language

This refers to language that has purpose, that is meaningful, authentic, and relevant. The reasons students have for using language must be more than simply to please the teacher and get a good grade. Students have many reasons for using real language: to order food, to ask a parent for an allowance, to convince the teacher to give them an extra day for completing an assignment, to tell a joke to a friend, and so on.

In the same vein, the language in which a student is being assessed must also have meaning and purpose. The context must be the type of situation he encounters in everyday life, rather than contrived language used to illustrate a phonic principle or language someone has decided is "easy." Research shows that students often perform more poorly on tasks that are dull, uninteresting, meaningless, purposeless, boring, or frustrating than they do on tasks that have a purpose (Smith, 1998). When the student cannot see a purpose for what he is doing or, if the cost of trying is too high compared to his expected rate of success, he may not give the task the time, attention, or effort it requires. Forester and Reinhard (1989) write:

> *Evaluation of children's reading and writing should take place while they are actually reading and writing and not in situations that are supposed to simulate reading and writing. This makes it possible for the teacher to learn about how children use the many resources that are available to them from their classmates and from print material.*

Real assessment, then,

+ is realistic. Tasks being assessed closely follow the ways in which our ability is tested in the real world
+ requires judgment and innovation on the part of the student
+ measures the progress of students engaged in authentic tasks
+ involves tasks that have meaning for the student
+ is dynamic and flexible. It can vary in time, context and demands
+ uses multiple means of measuring knowledge and skills

Integrated and Whole Language

For many years it was thought that language and literacy skills equaled the sum of their parts, that teaching the parts would lead to adequate understanding of the whole, and that testing the parts would give us insight into a student's grasp of the whole. We now know this is not true. Davies et al. (1992) write that "language is not a set of unrelated bits. It forms a whole...the bits must be integrated and tested in combination with one another." Assessment tools do not fragment language. They do not measure just spelling, or grammar, or word lists, or comma splices; they measure language use as a whole. Shuy (1973) writes:

> *Tests of grammar and phonology are not accurate predictors of effective participation...functional language competence is far more crucial. That is, a child's ability to seek clarification or get a turn seems much more critical than his ability to use past-tense markers.*

In *The Primary Language Record: Handbook for Teachers*, Barrs et al. (1989) state that "reading cannot be examined in total isolation from talking, listening and writing, so it is important to consider each child in the context of her/his language and learning experiences." As well, language is assessed within the context of the surrounding environment, not divorced from it.

According to Gumperz (1964):

> *Context is thought of as the physical setting, the people within the setting, what the people are doing and saying, and where and when they are doing it. Language is embedded in the flow of daily life.*

Assessment, then, does not isolate one skill from another. Reading is not separate from writing, listening, and speaking. What a student says about what he writes is important. His comments about what he has read reveal much about what he has understood. The drawings that illustrate what he wrote, and the actions he pantomimes to explain a situation are all clues to competence.

Integrated assessment, then, means

+ the context of the situation is as significant as the task itself

+ tasks consist of more than just rote memorization

+ individual tasks are not isolated from other people or from other skills

A Facilitating Environment

The learning environment must be conducive to learning. A facilitating environment means several things. First, it means a positive orientation on the part of the teacher and classmates that allows a learner to behave naturally and feel truly capable of expressing himself openly without fear of ridicule or punishment. Second, the environment and, consequently, assessment, should focus on positive achievement rather than on negative failure. Too much testing can be punitive, focusing on errors and a student's failure to measure up to a standard. According to Murphy (1992), emphasis should be on "meaningful and positive descriptions of what pupils know, understand, and can do." Facilitative assessment, then,

+ is constructive, not destructive

+ recognizes the student's achievements, not his failures

+ treats the student as a person worthy of respect, not a number

+ gives the student a chance to experience success in a wide variety of contexts at many different levels

+ provides a continuous record of tasks and stages of achievement that the student demonstrates

+ takes into consideration students' learning styles, language proficiencies, cultural and educational backgrounds, and grade levels of students

Observe Song Jo's writing.

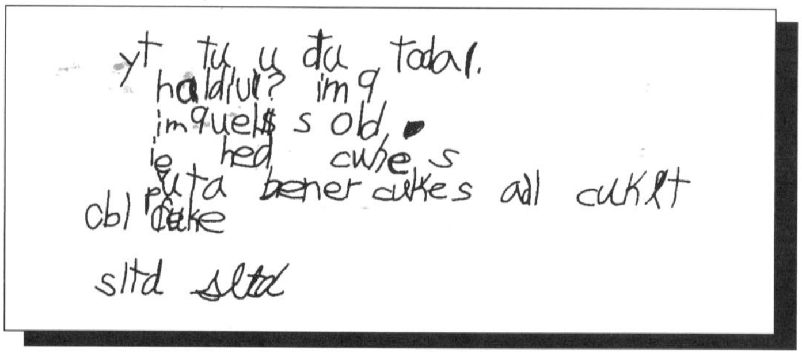

Figure I.1 Song Jo's writing

4

Song Jo meant to say:

> **What do you do today? How old are you? I'm 9. I'm 9 years old. I had cookies. Peanut-butter cookies. Salted.**

Although it is easy to be taken aback by the errors and to look at his language deficits, it is important to focus on what he *can* do. So, what *does* Song Jo know?

+ He knows word boundaries.

+ He knows cursive writing.

+ He knows the correct orthography of several English words: *I'm, today, old.*

+ He has a strong grasp of English phonic principles. For example, *yt, tu, u, du* and *cukes* reveal that he understands the concept of sound/letter correspondences and can make reasonably accurate guesses.

+ He is familiar with English punctuation. He uses a question mark.

Learning Is a Continuum

Forester and Reinhard (1989) speak of learning as a journey: it is not enough to note that students are giving correct answers on exercise sheets, reading well orally, copying words correctly, or spelling words from a list correctly. The question is, can they readily transfer that knowledge to new and different situations? Or, do they simply know it at the imitation or product level? Observing students' small steps forward will tell you far more about who has truly internalized knowledge and where individual students are along the learning continuum.

Every student travels along the learning continuum at his own pace. Although Nok and Veapasert are both ten and arrived in their new country at the same time, that does not mean we should expect them to be at the same level of proficiency. We cannot be concerned that it takes one longer to get there than it takes the other. We cannot judge developing English students according to a preset timeline, considering them failures or disabled because they do not achieve competence as quickly as we would like. For example, when Isabella says, "Tengo toys" (*tengo* is Spanish for "I have"), she is demonstrating progress. She is making the transition from monolingual Spanish to English, a piece at a time.

This also means that errors are not necessarily indication of a problem. Errors do not denote failure to learn. According to Goodman (1988):

> *Errors, miscues, or misconceptions usually indicate ways in which a child is organizing the world at that moment...Errors also indicate interpretations which may in no way be wrong, but simply show that the child has used inferences about reading or listening which were unexpected...the [observer] who understands the role of unexpected responses will use children's errors or miscues to chart their growth and development and to understand the personal and cultural history of the child. Often errors signal the onset of leaps in knowledge, as, for instance, the explosion of invented spelling with children just on the verge of putting reading together. Teachers who are familiar with the bumps and quirks of language and*

literacy learning encourage approximations and invented spellings with the faith and certainty that, over time and with continued exposure to the desired and ideal forms, children will learn them.

Teachers of ESL students also encourage approximations, sentences that contain both languages and creative grammar, because they know that these features indicate the student is moving forward toward proficiency.

Understanding that learning is a continuum means

how do we get the yahoos running the show to get this,

- all students are given the time they need, independent of what the policymakers think is a reasonable amount of time for mastering English or what other students are doing

- there is a place for errors

- errors can be considered indicators of progress rather than failure to learn

- errors are roadmaps for teachers, telling us where the student is now and where we need to go next

EQUITABLE ASSESSMENT

It is upon this conceptual framework that we will build our case for alternative assessment and demonstrate how to do it. Today's students will be assessed through testing. That is a given. What we want to ensure is that the assessments they undergo are *equitable*. The movement toward raising standards for all students, English language learners (ELLs) included, does not necessarily mean it will happen, particularly if the tests used are not accurate indicators of what the learners know or can do. Meisels et al. (1995) write:

> *Tests that do not accommodate crucial differences between groups of children are inherently inequitable. They do not give all children a fair chance to succeed because they assume that all children come to the testing situation with roughly the same experiences, experiences that are crucial to success.*

The needs of English language learners vary along a wide continuum. "To establish standards as though all students have had access and opportunity to learn from a common curriculum is to deny the reality that exists in most schools," writes Brown (2001). He continues that it is not possible for a single standard "to represent an appropriate expectation of academic quality…and still be fair for all the individuals in that school." Neither is this possible for a test.

The most fundamental premise underlying equitable assessment is that a student does not come to the classroom "alingual," without language. He usually comes with the ability to speak and with varying levels of competence in one or more languages. Therefore, we must observe him and assess his abilities where he is on the learning continuum and use our observations to make decisions about what to do with him next.

To assess a student accurately and equitably and to make fair decisions about him, we need to gather as much information about him as possible, including what he has accomplished and where he is on the learning continuum. But it is not enough to gather data for its own sake. It does no good to have piles of notes, or bursting portfolios that sit on the shelf. The data needs to be catalogued for accessibility and presented in useable ways. This information must then be used to help the student progress.

The ultimate purpose of any assessment or evaluation is to improve learning. If it does not further a teacher's understanding of where a student is and what he needs to do to improve or develop, if it does not inform students about themselves and their mastery and capacity, then assessment, in any form, whether it be testing, portfolio development, anecdote collection, or narrative writing, is a wasted endeavor.

CHAPTER OVERVIEW

In **Chapter 1, Kiss Me Teacher: WHAT TEACHERS NEED TO KNOW**, we discuss why we assess, what kinds of information educators need to find out about their non- or limited-English-speaking students to make appropriate decisions about placement, curriculum, and educational objectives, and what effective assessment is and does.

Chapter 2, What Shape Will We Use? Red! TESTING VS. ALTERNATIVE FORMS OF ASSESSMENT, explores what good data is and the problems traditional standardized testing poses for ESL students. We propose that alternative assessment can lead the way toward fairer and more accurate assessment in order to showcase a student's actual abilities as well as proficiency and development in language and academic content.

Chapter 3, Determining the Navel Assigned to the Factor: PLACEMENT, examines how to identify students whose primary language is not English, the steps to take in assessing proficiency and literacy levels, and factors to consider for placing students appropriately. We provide three placement scenarios to illustrate some of these factors or issues.

Chapter 4, We're Working Hardly: EMERGING LITERACY, explores the importance of both context and the concept of emergence with regards to language and literacy acquisition. We discuss the levels of emerging proficiency and literacy as well as the theoretical framework or standard against which to evaluate student proficiency or achievement. We provide a basis for understanding emerging proficiency and literacy by exploring the research and providing examples of growing competency and mastery in both oral and written expression.

In **Chapter 5, Diving for Pearls in their Shelves: HOW AND WHERE TO FIND INFORMATION**, we address how to find important information about students through observing them working, sampling their work, talking with them, and using traditional measures. From this, we can determine the strategies they are using as well as their understanding, attitudes, interest, and degree of control over language forms. We also explore opportunities for collecting information about students and how to analyze and interpret the information.

Chapter 6, The Santa Maria, the Pimpas, the Ninny Sailing with Baflaf's Dog: RECORDING YOUR OBSERVATIONS THROUGH CHECKLISTS, RUBRICS, ANECDOTES, AND CONFERENCES examines these four ways of collecting and documenting important information about student progress.

Chapter 7, Finding the Perimeter of a Pollyollygon: EXITING, is about deciding when a student is ready to function in a mainstream class on a level with his peers. We explore how to determine when a student no longer needs second-language support, as well as exiting criteria.

Chapter 8, The Final Nail in the Coffee: GRADES, presents the problems and issues involved in grading ESL students, the decisions you must make to grade fairly, and setting standards that can include ESL students.

Chapter 9, Lunching Several Measures: PRESENTING THE INFORMATION TO STAKEHOLDERS, is about systematizing the information you have gathered about your students, presenting the data in forms that are usable to the stakeholders, and how to hold conferences with the stakeholders.

Chapter 10, Converting Fahrenheit to Cellulose: STANDARDS, tackles the sticky issue of standards, what they are meant to do, and what they mean for ESL students.

Chapter 11, Fight to the Spinach! MAKING THE CHANGE, offers suggestions for changing methods of grading and assessment and for collaborating with partners in the educational system to make these changes reality.

Why We Have Written this Book

We have written this book so that you, the reader, equipped with tools and knowledge, can confidently document the development and progress of second-language learners, help to further their growth, and comfortably welcome all learners. We have filled these pages with many of our own experiences as well as struggles and mistakes we made over the years. We include numerous case examples and anecdotes*, which make the theory real and illustrate the sometimes uneven, often arduous path toward mastery of the English language. This book itself has been a struggle, and while we learned a great deal, we also discovered that as teachers we—like all other teachers—already knew the basics of assessment: observing students closely for signs of growth and mastery, and finding joy in that growth.

And so, in the overwhelming avalanche of publications and opinions about assessment, testing, and standards, we can add personal stories. We can add glimpses into the lives of students. We can make real the statistics and the theories. And we can put a human face on the endless debate—about the effectiveness of various forms of assessment—taking place across a great chasm of disagreement.

---

*Please note that names and minor details from some of these case examples and anecdotes have been changed.

Kiss Me Teacher

WHAT TEACHERS NEED TO KNOW

Daniel, Martha, and Elsie were brought to the middle school of the small, Midwestern college town with no warning and no school records. Barb was summoned from the "Boogie Room"—the tiny windowless classroom to which she had been assigned, found along an unlit corridor on the second-floor landing. Standing in the hallway outside the office with the principal and the counselor, she had to make an on-the-spot decision about where to place the three newcomers. According to their father, Daniel and Martha had a solid learning foundation, and he thought they would do well in seventh and eighth grade respectively. Elsie ought to be in sixth grade, he said. Everyone took his word for it. No one had any idea how to find out at what grade level they were or how much English they knew. Besides, the older two looked mature enough. So that decision "felt" right. But then Barb looked at Elsie. She was very tiny. She looked nine, not eleven. She hid behind her father, peering at Barb with large, frightened eyes. Instinct told Barb that Elsie would do better at the elementary school. But Daniel and Martha were going to be at the middle school. Maybe it would be better to keep her with her brother and sister. She might feel safer there. Stifling her apprehensions, Barb agreed to place Elsie in the sixth grade with the other eleven-year-olds. That, it turns out, was a decision that was to go very wrong.

What's in this Chapter

+ Why we need to assess
+ Questions we need to ask about our students
+ What we are looking for when we assess
+ What effective assessment is and does

HOW WE GOT HERE

Barb's Early Years

The seed for this book began long ago with Elsie. Barb's instincts were right. Sixth grade was too much for Elsie: she was too immature and her academic background was too spotty. As a tiny eleven year old, all she did was smile shyly and whisper. Two years later, she was still smiling shyly and whispering, but she had grown into a very large girl whose helplessness and unwillingness to try drove everybody crazy. She never seemed to pull it together and floundered for all the years she was at the middle school, only to return to who-knows-what in her own country. Barb has been haunted by the sense that if she had to do it over again she would have done it differently—and that the outcome for Elsie might have been different, too.

If she had known more about Elsie's background, her reading ability, and her grasp of basic academic skills, Barb would have asserted her apprehensions, articulated her rationale, and, perhaps, just as important, justified her decisions, then taken stronger measures when Elsie did not begin to make progress.

But Barb was woefully ignorant about what resources were out there, what she needed to do to help Elsie, and how to go about making well-informed decisions. She needed information and did not know how to get it.

In those days, Barb was one of three ESL teachers in the entire town. She was assigned to seven elementary and two middle schools. All students were mainstreamed, and Barb met them whenever and wherever they fit into her busy schedule. If the state had a policy concerning non-English-speaking students, nobody knew what it was. Often, decisions about kids like Elsie were made standing in the hallway while the parent disappeared out the door. No initial placement tests were given. There was no curriculum, no guidelines to follow. Once the student was placed, it was difficult, if not impossible, for Barb to schedule time with the classroom teacher to find out what and how the child was doing.

During Barb's third year in the district, she was given a self-contained classroom of second-language learners, thirty or so children from grades one through five, who arrived at her classroom soon after the tardy bell, to stay until lunch. Among them, they spoke eleven different languages. There were thirty different levels of English proficiency and thirty different sets of needs. Barb was

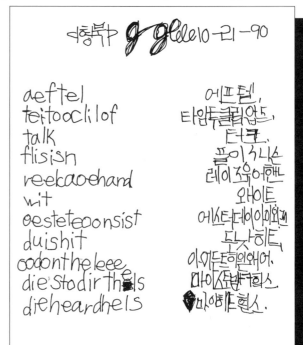

Figure 1.1 Jung's writing

sounds like my reading classes.

10

instructed to "teach them English" so that sooner or later they could return to the regular classroom fulltime.

Figure 1.1 illustrates the work of one new immigrant, Jung. Based on the work sample, Barb had to ask: How much does he know? Can he function in the regular classroom? Am I willing to set him adrift in a classroom when the options are pretty much all or nothing—either my class or alone in the mainstream?

Looking at the work sample, Barb could tell that Jung was literate in his own language. She could tell from his attempts at writing that he had some experience with English. When she questioned another individual, whose primary language was Korean, about what Jung had written, Bong Hee told her that Jung had listened carefully to the English words and phrases Barb had dictated, and he had written them first in Korean (which necessitated his understanding of her words). Then he had transcribed the words and phrases, as best he could, into English.

The first word Jung wrote is *after*. The second item is the phrase *time to clean up*. After some consultation with Bong Hee, Barb discovered that Jung knew quite a bit of English, but she was not ready to let him struggle alone in the mainstream classroom until he had gained more English. Jung, however, was one of those students who made great strides very quickly and was soon sailing along in the mainstream classroom with little or no additional help.

But Barb was privately overcome with questions about her second-language learners: **What would she teach the students?** There was nothing to help her establish what her priorities were and no one to help her decide where to start. Barb looked at John and Laban, who could read and write in Chinese but knew no English; at first-grader William who was on the verge of reading in English; at Chatphet, who would be going on to the middle school next year; at Vaji, who did not seem to be doing much in either Farsi or English. Barb sensed these children did not only need to learn to speak English, they needed to learn how to read and write in English. Time was passing. A year spent simply learning how to speak correctly was a year lost on learning the content of the curriculum.

Once Barb decided what to teach, **how could she be sure it was relevant and aligned to what the students were doing in the mainstream curriculum?** She rarely knew what was going on in the student's regular classroom. With her mornings filled and her afternoons occupied with kindergarten and students needing extra help in reading, content areas, or language skills, she had little time to talk to classroom teachers. Communication was catch-as-catch-can in hallways and the teachers' lounge. Conversation was often limited to "How is he doing?" "Oh, fine."

How could she be sure the students were learning? Barb watched. She listened to the children as they worked, studied the writing they did, and observed their behavior throughout the morning. She talked to her aides and compared notes on what they had seen. Documenting that progress was another issue altogether, however, and the idea of portfolios in the classroom had not yet been developed. She attempted to put together a report card but was not happy with it because it did not reveal much.

How was she to decide when to send the students back to the mainstream classroom fulltime? There was no established procedure or criteria for exiting students in her class, and so it was a struggle to mainstream them. William, for instance, was a problem. He

11

talked constantly while Barb was trying to lead a lesson, got up and ran around during rug time, picked fights with other students, and would not stay on task during group work. He had entered school in the United States in kindergarten, had been in the self-contained classroom since his arrival nearly a year and a half before that, could speak English fluently, and was ready to read. It was clear to Barb that he could be successfully mainstreamed. However, when she approached the classroom teacher with the idea, Mrs. Smith curtly stated that they would have to meet with the principal. At the meeting, Barb presented her case. But because she really did not know much about assessment and could not document in any concrete way what William was capable of doing, she was unable to convince them. Mrs. Smith accused Barb of trying to get rid of William because he was a behavior problem (which he was); Barb secretly harbored the notion that Mrs. Smith did not want him back for precisely the same reason. So, over Barb's objections, and what she intuitively knew was the right decision, William stayed in ESL.

Was the self-contained program the right program for the children? The logistics were overwhelming for Barb, with so many students at so many different levels. The children, isolated from their peers for half the day, made few English-speaking friends. And all but a few teachers seemed to relinquish responsibility for them, leaving the entire burden of teaching to Barb. Worst of all was the one-size-fits-all mentality that assumed that since the children all had the same "problem"—not knowing English—one teacher could, in the course of a morning, adequately teach five grade levels of children.

Mary's Early Years

Mary had a different experience. Her first ESL assignment was at the Language Assessment Center (LAC) in southern California. The center provided intensive ESL instruction for newly located Indo-Chinese refugees. Every day, they attended a four-hour class split into two two-hour shifts shared between two teachers. The students were grouped according to capabilities, and the classes were open entry—students could come in at any time during the semester, and teachers could move them from level to level when they were ready. The students stayed in the program for approximately six to nine months and then moved into other programs or job training.

The curriculum at the LAC focused on survival skills the students would need to succeed in their new environment. Teachers had six major themes they were supposed to cover, but the materials they used and how they used them were left to them. They had access to the resources the center provided, or they could create their own. Texts were available, but the director discouraged teachers from using them too frequently. They were encouraged to keep the English meaningful and tangent to the students' experiences. Teachers met every day to coordinate during the students' twenty-minute break. This gave them time to share materials, ideas, observations, and so on. Once a month, the break was extended and a few teachers were asked to present a successful technique or observation to the entire group of about twenty teachers. They were kept abreast of ESL theory by presentations from experts in the field, by publishing companies who wanted feedback from them on new materials, and by interested professors at the nearby universities. They were encouraged to attend ESL workshops and to share what they learned with the rest of the group.

this would be excellent

What made this program such an essential part of Mary's growth as a teacher was the constant input and support built into it. She never felt she taught in a vacuum. She knew she could get support from her supervisors and peers when she needed it. If she felt stumped, she could bounce ideas off her partner or other teachers for help. She also thrived on the access all teachers had to theory, methods, and people in the newly developing ESL field. With so many different personalities and backgrounds, the diversity was wonderful, the ideas challenging, and the pace frantic.

The center had a plan, well-defined levels of students, a curriculum, built-in time to connect with other teachers, and specific means for placement and exiting. By the time she moved to northern California four years later, Mary's teaching abilities had broadened and deepened to prepare her for the less supportive assignments she would encounter there.

The Reality Today

Mary's experience was the ideal; Barb's, unfortunately, was all-too-common, even today. In the past decade, states and provinces, under pressure from the federal government, have developed policies; districts have plans. TESOL has defined standards. However, working in a vacuum with large numbers of students and teaching populations that change year by year, many teachers face the same or even worse challenges than Barb did. And the number of students who enroll in schools and speak languages other than English continues to spiral. Rural schools and small towns, unprepared for newcomers, find themselves scrambling to meet legal mandates.

Different schools, districts, states, and provinces have responded differently to the influx of non-English-speaking students. Some districts have well-planned curriculums and programs, with coordinators and placement procedures established. Many others have chosen not to deal with the situation at all: the ESL teachers themselves assume the burden of testing, placing, monitoring, and exiting students from classes or programs—if there are any.

Whether or not you are responsible for testing and placement, the challenge of assessing student progress is still your job as a teacher.

WHY WE NEED TO ASSESS

Before we answer why we need to assess these students, even more fundamental is the question: Who cares?

Various stakeholders—each with different needs, philosophies, and issues with which they are grappling in the lives of our students—must make different decisions with the information they receive. These stakeholders include

- the federal government *- don't know, but make all the rules*
- administrators *- seem to get involved if issue arises*
- teachers (mainstream, next year's, ESL, or aides) *} these seem to make the best decisions because they actually know what is going on*
- parents
- students

Stakeholders demand accountability. They want to know whether the money pouring into school districts is producing the kind of learners that societies want and need. Nowadays, within the mission statement of almost any school is the goal for all students to be proficient in reading and math. This is a very tall order at the best of times. In schools with large populations of immigrants, it gets taller. Implicit in this goal is the assumption that schools can adequately demonstrate that they can teach these competencies. This means enormous pressure on schools and on you, the teacher, to help these kids succeed.

Administrators must decide how and into which programs to place these students. They must know how much money, planning, and personnel to commit to the education of non-English-speaking students, based on their numbers, learning needs, and literacy levels. They must know when and how to adapt to the changing populations that arrive and leave. They need to know that the programs they have implemented are the most appropriate ones.

You, the teacher, need to know how to plan instruction. You need to find out how much English these students know. You need to know whether your students can read or write when they enter the classroom. You need to determine whether students are learning and, if not, why not. And, you need to know how to document what and how much students have learned in order to promote, graduate, or retain them.

Parents need to know what their children are doing in school, what they are learning, and what the goals of the school are for their children. They also need to know how and why their child got the grade he did.

Students need to know what they have accomplished, understand what they need to develop further, and have a concrete record of what they have mastered so that, when they move on, they can demonstrate what skills they have.

But why should we care about any of this? Why should we worry about these students when, in some cases, they are not graded or assessed until they are totally mainstreamed, or, in other cases, they simply become the charges of the ESL teacher or the mainstream teacher until they become proficient?

The answer is very simple: the future of our students rides on our ability to make well-reasoned and appropriate decisions about their academic futures. Gullickson (2003) writes:

> *Evaluation of students is central to student learning in every school and classroom. Without evaluation, we do not know if learning has taken place, nor can we plan for future learning opportunities.*

In fact, for our students, it is even more critical than that. Gullickson continues:

> *Evaluation results and findings that are incorrect or unsound, or evaluation conclusions that are meaningless or unjustified are likely to be detrimental to a student's progress and future development.*

Erickson (1982) writes:

> *The consequences of misclassifications due to inadequate or inappropriate tests may include improper placement, insufficient instruction, and, as a result, lower academic achievement than would have been reached if appropriate instruments and proper placement had occurred.*

14

Erickson's prediction that the consequence of this sort of testing would be increased dropout rates and the perpetuation of unequal educational opportunity for language minority students has, unfortunately, come true. The irony is that in the United States it has resulted in increased testing!

[handwritten: WTF 4]

[handwritten: like I said before]

With so much at stake, we must gather as much information as possible about our students through assessment. The instruments we use must be able to tell us accurately and reliably how much a student knows upon entry and how well he is doing in our classes. Assessment

- helps us make informed instructional decisions, set learning goals, and shape a curriculum based on strengths and needs of the learner
- helps us gather evidence on what a learner can do and determine individual strengths and educational needs
- describes a learner's growth and development
- provides feedback for the learner
- provides a basis for communicating progress to the stakeholders
- acts as a method of accountability

WHAT EDUCATORS NEED TO FIND OUT

You may or may not be faced with testing and placement decisions. We feel it is important to present all the different types of questions asked, however, so that even if you are not responsible for these issues, you are aware that they exist. Somebody must make these decisions and needs certain information to make them wisely. They affect you in terms of who enters your classroom, the resources you are allocated, and the responsibility you have for these students. Stakeholders need answers to several questions:

Which students come from homes where English is not spoken?
Identifying a student who comes from a home in which English is not spoken sends up a red flag announcing that he might need services. You need an initial sorting mechanism as a front-line device to alert administrators of special needs.

You cannot assume, however, that a student with a foreign surname will need special help with the language, or that someone with an English surname will not. Nathan Sims is the son of an American marine and a Panamanian. His mother speaks to him only in Spanish. Helga Rodrigues is from Brazil but is of Swedish-Portuguese ancestry. A home-language survey (see chapter 3) for each of them would be the first order of business to find out which language they speak primarily.

How much English does a given student know?
Does he know enough (particularly academic English at the higher grades) to be placed in a mainstream class? Can he read and write English at a level similar to his grade mates, or is his English so limited that he needs special attention?

Effective assessment helps the school place students who are not proficient in English into programs and classes that are appropriate for their needs. Eighth-grader Ichiro's home-language survey revealed that his parents spoke to him in Japanese. However, further investigation showed that his father had been a psychology professor for several years and that Ichiro was fluent in English and read and wrote English at grade level. His parents spoke nothing but Japanese at home to instill respect for his culture and maintenance of their language. He also went to Japanese school every day after school.

Richard spoke and was spoken to in English at home. His parents insisted, because they had been told by a teacher not to speak their own language to their son. However, their English was slow and halting, and although Richard was in the fifth grade and was orally fluent in English, he could not read or write in either language.

This is sad

Which aspects of the English language or of content material does the student need to learn?

Yung Tae seemed to have a fairly adequate mastery of spoken English—if you could understand him. He used words like *therefore* and *consequently* correctly. However, his pronunciation was so atrocious that few could understand him. Sotir could read at grade level in his primary language, but he had a very limited vocabulary in English. Although he was in high school, he ran aground on many words in texts suitable for third-grade readers. He could do advanced math, but with word problems, his lack of vocabulary got in the way.

Are his academic skills at or near grade level in his primary language?

Michael Dylan

How much content and what concepts has the student learned in his own language? Does he read and write at grade level in his primary language?

With this information, you can decide where to begin and what to teach. Tenth-grader Martin had been to school in Mexico City and read fluently at grade level in Spanish. He had taken world history, algebra, and geometry. Sixteen-year-old Maria, on the other hand, had had less than two years of schooling and was barely literate in Spanish. Although they were both beginning speakers of English, it would have been inappropriate to begin teaching Martin at the same level as Maria. Effective assessment allows you to make these kinds of instructional decisions about students.

How well is he doing?

How much has the student learned since his arrival? Are the methods currently being used working? Or should other methods be used instead?

James, from Taiwan, had been to school in his own country until he was ten and was far ahead of the class in math and science. Although he was quiet and did not speak often, he understood what was said to him. And, while he read fluently in Chinese, he just could not seem to make the transition to reading in English. Barb, his tutor, tried many methods, but James could not seem to put it together. Finally, they returned to a method that seemed to fit in with how he had learned Chinese characters: working on sound-letter correspondences with rhyming words and memorizing frequently used words. He found success with that, and they built from that small start. Assessment, through careful observation of what James knew and which methods had been successful, helped Barb decide on a plan that eventually helped James acquire the reading skills he needed.

How and when are students reclassified?

How do you determine who has achieved enough proficiency in English to be reclassified? Who would continue to benefit from ESL or bilingual classes?

Margarita had made remarkable progress in just a few months. She spoke without an accent and could carry on a fluent conversation. Her mother requested that she be mainstreamed. The teacher had to be able to document just how much Margarita knew and whether her reading and writing skills were strong enough to transition to a mainstream classroom.

How can you tell if a student is progressing in the ESL and/or the mainstream classroom?

Tari was extremely shy and quiet. He failed the tests and did not turn in his homework. By these indications, he was failing his classes and had not learned anything. However, his science teacher noted that during lab work, he conducted the experiments competently. He drew well, and could demonstrate his understanding through drawing. He could also answer questions to the tests orally. Through careful observation, allowing Tari alternative methods to demonstrate his understanding and creating situations where he could contribute to class discussions and projects, his teachers were able to document that he was meeting the base-line competencies required for the courses he was taking.

How do you keep track of a student's progress after he has been exited from special programs?

Is he functioning at grade level? Or has he slipped behind and is not doing well in mainstream classes?

Effective assessment would reveal how well he is doing in relation to what is expected of him and his classmates, and what kinds of additional support he may need. Loan, for example, had tested fully English proficient (FEP) and was no longer eligible for special ESL services. However, she had failed her mainstream English, history, and science courses. She could not cope with the content courses and eventually dropped out of school, saying that she had a job in a local factory. Careful monitoring, extra help, and a contingency plan could have been worked out to help her get through the content courses and meet the requirements for graduation.

Does a student who is not achieving have problems with language, or do his difficulties stem from psychological, physical, or emotional problems that necessitate different supports?

Effective assessment, writes Alvarez (1991), helps distinguish between "real handicapping difficulties and transient difficulties the students might be having due to language, adaptation, or curricular mismatches."

Yebio was nine years old, in a third-grade class, and reading at a first-grade level. His tutor discovered that his attention span was, at best, five minutes on a good day. Yebio quickly lost interest in anything. He dictated one letter to his father and would not do any more. He typed one line and skipped off to another activity. He did not like to read and could not sit still to listen. His teacher finally resorted to doing simple activities with Yebio such as taking walks and discussing environmental print (street signs, advertisements, and words he would normally encounter during the day) and by playing the board game "Sorry!" Yebio could not remember the game rules from one day to the next; he needed them explained to him every time they played, and he had great difficulty counting the correct number of squares during his turn. Months of individual work did not seem to make a difference in his progress. After careful questioning of Yebio's mother, the teacher learned that he had been in a refugee camp for his first four years of life and had had malaria from eighteen months until he was three years old. Clearly, there was more going on with him than language problems. After lengthy deliberation and testing, Yebio was referred to a special-education class at another school.

TC was nine when he arrived and was placed in kindergarten. Now in the third province within the past three years, his family had moved four times; he was shunted from school to school, placed in fourth grade in one school then dropped to third in the next. He was tested and labeled "borderline retarded." The ESL teacher tried everything she could think of to help him learn English and how to read. When he moved to another district, he was retested as learning disabled.

By sixteen, TC still could not do the basics in his own language. Something seemed to be going on besides limited English. His interpreter and advocate believed the schools had misclassified him and felt he should be in a regular classroom. But could he handle the content required of most sixteen year olds? He still could not tell time, read at a first-grade level, or give directions from his home to school. He did not talk in complete sentences even in his own language.

After careful observation and documentation of both Yebio and TC's learning by ESL, mainstream, and special-education teachers as well as by tutors, Yebio was placed in a program designed to meet his particular needs as a learner. These measures then helped teachers begin to figure out how to support TC.

These scenarios are rooted in the common theme that decisions must be based on effective assessment. But what is effective assessment?

EFFECTIVE ASSESSMENT

Effective assessment involves obtaining enough essential and accurate information about your students. It depends on acquiring what Stiggins (1991) calls "good data." Good data contains the following features:

+   **A clear target.** Know what it is you are looking for.

+   **An appropriate sample.** Is the data you have collected truly representative of what the student is capable of doing? Is it enough?

+   **Known sources of interference.** What gets in the way of obtaining a good sample of what this student knows and can do? Is the test faulty? Are you looking in the wrong context? Are you current with the latest research concerning language learning and literacy development? For instance, research shows students learn large issues first and gradually refine grammar, and so on. A teacher who focuses on word endings or grammar errors and insists on perfection while overlooking content is focusing on the wrong issues.

+ **Usable results.** Can you use what you have found in a way that is valuable to you (as the teacher planning your student's learning), to other teachers, to parents, to administrators, and to the student himself?

CONCLUSION

ESL students bring a complex set of issues with them when they arrive at any school. To understand what a student knows and how much English he understands, schools need assessment procedures that provide stakeholders with accurate information. Being prepared for these students before they arrive means working out what you need to know about them so that placement and teaching is as effective as possible. Beyond the required tests, how will the additional information be gathered? Placement needs to be appropriate, teachers need accurate methods of assessing and recording their students' development, and documentation needs to reflect the students' progress through and beyond any ESL program. Each assessment issue needs to be addressed. That is why understanding the difference between the role of testing and the role of alternative assessment is an important first step.

2

What Shape Will We Use? Red!

TESTING VS. ALTERNATIVE FORMS OF ASSESSMENT

Irasema was a good student. She was attentive, worked hard on assignments, and helped the other students, translating for Rosie when the assignment was not clear. She willingly worked with other, weaker students, and took on the lion's share of the work in group projects. She read the seventh-grade literature book with comprehension and could discuss the stories with more understanding than some students whose primary language was English.

However, when the scores of the standardized Gates-MacGinitie reading test came back, Irasema scored very low. Although she showed impressive gains from the previous years, she still did not "close the gap" that had been mandated for every student in that inner city school—which meant more sanctions against the school. The teacher did not relay the scores to either Irasema or her parents, because they would have been very discouraged.

	NQ	NA	RS	NCE	National PR	S	GE	ESS
Vocabulary	45	45	15	35	24	4	5.0	497
Comprehension	48	30	8	10	3	1	3.1	458
TOTAL	93	75	23	17	6	2	4.0	478

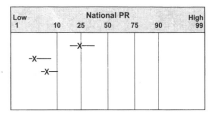

LEGEND: NQ = Number of Questions; NA = Number Answered; RS = Raw Score (Number Correct); NCE = Normal Curve Equivalent; PR = Percentile Rank; S = Stanine; GE = Grade Equivalent; ESS = Extended Scale Score

Figure 2.1 Irasema's Gates-MacGinitie scores

✦✦✦✦✦✦

Juan had been in a beginning adult literacy class for four semesters and had not made any progress. He could barely finish ten percent of the standardized placement test and was continually classified as non-literate and non-English speaking. Because he was nearly sixty, and chances of graduating high school were slim, counselors were beginning to make rumbling noises about his "educability." He did not turn in homework and could not read even the easiest of texts. His favorite sentence was, "I don't know."

Every day during spring semester, while driving through prune orchards to work, Juan's teacher saw something different happening. She asked him about what she saw. Juan answered all her questions in English, showing a remarkable knowledge of the cultivating, harvesting and processing of prunes. His teacher decided to abandon the class textbook and introduce projects on agriculture, reasoning that this was what her students, mostly migrant workers, knew best. And, although Juan needed a great deal of assistance, his project revealed just how much he actually knew, which none of the other assignments or tests had been able to reveal.

These stories illustrate the twin horns of the dilemma of testing: it frees us and it hogties us. Testing serves as a gatekeeper; it allows those, who can run the gauntlet, in at the door while effectively, efficiently, and anonymously barring others who would get in.

What's in this Chapter

✦ What good data is

✦ Why standardized tests cannot give us good data

✦ Why the data we gain from standardized proficiency tests is incomplete

✦ Alternative ways of assessing

The Importance of Good Data

To be fair and reasonable, to show what students can do, assessment must be effective. Effective assessment is the key to finding answers to the questions raised in chapter 1. Stiggins (1991) writes:

> *Important instructional and policy decisions are based on information about students' achievement. If those decisions are made well, students benefit. If they are made poorly, students suffer. But those decisions can only be as sound as the data on which they are based.*

But how do we make sound decisions? How can we keep from being biased? How can we prevent our own lack of knowledge or our personal feelings from getting in the way? How can we ensure that tests are selected properly, or read the way they were meant to be read, or used for purposes for which they were intended?

To make good, fair, reasonable, and sound decisions, we need the "good data" discussed in chapter 1 (page 18) based on Stiggins criteria of a clear target, an appropriate sample, known sources of interference, and usable results. Given these criteria, what are our options?

STANDARDIZED TESTS

The Hazards of Standardized Tests

Standardized testing has become a fixture worldwide. Tests have assumed more and more importance and carry ever more weight concerning who passes, who graduates, who gets into college, who gets the scholarships, which schools get funding, and which schools get shut down. The stakes have gotten higher and higher.

When tests are used properly, they can provide some useful information. However, when they are used exclusively, they cannot provide fair and useful information about students, particularly limited-English-proficient (LEP) students. We will attempt to clarify this through a careful discussion of tests according to Stiggins's four principles of good data.

Do tests have a clear target?

Yes. Standardized tests are

+ designed for what is called "summative" data and to determine how much a student has learned

+ used to compare a student's knowledge against a set core of knowledge and skills deemed essential for him to know. For instance, a state math test for eleventh graders will probably measure students' knowledge of geometry, graphing and plotting points, and using equations. If they have learned them, they can do the operations; if they have not, they cannot

Can you obtain an appropriate sample from standardized tests?

Many say, emphatically, no. Here is what the experts (Gould, 1995; Johnson and Johnson, 2002; Neill, 2003; Popham, 2003) have against standardized tests:

+ Norm-referenced tests are designed to sort and rank students from highest to lowest. This means that questions everybody can answer are left out, and someone *has* to fail. Half the students must fall below the fifty percent mark.

+ Multiple-choice tests cannot tell you whether your student knows the material or not. When he can choose among the answers, even if he chooses randomly, he has a good chance of choosing the right one. Mark, a grade-eight student, was taking a standardized test. Barb watched with dismay as he simply ran his pencil down the page, randomly checking off answers. When she asked him why he did not try, he countered, "Why should I?" He was not a good student; he knew he had as good a chance of getting an answer right by hazarding a quick guess as he did by laboring over each answer (and probably guessing at the end anyway.) This way, if he failed, he could save face by saying he had not tried.

+ From the test, you cannot tell where exactly the student failed. Conversely, you cannot tell what he does know. Because the scores are usually calculated by percentage points and do not tell you where the student had difficulty, you, as teacher, have no concrete starting point to begin teaching.

- Standardized tests have arbitrary cut-scores. A cut-score is a point on a scale, a boundary. Those who perform above the cut-score have met some set of requirements; they are supposed to have the knowledge, skills, and abilities that are being assessed. Theoretically, those who perform below it have not demonstrated that they do.

But who decides when a score is passing and when it is not? What if a student gets a forty-two, and somebody in some office somewhere has decided that forty-three is the passing score? Kane (1994, in Cizek, 2001) pointed out that setting a standard is tantamount to making a policy decision. He states:

> ...where individuals are to be categorized differently depending on their tests scores...the values of the cut-scores can have a major impact on individual decisions. Even a small change in a cut-score can produce a substantial change in the results.

The establishing of cut-scores is a political issue. If a state or province sets the cut-score for a high-school exit exam too high, a significant number of students will not pass, and politicians will have outraged parents screaming. The score has to be just high enough for some to fail—but not too many, or everyone will know it is a sham and the emperor has no clothes. If there is no consensus among experts and establishing validity is punishingly difficult, then it would seem wise to proceed slowly and carefully.

- Tests are one-shot deals. You either do it right when you sit down at that desk on that particular day, or you do not. The curriculum for each grade covers a wide range of topics. If students happened to have studied gravity that year, they got the question right. If they did not get to it yet, too bad. The plaintive, "I did not lern that rael good," says it all. There are no second chances.

Vocabulary
Choose the word that has the same meaning, or almost the same meaning, as the underline word.

11. at the nearest corner
    - Ⓐ farthest
    - Ⓑ latest
    - Ⓒ closest
    - Ⓓ widest

12. treated me fairly
    - Ⓐ gently
    - Ⓑ loudly
    - Ⓒ justly
    - Ⓓ surely

13. will be delayed again
    - Ⓐ late
    - Ⓑ hurried
    - Ⓒ started
    - Ⓓ early

14. stroll in the park
    - Ⓐ plow
    - Ⓑ dash
    - Ⓒ work
    - Ⓓ walk

Figure 2.2 How did the student arrive at the answers for this test? Did he know them? Did he guess? Did he copy from his neighbor?

What are the known sources of interference?

What gets in the way of a student performing well? Is the data collected representative of what this student can do?

In many ways, no, for the following reasons:

- Tests are biased. The tests are normed for a particular group of people, usually middle-class, white students from the East Coast of the United States where the testing companies are based. These tests are not normed for English language learners, who comprise an extremely large and diverse group. Hakuta and Beatty

(2001) write, "Little confidence can be placed in tests that assume a mastery of English skills and that were never designed with English Language Learners [ELLs] in mind." This principle holds true not only in reading/language arts assessment but in mathematics assessments as well. And the tests are biased in more than one way.

1. They are culturally biased. Many tests simply show how familiar students are with mainstream cultural knowledge (Estrin and Nelson-Barber, 1995). The norms are set for students from the mainstream culture, and the tests do not address the cultures and experiences of poor and minority students. On one test, Chilean students were asked to complete the following: "You walk with your feet and throw with your_____." Since the dominant and most popular sport in Chile is soccer, many students completed this sentence with feet, a logical answer. However, the test was written in the United States where baseball and basketball predominate; therefore, the "correct" answer was hands.

    Here is a fourth-grade sample reading selection from the National Association for Educational Progress (NAEP) about an incident that occurred in 1777, called "Sybil's Ride":

    > Sybil, at sixteen, the oldest of eight children, could read the question in her mother's worried eyes. Would Henry Ludington have to go away again? As commander of the only colonial army regiment between Danbury, Connecticut, and Peekskill, New York, Sybil's father did not have much time to be with his family.

    Implicit in this text is the cultural understanding that in 1777, the colonies were at war with England; that being a commander, Sybil's father was often away with his troops; and that another battle meant he would have to leave again. Students who did not know these facts would be confused by the story and miss most of the meaning. In the story, Sybil's horse, which she rides to warn neighbors of the approaching soldiers, was named Star. One student, in response to the question relating to Sybil's ride, wrote:

    > **She have said a thing truth. Also she will hope Hollowood stars but. The parents haven't allow for beomce stars. After the parents finish a story, she said exactly said, "I can do it." Therefore she went studio in star.**

    This student read "Star" and immediately thought Hollywood; that her parents did not want to send her there, but that she said she could do it, and went on to be a star.

2. They are linguistically biased. The way questions are worded slows readers down, adds to their cognitive load, and makes it more likely the reader will misinterpret the reading. Major trouble spots for students include word length, sentence length, complexity of sentences, word frequency, and word familiarity. Use of passive voice, difficult negative sentence construction, subordinate and coordinate clauses, and comparative structure are problematic both for students whose primary language is English as well as for ELLs.

    As another example, consider the following very complex sentence: "Adolescence, or the transitional period between childhood and adulthood, is not only a biological concept but a social concept." It requires a knowledge of what a biological concept is as well as what a social concept is, the ability to hang on to the subject while reading through the embedded clause, and the ability to understand sophisticated vocabulary.

As a third illustration, a high-school exam included the following question:

Mercantilists believed all of the following except…

a. Wealth was as important as power.
b. Manufactured goods should be sold to foreign countries.
c. Governments should not restrict or tax trade.
d. Colonies existed to serve the parent countries.

Many ESL students, even though they might know the content of such a question, do not understand and recognize the importance of words such as *except*. In addition, each choice includes advanced language structures including the subjunctive and infinitives.

- Tests happen in a vacuum. There is no context to them. The teacher is not allowed to intervene or have any interaction with the students outside of, "Do your best!" Here are a few students' answers to a question about the difference between the sun and the earth, all of which reveal profound misunderstandings:

    The sun don't come out in winter. The sun goes away and comes back in summer.

    The sun and earth are similar because they are both here in the morning.

    The earth can't change like the sun can turn night and the sun can turn day.

    The earth spins every 24 hours and the sun goes up and down.

An outsider might blame the errors on poor teaching, but they probably result more from basic assumptions teachers make about what kids understand or do not understand about the nature of the sun and earth. Note that these answers did not come from one classroom; they are from across the state, mostly from poor districts. Other students within those classrooms wrote thoughtfully and correctly on the same question. Any teacher, upon hearing those answers within the context of a classroom discussion, would instantly clarify and re-teach.

- Students can misread test questions. There is no chance to redirect if they do; no chance to correct errors. In another example, a student linked a test question concerning how humans use plants with the question before it, which involved differences and similarities. Here is the student's response:

    Humans walk, eat, sleep and throw up. Plants grow leaves and humans don't. Plants make food through photosynthesis not an oven. Plants make fruit and humans don't.

These are all true. They are also wrong within the context of the question, and the penalty is heavy.

+ Some questions are poorly written. Questions can be unclear and just plain dumb. Students get them wrong, because they just cannot figure out what is being asked of them. They take the blame.

+ Testing companies make mistakes. The National Board on Educational Testing and Public Policy (NBETPP), an independent organization that monitors testing in the U.S., has documented the horrific errors that have sidelined tens of thousands of futures and ruined lives. Programs can have glitches, scores can be calculated incorrectly. *The Sacramento Bee* detailed errors made in calculating district performance in California. Districts that believed they had failed to meet performance standards later learned they had not; other districts were dismayed to find out that instead of celebrating their good performance, they had to report to parents that they were now considered underperforming schools (Wiener, 2005).

+ Test readers can make mistakes. They get tired, hungry, bored. They can lose their train of thought. Sometimes they feel like giving the student the benefit of the doubt, sometimes not. Sometimes they are just not sure what a student meant. Two students from separate schools across the state from each other wrote that dandelions could be made into treads for tanks. They certainly did not make that up. Where did that information come from? How can one look that up? It was marked wrong. Even the best-intentioned reader sometimes cannot decipher what students have written. *Healfy, pinsos, chruk, strean beans* are not too bad, but what about *bricis* and *blath*? It took a thoughtful reader days to figure out that "send it to the pincle company to make pincles" meant *pencils*, and she never did figure out what "it's got hiiantcke" meant. Whoever wrote it knew. But it was too late. It was not given credit. It was marked wrong.

+ Tests lack predictive value; they cannot tell you how well your students can perform in real-life situations. It is one thing to recognize the answer from a field of four choices but quite another to formulate a reasonable answer from one's own knowledge base.

Shown here are the Gates-MacGinitie predictions about Irasema, whom we discussed at the beginning of this chapter.

> **Irasema's Vocabulary scores suggest that, for her grade, she has a below average knowledge of word meanings.**
>
> **Irasema's Comprehension scores suggest that she reads typical school materials with low understanding.**
>
> **Irasema's Comprehension scores are lower than her Vocabulary scores. This difference suggests that more emphasis might be placed on reading for meaning in Irasema's instruction.**

Figure 2.3 Gates-MacGinitie predictions about Irasema

But take a look at what Irasema was truly capable of:

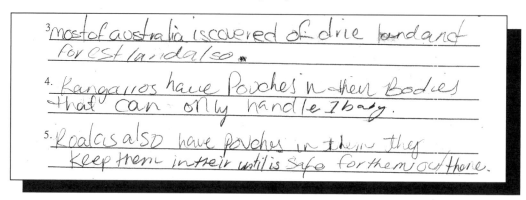

Figure 2.4 Part of Irasema's "What I Learned about Australia" assignment, which shows that her vocabulary and comprehension were nowhere near as poor as the Gates-MacGinitie predictions suggested they were

Are the results usable?

Stakeholders want to know: Is my child learning the required curriculum? Is he achieving at grade level? Are students meeting standards mandated by the state? Are schools doing their job of educating children?

So are the results usable? That depends. Traditionally, test results have been used to measure whether or not students have mastered a core of skills and knowledge or to rank students. Over time, however, tests have also come to be used for purposes for which they were not designed. If this is the case then no, they cannot produce usable results:

- No one gets to see what they did wrong or right. What they see is a number representing a score. There are no teachable moments.

- Tests do not provide teachers with immediate and/or meaningful data. Sometimes it is months before teachers get the reports. Learning in January that Juana scored twenty-six percent on a standardized reading test does not provide her teacher with anything meaningful from which to go.

There are also several fundamental problems with tests:

- They do not measure aptitudes like creativity, initiative, curiosity, independence, imagination, effort, judgment, or ethics.

- They define students by those who are making it and those who are not. Hebert (2001) writes:

    Children experience standardized tests as a means to sort the competent and the less competent. Such testing encourages them to view their own learning and that of their peers as fitting into a high, medium or low level of performance according to preordained expectations of these measures.

- Tests take the decision-making out of the hands of those who could effect the most change. "Decisions," write Tucker and Codding (1998), "ought to be made by the person who will be held responsible for the results." Tests are being used to replace decisions rather than to inform.

+ Tests divert money from other resources that contribute directly to learning. Some critics of testing (for example, the Center for the Study of Testing, Evaluation and Educational Policy [CSTEEP] and the National Center for Fair and Open Testing [FairTest]) calculate the cost of tests between $800 and $1800 per student. These estimates are based on dubious criteria however, and do no favors because of their speciousness. Others calculate the cost to be as low as $50 per student (Phelps, 1997). Even at that rate, however, it costs states millions of dollars that could be spent on books, paraprofessionals, special services, and training.

The Consequences of Tests to Schools

Anyone who has been even tangentially involved with schools knows what the upshot is. If tests are high stakes with significant consequences (Worthen, 1993; Brown, 2001) then one or more of the following is bound to happen:

+ Teachers are going to tailor their teaching to what is on the test. Drill, drill, drill. Brown (2001) writes:

> *Even though minimum standards are low, they are high stakes, and teachers often respond by altering their instruction. An inordinate amount of instruction may be focused on the objectives needed to pass the test. Because most of the students in a school are already beyond this level, the full range of their instructional needs are unmet. Ironically, the practice of teaching to the minimums can have the unintended—and negative—educational consequence of lowering expectations for the majority of students.*

+ The curriculum will narrow as a result. Classroom time is devoted to what is going to be on the test. A National Council of Teachers of English (NCTE) position statement asserted that "high stakes testing often harms students' daily experience of learning, displaces more thoughtful and creative curriculum" ("On Urging Reconsideration of High Stakes Testing", 2000). It is axiomatic that if something is going to be tested, that something is going to be taught. If capitalization and end punctuation are on the test, the tendency will be to focus on those items.

+ Creativity, richness, experimentation, and risk-taking go by the wayside. Hillocks (2002) notes, "The more time that is devoted to drill, the less time is devoted to high level thinking."

+ Schools and districts find ways to make test scores look good. Nifty ways to pad scores include:

  + Putting ESL/bilingual students in special ed, Title VII, and Chapter I (see glossary) programs

  + Putting all the "dumb" kids in the same classroom so they will not hold back the "smart" kids

  + Lowering the cut-scores so it looks like students have improved

- Encouraging students to stay home or suspending them just before test dates so their scores will not be figured in
- Encouraging low-scoring students to drop out
- Cheating

Standardized Proficiency Tests

Standardized proficiency tests exist as a subset of other standardized tests. These tests share the same characteristics of other standard tests; to ensure consistency so that scores are not skewed, all students take the same tests, under the same conditions. Standardized proficiency tests are designed specifically to measure an incoming student's level of proficiency so that teachers know just how much English he knows. They are also often used for monitoring progress and making exiting decisions. Knowing a student's level of proficiency, one can theoretically make an informed decision about placement and programs. States and provinces often mandate which proficiency tests schools are allowed to use when students enter and exit programs.

Do they have a clear target?

Yes. They are designed to measure proficiency in English.

Can you obtain an appropriate sample?

Not really. Proficiency tests have the same faults as standardized tests:

- They are single-occasion. They tell you only what that student can do at that particular time. Many places mandate that the tests are administered within a certain amount of time after the student enrolls. That newcomer might be frightened, confused, vulnerable, defensive. Ahmer had arrived from Pakistan at midnight the night before. He was exhausted, but his uncle insisted he take the tests. He did not do well and declared that his math and reading skills were rusty; he had not had to use them in a long time. If Ahmer had taken the tests on a day he felt rested and competent, he could have done much better.

  Hiro's mother registered him at school. When she left through the front door, Hiro bolted out the back. It took several hours to find him, several days to calm him down enough so he could be left alone in the classroom without constant attention from the parapro, and several weeks before he would speak. Testing him would have been pointless on the day of registration.

  Many school districts, saddled with state and provincial mandates that approve only a limited number of tests, make both entry and exit decisions using the same test. Students become "test-wise" and learn, through several trials and through the grapevine, the right answers to the questions. Michael registered at the local university and took the ESL placement tests. He wrote an essay with great fluency and ease. The problem: he had answered the prompt from last year's test.

- Proficiency tests fragment skills. One test may measure grammatical knowledge with such questions as "He is _____ carpenter." Mastery of grammar is only one facet of

---

1. Amy _____ her new dress to the dance last night.

   a) wear   (b) were   (c) wore   (d) went

2. The clouds looked threatening, but _____ the sun came out.

   (a) then   (b) when   (c) than   (d) where

Figure 2.5 Proficiency tests fragment skills.

knowing a language, and a student's apparent success or failure is not an indication of his ability to use the language in a different context, such as in a conversation or when reading a book.

+ Proficiency tests also have arbitrary cut-scores. This has a major impact not only on who gets put into what program, but who is eligible for which services. For instance, in Wisconsin, a level 3 or higher (see chapter 3) means that a student is required to take the reading comprehension test and the Wisconsin Knowledge and Concepts Exam (WKCE) along with his English-speaking peers.

Although the cut-scores are established through a Modified Angoff (a complicated procedure requiring a panel to rate questions according to basic standards and a projected percentage of success) and compared to test publishers' technical manuals, they are based only on a broad prediction that students who achieve a certain score should be able to function at such and such a level. More important, they determine whether a school is meeting its yearly progress quota.

Baker (1991) reported that the Office of Civil Rights decided to use the forty-percent cutoff to classify students needing services. When asked to justify the percentile cutoff used, staff responded that a consensus had been reached for the score that would identify a student who was not doing well in school. Baker wrote, "While that may very well be true, such a score does not tell us whether this student needs special language instruction, because a single score alone cannot differentiate among the several possible causes of a low score."

Arbitrariness has no place in the lives of students, especially those who depend so heavily on what we do in school to help them further their dreams of a decent future. Gullickson (2003) states, "The adequacy of information gathered should be ensured, so that good decisions are possible and can be defended and justified."

+ Proficiency tests are removed from a meaningful context. Studies have demonstrated the vast differences between what a person can produce in the classroom, in the hallways, and at home, and what he can produce in response to stilted, isolated prompts from an examiner. For instance, one seventh-grader who did poorly on a proficiency test also produced these sentences during one recess on the playground:

> **Where you going?**
>
> **Are you graduate this year?**
>
> **What is you eating in the lunch yesterday?**

When you go back to Mexico?

Why you not stay in Mexico?

Who broke pencil yesterday?

Will do you go to the park?

Who is not going to the store today?

Individually, the questions reveal that the student has not grasped English tenses. Together, however, they reveal that his command of grammar, such as word order in question-making, is quite advanced. His final sentence is correct.

♦ You cannot tell how or why a student reached the answer he did on a proficiency test. He may have guessed; he may have been savvy enough to find the answer without being able to read. For instance, in figure 2.6, the student could pick out the correct answer (popcorn) simply by looking through the text, without understanding. Her score sheet reveals simply that she did poorly, not why; nor does it tell what she actually could do.

Popcorn is a popular American snack. It is made from corn kernels that are heated until they pop. Most people add butter and salt to the popcorn before they eat it. Americans love popcorn so much that they eat about 450 million pounds a year.

The American Indians showed the first settlers how to make and eat popcorn. Some Indians used popcorn for soup; others used it for jewelry. Now it is mainly eaten, but sometimes children put popcorn on a string to feed birds or to decorate a tree or window.

1. Americans eat 450 million pounds of:
(a) butter   (c) popcorn
(b) salt   (d) soup

Passage 2: Popcorn ....
1. a
2. d
3. d
4. d

Figure 2.6 Excerpt from a reading comprehension test with student's answers

What are the known sources of interference?

♦ Proficiency tests are biased in two ways.

1. They are linguistically biased. Some tests are translated into Spanish and a handful of other languages. If the instructions are not translated into the language of the student, the teacher has no way of knowing if he understood.

2. They are culturally biased. Asking children to identify a picture of a camel, an octopus, or men panning for gold or to listen to a story about computer matter that may not be within their frame of knowledge does not tell us what they can do in English. They may not have words for snow or snowman in their own language and would, therefore, find it impossible to identify either (see figure 2.7).

Figure 2.7 This portion of the Cambridge Young Learners English test includes pictures of snowmen. For those students who have never seen or experienced snow and cold, this set of pictures would be out of their range of knowledge, and they would likely have great difficulty discussing the content.

+ Proficiency tests do not tell us what we want most to know: Can this student succeed in a regular English classroom? Can he successfully perform the same tasks as can students whose primary language is English? In technical terms, proficiency tests lack "predictive validity." A student who gets a good score on a proficiency test may or may not actually be at the level the test places him. He may not be ready to compete with fully proficient students in the regular classroom. In the same vein, a low score does not necessarily mean he is not ready to be mainstreamed.

One test, which asks students to read words such as *moustache, cologne, sufficient, bouquet,* and *stochastic,* was ostensibly testing reading but was really testing decoding skills and measuring experience in the vagaries of English. This sort of test gives false scores. Japanese students, for instance, do well on this portion but understand very little of what they read, even at a basic level.

Are the results usable?

Yes, to a certain extent. Proficiency tests can give a basic picture of the student, a ballpark classification of his language capabilities, such as NEP (non-English proficient) or LEP (limited-English proficient). However, since they are often used again and again to classify and reclassify students into and out of programs, the results may not be usable. A student labeled FEP (fully-English proficient) is no longer eligible for services, but he may have acquired the label simply because friends told him the answers or because he has taken the same test over and over and knows the answers.

Many assert that not only are such tests unusable, they are dangerous. The United States Department of Education administered a test called the Language Measurement and Assessment Instrument to a nationally representative sample of students whose primary language was English and classified forty-two percent of them as LEP. And, in a little experiment completed a few years ago, Barb and the principal of an inner-city school asked the third-grade teachers to administer the written portion of the Language Assessment Survey (LAS) to their students. A great number of them scored in the LEP range. To the right is a portion of one of the mandated tests.

wow

1. First pet the horse and then *the sacen pet is the hand.*
2. Nobody answered the door, so *I don't haff to answered my door?*
3. When the newspaper comes, *My dad will read the paper comes my dad will read it.*
4. After the storm is over, *I will see what ampon waen storm hant.*
5. He is afraid of dogs because *maybe he geats afraid of dogs.*

Figure 2.8 After completing this mandated, standardized proficiency test, this little girl was labeled LEP, needing services. Interestingly, her primary language was English.

Many teachers confide that since the tests are mandated and they must use them to gather information about a student's proficiency, they pay more attention to how the student takes the test and what he does while taking it than to the actual test scores.

Testing Is Here to Stay

If these criticisms are valid and pressing, why do politicians and taxpayers continue to insist on using standardized tests? There are several reasons.

- Likely the most important reason is our confidence in tests. As Hebert (2001) writes:

  We have devoted close to a century of experience toward the development of the form, data, and conduct of standardized testing. The content of evaluation and the explicit standards for achievement on these measures have been clearly defined.

- Reluctance to change. Change is hard. Change takes time. Change takes a lot of energy and motivation. Try changing your partner sometime.

- Because change is difficult, cumbersome, and time-consuming, tests offer a comparatively cheap way to measure progress and adherence to new rules.

- Tests offer the appearance of hard data. Alternative assessment seems "squishy," unscientific, and too subjective.

- Accountability. We can hold teachers, schools, and districts to task based on the outcome of the tests. Falk (2000) writes that "test scores are the loudest voice in the public conversation about teacher and school accountability."

- The need to demonstrate competence. The public wants ways to identify whether or not students are learning what they are supposed to.

- They have the appearance of scientific objectivity. People trust the results more than simply trusting the teachers.

- Tests provide information that stakeholders want.

- Both the language and the format of tests is something we have all experienced and, therefore, something we understand.

- The assumption is that tests can measure student learning. In a brochure called "A Parent's Guide to Standards and Assessment (1999)," the Wisconsin Department of Public Instruction, warned, "The test scores will show how each child is doing in the tested areas…If your child scores in a lower proficiency level, even in grade 4, you should be concerned. A low proficiency score in grade 4 is an early warning that your child may need help to develop the knowledge and skills required for that grade."

ALTERNATIVES TO STANDARDIZED TESTING

The criticisms we have presented demand that we ask, what other means of gathering information are there? There has been much discussion about additional forms of assessment. Do they do what we need?

To begin, we can clarify the similarities and differences between assessment and testing. Both share the same goal: to collect information in order to make a decision. They also share several fundamental characteristics: in each method, you are getting only a sample of the student's knowledge, skills, and abilities; and, just as important, you have to make an inference from that sample. It should be clear from those features how important it is to get a range of samples from several different tasks and contexts. It should also be apparent how crucial the means of gathering information are to getting a true picture of that student, and just how much the tester/assessor's assumptions factor into making the inferences.

While assessment and testing share some fundamental qualities, there is an important difference between the two. Mitchell (1992) defines a test as a "single-occasion, unidimensional, timed exercise, usually in multiple choice or short-answer form." Testing is formal, and is often standardized. Everyone takes the test under the same conditions. In other words, everyone is given the exact procedures for administering and scoring, the same test materials and items, and the same norms against which the student is compared.

Assessment is a broader term. It implies evaluation based on a collection of information about what students know and can do. This means many ways and methods of gathering, at different times, in different contexts. Testing is part of assessment, and using additional forms of assessment does not mean total abandonment of standardized testing. But, as we demonstrate with the Quad (see page 117), testing is only one means of gathering information about a student. The focus in testing is on finding the norm. Assessment is broader; you are looking at progress over time in a variety of contexts. As Neill and Medina (1989) point out, assessment is about the *how* of learning as well as the *what* and *how much*.

Finding Additional Ways to Assess Student Competence

Not a single piece of research says, "Use only one form of assessment to gain information about students." Not one. Even government forums call for multiple forms of assessment. But all too often, high-stakes tests are used as the sole criteria for "life event" decisions including graduation, promotion, or retention. Negative decisions can be catastrophic for individuals.

Nobody disputes that parents, districts, and the government need to know how students are doing. Nobody argues with the concept of accountability. What we need is a way to answer the needs of all the stakeholders. We continue to assert that teachers' needs for accurate information are of paramount importance, but we have to answer to the public as well. Kohn (1999) writes:

> *A teacher designed—and perhaps externally validated—assessment doesn't meet only the teacher's needs. If it's done right, it also meets the needs of parents and citizens to make sure that the teachers and schools are doing a decent job. Parents want to be reassured that the teacher's judgment is reasonable and that, in the face of largely exaggerated press reports about the failure of our schools, our kids are being well educated.*

Assessing Alternative Assessment

Alternative forms of assessment are not without their faults, and they should be afforded as much critical and stringent scrutiny as are standardized tests.

Do they have a clear target?

Yes. We want to know more than simply scores. Alternative assessments are designed to reveal a broader range of information that will give us not just a snapshot but a dynamic picture of students' development, both academic and linguistic. Our target is to

- find out how the student learns, and reveal the strategies he uses
- determine whether the student actually knows the material or not
- reveal higher-order skills
- see how much progress a student has made over time; demonstrate growth
- find information within the context of the regular classroom
- learn about each student's individual needs
- gain knowledge that we can apply to our teaching

Can we obtain an appropriate sample?

Again, the answer is yes. Alternative assessment

- can provide data that truly represents what students' capabilities are. We can directly determine whether the student has synthesized information or made proper inferences about the material. We can differentiate between competence and performance.
- allows us to continue to look for answers if one method does not give us enough information. If the student cannot perform a task on a particular day, we have the time and the opportunity to discover whether he can perform the task at a different time, in a different situation, perhaps with different instructions or media.

What are the known sources of interference?

Unfortunately, this question is the major hurdle that must be addressed by those who use other forms of assessment. The criticisms are as follows.

- **Manageability.** Methods of alternative assessment are cumbersome. They require lots of thought, space, logistics, and training. If you are already "taxed to the max" with other duties, you must be able to incorporate assessment into your classroom schedule and do it justice. Assessment must be doable, manageable, readable, and valuable to the next teacher and to the parent, both of whom question what and how the student is doing. DRESS does a good job I think

+ **Reliability.** This refers to the dependability and consistency of scores or information. A test is considered reliable if, for instance, a student takes the same test at different times and the scores he achieves are roughly the same. It is reliable if two or more raters can agree on the scores. Because alternative assessment is a much more subjective process, critics argue that it cannot be held to the same standards of reliability as tests.

+ **Bias.** Bias is when "irrelevant or arbitrary factors systematically influence interpretations and judgments made in evaluations in a way that differentially affects the performance of an individual or subgroup" (Gullickson, 2003). Assessments done in the classroom by a teacher are subject to the biases, beliefs, likes, and dislikes of that teacher toward the students, as well as her knowledge about language learners and their error patterns. Gullickson continues: "Bias can undermine the fairness of a student's evaluation and distort the assessment process and corrupt judgment and decisions leading to potentially faulty follow-up to the detriment of a student."

1. Alternative assessment can be culturally biased. Just as standardized tests are known to be culturally biased, so too can be other types of assessment of non-English-speaking students by untrained, insensitive, or ignorant teachers. Misunderstanding of ways of speaking, turn-taking rules, norms for politeness, or simply a bias against an ethnic group can lead to avoidance, lowered expectations, or rejection of the student. This can lead to failure for reasons divorced from the student's abilities.

   uh between each word when Lily tested girl, we didn't count as errors

2. Alternative assessment can be linguistically biased. A student's English proficiency and a teacher's ability to understand his attempts can have a profound effect on what she sees and interprets. One teacher can deem a paper wholly unreadable and riddled with errors where another can see creativity and depth of thought.

   Franco wrote this paragraph as part of an English essay on "Dover Beach" by Matthew Arnold:

   > **Dover Beach beattiful beach in England were the sea is beautiful at night when the moon lies in the ocean and the cliffs of England shine at the forness. Dover Beach talks about how in one time everything was beautiful and the only thing that we had was faith but now what is left is hatred and war, that beauty can come if we only love.**

   Most of Franco's essay contained run-on sentences and errors in syntax, grammar, and spelling. His twelfth-grade English teacher may have been overwhelmed at first reading of this essay. How does she go about grading a paper like this? The surface errors detract from what is really going on. If she had given equal weight to fluency and word choice as she gave to understanding and organization, he would have received a low grade. However, to a trained eye, it is clear that Franco knew what the poem was about. He understood the sense of melancholy and loss.

   ↳ this is what is more important.

Here is another student's writing sample:

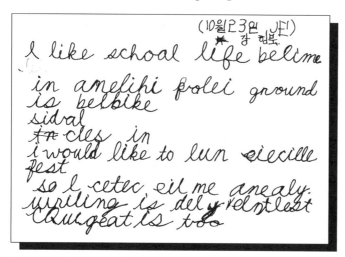

Figure 2.9 Student's writing sample

In figure 2.9, the writer was saying, "I like school life because in America, playground is very big. In school class I would like to learn English fast so I can talk to my American friends. Writing is the hardest. Speaking is tool." A teacher tuned into the idea of language learning as a continuum—whereby a student grapples simultaneously with syntax, vocabulary, and transcription in a language in which he is not proficient—will be able to see through the errors to an admirable attempt at conveying meaning rather than a woeful lack of proficiency in spelling and grammar. The school that espouses the drill-and-kill method of teaching will have a difficult time using assessment to measure real progress in learning accurately.

- **Validity.** This refers to the trustworthiness of the inferences a teacher draws from the assessment. The method itself can be valid, but the inferences drawn from it can be invalid. If we are to trust other measures of collecting information, we have to believe that the inferences individual teachers draw from them are also true and defensible. Otherwise, they will do as much harm as any other form of assessment.

- **Standardization.** This is the biggie. Teachers vary in an infinite number of ways. First and foremost, they are people who bring their own value systems with them to the classroom. Governments have tried to instate assessment systems rooted in a common core of values and knowledge, built on uniform and public standards, intending to effect systemic reform and hold students across the nation accountable to the same expectations. But teachers are, and should be, unique individuals, each with their own way of doing things. It is almost impossible to get consensus and have teachers adhere to uniform methods of anything, much less testing and grading. Herein lies both the beauty and the burden of additional or alternative forms of assessment.

Are the results usable?

Yes. The benefits outweigh the criticisms. Alternative, balanced assessment focuses on the learning strategies a student employs, an inventory from which new strategies and new learning develop. With the results, you can make appropriate decisions about what to teach next based on which areas need more work and which areas the student has mastered. Alternative assessment

+ allows us to diagnose, prescribe, intervene, verify, and certify progress in a continuous cycle

+ provides the information now, not after the fact

+ provides a continuous flow of information, not intermittent bursts. Only classroom assessment can do this, not once-yearly checks

+ provides information that is accurate enough to be useful

+ encourages learning by "helping teachers and students believe that their continued efforts will result in success" (National Education Association [NEA], 2003)

+ supports and enhances learning instead of simply verifying that learning has taken place

+ is driven by the concept of improvement. Balanced assessment means "teachers can use the classroom assessment process and its results to support each student's specific learning, regardless of where the student falls along an achievement continuum" (NEA, 2003)

+ informs students about themselves IMPORTANT

+ gives students and teachers control over their learning

+ balances the equation. No single assessment can meet everybody's information needs

When we rely on a lone piece of evidence, critical bits of information do not reach the crucial decision makers.

Most importantly, perhaps, "improved formative assessment helps low achievers more than other students" (Black and William, 1998). ELL students often fall into the low achievement category simply because they have not achieved the language yet to compete with their age mates. — *probably will use in paper*

BALANCED ASSESSMENT

What we are calling for is balanced assessment or, more specifically, counterbalanced assessment. In chapter 5, How and Where to Find Information, we discuss the "Quad" (page 117), which offers details of the breadth of data required to provide comprehensive, balanced assessment. A complete picture of a student can be created by piecing together data, including test data, garnered from assessment methods found in all four quadrants. This picture can help teachers and administrators identify both areas where students are functioning well and those where more intensive teaching or re-teaching is necessary. Intervention strategies can also be developed for students who are being left behind.

Balanced assessment focuses on the strategies a student employs and helps you to create an inventory from which new strategies and new learning can develop. Students can leave school or go on to the next grade with a record of what they *have* mastered and *can* do, rather than with a simple list of scores that reveal only failure to succeed on one type of assessment. Using balanced assessment

- gives a fuller and fairer account of a wider range of experience than standardized testing can

- recognizes types of achievement that are not always evident with conventional methods of assessment

- can be adapted to different teachers, styles, classrooms, purposes

- fosters a learning-through-success pedagogy that provides a continuous record of tasks that the student has achieved

When we use balanced assessment, educators, administrators, parents, students, and the general public have concrete data by which to judge a student's success. You, the teacher, have

- a clearer picture of the student's proficiency level and capabilities

- data on which to base decisions about curriculum, matriculation, retention

- a course of action to follow

- doable options for teaching and assessing

Students have

- a clear picture of their own capabilities and levels of proficiency

- a positive record of what they have accomplished

- a sense of control and power over their own education and their future

Parents have

- a concrete record of their child's learning and capabilities

- an awareness of the level at which their child is functioning *now*

- a sense of direction for their child

- clear expectations for what their child will be learning and how they have been evaluated

Administrators have

- a concrete record of each student's accomplishments and proficiency level

- a set of records from which to base larger programmatic and curricular decisions

- clear data that either support or refute the model upon which the programs are built

- a sense of security that students will benefit because they feel good about themselves

CONCLUSION

Even in the early 1990s when educators were excited and optimistic, we recognized that alternative assessment had a long uphill climb ahead of it to iron out its inherent difficulties. By the end of the decade, experts were realizing just how difficult that change would be. Lachat (1999) writes:

> *...shifting from a testing to an assessment culture involves changing assumptions* *about the nature of intelligence and about how people learn. Because testing and assessment cultures have radically different belief systems and goals, helping educators and the public understand the implications of this change in point of view is an important part of education reform.*

→ My undergrad portfolio.

Since the turn of the century, however, the testing culture has won out in the realm of policymakers in the U.S., Canada, and abroad. Consequently, the focus is on standardized test results to the exclusion of all other pertinent data. William Ayers (in Cizek, 2001) writes, "The American school crisis is neither natural nor uniform, but particular and selective; it is a crisis of the poor, of the cities of Latino and African American communities" (and, we might add, the immigrant communities). He continues:

> *By failing that huge group without seriously addressing the ways school has failed them—that is, without changing the structures and cultures of those schools— is to punish those kids for the mistakes and errors of all of us. Further, the vaunted standard turns out to be nothing more than a single standardized test, a relatively simpleminded gate designed so that half of those who take it must not succeed.*

We are advocating a return to a more level-headed approach to assessment, in which multiple forms of assessment are used to gather information about students. How else can the varying stakeholders make informed decisions? Each stakeholder must make choices that will affect what happens next. They need *all* the information in order to succeed. Orfield and Kornhaber (2001) write, "If we are going to put a serious emphasis on tests, it is very important that they be good tests, and that they assess material that students have actually been taught." This is true for all forms of assessment and should be our ultimate goal as we explore ways to document learning and inform teaching.

Gullickson et al. (2003) write, "The adequacy of information gathered should be ensured, so that good decisions are possible and can be defended and justified." The following chapters are designed to help you gather adequate information so that you can make good decisions.

Determining the Navel Assigned to the Factor

PLACEMENT

3

W hen fifty new students arrived unexpectedly in the school district, all the teachers at elementary, middle, and secondary levels were caught off guard. A local meat-packing plant had recruited and hired from abroad but neglected to tell the schools that workers were arriving with their families. Panic ensued. No one knew what the laws were regarding non-English-speaking students. No one had any idea how to go about placing them in the right classes. No one knew how to determine their levels of English proficiency. Amid ringing phones and swinging doors, the secretaries meted out placements as they saw fit: according to who might have an extra seat in her room or even which teacher happened to walk through the office door, making quick judgments based on age and size and sending students down the hall with notes to their new teachers, leaving terrified kids facing dumbfounded teachers.

What's in this Chapter

+ A process for identifying Limited English Proficient (LEP) students
+ A process for determining the oral proficiency of LEP students
+ A process for determining the literacy levels of LEP students
+ Guidelines for where students should be placed, based on the results

Being Prepared

Districts that are prepared for ESL students have two procedures in common. First, they have an established sequence for testing and placement. Second, they use a battery of assessment instruments to gradually sharpen their focus and profile of each student, making placement into programs and grades as accurate as possible. Even if you are the only one who teaches ESL at your school, it is critical to establish a process that all personnel can follow, ideally at the district level as well as at the school level. This process includes the following components:

+ A list of available interpreters

+ (A) designated individual(s) responsible for overseeing intake, administering tests, keeping records, requesting records from previous schools, placing students, and ensuring that teachers receive appropriate information about those students

+ A home-language survey

+ A list of tests or assessment instruments to use in the initial placement decision

+ A step-by-step procedure for how and when to administer these tests

Making Informed Placement Decisions

Information is the key to addressing the challenge of appropriate placement—adequate information with which to make reasoned, well-thought out decisions. Schools need to collect pertinent information about each student and then share it with all individuals who have an interest in or influence on the student's learning future. Only then can sound placement decisions be made. In this chapter, we present an ideal procedure that removes much of the guesswork and can help you make informed placement decisions. Each step narrows the field and focuses more closely on the student, on his abilities, and on his level of English proficiency so you can collect enough information to make decisions that will benefit the student.

Step 1: Identify

Who: All new students enrolling in K-12

Why: To establish who is potentially eligible for ESL services

What to use: Home-language survey

Step 1a: Decide

Register in regular program students who speak English only. For students whose primary language is other than English, go to step 2.

Step 2: Assess oral proficiency

Who: All students whose home-language survey reveals their primary language is not English

Why: To determine their English language proficiency

What to use: Oral interview or standardized form

Step 2a: Decide

For students entering grades K-2, or if fluent in oral English (fully English proficient, or FEP) and entering grade three, enroll in regular program. For all others, go to step 3.

Step 3: Assess literacy

Who: All students in grades 3-12 who are non-English proficient (NEP) or limited English proficient (LEP)

Why: To determine the level of academic assistance students will need

What to use: Mandated standardized tests, writing samples

Step 3a: Decide

Enroll in regular program those students who are fluent in written English. For students NEP or LEP in written English, go to step 4.

Step 4: Tentative placement

This step is not fixed and can involve moving students should you find they are too advanced or too limited in proficiency or content knowledge.

Step 5: Learning more: narrowing the field

Who: All NEP, LEP, and FEP students

Why: To gain more insight into what strategies students use for reading and writing

What to use: Concepts of print test, reading samples, writing samples

The who, what, what to use was a little confusing Flowchart would be better. VISUAL.

DEFINING PROFICIENCY

Before we talk about assessment and placement, we need to discuss what an LEP student actually is. We want to prevent misplacing a student due to improper identification or operating under the assumption that he automatically needs services because his name is Roderigo Lopez or Mai Xiong. The old "if it looks like a duck, walks like a duck" strategy does not work if you have not figured out what a duck is. Definitions are in order first, because they lay the foundation for determining who needs services and what type.

A limited-English proficient student, according to the United States Department of Education (1994), is:

> *A person who was not born in the [country of residence] or whose native language is a language other than English and comes from an environment where a language other than English is dominant; or…has had a significant impact on such an individual's level of English language proficiency…[a person] who has sufficient difficulty speaking, writing, reading or understanding the English language, and whose difficulties may deny such individual the opportunity to learn successfully in classrooms where the language of instruction is English or to participate fully in our society.*

Currently, there are no universal definitions of the levels of English language learners. This is problematic for several reasons.

+ What one state or district determines to be a functioning student may be different from another

- Some states and some of the more frequently used standardized tests designate only three levels: beginning, intermediate, and advanced, or NES (non-English speaking), LEP, and FEP. This is inaccurate and much too simplistic. The range between a low intermediate student and one who is bordering on advanced can be vast. Learning that a student is "a limited reader and a limited writer with a score of 78" is not helpful information

- It hampers decision making about which services are appropriate for which level of proficiency

- It muddies the task of trying to decide when a student can be weaned from special services

Why Definitions Are Important

- Using the same definitions keeps everyone who is involved in the assessment, placement, and exiting of students on the same page, particularly if the definitions include both oral and academic proficiency. If, for instance, Patty at Meadowview and Cathy at Riverdale perceive "level 1" (see page 47) differently, Patty might keep a student in an ESL or bilingual program whereas Cathy might have exited this student long ago.

- Programmatic decisions are tied not only to students' level of functioning but also to the number of agreed-upon levels. One small city in the Midwest had built their ESL program around large numbers of preliterate Asians. Eventually, the students mastered English, grew up, and graduated. When their children came to the same school speaking English, there was no longer a need for as many teachers working on basic literacy and survival skills at levels 1 and 2. Then, the town experienced an influx of Eastern Europeans, many of whom had had schooling in their own countries; thus, the ESL program focused on academics, core classes, and support for the mainstreamed students. Soon after, an influx of Kurdish and African refugees resettled in the town and, again, the program had to retool.

- Funding is tied to numbers. A district's funding for special programming and services is determined by the students' levels of proficiency and the programs into which they are placed.

You may live in a jurisdiction that has its own standards and definitions of levels of proficiency. For illustration purposes, we offer what we think are ideal definitions of the various levels of English language proficiency. Even if you live in an area that employs only three levels, you can use these to be more precise about what your student knows and can do.

We use definitions employed by WIDA (World-class Instructional Design and Assessment), which we think are exemplary because they define proficiency in terms of both oral and literacy skills. We also incorporate Michigan's sensible division of WIDA's proficiency level 1 into two distinct groups of newcomers.

The idea that English proficiency is defined by more than an ability to speak well and clearly is significant for teachers and students alike; too often, students are exited from programs solely on the basis of their speaking abilities. They enter the regular classroom and flame out spectacularly or simply fade away and disappear because they cannot keep up. Also important is the introduction and emphasis of both academic skills and literacy right from the beginning.

Here are WIDA's definitions of the five levels of English language proficiency. Later, when we give examples of student interviews and writing samples, we include detailed descriptors of each level to help you see concretely what we mean.

Level 1: Entering

Level 1a

Students have extremely limited educational experience. They may have had seriously interrupted schooling, be pre-literate or semi-literate in their native language, and/or have minimal understanding of the function of literacy. Their performance is significantly below grade level, and they may lack awareness of the organization and culture of school. They cannot participate meaningfully in testing and need time to adjust to school and their new cultural surroundings.

Level 1b

Students do not understand, speak, read, or write in English with any degree of fluency but may know a few words or expressions in English.

Level 2: Beginning

Students can understand simple sentences in English but speak using only isolated words and expressions. They are at an emergent level of reading and writing in English and understand parts of lessons.

Level 3: Developing

Students understand and speak conversational and academic English with hesitancy and difficulty. With effort and assistance, they can carry on conversations in English, understand at least parts of lessons, and follow simple directions, but they make noticeable errors in grammar. These students are at a beginning level of reading and writing in English, and they need assistance in content areas (for both reading and writing) to achieve at a level appropriate to their grade and age.

Level 4: Expanding

Students understand and speak conversational English without apparent difficulty, but they understand and speak academic English with some difficulty. They are at an intermediate level of reading and writing in English. They demonstrate some skill in selecting language appropriate to any given situation, can organize ideas in writing, and can read a variety of authentic materials. They still read significantly below grade level.

Level 5: Bridging

Students understand and speak both conversational and academic English well but need assistance with reading and writing in content areas to achieve at a level appropriate to their grade and age. They have mastered the technical language in content areas for comprehension and speaking, and they are making the leap to meeting state academic content standards for reading and writing.

With these definitions in mind, teachers and schools can begin to learn who their students are and what they need. The definitions are quite general and cover a lot of ground, allowing for a great deal of latitude and range among students. They also build in the assumption that even students who are highly proficient and may be mainstreamed must be monitored and receive assistance when necessary. Too often, because the needs of less proficient students consume our full attention, the more proficient learners are left to cope on their own when they still need help and guidance from teachers.

[handwritten: we do have monitoring for exited students]

PLACING A NEW STUDENT

Step One: Initial Identification

When a new student arrives at the school or district, there are certain basics you need to know about him:

+ Does he speak a language other than English?

+ Does he speak any English?

+ Can he read in his own language?

+ Can he read in English?

+ Can he function on his own in the mainstream class, or does he need help?

+ How much help does he need?

The Home-Language Survey

The first step in assessing an incoming student is finding out what language(s) he knows and speaks. Most school districts routinely administer to parents a home-language survey as part of the enrollment procedures for new students. In the United States and Canada, the law requires this. Although the questions vary, here are the five standard ones:

1. Which language did your child first learn?

2. Which language does your child use at home most often?

3. In which language do you speak to your child most often?

4. Does your child know any other languages?

5. In which language does your child speak most often with friends and neighbors outside your home?

Why the home-language survey matters

The home-language survey provides you with a baseline idea of *potential* LEP students. It is a quick-sort mechanism that tells you who is a proficient speaker in English as a primary language and who is not. The survey

+ is an initial red light that helps you identify who needs testing and who is competent enough in English to be immediately mainstreamed. For example, you do not need to further screen Mara when you know she comes from an English-speaking background. You can then focus your attention on Vladimir who is not fluent and needs to be assessed for his capabilities.

+ helps you get a lead on what resources you will need to work with the student, so you can begin amassing materials in the student's home language.

+ helps you determine which local language group to alert. For example, a school district in the Sacramento area saw the beginnings of a trend in Russian-speaking students and began searching for interpreters *before* the wave hit. When the real need arose, the school district already had resources to contact for translation purposes.

+ identifies what language(s) the student can speak, including his first language. You cannot always tell what nationality a student is or guess their primary language by their last name. Michael Young might be Chinese, he might be Dutch. Ahmed Mahjour has a Persian name; his Iranian father speaks Farsi, but his mother is Japanese, and he has reached school age fluent in Japanese with only receptive proficiency in Farsi.

  This information is also useful when you do not have an interpreter for the student's first language. For example, a student who speaks Khmer, for which you have no interpreters, may also speak Thai because he grew up in Thai refugee camps. You can try to find an interpreter with some common ground.

+ indicates how much English the student hears at home and whether the English he hears at school is the extent of his exposure.

What the home-language survey does not tell you

+ *How much* of any language the student knows
+ In which language the student is dominant
+ Which language the student prefers to use
+ In which language the student was schooled
+ Whether or not the student is fully proficient in English

A home language survey tells you what language is used at home; it does not tell you *how* it is used, by *whom*, for *what purposes*, and so on. Baker (1991) cautions:

> *Since there are large intergenerational differences in language use in immigrant groups, knowing that a child's parents or grandparents speak Spanish, for example, provides no information as to what language the child speaks. A monolingual English-speaking child could answer yes to the question whether someone in the home speaks a language other than English.*

The wording of the questions is, therefore, important, and it is critical *not* to assume the student speaks other languages that are spoken in the home. For answers to the above issues, and to determine whether or not the student is dependent on a language other than English, we must look further.

Step Two: Oral Proficiency

The next step in the placement procedure is to determine the spoken language proficiency of each student. While it is mandatory in most North American districts to administer some formal tests (and there are usually only certain ones that states and provinces use), these are time-consuming and tiresome. In addition, often they tell you only what you already know, and worse, you spent a great deal of time on activities that are ineffective and focus on fine-tuned, minor details.

Moreover, the tests are tests—there is very little about them that are natural. To get a clear picture of what a student can produce, you want to engage him in as natural a discussion as possible. This is tricky. As Underhill (1987) notes:

> Two people having a conversation on a topic of common interest…is also the hardest to make happen in the framework of a language test; it can only occur when both parties are relaxed and confident and something sparks between them…the oral test then reaches its highest degree of authenticity by no longer being a test.

You need to take some steps to create a relaxed setting. Try choosing a non-threatening environment: a room with a window that looks out onto a natural setting or a space with few desks and some pleasing posters, away from the hustle and bustle of the front office or students coming in and out.

When you are in this testing situation, limit your own talk so the student can speak. Allow him time to hesitate and to sort out what he is trying to say.

Over the years, we have developed a quick-and-dirty method that will tell you, within a few minutes, what you need to know about a student's oral proficiency in English. Five questions ought to do it.

1. What is your name?

2. How old are you?

3. Tell me about your family. *Or,* Do you like_____?

4. What will you do (after class, when you get home, and so on)?

5. What would you do if (the school caught on fire, you saw a bear, and so on)?

We like these questions for several reasons.

+ They focus on the student and not on the language per se. It is very tricky to engage in a natural discussion when a student knows he is being tested, he is new to the country, and he is in an unfamiliar situation with a stranger. These questions allow him to talk about something in which he is interested and with which he is comfortable.

+ They are designed in an ascending order of difficulty. If, as Underhill (1987) suggests, you begin with easy questions—such as the first one, to which the answer is a simple statement of fact, and build up to harder and more linguistically challenging ones, such as "why?" and speculative questions—you can stop when the student's language fizzles out. Or, if he shows proficiency, you can ask all the questions. You can even expand on simpler topics to gain more information.

+ They are designed to elicit a range of grammatical abilities that will become evident if the student has the knowledge.

+ They are open-ended so that you can expand on them and elicit more conversation if the student is willing and capable, if he or she expresses interest in a given topic, or if a particular situation presents itself (such as a student's arrival in the dead of winter).

+ You can add to them with a question such as "Why do you think so?", which is a more sophisticated question requiring a more sophisticated knowledge of English structures.

+ You can add to, subtract from, or change questions according to the student. You can expand certain questions if you suspect he can answer in more detail, or, you can add different questions for the same reason. You can follow a line of conversation if it is going well, or abandon the questions altogether if he cannot get past "What is your name?"

You can also explore how well your student can ask you questions. Suggest that he ask you about the school routine, your family, a hobby, or something general about you. Observe how your student responds to your answers. Can he respond with a statement of his own? What the student says, how he says it, even what he does physically (for example, he continually shifts in the chair) reveal much and give you data to support your instincts.

Assessing for oral language is only one part of the picture. Oral proficiency is not an indication of total grasp of English: there are many who have learned English as a subject in school and are very literate in the language while their spoken English is abysmal at best. Conversely, there are those who have impressive speaking abilities in English but they can neither read nor write in the language. It can present great difficultues if students are exited from support programs based on their oral output alone. It is important to get a complete picture by assessing both oral proficiency and literacy. Here are some case examples of oral proficiency interviews (tests) at each level of English-language proficiency.

Level 1: Entering

Characteristics

Students have little English comprehension or production. They may have memorized some phrases. They may be able to answer simple "yes" or "no" questions and follow simple directions. They respond nonverbally to simple commands, statements, and questions. They may be able to follow simple instructions and demonstrate their understanding nonverbally. For example:

> What is your name?
> **Judy.**
>
> How old are you?
> **I'm fine.**

Do you like Michigan?
I don't know.

What will you do when you go home today?
I don't know.

Judy gave a correct response to the first question only. It was apparent that she had memorized some stock phrases such as "I'm fine" and "I don't know." She was unable to carry on even the simplest of conversations.

Level 2: Beginning

Characteristics

Students can comprehend and repeat simple sentences. They can follow simple instructions to complete a task. They make many errors in grammar. Tenses are usually limited to present and some future and regular past tense. They rely on familiar structures and utterances. They use repetition, gestures, and other non-verbal clues to sustain a conversation.

What is your name?
Kim Yung Tae.

How old are you?
I'm fifteen. I'm coming fifteen.

When did you arrive here?
Junior five days. I'm three month decide come from.

Do you like Michigan?
I don't know. No, it cold.

Yung Tae responded meaningfully—he understood three questions—but his response to the third question was unclear and awkwardly phrased. His vocabulary was elementary. It was difficult to carry on a conversation with him beyond simple factual topics.

Level 3: Developing

Characteristics

Students understand standard speech with some repetition and rewording. Their oral communication is adequate in most settings. They can express their thoughts in complete sentences. They use vocabulary relevant to the purpose of the conversation, but it is often awkward and influenced by their primary language. They can participate in class discussions.

What is your name?
Sotir Davidhi.

How old are you?
I'm sixteen.

Do you like Michigan?
(Shrugs) **Yes, I do not like the cold, but is okay.**

Where are you from?

I'm from Albania.

Why did you move to this country?

For study. My trip is for study in American school. Because in this country people have open and clear mind, and my parent they want for me to be a professional. Here you have what I can need.

Sotir's responses were meaningful and comprehensible. He made errors in grammar, but he could carry on a reasonable conversation with the other person in English.

Level 4: Expanding

Characteristics

Students are beginning to produce complex sentences. They can use most tenses without errors. They have acquired an extensive vocabulary, although they may need explanations of abstract academic concepts. They are beginning to understand and use idiomatic expressions, figures of speech, and words with multiple meanings. They can participate actively in cooperative group projects and activities.

What is your name?

Silvia Gomez. I'm from Puerto Rico and Colombia.

How old are you?

Ten.

Tell me about your family.

Most of my families are moved from Puerto Rico. Everyone moved down to here from Puerto Rico but most of my father's family is still in Colombia. Fifty percent each.

What are you going to do after school today?

Do my homework and watch television.

Silvia's responses were very clear. She made few grammatical errors of any kind, with a good command of vocabulary. Her sentences were complete.

Level 5: Bridging

Characteristics

Students approximate primary language speech with a few errors. They can carry on a sophisticated conversation and can speculate using conditionals. They use precise and extended vocabulary. They are considered proficient in English.

What is your name?

Vlady Paredes.

Where are you from?

I'm from Peru.

How old are you?
I'm fifteen.

How long have you studied English?
I don't know. About three to five years. I forget. Maybe five.

Do you like Michigan?
It's not so bad. Yet. It's still summer. Ask me again next May.

Are you going to stay here until you graduate?
Yup.

How does your mother feel about you coming here?
(Grins) **She said, "Oh, my baby son!" and cried a lot.**

Vlady's response was nearly on a par with that of a student whose primary language is English. There were no errors in grammar or syntax, and he could elaborate with ease and fluency.

Step Three: Assessing Literacy

The next step in the placement procedure is to determine if the student can read and write. Why? Because

+ preliterate students (who have no experience with the written word) and non-literate students (who are from a culture with a written script but have not learned it) require different services and strategies than those who have learned to read and write in their primary language.

+ if a student is literate, his literacy skills will transfer to the new language (English), and you do not have to start at the beginning.

+ you can make assumptions about schooling based on how well a student reads and writes.

Home-Language Literacy

Determining a student's level of literacy in his home (primary) language provides further valuable information about his background. If he is literate in the home language, it is a safe bet he will be able to transfer those skills to a new language. You can also establish what the student can do when lack of English proficiency is not a factor. Knowing what he has learned to date provides the classroom teacher with a starting point for instruction.

Again, it does not take a sophisticated instrument to learn what you need to know about a student's level of literacy to get you started. Open questions can give you a rough view of your student's capabilities. The choice of topics should ideally respond to a subject in which he has an interest or with which he has experience, such as

+ My best friend

+ My first day in America

+ The worst day of my life

The strengths of this straightforward format are the following:

+ It is a relatively simple task to have questions about these topics, which are short and to the point, translated into the language in which you need to assess.

+ You do not need to be proficient in that language to note whether the student is literate or not.

+ You can quickly establish whether the student is literate, has limited literacy, or is non-literate in his primary language. Even if you do not get the student's writing translated, you can still make a determination based on how he responds to a paper-and-pencil task. How much or how little he wrote will tell you something about his level of literacy. For example, Thanousi's primary language was Lao. His teacher had no formal tests translated into Lao, so she gave him paper and a pencil and, through gestures, asked him to write a short sample in Lao. Thanousi took the pencil tentatively and held it awkwardly. After much hesitation he scrawled a few symbols. The simple maxim, "If he can write, he can read," applied to Thanousi. Even though she could not read what he wrote, Thanousi's teacher knew he had limited literacy in his own language. She was also certain he would not be able to read or write in English. She could make a fairly confident placement based on this very basic test.

In figure 3.1, Sotir was given the topic "My First Day in America." Even if it is all Greek to you, you can deduce that he was literate in his own language, could formulate complete sentences, organize his facts, and write more than a few words. You can assume that he did not need basic survival measures, could build on his skills in Greek, and could begin transferring those skills to English.

> My first day in America
>
> Dita ime e parë ne Amerikë
>
> Ishte 3 Janar, 2005. Japo mbërrita në aeroportin e Nju Jorkut. Në Anglisht dija të flisja shumë pak, vetëm disa fjalë të cilat më duhej t'i thoja shumë herë bashkëbiseduesit që të mund të me kuptonte pak a shumë.
> Nga Nju Jorku më duhej të merja aeroplanin tjeter për ne Sinseneti, dhe që andej të merja merja nje tjeter aeroplan për ne Grand Rapids.
> Ishte nje dite e gjate dhe e lodhshme që do ta kem të vështirë që ta harroje.

Figure 3.1 A portion of Sotir's "My First Day in America" assignment

Standardized Proficiency Tests

Most districts use standardized proficiency tests to determine students' academic language capabilities and educational background, and it is now, in fact, federal law in both the U.S. and Canada to use them in placement decisions. A number of these tests are available; check with your district to see which ones it has approved.

Although standardized proficiency tests have significant limitations and are often misused, they offer many of the same benefits as do definitions of the levels of proficiency, including

- Keeping everyone involved in the assessment, placement, and exiting of students on the same page
- Providing parameters within which to assess students

What a standardized proficiency test can tell you

In a general way, they reveal

- how much English a student knows
- whether a student is literate
- whether a student has any command of English grammar, idioms, or Western culture

The test's intent is to give a broad view of what the student is capable of in English.

What a standardized proficiency test cannot tell you

Because of all the disadvantages listed in chapter 2 (see pages 30 through 33), standardized proficiency tests will not

- tell you whether a student did not get an answer because he does not know the concept, does not know the language, or does not have the content-based or cultural vocabulary
- give you important information about the strategies the student uses to gain meaning from the test. They only label right or wrong
- tell you in which language the student is dominant in terms of academic skills

Proficiency in Written English

You want to determine your student's ability to write coherently. A sample of his writing can give you a good look at his productive proficiency and his grasp of English syntax, vocabulary, conventions, and organizational skills. If he is functioning at the higher levels, you want to see whether he can write on par with his English-speaking classmates. Knowing what you can expect from the student will help you determine what sorts of interventions you need to make.

Prioritize your scoring criteria for the writing, beginning with the most important writing skills—content, organization, and vocabulary—and ending with the spelling and mechanics. It is very easy to become overwhelmed by errors and then find little good in the writing. But once you get past the first gasp, you can look beyond surface errors. Here are some writing samples at each level of English language proficiency:

Level 1: Entering
Level 1a
Characteristics

Students may leave the page blank. Or, they may write in a foreign language. They may display writing that is indecipherable or that consists of letter-like forms. They may copy writing from a model. Figure 3.2 is a small boy's attempt at a signature. He had had little experience with print and simply produced a series of letters from words that appeared on the walls of the classroom.

Figure 3.2 A young boy's signature

Level 1b
Characteristics

Students may write single words and word combinations. They may use letter strings or symbols or draw pictures to convey meaning. They may copy from a model but add a few of their own words or phrases. The language level is so low that it is difficult to derive meaning.

Richard was a small boy of eight who came to the United States for ESL Summer Camp. He was writing about his first experiences in America:

Figure 3.3
Richard's writing

Richard's sentences are short. His letter formation is awkward and elementary. There is little organization, except for a list of thoughts, and many words are unrecognizable. There is no punctuation.

Level 2: Beginning
Characteristics

Students may write phrases or simple sentences, and they might list related ideas. They may use repetitive vocabulary and utilize few or no mechanics. They may use temporary or invented spelling. A primary language influence may be evident in syntax, spelling, and word choice.

Odette was a teenaged refugee. On the next page is the story of her first day in America, arriving in the middle of January from the Sudan:

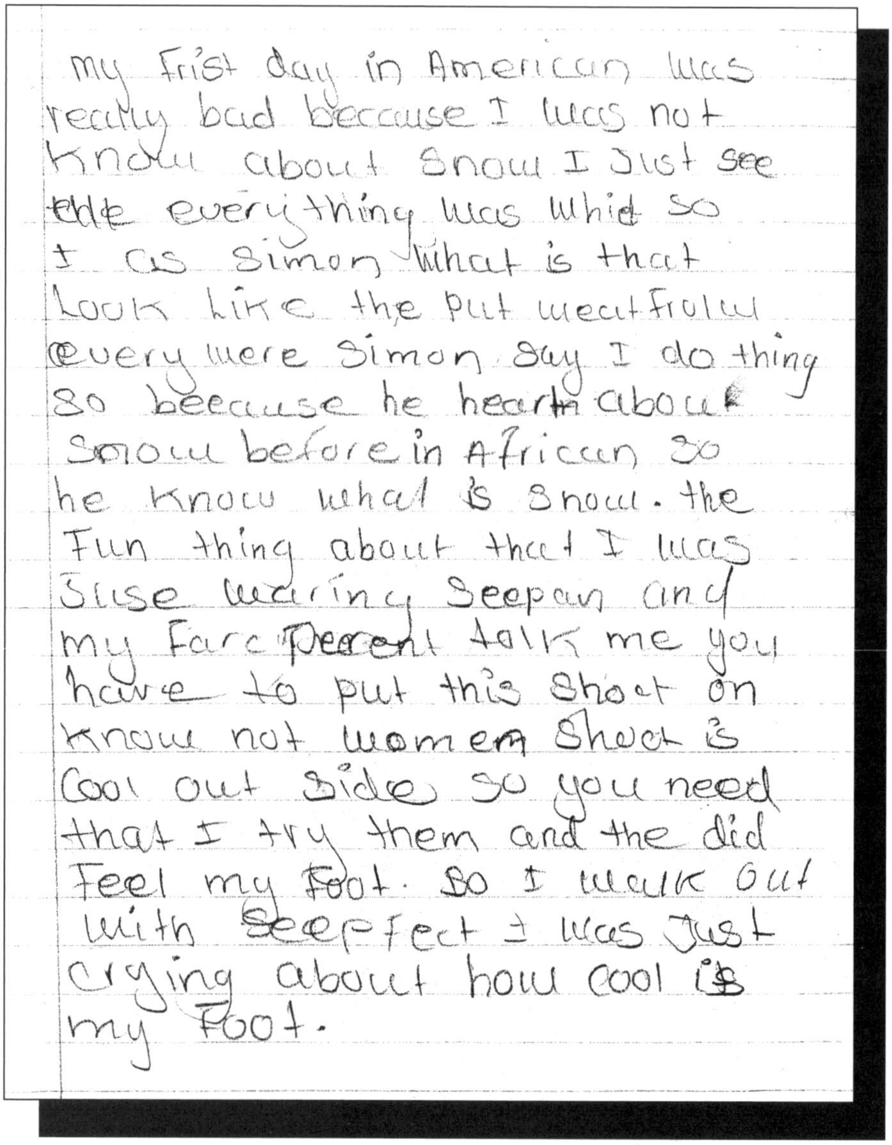

my Frist day in American was
really bad beccause I was not
know about Snow I Just see
the everything was whid so
t as simon what is that
Look like the put meatfrolw
every were Simon say I do thing
so beecause he hearth about
Snow before in African so
he know what is Snow. the
Fun thing about that I was
suse waring Seepan and
my Farc Perent talk me you
have to put this Shoet on
know not women Shoet is
Cool out Side so you need
that I try them and the did
Feel my Foot. So I walk Out
with Seepfect I was Just
crying about how Cool is
my Foot.

Figure 3.4 Odette's first day in America

There are many serious errors in Odette's writing, both in spelling and in grammar. She apparently did not know how to form the past tense, and so she wrote consistently in the present tense. Many of her spellings are invented, although they do show a familiarity with English.

Level 3: Developing

Characteristics

Students may convey a single idea using multiple sentences that may lack cohesion. They may use some complex, compound sentences but may also have difficulty with grammar. Students will write with frequent punctuation, spelling, and capitalization errors and will likely use high-frequency vocabulary, sometimes omitting words.

Wes, thirteen, also came to the U.S. for the summer ESL camp from Taiwan. He had had three years of English instruction. He was an optimistic, happy kid.

My trip in America

In America, we usually ate a lot. The food be great! I like it so much. We usually happy all day.

We went to a lot of place, like sea world….It's all very good. In sea world. We saw a lot of fish and show.

We went to shoped every day. We bought a lot. Any thing were cute. So I want bought any thing. But I don't have a lot of money. So this is not happy to me.

Every day, I saw a lot American. In Taiwan don't like it. Every American is fine. I like they very much.

In America, I miss a lot of new firned. They all like me, I like they too.

In the first day. The driver took we to his home. And his family are great to we. His daughter is cute.

Wes's writing conveys his enthusiasm for his experiences in America. He gave detailed examples of what he did and how he felt. His sentences are simple, using only basic vocabulary and verb tense, and he made some spelling errors. However, he was able to effectively describe his trip to the U.S.

My Portugues writing is probably developing
my oral is probably expanding

Level 4: Expanding
Characteristics
Students begin organizing ideas in paragraphs and use some complex and compound sentence structures. They may have errors in grammar, punctuation, spelling, and capitalization. Vocabulary and organization are beginning to approximate the writing of students whose first language is English. Here is Mimi's writing:

Mimi	My trip in America Seaworld, Disneyland. Los Anger. I see many something. and understand American life. In Seaworld, I saw many fish and shake. I wet my shirt. it's great. America's trafic is good. and food is very great. so I eat many food, I'm fat. In Disneyland: I played any games. and looked many show, that's good. America girl is beautiful. I want like them. I meet much friends in America. they all handle me very good. But I don't like this weather. because it's too cold. I pdis fill cold. it's bad. I buy many gift for my friends. they all glad. In the car, I headack. because yestday I non sleeping.

Figure 3.5 Mimi's trip to America

Mimi's description offers many particulars about her trip to southern California, and her sentences provide both detail and support for her statements. She organized her paragraph into what she liked and did not like about her visit and was able to use the simple past tense correctly. Her sentences might look short at first glance, but she often used periods in place of commas.

Level 5: Bridging

Characteristics

Students write multiple paragraphs with a variety of sentence structures and using transitions. They use precise, varied, and descriptive vocabulary but may still have grammatical errors. They still write with a "foreign accent" although they make few errors in punctuation and spelling.

Ghazi was a recent emigrant from the Middle East. Energetic and funny, he was raring to dive right into his new life. Here, he was responding to the question: What advice would you give to a friend who is going to come to the U.S.A.?

> No sooner had I arrive U.S.A., I realized that I should have some good advice from any friends who had ever been to US before. Although everything seems to be all set very well (on my behalf), but I saw many unexpected problems arised when some of my friends arrived here with me simultaneously...
>
> The most important thing is you should understand what is your real aim, your ability and how to reach your final goal (otherwise to dream the impossible dream; to fight the unbitable foe; to bear the unbearable sorrow; and to reach the unreachable star will be a painful and terrible thing)...
>
> Anyone who is going to come should know very well about his own culture, and a rough concept about America culture...to compare the America culture with his own culture and dwell in America without any culture – shock!
>
> Finally...please learn your English very well in your own country, otherwise you'll have to take a test, and just can't sleep at night for at least 2 days...

Ghazi's paper has a few errors, but they do not get in the way of meaning. It has a voice, humor, it is well-organized, and it reaches beyond the expected to grip the reader and shake him out of his ordinary perceptions.

Step Four: Tentative Placement in the Proper Grade

The reality of the placement issue is that it is often rooted in the hazy realms of intuition and judgment calls. Even if your state has a very rigid code that requires placement according to percentile rankings in mandated tests, you cannot be assured

+   that teachers know what the student knows and can do

+   how best to teach the student

- that a student will be successful in an age-appropriate or mainstream class, even if he scores above the passing percentile and is, therefore, ineligible, for ESL services

The Issue of Grade Levels

One of your most important jobs is to place each student in the right grade with the right teacher. It is often tempting to place a student in a lower grade simply because his English is low. But this can backfire in a big hurry. It may seem alright to put Dave, who is nine and small for his age, in the second grade because he can neither read nor write, but when he suddenly shoots up, can no longer sit comfortably in his desk, and becomes interested in girls, everybody will be in for trouble.

As much as possible, it is important to put students with their age-mates. There are several important reasons for this.

- Many of students' emotional and social needs can be met only by being with their age-mates. Handscombe (1989) asserts that social integration is much more important than language needs. Students' self-image and motivation can be severely affected by being stuck with younger children when they long to be with kids their own age. Students model what their peers say and do, and they need the opportunity to share common interests with their age-mates. Depriving them of the opportunity to interact with their peers can hinder their adjustment to their new life.

- Lack of fluency does not indicate limited intelligence. Although some students may not be able to express what they know or are unable to cope with the tasks demanded in their grade, they are not necessarily lacking in cognitive development. It is a disservice to make a student repeat material he has already mastered simply because his language has not reached a level at which he can compete on a par with his age-mates. He can become bored and frustrated.

- Students beyond the primary grades can often learn to read faster than younger children, simply because they are more mature. *I think in English too, at adolesences many students comprehens in reading just clicks.*

Effective Placement

Successful programs consider the following when placing a student:

- The student. Age is a primary consideration.

- Available resources, including

   - **Options.** A school system with a number of alternatives for ESL students will obviously have more options to consider.

   - **Numbers.** The number of students of a particular language background attending the school and program affects the resources invested.

   - **Personnel.** How much experience the mainstream classroom teacher has working with ESL kids; how impacted the school and mainstream classroom are; how receptive the other students in the mainstream class are to working with ESL students.

- **Amount of outside support.** For instance, the presence of certified, bilingual teachers adds another dimension to what a school can offer students.

- **Training.** If mainstream teachers are untrained and unprepared in ESL, schools are less able to offer solid ESL programs than if teachers have significant, substantial experience and training under their belts.

same → for all other students also

More than any other factor, success with ESL students depends on a commitment by teachers and administrators to acknowledge and meet the students' special needs. Academic achievement is directly linked to the quality of instruction, not just the placement of the student.

It is also important to note that many placements need to be decided on a case-by-case basis. Odette, (see page 57), for instance, was in her teens. When asked to tell something about herself, she told a hair-raising story about being held in prison for three days when she was eight because she was the only person nearby when a man shot himself. She had many sharp edges and could get defensive and refuse to work if she was tired. She did not get along with her first foster parents and found a new place to live on her own. She was constantly waging a long-distance battle with her father, who sent her video tapes of men he thought she should marry (to which she replied, "*You* marry him."). Although her grammar was rudimentary and she consistently substituted *f* for *p* in her speech, Odette's conversational English was quite advanced, and her comprehension abilities suggested she could function at a level 4. Her writing (see figure 3.3), on the other hand, was at a very low level, making it difficult to keep up with her age-mates in a mainstream class. But a teenaged girl who is old enough to marry in her own country should not be put in a lower grade. Accommodations had to be made. She needed to be given work at which she could succeed, but content that would move her forward enough to satisfy the requirements for high-school graduation.

Placement of a newly arrived student is often temporary; with time, it becomes clearer whether the placement is actually a good fit for the student or not. Rounding out the picture with supplemental information about your student will help ensure that the placement is the best one possible—even if that means moving the student to a more appropriate class (or grade) down the road.

Step 5: Learning More: Narrowing the Field
Why test further?

Although you have used (and are required to use) a standardized proficiency test, you still need more information to get a complete and accurate picture of your student. You want to know enough about the student to be confident in your placement. You want to determine both the level at which he is operating as well as the learning strategies he has. You want to identify weaknesses up front so that you can quickly begin working on the areas in which he needs the most help. You want to have a basic idea of how much vocabulary, experience with English, and even knowledge of print awareness he has.

We have found that the Language Assessment Scale (LAS), and other instruments like it, generally do a poor job of revealing this information. Individual student's proficiency levels in listening, speaking, reading, and writing vary depending on his experiences both in North America and in his own country. Some might have advanced speaking and listening skills but poor reading and writing skills; others might be proficient in reading and writing but understand little spoken English or do not speak well enough to be understood by others. The LAS cannot reveal these subtle differences very effectively.

In the following section, we describe our struggles to find out what we needed to know, the different instruments we used, and the decisions we made. We want to point out again that although standardized tests deliver limited information, they have their uses. Teachers often sense that students know more than a test can demonstrate. Intuition raises flags that point toward further investigation. Because standardized tests do not accurately reflect a student's capabilities, it is often more instructive to watch *how* the student takes the test and to examine the strategies he uses. You can use multiple measures to get at the same question, how much does he know? *I do like to watch my students read to see what their reading behaviors are.*

We have added several more anecdotes to reveal just how complex it can be to get a whole picture of your student. We also want to demonstrate how you can (and should) adapt your testing methods and selection of materials according to the ages and proficiency levels of your students.

Note that you should only test reading strategies in English if the student is literate. If it appears that he does not know how to write or even hold a pencil, and you suspect he has no experience with print, you can still find out if he has some degree of English and alphabetic principles by observing what he does when he is handed a book. Does he know how to hold it correctly, right-side-up and front facing forward? Can he recognize any letters?

Barb spent two years volunteering in an inner-city elementary school where the turnover rate was a staggering seventy-three percent. Only one in about four kids who enrolled in September was still there in June. Because teachers could not stop their teaching long enough to do testing, and because records often took months to catch up with students, it seemed imperative to design some sort of assessment mechanism to give teachers enough information to go on—to find out what students knew and what they were lacking. After much trial and error and constant refining, and with the goal of gaining the most information in the shortest amount of time, a team that included Barb, the reading specialist, the principal, and several linguistics students developed a series of tests. These tests included, among other items, the following three questions to ask themselves, both for younger elementary students and for older, preliterate students:

1. Can he recognize and write his own name?

2. Does he have any print awareness?

3. Does he have concepts of print such as knowing which is the front of a book, where to begin reading, top left to right, return sweep, and word matching?

Here are some criteria we needed to fulfill with the series of tests:

• It had to be flexible enough to accommodate a range of ages and levels. We needed to be able to start low and work up. For instance, if a child was in third grade but unexpectedly could read at an advanced level, we needed something challenging.

Conversely, if we encountered an eleventh grader who had never sat at a desk, we needed materials that did not make him feel stupid, but gave us an idea of how much he did know.

+ Older students needed tasks that were different than younger students.

+ It had to be simple. Simple tests are easier and faster to administer, and do not tax either the student or the teacher.

+ It had to be reasonably open-ended rather than fill-in-the-blank types of questions. The more open-ended the tests were, the more students could demonstrate what they actually knew and could do. The idea was to get the student talking; the questions became more open-ended as the student's ability increased.

To follow are reading and writing samples of several students we tested and details about how we tested some of them.

Lower levels

Venus was five when she transferred to the school in February. She was orally proficient in English, and the teacher determined she was a level 5. She could tell you her name and how old she was, and she could discuss her family in great detail. Based on her age, she was placed in kindergarten.

Venus could write her first name, but she could not recognize it in a field of four names. She did not yet know how to write her last name. When given a page of letters, she recognized *O, S, A*, and three letters that were in her name: *V, E,* and *N*. She said, "This one and this come in my name. And this (she pointed to a G)." She could write *1, 2,* and *3,* and she correctly identified the numbers *1* and *2*.

 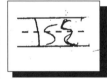

Figure 3.6 Venus's name and writing of 1, 2, 3

Venus recognized the front of the book, understood directional sweep, and knew where to begin reading. She was not yet tracking print; she did not look at individual words and get meaning from them.

Kindergarten was the right placement for Venus. She had not yet learned many of the basic kindergarten concepts. Because she was smart and motivated, catching up was achievable, particularly with an enriched or all-day program.

For first- and second-grade students, we wanted to see if they knew their alphabet as well as some sight words. We also wanted to know how much they could write, because a student's command of orthography and language is better revealed in what he produces than when he simply reads.

Salvador was about seven when he arrived from Mexico where he had been in a bilingual program. He was placed in the second grade and was determined to be a level 2. He could speak in simple sentences in English but preferred to be spoken to in Spanish.

When given a list of words, this is what he read:

the	(**I don't know**)
go	**go**
and	**a**
a	**a**
to	**o**
in	**i**
is	**issa**
you	**o**
me	**eme**
it	**i**
he	**h**
was	**w**
for	**r**
are	**a e**
his	**i**

Salvador read *go* correctly, and he read *is* and *me* as words, albeit incorrectly. With the rest of the words, he simply identified the letters that he knew, without attempting to read them as whole words or to sound them out. He wrote his first name correctly, and he left out the vowel in his last name.

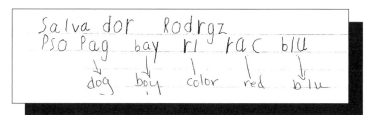

Figure 3.7 Salvador's signature and words

When asked if he could write any words, Salvador said, "pencil" and then asked, "In English or Spanish?" Then, he copied the *p* from the cover of a nearby book.

> Teacher: Do you know *perro?*
>
> Salvador: **Dog?**
>
> Teacher: How about *boy?*
>
> *Salvador looked for a* b *on the page.*
>
> Teacher: How about *color?*
>
> *Salvador made the* k *sound, but wrote* r *and then* l*. For* blue*, he looked for models of a* b *and an* l *but he knew* u*.*

Salvador would not attempt to read on his own, but when read to aloud, he would read along with the teacher while she pointed to the words. By the end of the book he could read the word *monster*, which was repeated in nearly every sentence. Because he would not attempt to read on his own, it was pointless to pursue it any further. It is important to stop when the student does.

Salvador had a strong awareness of print and knowledge of letters and sounds. He knew how to track from left to right. He was an eager learner who had some pretty crafty strategies such as searching for a letter he recognized to use as a model for writing. He was not yet secure in his reading, but he was looking at the words (a big step) and was getting a foothold.

Second grade was the right placement for Salvador, but because he was so far behind, he needed to be read to and to read along with others. (He liked to work one-on-one with someone and chime in when he was ready). He needed intensive help to catch up with his age-mates, in Spanish, if possible.

Higher levels

So that you do not waste time floundering around, trying to figure out where to start, you need a ballpark idea of the grade level at which the student is functioning. For level 2 and second- through fourth-grade students, we tried a list of spelling words devised by Manning and Manning (1992). This is a nifty test, because it offers a good way to determine students' phonological awareness, their knowledge of English spelling and, by inference, the amount of reading they have done.

With levels 3, 4, and 5 students, and with fourth-, fifth- and sixth-grade students, we tried the San Diego Quick Assessment of words. It was tedious, and, because the focus is on word-calling, it was not quite as useful as we had hoped.

After much discussion, we tried a standardized reading assessment devised by Flynt-Cooter (1998): the student read aloud while the teacher kept track of the miscues; then, the student gave a retelling of the story for comprehension. We do not necessarily recommend using the Flynt-Cooter and the San Diego Quick Assessment, but we used them with success. Their strength was in the fact that they had been developed with care and, as we discovered, they showed us quickly and easily what strategies students were using. They also offered a streamlined, efficient, and accurate way of making running records, which were very helpful for interpretation. When you are faced with incoming students, the last thing you need to do is spend a lot of time developing your own assessments. Here are some of the results.

Florinda had moved from California to the Midwest in the middle of the school year. She was eight but had been in the second grade in California.

Teacher: How old are you?

Florinda: **Eight.**

Teacher: When is your birthday.

Florinda: **Summer. I'm not sure what month.**

Teacher: Tell me about your family.

Florinda: **I don't got brothers. I have two sister. One she's nine. Another sister she's four.**

Florinda was a level 5 speaker. When given the list of spelling words, she produced the following:

punishment	**baneses**
cement	**samat**
vacation	**vekisen**
motion	**morsen**
ocean	**osen**
taco	**(did not attempt)**
karate	**crairi**
tomato	**tommiro**

Florinda did not seem to have a great deal of experience with English words. She got the initial and final consonant sounds right (except for *p* and *b*, which many children confuse early on), as well as the *"ee"* sound of karate and the *"o"* sound of tomato. It seemed that she was a beginning reader.

When asked to write, she produced the following:

> **I like to play with my frouands. Somese with frend in school. Wen I get home from school I play…**

Then, she did something surprising: Florinda read through level 3 in the Flynt-Cooter reading selection. Here is a running record of what she read (her errors appear above the correct words):

> *One day Mr. Wolf was walking through the forest. He was enjoying*
>
> **thinking**
> *an afternoon walk and not bothering anyone. All of a sudden it*
>
> **become**
> *started to rain and he became wet and cold. Just when Mr. Wolf*
>
> *was about to freeze to death, he saw a small house in the woods.*
>
> **Smoking**
> *Smoke was coming from the chimney.*

Florinda's story retelling was as follows:

> **He one day he was walking then he got to a house and they left him a note so he sit down and then he went to sleep. And the little girl said she was going to kill him and then he run and then he got back home.**

From this assessment, the teacher deduced that Florinda was reading at or above grade level for grade two. She was a confident reader, and if she made errors, she offered meaningful substitutions. It is very possible that her familiarity with the variation of the fairytale in the reading selection made it easier to read. However, she still had to get through words like *chimney*, and *freeze to death*, which were unfamiliar.

One wonders why an eight year old was placed in the second grade. However, since no school records arrived with her and it was already the middle of the year, it was too late to consider making a change. Florinda needed more practice in what she had already been exercising in abundance: reading.

Middle school, high school, and beyond

As a student gets older, the Manning and Manning spelling test becomes less and less useful. Unless a student has had limited schooling or comes from a preliterate or non-literate background, he is no longer learning to spell; spelling sorts itself out after about eighth grade. As students get into the higher grades, it makes sense to choose something else. The Flynt-Cooter is one place to start. You can also select essays or stories from other texts such as readers or literary books. Or, you can give a student a reading from an academic text to determine his level of comprehension. At this level, it is probably better to select texts that are several grades below the grade in which a student has been placed. A simple reading selection will suffice.

Here is Yung Tae, writing the answer to a question from a reading. Yung Tae was determined to be a level 2 in oral skills. He was literate in his own language:

> *Prompt: If you agree, write 10 sentences saying why. Use the ideas in the text and the phrases in the list.*

> I was agreed in sentences. I think of small the country. All people and special things were living in the life. Other peoples was advises in people. They was felt in social to groups. They was efforts the job and family. In part a sentence. All write a life and family, job, finances condition etc. We were knows important in social. It's teaching to important in social.

Yow! It seems Yung Tae can understand what he read. He is not a beginner in English: his syntax is correct, but the errors are more than noticeable; they threaten to drown the writing altogether. He has a substantial vocabulary, but untangling the overall message is difficult. One can infer that he had probably had extensive schooling in his own country and language but would not have been able to function in a mainstream classroom here. He needed extensive work to build his English reading and content skills.

Here is Sotir again after reading a selection about the importance of grandparents in the lives of children:

> In my country the people is not so reach, so then is difficult to live apart from their parents or their Grandmothers. Everybody need some help and when anybody can help you, you feel better, you feel wormer.

I remember my Grandmother from my father. She was told with black along here, brown eyes…She was beautiful, sweaty and very lovely. When she was sick I had slept with her. I know her antibiotics and I had helped to drink that. Her hart betrays when I was 7 years old. I mess her.

My Grandmother from my mother is not so lovely with all her Grandchildren's. She has 5 girls and 2 boys, so she has many grandchildren. She helps only some of them. I love her but I don't like what she doing her whole life.

When I will be Grandfather, I will love my children, but my grandchildren I will love more. In my country people say: "My children's children are two times my children" and I believe that. All my family believes that too."

Sotir read the selection with comprehension, and he wrote with great feeling, in spite of the charming errors. He presented a different problem for educators: with a student who is literate and who obviously comprehends and can adequately write understandable prose, it may be tempting to place him in a mainstream class with a sympathetic teacher. And, if you are flooded with kids at the lower levels, this may be an appealing alternative. But this was not a fair or reasonable option for Sotir. He still needed a lot of help. During the school year, it became apparent that Sotir, who labored over every assignment and left nothing to chance, would also get frustrated and throw down his pen if the teacher was going too fast and he could not keep up. It was better to place him in a lower grade and give him time to consolidate his skills. He had the foundation, but he needed time to build his fluency.

To follow are writing samples from two students who were determined to be level 4 and level 5, respectively, in oral proficiency. They were given a small reading selection from *The Autobiography of Malcolm X* and two questions to answer. In the reading sample, Malcolm talks about his time in prison, where he teaches himself to read by copying the entire dictionary.

Response Sheet for Malcolm X Essay

Name

1. Read the essay.

2. Describe as carefully and completely as you can, the significant point or points Malcolm X is making in this essay.

3. As carefully and completely as you can, write about whatever in the article is significant to you. Be sure to explain why it is important or significant.

2: The best way to study and learn some words is to get hold of a dictionaly that is like a miniature encyclopedia

---

Figure 3.8 Noriko's responses to questions about *Malcolm X*

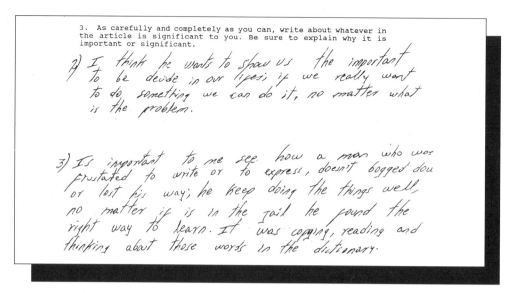

3. As carefully and completely as you can, write about whatever in the article is significant to you. Be sure to explain why it is important or significant.

2) I think he wants to show us the important to be decide in our lifes; if we really want to do something we can do it, no matter what is the problem.

3) Is important to me see how a man who was frustated to write or to express, doesn't bogged dou or lost his way; he keep doing the things well, no matter if is in the jail he found the right way to learn. It was copping, reading and thinking about those words in the dictionary.

Figure 3.9 Naoki's responses to questions about *Malcolm X*

Noriko (previous page) attempted to describe the significance of the points Malcolm X was making, but did not go on to explain what the wisdom of Malcolm X meant to her. It would take more information to determine if she could function on her own in a mainstream classroom, but this small sample raised doubts.

Naoki (above), on the other hand, answered in more detail. He showed a good understanding of the text, and articulated this with few errors. He was operating at a high level 4 if not a level 5 and, with further investigation, the teacher may have decided he could be mainstreamed.

PLACEMENT SCENARIOS

To illustrate the assessment and placement procedures in more detail as well as the real dilemmas that teachers face, we present three students from a made-up town we have called Elizabeth Arbor—a moderate-sized city that has experienced a steady number of newcomers over the years. The school district has two ESL teachers serving nine elementary schools, a bilingual Spanish program, and another ESL teacher (Eloise) who divides her time between the middle school and the high school. Eloise also sometimes assists the ESL teachers at the elementary school level when, for practical reasons, this makes the most sense.

The three students are Boris, May, and Elsie; the ESL teacher in charge of all decisions regarding their education, placement, and welfare is Eloise. We are attempting to demonstrate that the choices teachers make are often not the ideal—but ones they are forced to make in the real world when school districts do not have programs or plans.

Boris

Boris, seventeen, and his father arrived unannounced at the principal's office of the high school. Since Eloise, the ESL teacher, was teaching her home economics class, the secretary had them fill out a home-language survey. It was revealed that Boris was born in Russia, he had learned Russian as a child, and his parents spoke exclusively Russian to him.

When Eloise came in, she asked Boris to take some tests. His father said, "I'm not really sure that's necessary," revealing that he had emigrated from Moscow and was now an engineer in a local firm. Although the family spoke fluent English, Boris's parents, who wanted him to retain his home language, had imposed the rule that only Russian be spoken at home. Eloise decided to abandon her agenda of formal testing and, instead, asked Boris a few questions. He was at ease, slightly cocky, and sat back in his chair with his arm dangling casually over the back.

> Eloise: Were winters pretty hard back where you grew up?
>
> Boris: **Well, it got below zero Fahrenheit by November. So I'm pretty used to the cold.**
>
> Eloise: What kinds of things did you study in your last school?
>
> Boris: **Everything. I think this school will be too easy for me.**
>
> Eloise: What kinds of things do you like to do for fun?
>
> Boris: **I like soccer. I'm pretty great at it. I was captain of my team.**
>
> Eloise: Would you like to ask me some questions?
>
> Boris: **I heard the soccer team here really sucks.**

Boris's main obstacle was a rather large chip on his shoulder. Although he had a marked accent, his English was decidedly fluent, even colloquial.

Boris had brought with him a cumulative file of his school records. Eloise determined that most of the courses he had completed in Russia were equivalent to the required courses at this school, but he still needed to take United States history, civics, family life education, and several math and science courses. She suggested a course or two at the grade-nine level in English, but his father objected; he insisted that Boris could handle higher-level requirements.

In response to the prompt, "What are your goals in life?" Boris wrote a rather poignant essay that gave Eloise a clear idea not only of his capabilities, but of Boris himself:

> Our life is a very short period of time given to us by God and probably everyone drims about a better place in it.
>
> Everyone has the right to be born and to die, but people who are born in the state of Russia seem to be extraordinary because from their birth, these rights were taken off them by the leading group of the country. And then appears the feeling of struggle, struggle for just a normal human being existance, for just a quiet, peaceful life and love. And that straggle continues all their life...
>
> I always was one of these and straggled a lot for reaching a better life, I and my father, and he did everything possible in order to overcome all the difficulties in order our dream came true...He overcame all the tense

relations with officials, sometimes with close people that refused to understand us, but we saw the right of our purpose ahead of us and in spite of all opsticals we went to it and now we are here.

Now I have another goal in my life—to occupy a better place in a social staircase of American society and to be happy man and citizen of this country.

Eloise wanted to be sure Boris could read content at grade level, so she gave him the *Malcolm X* selection in which the human rights activist discusses how he learned to read and write in prison by copying a dictionary word for word. Here is Boris's response to the reading:

So I have read Malcolm X essay and I can say that I completely agreed with his point of view. They are a lot of examples that can tell us how people have changed of reading books. I think he had done a good job. Also it was very difficult. But I can say I found this article very interesting. When I read this article I finded his way of learning very alike to me. I know that people can have different ways of memory. For me it is very similar because I always learn words in such a way. I find it more progressive. Another point is that the author wanted to say that if you want to do something (to learn, to get job, to have interesting life,) you must always try to do this, even if it will be difficult for you. And I think the third thing is that all the time when he saw that he made progress, he got more real to do it more, to make higher his knowledge.

Eloise could see that Boris could write capably and with power, passion, and the ability to move his reader. This was more than we see in many students whose primary language is English. Boris was a young man with a superior grasp of English and real abilities. As well, he could read for information and articulate the important ideas in a reading selection. Eloise decided that mainstreaming Boris was the best choice.

May

May was fifteen and in tenth grade when she arrived in Elizabeth Arbor. Her parents spoke no English and could not complete the standard home-language survey, so Eloise gave May a different version, which directed questions to the student.

May's last name was Laotian, and so Eloise had attempted (unsuccessfully) to find a Laotian interpreter. To her surprise, she discovered that the primary language for May and her family was, in fact, Hmong. (Unless an interpreter had spoken Hmong *and* Lao, he would have been useless. In addition, attempting to amass materials in Lao would have been a mistake.) May explained that their grandfather had been a freedom fighter for the French and had taken a Laotian name.

Eloise gave May a home-language interview followed by several questions about the school environment.

Home-Language Interview

Student's Name __May__   Date _Feb. 19/95_ Age _15_

1. Which language do you hear most at home? _Hmong_.

2. Your father speaks to you in _Hmong_.
   underline: 1. Always   2. Often   3. Sometimes   4. Never

3. Your mother speaks to you in _Hmong_.
   underline: 1. Always   2. Often   3. Sometimes   4. Never

4. Your brothers and sisters speak to you in _English_.
   underline: 1. Always   2. Often   3. Sometimes   4. Never

5. Does your father ever speak English to you? _No_
   How often? _____ When? _____

6. Does your mother ever speak English to you? _No_
   How often? _____ When? _____

7. Do your brothers and sisters speak to you in English? _Yes_
   When? _All the time_

8. Which language does your parents consider most important for you
   to know? _English_

9. If you have a TV at home, what channels does your family watch
   most often? _8, 5, 12_

Figure 3.10
(a) Part one of May's home-language interview (b) Part two of May's home-language interview

Then, Eloise administered the Language Assessment Scale (LAS), which rated May "limited proficiency."

Next, Eloise read *The Crow and the Pitcher* to May and then asked her to retell the fable. May responded:

> He's looking for water...she... He saw a pitcher looked like a water. Find water...He drink he go...She go.

May understood at least part of the story, even if she was not able to articulate what the crow did to get water.

Questions about the school environment

1. Do you hear _English_ during class breaks? _Yes_

2. Do you speak _English_ during class breaks? _Yes_

3. Which language do your three best friends speak to you?
   a. _English_
   b. _English_
   c. _English_

4. Are you participating in any clubs or activities that use English? _Yes_

5. What other languages do you speak besides English? _Hmong and Thai_

Finally, Eloise asked May to write about her first day of school:

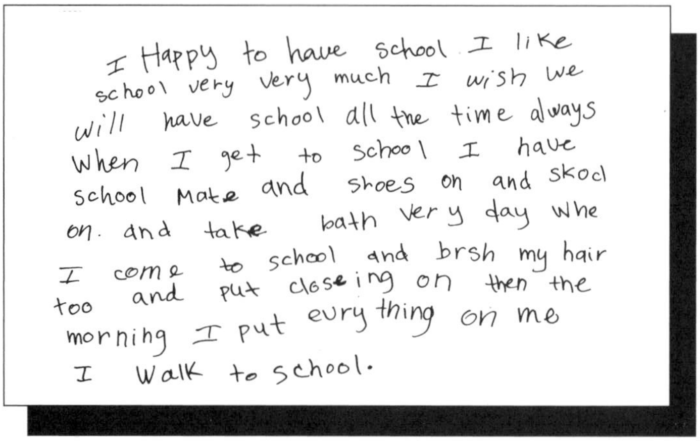

> I Happy to have school. I like school very very much I wish we will have school all the time always When I get to school I have school Mate and shoes on and skool on. and take bath very day whe I come to school and brsh my hair too and put closeing on then the morning I put every thing on me I walk to school.

Figure 3.11 May's writing sample

The writing sample shows that May's knowledge of grammar and sentence structure was limited and that her organization meandered. Her writing was at an elementary level, somewhere between second and fourth grade, and not what one would expect of a tenth grader in the regular curriculum. She could carry on a conversation with assistance, but she needed a lot of help in reading and writing in the content area.

This created a dilemma about where to place May. If there had been a fully developed ESL program in town, with instruction at all levels, Eloise could have placed May in content-area classes geared to her level of functioning. But Eloise was the only ESL teacher for the upper levels. After reviewing May's transcripts, Eloise found that she had taken sheltered classes in biology and history at the beginning literacy level. She had taken no mainstream courses except for art and music, and she had completed most of those requirements for graduation. The "heavy-duty" content courses, including government, history, science, and English, were left.

Eloise consulted the counselor, Carol, who recommended what most students call "flunky English" (a lower-level English class, which generally goes through the literature at a slower pace). But Eloise knew that plowing through *Tess of the D'Urbervllles* was not what May needed. She did not have the reading or writing proficiency to benefit from a class for mainstream English-speaking students, and she needed to focus on literacy skills.

"What about college?" Carol protested. But it would have taken May much longer to acquire a level of proficiency required to function and compete at the standard expected by the district. She needed more time, and time was what she had not received in the regular school system. College might have been an unrealistic goal at this point.

Statistics show that in the past, many schools have placed students like May in special education classes. There have been several lawsuits in the higher courts about placement of ESL students into the wrong programs; students who needed English-language support could not get it because they were placed in a program with a completely different objective. But Eloise did consider special education carefully for May, because it would mean small classes and attention to her individual needs. In the end she abandoned the idea because, although special-education teachers can adapt the curriculum to the needs of special students, the teacher in this district was not familiar with the issues and challenges of working with ESL students. Eloise knew that May needed meaning-based language activities. Her difficulties were related to gaps in her knowledge base, not to intrinsic disabilities. Eloise also decided that the potential risks of special education outweighed the possible benefits.

Eloise was troubled about where to place May. Realistically, she knew that the school system, although well-meaning and concerned, was not about to mount a special program and hire teachers until the number of students at this level of proficiency and literacy reached a critical mass. She had to cope with them herself.

Eloise had no experience with this low level of literacy. She decided to get help and called a school district in Ontario for advice. The administrators were very helpful. With their help, Eloise established two central and realistic goals for May: (1) to develop her skills so that her limited proficiency would not be a barrier to achieving her own personal goals; and (2) to help her acquire the basic academic skills that would allow her to continue her education beyond high school if she chose. With those goals in mind, Eloise elected to schedule May for as much ESL help as possible as well as time with the reading specialist. She found a buddy to tutor May in study hall and scheduled her for health, computers, and home economics classes. Eloise chose a course with expectations that were neither too high nor too low for a girl who had arrived at the eleventh hour.

Elsie

We discussed Elsie in chapter 1. She and her siblings, Daniel and Martha, arrived from Ethiopia at the middle school, and Barb had to make an on-the-spot decision about placement. Since Elsie's story has haunted Barb for so many years, and since the issues and problems confronting the school were so complex, we decided to recreate Elsie and a what-we-might-have-done-if-we-had-known-more scenario, replacing Barb, the actual teacher accountable for Elsie's education and placement, with Eloise. Regrettably, there are no what-ifs in the real world, and there is no turning back the clock to straighten out a life that has taken a wrong turn. Elsie's unfortunate story was a combination of a lack of knowledge on the part of the school system, a profoundly disrupted school and home life, and a small girl who would not or could not take ownership of her own learning.

Eloise gave Elsie the Idea Proficiency Test (IPT). She responded correctly to only two questions: her age (in a barely audible whisper) and the word *banana*, when shown a picture. The test registered Elsie as NEP. (Daniel and Martha breezed through the IPT, and placed quite high in reading and writing. The test indicated that they were both high level 2s: they needed assistance, but they were both ready to tackle many of the classroom tasks. Eloise tentatively followed Elsie's father's wishes and placed Daniel and Martha in seventh and eighth grade.)

To learn more about Elsie's schooling background, Eloise spoke to Elsie's father. She found out he had been in Oklahoma studying when Daniel and Martha were preschoolers, and so they had learned English. Then, they had returned to Ethiopia. Daniel and Martha had both had a good start in their formal schooling and had learned to read and write in their own language. When Elsie was just beginning school, fighting had broken out. Her formal education had been disrupted, and much of her schooling had consisted of marching and singing patriotic songs. Several times they had had to flee their home. Their mother was still in Ethiopia, literally being held hostage to ensure the father's return.

Eloise began with some very basic testing: First, she conducted an oral interview with Elsie, but it was not very revealing—it was hard to tell whether Elsie did not know or was just extremely shy. For instance:

> Eloise: What will you do after school today?
>
> Elsie: **Play.**
>
> Eloise: What would you do in case of a fire in your home?
>
> Elsie: **I don't know.**

Next, Eloise gave Elsie the Concepts about Print test (Clay, 1979), designed to reveal what learners know about literacy materials. Elsie's father translated to be sure Elsie understood the questions, and the test actually checked her skills, not her English proficiency. The results were very revealing:

> Eloise (*showing her a book*): What is this called?
>
> Elsie (*tentatively*): **Book.**
>
> Eloise: What do you do with it?
>
> Elsie: **Read it.**
>
> Eloise: What is inside it?
>
> Elsie (*after a long delay*): **Letters, picture.**
>
> Eloise (*gave Elsie the book upside down*): Show me the front of the book. (*Elsie found the front cover and turned it right side up.*) Show me a page in this book. (*Elsie pointed to a page.*) Read this page to me. (*Elsie shook her head. Even with encouragement from her father, she would not attempt it. Elsie was able to show the top and bottom of the page, the exact place where Eloise should have begun reading, and which direction Eloise should move her eyes as she read the page.*)
>
> Eloise: Now, I want you to point to the story as I read the page to you.

Up to this point, Elsie had been doing fine. However, as Eloise began to read, she saw that Elsie was not matching the spoken word with the written word. She moved her finger smoothly across the lines on the page, not noticing that her finger was not on the correct word. She had finished sweeping her finger across and down the page before Eloise had completed reading the second line. Elsie understood that print had meaning and she knew how to use a book, but she was not actually looking at the words yet, and she had not connected print to meaning. She was a level 1, still a beginning reader. She had a long way to go before she could begin work at the sixth-grade level.

Eloise now had to decide whether to place Elsie in the middle school or at the elementary level. Three of the district's elementary schools had an early-exit bilingual program for the Spanish-speaking population, but Elsie did not speak Spanish. There were no known interpreters available for Elsie's native tongue.

The closest elementary school was Lange Street Elementary, with three fifth-grade classes. One was a split-contract fifth, with two teachers each working half-time. Although one of the teachers had taught sheltered English before in pull-out classes, she was pregnant and would be on maternity leave beginning in December. Her partner was an enthusiastic teacher, but this was her first year teaching.

The second fifth-grade teacher at Lange had an excellent reputation. He was a creative individual and had had great results with mainstream students. But he had no ESL experience and already had enough students. He also had a number of special day students and a few students with challenging home problems.

The third fifth-grade teacher was low on the list of options. She was ready to retire at the end of the year and had made it known she would not take on any new challenges. She did not have the experience or flexibility for someone like Elsie.

Austin Elwin Elementary, located within walking distance of the middle school, had a combination of East Asian and Latino students, so teachers were experienced working with ESL students. The itinerant ESL teacher provided pull-out ESL classes and newcomer initiation for the NEP and LEP students.

Another choice was Rowland Elementary, eight miles southeast of the middle school. Rowland had two Latino students and one from Eastern Europe. The ESL teacher, with her heavy schedule, made it there about three times a week for an hour. This school also had a fifth-grade teacher who had had LEP students in the past. He had a great reputation and was receptive to taking on a student like Elsie.

Meyer Middle School covered sixth through eighth grades. Offering seven period classes each day, Meyer also provided a few sheltered-English classes for LEP students consisting of content classes (science, math, and so on) designed to teach the language and content concurrently. Eloise taught two of these sheltered-English language arts classes; these were not large classes, and she could provide support for Elsie at the middle-school level. Elsie would be attending the same school as her brother and sister, who would provide some emotional security for her, as well as help with translation, if necessary.

Faced with these choices, Eloise knew there were no clear answers to proper placement. It all boiled down to priorities. Proper placement was critical, and each placement had to be made according to the specific needs of the student.

The drawbacks to placing Elsie in the middle school were her young age and the intensity and immensity of a seven-period day. The sheltered English may have helped Elsie, but the language and content may have been too difficult. Elsie still needed many basics; sheltered English was designed to make content classes more understandable. If she placed Elsie in this class, the teacher would have to spend a lot of time trying to fill in all the gaps, which is not the intent of a sheltered class.

Eloise decided to place Elsie in Austin Elwin Elementary. That extra year at the elementary level would give Elsie some much needed time to catch up with her peers. It would offer the individualized services that Elsie so desperately needed. The school was not too far from Elsie's siblings' school, so she would be able to ride the bus with them before and after school. A drawback was that she would be removed from class for some of the day for pull-out ESL classes. She would, however, still have time in the mainstream classroom, and if she was going to make the strides she needed to make before middle school, time was of the essence. The staff's experience, as well as the possibility of a newcomer program, seemed to outweigh all the other advantages of the other schools. Elsie had much ground to gain, not only in English but also in content and literacy. As well, having tested NEP, she was eligible for tutoring. Because the dropout rate was so high among secondary students who had weak educational backgrounds, Eloise felt that the extra elementary year, tailored specifically to Elsie's needs, would be the best plan for her. She contacted the ESL teacher who worked at Austin Elwin and together, they made the rest of the arrangements for Elsie's placement.

No environment has the perfect solution. Once the pros and cons are evaluated, the school *and* the parents need to decide on the best placement situation. This means the parents' priorities and issues must also be carefully considered.

CONCLUSION

Placement procedures must be clearly defined so you are prepared to deal with incoming ESL students efficiently and humanely, no matter what the situation in your district. All members of the school team involved in placement—administration, teachers, and office personnel—share the responsibility of placing that student into a program that fits his individual needs and must work together toward that goal. Communication and knowledge of available resources are critical before an informed and logical decision can be made.

Proper placement is one of the most critical issues facing schools today. When a student is in the best place possible for him and there is care and concern that he succeed and improve, then the school's ultimate goal—to educate all—can begin. When all levels of the team aim to place a student where success is most likely, then success is probable. However, the opposite is also true. When placement is haphazard and no one takes responsibility to find the relevant facts or to foster the student's success, then the likelihood of the student falling through the cracks and eventually dropping out is far, far greater.

One of the greatest joys and, conversely, one of the greatest challenges of teaching newcomers is that every student is different: pre-literate, highly-educated, victims of interrupted schooling, better grammarians than all of us combined. You can make no assumptions. They are what they are, and we have to meet them at whatever stage they are in their education and figure out how to move them on to the next stage. Having clear definitions makes the job easier. Having a clear and workable intake procedure also eases the process. However, the sheer number of variables that exists among students means that many decisions need to be case-by-case decisions. Moreover, teachers are part of the mix too: their needs, level of tolerance, and strengths and weaknesses must be taken into consideration as well as the makeup of the students they already have.

Our goal is to prepare all students to participate fully in society. This goal might seem overwhelmingly idealistic when we face the realities of the students we serve. That is why a clear, unified, and consensual plan is the best hope for meeting the challenge.

We're Working Hardly
EMERGING LITERACY

Miss Nguyen was the bilingual teacher at Sherwood Park School. She worked with forty children of non-English-speaking background. Most were Vietnamese, but recently, several Russian children had enrolled in the school, and she had taken over responsibility for them, too. The children, from first through fifth grade, came and went at various times of the day in what, to an outside observer, might have seemed like an extraordinarily complicated system of groups and individual programs.

When asked how she decided to which group students belonged, Miss Nguyen said, "I watch them."

How do you know when they can be mainstreamed?
"I watch them."

What do you look for?
She shrugged. "English competency. Readiness."

Though her answers sound vague, Miss Nguyen was observing all day, every day. She knew what each child could or could not do, and whether or not he would be able to succeed on his own in the mainstream class.

What's in this Chapter

+ The importance of context
+ The concept of emergence
+ Levels of emerging proficiency and literacy

This is my best source of assessment

- Examples of student work
- Activities to enhance each level of emerging proficiency and literacy

All teachers observe. Every teacher watches her students and can tell where they are on the learning continuum and what they are capable of doing. Observation, ongoing assessment, and reassessment are all part of every teacher's daily role. However, Miss Nguyen's situation brings up two key issues.

1. Teachers see what they believe. How you view the learning process depends on what you believe about it. *or believe what they see*

2. In today's world, with the emphasis on accountability and the press for inclusion, vague answers (such as those given by Miss Nguyen) are not sufficient and will not satisfy principals, ESL teachers, or mainstream classroom teachers who want to know how well their students are gaining proficiency outside their own class.

Ways of Seeing

No matter what role you may play in your ESL student's learning—whether you are the classroom teacher, the ESL specialist, or the provider of some other support—you need to assess your student with an understanding of the language acquisition process. This process has qualities as unique as each individual who struggles to acquire the language. Therefore, before we can discuss how to document what your students are doing, we need to consider the big picture, what we see when we work with the students who learn from us.

Before you can see how much progress a student has made, or what level of understanding that student has about what he is doing, you must have some sort of framework or standard against which to judge the work or the output. Routman (1991) writes, "good observation, the most critical component in evaluation, is only as good as the teacher's knowledge base." Teachers see what they believe; in other words, what they believe about learning, errors, and language all influences how they view a student's productions. Thus, having a way to "see" what you are looking at is of absolute importance. Galda, Cullinan, and Strickland (1993) write:

> *Early childhood educators long have operated on the premise that children's language and literacy development is interwoven and continuous from infancy... Literacy develops concurrently with oral language. Fluency in oral language is no longer seen as a precursor to literacy, but as a goal to be accomplished with and through literacy as each language process informs and supports all the others.*

For ease and simplicity, we divide our discussion into a framework for the development of speaking proficiency in another language, and into a framework for the development of literacy.

THE IMPORTANCE OF CONTEXT

In the introduction we discussed our four themes (page 2) and asserted that effective, facilitating assessment means assessment that occurs within a context. This concept is so important that we have devoted an entire section to it. As Braun (1993) says, "Everything hinges on the context." Context, as defined by Gumperz (1964), is "the physical setting, the people within the setting, what the people are doing and saying, and where and when they are doing it. Language is embedded in the flow of daily life."

There are many contexts in life. Many of these are embedded within others. Your student must be seen within the larger context of his family, his culture, and his language. Reading groups, show-and-tell, centers, and seat work are all contexts within the context of a particular classroom. The classroom operates within the larger context of a particular school, with its individual teachers, principal, and population. The school operates within the larger context of a school district, with its policies and programs for limited- or non-English-speaking students. The school district is embedded within the context of the community—whether it is a poverty-stricken port-of-entry city struggling with drugs, despair, and severely strained budgets, or a settled, middle-class community with pockets of low-income housing and a certain attitude toward immigrants. The districts are embedded within states and provinces, each with differing policies and laws concerning bilingual education and services for non-English-speaking students and different levels of funding for alternative programs. All these contexts are embedded within a country, such as the United States, with its prevailing attitudes toward bilingual students and its promise of education for all. Each context influences the others, and each has a history, or a set way of doing things, that makes change difficult and slow.

The Basic Features of Language in Context

All contexts have certain rules that one must know in order to operate successfully within them. A student's ability to perceive a given context, and to function within it, demonstrates both language and social competency.

All language interactions also have certain features. Years ago, Dell Hymes (1965) organized these features into a memorable form:

> *S — the setting*
> *P — the participants*
> *E — the ends (i.e., what the speakers hope to achieve)*
> *A — the act sequence*
> *K — the key or tone*
> *I — the instrumentalities (spoken, written, telephone)*
> *N — the norms of the interactions*
> *G — the genre (lecture, joke, round-robin reading)*

+ **Setting.** Where the interaction takes place profoundly affects everything else. The setting can be the classroom, the principal's office, the playground, the reading group. How the speakers interact with one another can change from setting to setting.

Students will be more informal and friendly to Mr. McMullin on the basketball court than when he is giving a science lecture.

- **Participants.** Who is speaking to whom also affects interactions. Georgia would not dare go up to Mr. Chang, the principal, and say, "Yo, Dennis, how's it hanging?" if she valued her free time. Talking with a superior necessitates a certain amount of formality. She would be wise to say, "Hello, Mr. Chang, have you had a busy day?" In a conversation between Georgia and her best friend, Nani, such formality would be inappropriate and unfriendly.

- **Ends.** What the speakers are trying to accomplish by this interaction also influences the conversation. Is Mrs. Law chewing out TJ for missing class, or is she asking how long his grandmother has been ill? Is Dan trying to help Taka learn the rules of basketball, or is he trying to convince his teacher that he had a good reason for being late for class?

- **Act sequence.** The rules of procedure are a silent partner to any conversation; no one pays attention unless they go awry. Procedure is determined by our understanding of how an interaction should proceed, from beginning to end. Americans begin conversations with hello and a certain amount of small talk, and end them with a *pre-closing* like, "well, gotta go," before walking away or "I don't want to run up your bill," before hanging up the phone. Children familiar with school routines know that, for instance, when they enter Mrs. Delp's kindergarten classroom they are to check their desk first, and if there is seat work, they must finish that before doing anything else. This act sequence is particularly important for students who have little knowledge of schools or in places where students get little or no structure at home. Training in how to begin the day, how to respond to teachers, how to pack up and leave, once simply taken for granted, is imperative in some places.

- **Key.** This is the *tone* of the interaction. Many teachers, especially ESL teachers, work hard at setting up a comfortable, warm atmosphere where the students feel safe and free from ridicule and pressure. The key of an interaction can be formal or informal. It can be sarcastic or playful. Often the more subtle keys are lost on second-language learners. Saying, in a joking voice, "You cannot tease a teacher," could lead Chai to never tease again if he misunderstands the tone.

- **Instrumentalities.** This is the channel or the medium by which the message is transmitted. Is this interaction written or spoken? Many of our students master oral communication long before they can write, while others write well but are hesitant to speak.

- **Norms of the interaction.** These norms are often the most fraught with peril for newcomers. These are the basic, underlying, unspoken rules we bring to the conversation, to the classroom, to the school. We make assumptions about how far a person should stand away from us, whether touching the other person is appropriate, how much eye contact indicates shiftiness as opposed to staring. These assumptions are culturally relative—they differ from one culture to another. Studies show that North Americans think eighteen inches is the appropriate distance to stand from

82

another; alternatively, we can be edged down the hall by a bewildered person who wants to move into the closeness of his comfort zone—one that is a lot closer than the North American standard. If a teacher asks, "what is the procedure?" the implication is that it has already been stated clearly.

- **Genre.** This is a class of interactions, such as a sermon, a joke, a lecture, that dictates different kinds of responses. No one expects someone to interrupt a preacher and ask questions in the middle of his sermon. A joke teller feels annoyed if someone jumps in with the punch line.

All these language features influence each other and necessitate that the speaker reacts to the language context appropriately. Because the features are culturally relative, they change according to the context. Understanding the rules means more than linguistic competence—knowing the grammar and the words. It indicates *communicative competence*—understanding, within the particular context of a classroom, what the routine is: how to say something, how to understand what was said, when to speak, when to keep one's mouth shut, and how to say what to whom. Each classroom has its own set of rules. In Mr. Trinh's class, the children wait their turns politely and raise their hands before speaking. In Mrs. Barker's class, they feel free to jump in with their own opinions at any time during the discussion. These rules may be explicitly stated—for example, in a list drawn up at the beginning of the year, or they can be inferred as students become used to the teacher. An example of a set of elementary-school classroom rules is

- Observe your own space.

- Use an indoor voice.

- Stay on task.

- Respect all property.

These rules are probably standard for any classroom. However, the wording assumes a certain amount of cultural background knowledge; although a fairly proficient newcomer may be able to read the words, he may be mystified as to their meaning. What does "observe your own space" mean, anyway? How can you explain what "indoor voice" means to a non-English speaker who has never experienced a school setting before?

Understanding these implicit, governing rules is like wearing comfortable clothes in which you can operate freely and successfully within the context. Not knowing or understanding these rules can be a major source of failure for non-English-speaking students, or students from cultures different from the mainstream. Boggs (1985), for instance, found that within the context of the family, overt, direct questioning by Hawaiian parents is considered an inquisition, a search for a culprit, and a prelude to punishment; therefore, within a school context, Hawaiian and part-Hawaiian students would not respond to direct questioning from the teacher. Heath (1983) found that African-American children did not understand indirect questions such as "Is this where we put our toys?" and had a great deal of trouble with the concept of "it is time to put away the games." In their homes, they lived in a free flow of time in which an activity was finished when the child tired of it or it had come to a logical end that was not determined by the clock.

Context and assessment are interrelated

Because what we do and say is profoundly influenced by the context and the guiding rules within it, we cannot separate what we are assessing from the context within which it is spoken, heard, read, or written. Barrs et al. (1989) write, "Children's talk in small groups will be affected by the membership of the group—by personalities that are compatible or not; by relationships between girls and boys; by attitudes to race and culture."

We cannot use what a student has said in one context as an accurate indicator of what he can do overall. Teachers often create a picture of a learner's reading level based on how he performs in a round robin or on the seatwork he does. But these pictures are incomplete and often inaccurate. We need to look at many different contexts and build a portrait of the student and his capabilities based on how he functions in all of them.

Lan, for instance, was very shy. She never spoke up in class, preferring to approach the teacher privately to ask questions. However, her journal entries about her reading were filled with insights and a depth of understanding that many other students do not reach. When the class began role playing characters from *To Kill a Mockingbird*, the part of Bob Ewell fell to Lan. Taking on Bob's persona, she became loud, aggressive, and filled with hatred for Atticus, Tom Robinson, and the Finch children. The transformation was remarkable and a little scary from such a hitherto quiet, unassuming person. The teacher was now aware that Lan had understood the character—only too well!

The Language Framework and Traditional Testing

As teachers, we want to know what our students have learned, how much English they have acquired, and how much content they understand. Reviewing the language framework we have just discussed along with the common procedures for traditional testing, it is now easier to see why traditional tests are problematic for non-English-speaking students in one or more ways:

- **Setting.** The setting for test-taking may be unfamiliar. Students are often taken to a room away from others. For students whose tests of skills may have taken place within the marketplace ("Did you give that man the right number of fish?") or the field ("Dig small holes, and put six seeds into each hole"), the change to a classroom environment for testing makes the entire physical and psychological setting confusing and threatening.

- **Participants.** Within this unfamiliar and unsettling situation, the student interacts only with a stranger, a voice from a tape recorder, or a piece of paper, in a language he has not mastered.

- **Ends.** The students are given tasks whose purpose and meaning are often unclear to them and, unless there is an interpreter present, cannot be explained adequately. There are larger ends, beyond the classroom, for standardized tests, such as accountability to districts, states, and government bodies.

- **Act sequence.** In test situations, westernized students become accustomed to sitting down, pencil ready, waiting for the teacher to say, "Ready, begin," and then proceeding with the test until told to stop. Many students from nontraditional, non-Western societies have never been exposed to this.

- **Key.** The key is formal, often ritualized. There is little opportunity for laughter. There is rarely an opportunity to try again.

- **Instrumentalities.** The channel is often limited to one form, such as writing, or reading, or oral production. For students whose progress needs to be demonstrated in an ongoing way, this type of testing is limiting and unnatural. In addition, and, perhaps, most important, the channel is a different language, one in which the student may have little or no experience. For example, Mary worked in a school with a policy that allowed foreign students to attend ESL classes for two years only. Within those two years, they were expected to have acquired enough proficiency to move into the mainstream. Mary worked with many non-literate students whose progress was almost imperceptible by the standardized tests she had to use. It took nearly a year for students to absorb the language before they could demonstrate anything on the prefabricated tests. Yet she had to show that they were learning in order to secure them an additional year in the program. She kept reports, which documented each student's progress in the listening and speaking areas, but it took some lobbying to get the supervisors to agree to a change.

- **Norm.** The norm for most tests is "no talking, no looking at your neighbor's paper." This is incomprehensible to students who come from cultures where collaboration and sharing are valued and expected. There are also implicit norms, such as, "this is a one-shot measure. If you blow it, too bad." The norms do not take into account the fact that Serge might be suffering from recurring malaria, that Bertha had to stay up all night working in a factory because it is pumpkin season and her family needs the money, that Kao is so worried about his father that he cannot think straight. Standardized tests are impersonal and deal only with what the student purportedly can do, ignoring the person and the personality that confronts the test and the testing situation at the particular time.

- **Genre.** The genre is frequently multiple-choice. As with the setting, it is often unfamiliar to students (as well as a narrow, restrictive method of gaining information).

By understanding and paying attention to the contexts within which each person resides as well as to the contexts within which we operate as students, teachers, and ordinary citizens, we can better understand how and why people react as they do, and how context influences not only who we are, but how and why each learning situation succeeds or fails.

EMERGENCE

In addition to context, the continuum of language learning is important to understand while observing the learning processes in students. In the late 1970s and early 1980s, Krashen and Terrell (1983) developed the "natural approach" to language learning, defining several stages of developing language skills, including: preproduction, early production, speech emergence, intermediate fluency, and fluency.

Although some states still use these stages as guidelines for their ESL programs, there are problems inherent to them, particularly in the concept of preproduction—the idea that "comprehension precedes production" and that there is a stage where the learner does not comprehend and cannot produce any meaningful strings in writing or speaking. Research has shown that production and performance in reading, writing, and speaking often precede comprehension. Children will experiment and play with forms before they understand what they are doing. They will practice before they have been deemed "developmentally ready" for that form. How many children chant *ABCs* (or swear) before they have a clue what it is they are saying, or memorize long poems without understanding a word? (Witness such lines from songs as "low in the gravy lay Jesus our Savior" or "strumming on the old bad Joe.")

That proficiency emerges with exposure and practice over time is an attractive concept for us for several reasons. One of the most important is that this implies a *continuum of learning*, not an all-or-nothing focus with the perception that the student is somehow lacking until he gains proficiency nearly equivalent to that of a native-English speaker. Rather, a student arrives with little or no English and gains proficiency over time.

Another reason involves the concept of emergence. William Teale (1987) writes that *emergent* describes something "in the process of becoming." The idea of a learning continuum suggests the reaching of general milestones along the way rather than stages to which one must rigidly adhere. This is useful for looking at both speech development and at development of literacy and/or proficiency in students learning English as an additional language.

Following Teale, we can demonstrate four reasons why the concept of emergence is important and useful.

1. It emphasizes the notion that students are in the process of becoming proficient and literate in English at whatever point in development we look. It is not reasonable to point to a time when literacy begins, nor is it reasonable to think of a student coming to school either alingual (without language) or with absolutely no exposure to English. Learners are not transported to the school doorstep in a vacuum. Newcomers generally arrive at school having heard their primary language since birth and arrive in North America having seen street signs, billboards, immigration papers, and probably advertisements on television.

2. It emphasizes the continuity of development, from a beginning toward more proficiency and mastery.

3. It suggests discontinuity. Development is taking place and lack of mastery or proficiency is left behind.

4. It suggests that growth occurs without a prerequisite and overriding emphasis on formal teaching. Language learning and literacy development take place at home, at school, on the playground, and at work.

Emergence and Second-Language Learners

With second-language learners, the gathering of knowledge, skills, and proficiency does not happen in isolation but in orchestration. They develop concurrently, each one dependent on and influencing the others throughout life. The mastery of reading depends on the knowledge of vocabulary and syntax as well as on the skills basic to getting meaning from print.

PROFICIENCY

The term *proficiency* is a slippery one, which everyone uses but does not necessarily define up front. It implies having gained a certain mastery over material or skills, which opens doors to functioning on a level with others who have achieved that level.

English language proficiency, as defined by the Council of Chief State School Officers (CCSSO) (1992), is the ability to "use English to ask questions, to understand teachers and reading materials, to test ideas, and to challenge what is being asked in the classroom for both basic communicative tasks and academic purposes." Literacy is "the ability and willingness to use reading and writing to construct meaning from printed text, in ways which meet the requirements of a particular social context" (Au, 1993).

Proficiency in listening is defined as "the ability to understand the language of the teacher and instruction, comprehend and extract information, and follow the instructional discourse through which teachers provide information." Proficiency in speaking is "the ability to use oral language appropriately and effectively in learning activities (such as peer tutoring, collaborative learning activities, and question/answer sessions) within the classroom and in social interactions within the school" (Del Vecchio and Guerrero, 1995).

Emerging Oral Proficiency

It is nearly impossible for a student to come to school on the first day without ever having heard a word of English: he has been bombarded with the English language from the moment he set foot in an English-speaking country or community. The English he knows, however, may be so limited that it does not allow him admission into the arena of a school social life. When he first arrives, he may know no functional English, and he may be unable to do the simplest of activities. From that point on, he moves toward greater and greater command of his new language.

In appendix A2 (page 268-269) we demonstrate the emergence of oral proficiency. The terms we suggest are not necessarily aligned with state proficiency levels, although we have included several phrases from the Michigan state proficiency levels. Neither are they a precise organization of levels—it is not our intent or our place to be precise. Within each level there can be a substantial range of student performance. We merely use the levels to help define what teachers are seeing and hearing when they watch and listen to their learners.

Emerging Literacy

Teale (1987) defined emergent literacy as the period "between birth and the time when children write and read in conventional ways, ways that adults generally would identify as actually being reading and writing. Thus, emergent literacy represents the beginnings of reading and writing for the child." Literacy is not a state. Becoming literate is a continuous process. We do not achieve the ability to read and stop there; we grow as readers throughout our lifetimes. Beginning literacy, continues Teale, is not to be confused with beginning reading, which is closely associated with formal reading instruction in school.

Emergent readers from literate backgrounds

Many children, especially middle-class, mainstream children, come to school with a long history of exposure to print, and there is a gradual emergence of understanding about the concepts of reading and writing. Researchers find that literacy in the home mediates nine domains of activity: daily living, entertainment, school, work, religion, interpersonal communication, participating in information networks, storybook time, and literacy for the sake of teaching/learning literacy. Goodman (1988) writes, "The beginnings of reading and writing occur in individuals when they develop the awareness that written language makes sense."

ESL students from non-literate backgrounds

Many non-English-speaking or limited-English-speaking students do not have the luxury of being surrounded by reading and writing. They come to school with no background in print media or awareness that print has meaning, and they are suddenly immersed and expected to be productive in a literate environment.

With these learners, we cannot assume common assertions like "literacy development begins long before children start formal instruction" (Galda et al., 1993). Many have not learned reading and writing behaviors within the informal settings of home and community (some struggle with literacy into their high-school years). Their parents are illiterate; someone must translate for them, pay the bills, write the checks, interpret the laws. Beginning and emergent literacy for the student is often limited to situations that occur strictly within the school: storybook time and learning to read for the sake of learning to read.

Students of all ages entering our schools can fall anywhere on the continuum of literacy development. Teale and Sulzby (1986) write, "Although children's learning about literacy can be described in terms of generalized stages, children can pass through these stages in a variety of ways and at different ages." Exposure or lack of exposure to literacy early in life is a key factor in where, and at what age, preliterate and non-literate students enter the literacy continuum and how quickly they pass through the stages.

Secondary schools inundated with illiterate and poorly educated students face additional challenges. A fifteen-year-old refugee enrolling in school for the first time in his life is entering at the eleventh hour. Not only must he learn English but also some basic concepts we take for granted at the high-school level. The high-school curriculum demands that students know not only how to read (never mind knowing how to read in English) but also strategies for reading different genres at a fairly sophisticated level. A student must know how to skim; he must have a background knowledge in history, science, and North American culture; he must have years of practice not only in learning, but in learning how to learn. All of these concepts must be addressed for these students so that they do not simply fall through the cracks.

GAINING CONTROL OVER FORMS

It is critical to make both reading and writing essential components of a literacy program. Marie Clay (1975) writes, "For children who learn to write at the same time as they learn to read, writing plays a significant part in the early reading progress." There is strong evidence that learning to write helps provide experience with the basic hierarchical relationships between letters, words, and messages; when a student is attempting to write, he is compelled to pay attention to the significant details of written language. He *applies* the concepts rather than simply takes them in. As Forester and Reinhard (1989) point out, writing "requires greater attention to letters and their sounds than reading does."

What can a student learn about reading and writing by practicing print and by reading his work or having it read to him? A student can learn

- that print carries a message
- directionality—that print in English goes from left to right, and we read pages in English from top to bottom
- that letters are formed in a specific way, and that their form is unchanging
- what a word is
- what a letter is, and what sounds each letter can make
- the mechanics of writing, including punctuation and capital letters

Levels of Literacy Development: Writing

Research about the significance of literacy instruction, including what Cunningham et al. (2000, 2002, 2005) term the "Four Blocks" (guided reading, self-selected reading, writing, and working with words), has been well established. Reading aloud to students regularly has long been recognized for its centrality in helping students learn to read (Durkin, 1966; Elley, 1989; Stahl, Richek, and Vandevier, 1991; Morrow and Gambrell, 2000). The importance of these four components, particularly for English-language learners, cannot be overstated. When we compared the text produced by various levels of readers and writers, it was clear how much reading and being read to influenced the quantity and quality of work produced. Those who had been exposed to books had a much wider range of words and resources at hand than those who had not.

Mastery over the conventions of writing does not take place in a day. There are many models to show the stages of children's literacy development, each with its own labels for levels and divisions within the continuum toward mastery. We have adapted several of these models, most notably those of Teale and Sulzby (1986), Manning and Manning (1992), and Weaver (1994). This development toward mastery represents a continuum, and the leaps from one level to the next are never clear-cut.

[handwritten margin notes: "I do this even with my 8th/9th graders"]

[handwritten margin notes: "Um yeah I still don't have that"]

Drawing

Children from literate environments begin drawing very early. Before long, they can tell you what it is they are trying to draw, even if it bears no resemblance to the actual object. Soon, they announce their intention before they begin ("I am going to draw a cat"). Many second-language learners, who do not yet know how to write or who cannot write in English, can demonstrate their understanding of concepts by drawing. As we pointed out in *The More Than Just Surviving Handbook*, drawing is a terrific way of helping students whose intellectual capacity exceeds their English proficiency and of demonstrating their understanding of concepts.

Figure 4.1 This drawing was a response to the book *The Cat in the Hat*. The first grader who produced this loved to listen to the story and, although she could not write, she could demonstrate her understanding through her picture.

Scribbling

Many children from literate environments go through a period of what looks like scribbling that gradually evolves into letters and words. Numerous researchers (for example, Teale and Sulzby, 1986) have found that these early efforts reflect a very clear distinction between drawing and writing and conclude that the markings are intended to signify meaning. Usually, children can "read" what they wrote, showing that they have begun to understand the difference between pictures and print. *My niece writes story on the computer*

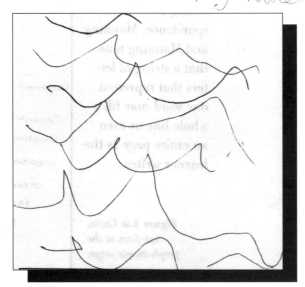

Figure 4.2 This is a letter written by a three-year-old English-speaking child: "Dear Jesus, Thank you for taking the spider away. You can come to my house. And you can come to my party with Lala and Robin and Sofie. Amen." Note that the writer has a sense of both the standard format of a letter and of prayers.

I have several ELL students do this for their first semester in their readers notebook

Students from preliterate and non-literate backgrounds, or even students from non-print home environments within the western culture, come to school without that all-important repertoire of knowledge about print. They are not afforded the time for experimentation, and because of the demands of school, most of them probably proceed directly to print.

Figure 4.3 This drawing was done by a new-to-the-country first grader. Note the wavy lines he used directly under the picture, which are clearly different from the non-English-script-like lines at the bottom of the page. His drawing shows skill, as well as an astonishing degree of Christian symbolism. He may have been attempting to depict writing both in English and in his own language, Lao.

Using letter-like forms

Gentry (1982) termed this stage "prephonemic" because learners know that letters can "say" something, but they have not yet learned that there is a sound-letter correspondence. Manning and Manning (1992) note that a string of letters that represents one word may fill a whole line or even an entire page as the learner writes.

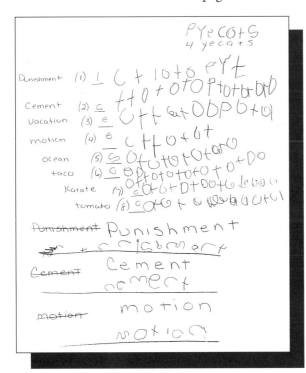

Figure 4.4 (left) Carla, age four, at the prephonemic stage

Figure 4.5 Choua is making the bridge to phonemic spelling. She has several sight words: "He is OK." The rest is indecipherable.

Copying

It is easy to overlook and minimize the importance of copying. However, a student's practice of and mastery over forms by copying is a major achievement in his movement toward literacy and proficiency. Clay (1975) continues:

> *If a child knows how to scan, how to study a word to reproduce it, and how to organize his writing of that word, he has the skills to deal with the detail of print. It is probable that early writing serves to organize the visual analysis of print.*

You can see real growth when a learner sees words written in uppercase and reproduces them in lowercase. This demonstrates a significant step in understanding.

Figure 4.6 A first grader's bat report. This child recognizes the significant features of letters but has not yet gained control of the forms. She is not aware of word boundaries.

Figure 4.7 This child recognizes significant features of letters but has yet to gain control of the formulating of letters. He is not aware of word boundaries.

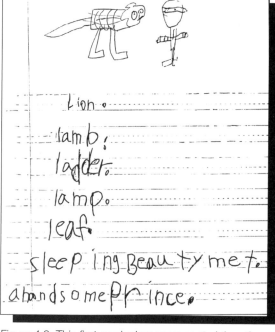

Figure 4.8 This first grader has more control than the student from figure 4.7. She is aware of punctuation and places periods after each word in the list.

Invented spelling

This is also called "phonetic spelling" or "constructive spelling" (the latter is probably for the benefit of doubtful parents and administrators). Researchers and early childhood experts contend that this is an important stage for learners, which should be encouraged. Weaver (1994) cites several advantages to promoting invented spelling.

+ It affords the student the freedom to explore his knowledge of sound-letter correspondences, to put his ideas down without worrying about rightness or wrongness. It also allows him to write long texts that would likely never have been produced if he was constrained by the needs to be exact and the teacher having to spell every word for him. For example, in figure 4.9, Katie laboriously sounded out every word in this story about Maleficent, after seeing the Disney version of *Sleeping Beauty*. It took her a very long time to write, and afterwards she wanted it read to her. Of course, it was almost impossible for anyone else to reconstruct, but she knew what she was saying when she wrote it and could read it because her own internal set of "rules" were consistent.

Figure 4.9 Katie's story about Maleficent

+ Students are encouraged to take risks and to construct knowledge for themselves. For example, Stan was in a class of beginners. In figure 4.10, he was not only demonstrating that he had a good deal of understanding of concepts like sound-letter correspondence, as well as a number of sight words, but he was also learning to apply this knowledge.

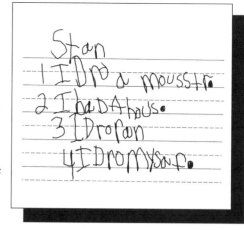

Figure 4.10 Stan wrote: "I draw a monster. I had a house. I draw rain. I draw myself."

+ Because they are constructing this knowledge for themselves, these spellers learn and apply phonics rules more readily than those who are simply given spelling lists to memorize. Spontaneously produced texts can reveal a greater understanding than those that were guided by the teacher. For instance, when we look at a list of spelling words from the test devised by Manning and Manning (1992) (see figure 4.11), we get a very clear picture of the learner's understanding of writing and his representation of spelling patterns and sight words. However, looking at a freely written text (see figure 4.12), we can see that a learner can reveal a much wider range of understanding.

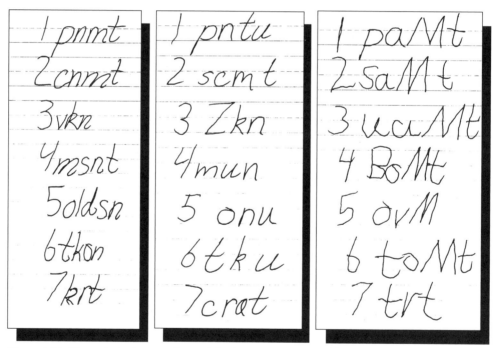

Figure 4.11 Three students were dictated the following words: *punishment, cement, vacation, motion, ocean, taco, karate, tomato*. Note the differences in their evolution.

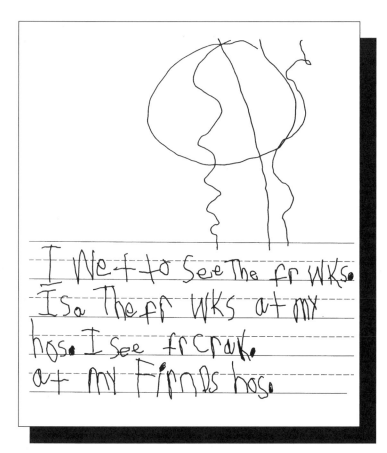

Figure 4.12 This spontaneous story about fireworks shows that the writer has a number of sight words in his memory and a good command of sound-spelling correspondence. It reads: "I went to see the fireworks. I saw the fireworks at my house. I see firecrackers at my friend's house."

+ Finally (and this can be used to "sell" administrators and parents to the idea), some research (for example, Clay, 1991) suggests that students who are encouraged to spell constructively do better on standardized spelling and reading tests.

? long term? When?/who? would spelling tests be helpful for

There are several levels that fall within the "invented spelling" stage of growth (Note that as learners progress and their experience with the written word grows, they include more and more sight words that they can recognize and produce independently.).

+ **Consonantal.** Writers at this level realize that there are letter-sound correspondences and use mostly consonants. This usually begins with learners using one letter to represent the word. As his understanding grows, he begins to include initial and final consonants.

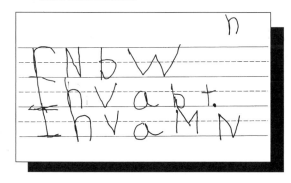

Figure 4.13 This beginner only used vowels in the word "*a*." Her sentences are strikingly consistent in their omission of vowels. When vowels are included her meaning is clear: *rainbow / I have a bat / I have a man.*

95

The test perceys :) ←

Figure 4.14 This child omits the vowels in words that are not in her sight repertoire. This reads: "My cat go find squirrel."

+ **Letter-name.** At this level, learners begin to use letters whose name sounds like the sound they are trying to represent: for example, the letter *c* for *see*.

Figure 4.15 This learner uses *z* for the *zzz* sound in *is* and a *t* for the ending of *liked*. She was at a level where *m* and *n* are confusing and continually asked, "one hump or two?" Her text reads: "This is my snake. I liked him, but we had move to a different house."

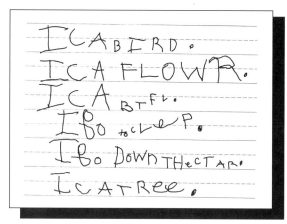

Figure 4.16 This beginner also uses the name of the letter to represent the sound: *c* for *see* and *c* for the *s* sound in *sleep* and *stair*. She has begun to progress beyond simple consonants to represent complete words.

+ **Vowel-consonant combinations.** Vowels start to appear in the middle of words. Many of the vowels reflect the letter-name strategy, in which the letter the student uses reflects the name of the letter.

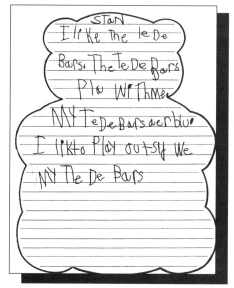

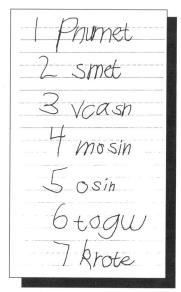

Figure 4.17 Here is Stan again, showing a lot of vowel names, such as the *e*-sound in *teddy* (made by the *y*), the *a*-sound in *play*, the *u*-sound in *blue*, and the *i*-sound in *like* and *outside*.

Figure 4.18 Bo is showing an understanding of the use of vowels in his words. The dictation was: punishment, cement, vacation, motion, ocean, taco, karate, tomato.

♦ **Words.** This is what Teale and Sulzby (1986) call "full invented spelling," where the learner indicates all the sounds represented by a word. If there are missing sounds, there is usually an indication that beginning, middle, and final sounds are present.

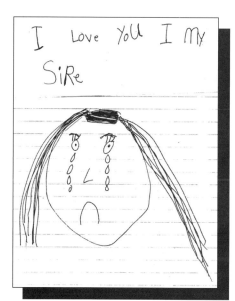

Figure 4.19 This reads: "I love you, I'm sorry"

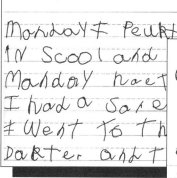

Figure 4.20 This reads: "Monday I puked in school and Monday night I had a sore ear. I went to the doctor and the doctor said you have to take ear drops and medicine, ok?"

In figure 4.20, the writer spelled some words just like they sound, such as the *k* in *doctor* and the *s* in *medicine*. He spelled other words exactly as he heard them, such as the *f* in *have to*. He approximated what he heard in the word *drops*. And he showed an awareness of the rules of vowel sounds, which are notoriously inconsistent. With more reading experience he would move closer and closer to standard English spelling.

Standard-English spelling

At this level, learners spell most words the conventional way. Forester and Reinhard (1989) remind us that "neat little printers lapse into quite poor performance when shifting from copying to composing...When composing, the attention of the writer is focused on the creative task at hand. Neatness of handwriting takes second place." *I do that*

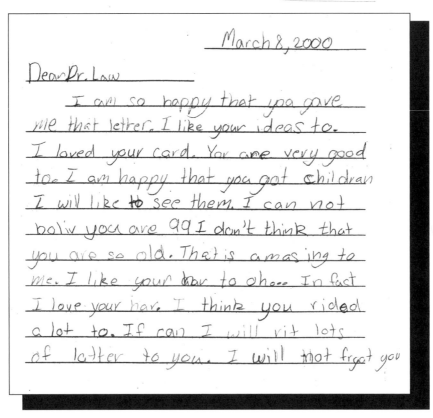

Figure 4.21 Here is a letter from a third grader who has moved well beyond the basics and is mastering grammar and spelling, as well as correct letter format.

Levels of Literacy Development: Reading

We already mentioned that students do not come to school alingual. Unless there are other factors operating, a student's first language is well developed, and now he is working at adding a second (or a third, or fourth) language. This is not always the case, however, with reading and writing. Mainstream, middle-class students usually come from print-rich environments, with a large storehouse of information about print. Many can read before they enter school; others can write their own names. At very least, most know that words convey meaning.

Not so with many immigrants. They enter school at the most basic level. The first major step toward literacy is the realization that print is meaningful. This may take a year or more. We cannot underestimate the importance of that breakthrough. Neither can we underestimate the time it takes to reach it nor should we start searching for underlying disabilities if it takes longer than we think it should. It can take a long time to reach this level; you cannot rush it.

I always assumed after several years it is a language problem

Based on a system used in Michigan, we have formulated the following levels of reading development to help you determine where your student is at, so that you can design activities to enhance the student's strengths and help him continue to build on them. The following levels overlap to a certain degree. Emerging readers do not make strict leaps and can have features of several levels all at once. A beginning awareness learner can also be aware of punctuation. An emergent reader can create long texts using invented spellings, while the repertoire of words he can spell correctly on his own is less than ten. Each student is different.

Pre-awareness

At this level, students

+ do not know that print has meaning; print is merely squiggles on the page
+ do not seem to know what books are and what they are for
+ do not know how to handle a book or how to turn pages
+ have not held pens or pencils
+ may not be able to look at pictures and see more than simple shades of color
+ cannot see drawings of objects and identify them for what they are
+ may or may not be able to copy words
+ may demonstrate understanding of a story by drawing a picture

Students at this level need to be inundated with print, even though they are not reading yet. It is only by seeing print in use that they can make that qualitative leap to understanding and eventual reading. For example, Kao picked up a book and opened it upside down. Then he looked at his neighbor and, examining how she was holding her book, he turned his own right side up. In another example, Ka Neng was contentedly reading *National Geographic*, not realizing that the magazine was upside down. When she reached a picture with people in it, she noticed and turned the magazine right side up.

In a third example, eight first-grade boys, whom classroom teachers Carolyn and Shirley called their "challenging group," had been matching words with pictures to practice classroom vocabulary such as *book, eraser, pencil, scissors,* and *color.* Today, for the first time, they were going to try a writing exercise. They were given a large sheet of paper on which several cloze sentences had been written. They were to fill in each blank with the correct name of the object and then draw a picture of and color the object.

This turned out to be a revealing exercise and was the first time Carolyn and Shirley could see whether the boys were actually making connections between the objects they saw and the words pinned above them. Peter, their most verbally proficient boy, was unable to fill in the blank. He could not connect the word with the object even though they were together on the wall. In addition, when he got some help using a pencil and forming letters, his writing showed a lack of skill. The letters were large, irregular, and unevenly spaced.

Students at the pre-awareness level often come from cultures and places in the world that have no written form of language; they have not connected print with meaning. This all-important leap in understanding may take several years; teachers often get frustrated during this phase and begin to look elsewhere for blame when the student does not seem to get it. It is only by seeing print *in use* that students can make the qualitative jump to understanding and eventual reading. Immersion in print means demonstrating to students how to make the connection between print and meaning and giving them many opportunities to try it out for themselves. We suggest the following teaching strategies to support pre-awareness readers:

+ Label items in the classroom.

+ Make lists.

+ Introduce environmental print in the classroom by pointing it out on posters, calendars, and so on.

+ Read to students in their first and second languages.

+ Work with sequencing.

+ Read predictable books (for example, pattern books).

+ Use the Language Experience Approach (LEA) (Van Allen, 1961).

+ Introduce songs, rhymes, and drama.

+ Provide many opportunities to draw, copy, and to practice writing.

Many of the activities and the reading can be done in orchestration. For example, Shirley and Carolyn devised a lesson using *Goldilocks and the Three Bears*. They read the story many times; the boys acted it out; they talked about the words *first, second, last,* as well as *big, bigger, biggest*; they made puppets, and they drew the bears' house and its contents on three-part folders. The boys could then tell the story to one another using the puppets and the folders.

Emerging awareness

At this level, students

+ understand that print carries a message

+ can demonstrate understanding of general terms like *read, page, story, book*

+ are beginning to construct meaning from text using non-print features like illustrations, graphs, maps, and tables

+ engage in pretend reading, often using proper intonation

+ can tell a story in sequence from pictures

+ can read and write their own names

+ begin to read environmental print

+ begin to track from left to right

- can repeat all or parts of predictable text

- become familiar with "story grammar" in English-language stories (for example, "Once upon a time..."; "In a land far away..."; "There once was..."; "...and they lived happily ever after")

- begin to write words

- can copy with relative ease

- are not fully aware of word boundaries

- do not understand the concepts represented by the terms *letter, words, number*

Students at this level have made the all-important first step of connecting print to meaning. Pretend reading is a strategy that should be welcomed and reinforced. Some consider this to be phony reading, but through this strategy, beginning readers are internalizing patterns and story grammar that form the basis for much that comes later. According to Doake (1985), children who engage in pretend reading:

> *...have been able to absorb the meaning of their stories, engage in deep-level processing, and generate meaningful written language on the run. They [are] not simply imitating and remembering but creating and composing their version of the stories using the written dialect and their knowledge of story structure to do so.*

Eventually, the readers will begin to attend to the print on the page as well as to the pictures and other cues. For example, Alexi proudly "read" the "Brown Bear, Brown Bear"-patterned book that he made in school:

> **Brown Bear, Brown Bear**
> **What do you see?**
> **I see a...** (*he turns the page to look at the next picture*)
> **...Red bird looking at me.**

Alexi could not track or point to individual words he was reading on the page. He had the right intonation and paused in the right places, but he was not at the level where he was attending to the print. By reading the patterned book again and again to Alexi until he had it memorized, the teacher had provided a scaffold on which he could build. She had modeled the reading and now he could imitate the correct behaviors and use the pictures as cues.

In another example, a class of beginning literacy students, who could barely read their own names, was able to recognize important words in the environment such as *Cub Foods, Kmart,* and *rice.*

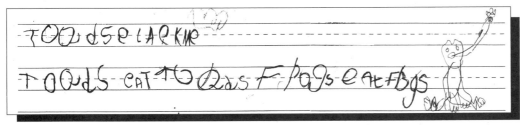

Figure 4.22 A third grader's writing

The third grader whose writing sample is shown as figure 4.22 had had little experience with print, and it was easy to sum up how little he knew. He did not yet have control over his forms and did not seem to be fully aware of word boundaries. However, the fact that he used a lowercase *a* in *toads* and a capital *A* in *eat* demonstrates that he did have knowledge of spelling and forms. If he had simply been copying, he would have been consistent with either upper or lowercase letters.

hadn't considered this

We suggest the following teaching strategies to support emerging-awareness readers:

- Do all suggested activities for the pre-awareness level.
- Use familiar patterned books for modeling.
- Use frame sentences.
- Read, read, read.

Emerging reading

At this level, students

- can recognize and pick out individual words within a text
- look at the text and words when reading
- can spell a few words on their own, remembering word forms and writing them independently
- understand that the sentence and the picture go together
- are familiar with the "story grammar" of English-language stories
- are developing strategies to predict meaning
- take information from a variety of sources, such as graphophonic, syntactic, and semantic
- still read aloud
- are aware of word boundaries when writing
- are beginning to understand the conventions of punctuation

many of my English Students still do this

Katie (see figure 4.9) was aware of print and "wrote" copiously in her journal—and yet it seemed she had not made the connection between words on a page and the meanings they were supposed to represent. She had had a lifelong experience with print and had all the right "behaviors." For instance, she knew how to track print in the right direction. But she simply swept her finger across the page without focusing on individual words. She had not made the leap to reading yet, and her teacher was getting concerned. Then, one day Katie sat down with a book and said, "I'm going to read this to you." She looked at the words and actually read the text. She had moved from emerging awareness to emerging reading in what appeared to be one smooth transition; however, all the pieces had been in place and she had had rich input and constant reinforcement all her life—something we cannot take for granted with many of our newcomers.

Figure 4.23 The first-grade class used patterns found in a silly story they had read to write their own stories. This student was very verbally proficient and was able to invent and illustrate his own story using the model. He was developing "story grammar" in his head.

At this stage, fledgling readers really begin to take off. There is a very large leap between this stage and the previous one—one that may take a long time to make. For older learners, this can be particularly problematic, as many programs only allow students a set amount of time to complete them—but it can take as many as two years for the student to simply recognize that print has meaning and to make the connection Katie made. Emerging readers are often bumped from classes and programs by newcomers whose needs seem to be more pressing. But they are not ready to make the transition to content classes; they are still transitioning from being dependent readers toward reading independently. You can observe them working with text, finding clues to predict meaning, sounding out words, succeeding in reading words outside of the story context. Learners are often word bound, focusing mainly on phonics skills to get meaning and laboriously sounding out words. They need to be guided toward using their predicting skills.

Teachers might be tempted to give emerging readers traditional Dick-and-Jane-type of books because these books have few words. We do not recommend it. An interesting storyline is more important than simple words. It may seem counterintuitive to give a student a book like *There's a Nightmare in My Closet* (who needs sight words like *nightmare* or *suppose* at this stage?). That is not the point. Enjoyment of reading is essential. Giving students books they can have fun with, that they want to read over and over, is a big part of the game.

Developing skills are reflected in emerging readers' writing as well. There is evidence of word boundaries, and learners show spelling abilities and can use word forms with more accuracy.

This is very true even for English students, especally struggling adolescents

My home was in Laos. It was made of bamboo and grass. It had a fence around it. We had a barn with chickens and six buffalo. We had an orchard of orange trees. Sometimes we grew rice. We grew everything we ate.

Figure 4.24 Lee's picture and transcript

Many students, including older ones like Lee, are much more proficient orally than they are in reading and writing. As well, many students from non-literate backgrounds are skilled artists. In figure 4.24, Lee drew a picture of his home in Laos and told the teacher about it. The teacher wrote down his words, and they revised them together, producing a clear, written description of his home.

We suggest the following teaching strategies to support emerging readers:

+ Do all suggested activities for pre-awareness and emerging-awareness stages.

+ Provide many reading models.

- Use frame sentences and patterned books.

- Set aside a silent-reading time.

- Read books to students that are of higher levels than those they are capable of reading on their own. This expands vocabulary and horizons.

A group of students of all ages went camping in the mountains of California. They hiked to their camping spot, cooked over an open fire, ate s'mores, and slept outside under the stars. The next morning, back at the classroom, they were given frame sentences to fill in, such as:

> *Last night I_____.*
> *I was brave when_____.*
> *I was afraid of _____.*
> *I liked when _____.*
> *I had fun when _____.*

Students were free to write their reflections and draw pictures, and they could expand as their English mastery allowed. Here, we show some students' responses.

Figure 4.25 Herman simply filled in the blanks with single words and enhanced his writing with great pictures.

Figure 4.26 Matt, too, was content to simply fill in the blanks.

The following year, we had students record their memories in the form of a book/sleeping bag. The front page was the top of the sleeping bag, and on the inside back page, students drew their heads. On each inside page, they drew their bodies and wrote about a different facet of the night they had enjoyed (see figure 4.27, next page).

Gaining fluency

At this level, students

- are confident when reading familiar texts

- pay attention to the words on the page

- achieve growing independence

- begin to read silently

- may use invented spelling

- can read for a variety of purposes (pleasure, information)

- select books that interest them

- can retell stories they read in their own words

- can extract the main idea

- use punctuation appropriately

Figure 4.27 Judy is at a higher level and adds more detail.

These students are becoming more independent and more confident as their proficiency and knowledge base grow. They still need support in understanding texts in content areas. They need structure, models on which to base their writing. This period can reveal a virtual explosion of errors in writing; the student is ungluing from the chalkboard or the book and taking risks by using knowledge of sound-letter correspondence to try spelling on his own. It is always tempting to correct these errors, but many teachers do not, unless the writing is for publication. We suggest the following teaching strategies to support readers gaining fluency:

- Provide structures and models on which students can base their writing.

- Have students write responses to readings.

- Concentrate more on revision and editing.

Louisa's story (figure 4.28) was a frame-sentence assignment based on the book *Rosie's Walk*. In a similar camping adventure, students went on a hike through a series of crevices and tunnels. They had reviewed safety factors—as well as prepositions—before they went. Students of varying proficiency levels had fun with this assignment because they all had a great adventure and could expand as they were able.

Figure 4.28 Louisa's sentences are very short, but the last one (at top) shows a sophisticated knowledge of English sentence structure and vocabulary.

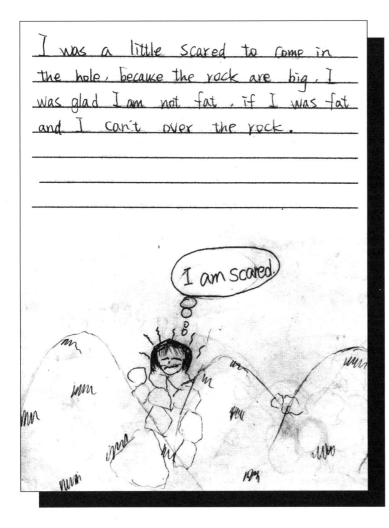

I was a little scared to come in the hole, because the rock are big. I was glad I am not fat, if I was fat and I can't over the rock.

I am scared.

Figure 4.29 Letty wrote a great deal more. She had a much greater vocabulary and knowledge of sentence structure, and she used this knowledge with ease.

Increasing fluency

At this level, students

+ can approach unfamiliar texts with a degree of confidence, but still may need support

+ begin to draw inferences from books

+ can use directories like telephone books and tables of content to find information

+ need support with cultural aspects of texts

+ can write quite sophisticated stories

+ pay attention to organization when writing

+ use context to predict meanings of unknown words

+ develop personal voice in writing   Alex

These students are well underway with reading and are increasingly confident, although they need to return to familiar types of materials to solidify their skills and increase their fluency. They may need support with unfamiliar texts. They know they must apply different styles of reading with different types of text.

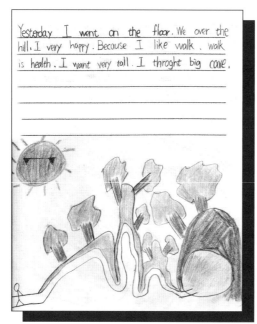

> I am bird butt because gam a
> Bird that bave a butt

Figure 4.30 This example, picked out of the recycling bin, shows a student playing with the language. When students achieve a certain threshold of proficiency, they can wield the language with a dexterity that lower levels are unable to do.

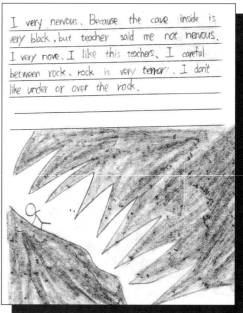

> Yesterday I went on the floor. We over the hill. I very happy. Because I like walk. walk is health. I want very tall. I throght big cave.

> I very nervous. Because the cave inside is very black, but teacher said me not nervous. I very nove. I like this teachers. I careful between rock. rock is very terror. I don't like under or over the rock.

Figure 4.31 Here is Linda's story of her walk in the mountains. The drawings, especially the jagged teeth in the cave, enhance the depiction of her fright. The excitement of the adventure gave her the opportunity to use her voice, which is very strong here.

We suggest the following teaching strategies to support readers at the increasing-fluency level:

+ Provide support for unfamiliar materials or content.

+ Allow students to choose to read texts at easier/lower reading levels.

+ Help with abstract, conceptual reading.

+ Help with cultural background of reading.

+ Work on higher-order skills such as making inferences, comparing, synthesizing, and so on.

+ Use stories and concepts students learned in their first language as a take-off point.

For example, Tong's sixth-grade class was studying parts of a story: main character, setting, conflict, *denouement*, and so on. To complement and extend this lesson, Mary, Tong's tutor, used fairytales to illustrate these features for her student. Tong was familiar with the Chinese rendition of "Little Red Riding Hood," "Lon Po Po." After reading the story in

English and discussing these concepts within the framework of that version, they moved on to "Hu Po Po," a Taiwanese variation of the "Lon Po Po" story, and then to a reading of the Grimm's version of "Little Red-Cap." Then, they did a chart of the three versions of the story to study similarities and differences and draw conclusions.

Advanced fluency

At this level, students

+ are self-motivated and confident readers in English and/or another language

+ can process material further and further removed from their own experience, and make links to personal experiences

+ can research topics independently, by formulating questions and finding relevant information

+ can tackle a wide variety of texts by employing various reading strategies

+ can make inferences and offer critical opinions or analyses

+ have sufficient understanding of content vocabulary to read and understand textbooks

+ can synthesize and expand on information

This fluency may or may not be in English. Many students come to us from countries with rigorous school systems. Often they can read and write at exceptional levels in their own languages. They may be far ahead of North American students in math and science, and it is only their fluency in English that holds them back. Other students can read and write in English and know grammar better than we do (often to our embarrassment when they try to discuss the finer points of English with us). Their English writing may be hesitant and filled with grammar that reflects their own system. Or, their writing might be vigorous and strong, even though their grasp of English is not complete. They need assignments that challenge them and that demand a higher level of thinking, analysis, and synthesis, which allows them to extend their capacities.

When Barb was assigned to work with a class of higher-level ESL reading and writing students, she assigned a simple text, *Sarah, Plain and Tall*, on the grounds that the theme of moving to a strange place would be something to which all students could relate. Students were required to write responses to the text before they came to class. In groups, they worked through questions that required them to go back into the text for answers. Those who understood less than others benefited from the discussions. Questions were literal and simple: "List as many characters as you can," "List in order the events as they occurred." Then the questions moved on to higher-level thinking: "Go back to your list of events and star the events that seem important in the evolution of Sarah." The book's simple prose gave students the confidence and practice to move through a text without stopping to look up every unknown word.

Then, the class moved on to *To Kill a Mockingbird*. Barb had much intervention to do in order to explain both the background and the text itself. Beginning questions were identical to the "Sarah" questions. Then, students were asked if they had experienced prejudice in their own countries and, if they had lived in Maycomb, what they would have done for Tom Robinson. Finally, students were randomly assigned parts. They were instructed first to go back to the text and write down as many facts as they could about the character and then to make as many inferences as they could about the character. As a culminating exercise, other class members brainstormed questions to ask them, and they were interviewed and videotaped as that character.

Figure 4.32 Pages from the retelling of an old folk legend by an eighth grader

LITERACY IN THE FIRST LANGUAGE/ GAINING FLUENCY IN ENGLISH

Superimposed onto the template of our discussion about the levels of literacy development is the phenomenon of students who enter our schools with varying degrees of literacy in their own language. They may read and write at grade level in their first language but have not yet achieved proficiency in English to read or write with ease. They are not learning to read all over again, so it is inappropriate to teach them as if they were illiterate. Studies show that a person only learns to read once, and the skills gained in the first language transfer to the second as mastery in syntax and vocabulary proceed. As the student gains control over grammar, vocabulary, and, often, the conventions of an alphabetic writing system with all its attendant punctuation and mechanical details, he can demonstrate more and more what he is capable of conceiving, and the gap between his thoughts and his production decreases. Barrs et al. (1989) write:

> *Bilingual children may well be developing as readers and writers in their first languages and, given the opportunity, can use this developing competence in the mainstream classroom...some children may also wish to write at length in their first language without necessarily recasting the writing into English. This kind of activity is valuable in itself but is also useful as a way of increasing a [student's] awareness of the similarities and differences between different language systems.*

It is not uncommon for students to want to write in their own language first. This should be encouraged. It is often easier for them to get their thoughts out in the language with which they are familiar than to struggle through the triple whammy of formulating ideas, finding the words in a language in which they are not proficient, and then transcribing these words onto paper. Writing first in their primary language gives students a chance to figure out what they want to say before struggling in English. For example, a seventeen-year-old boy, who had been placed in the eleventh grade but was reading at a much lower level, wrote his story first in Spanish, then translated it into English later:

> **The first time I come to the United States was in December. When I arrive where my brother was living I was impresionado of the beoric [indecipherable], and organized of this country. After I go to school to learn Inglish, this was very dificult for me the two first weeks, because I don't spoke Inglish.**

During their journey toward proficiency in English, many students use, as in the preceding example, an *interlanguage*. In appendix A2 (page 268-269), we discuss this concept as well as that of *interim grammar*—part one language and part another. This phenomenon can also be evident in writing. Using the tools they have at the level of mastery they have achieved, students may, for instance, use the spelling and conventions of their first language with English syntax. Or, they may intersperse their writing with words from their primary language for which they have not yet learned the English translation.

It is also critical to support growth in a student's home language. Although we may not be able to read it, we can encourage and celebrate the writing. Barrs et al. (1989) concur:

> *[Students] can be invited to choose to write in their community language(s)*
> *or in English...By encouraging bilingual [students] to talk about their writing,*
> *the ideas, the content and the way they went about the writing, a teacher who*
> *may not understand the language can become involved and give support to their*
> *developing biliteracy.*

For example, Song Jo, who came from a rigorous educational system in Korea and was new to the country, completed the following report on an animal:

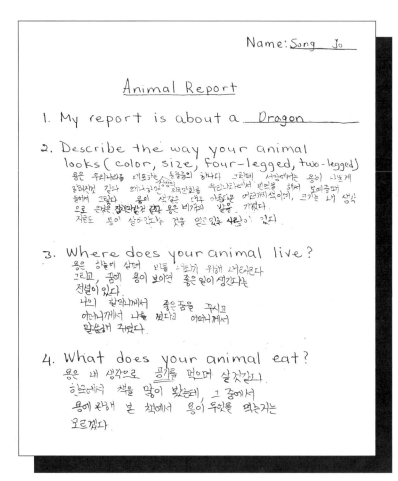

Figure 4.33 Song Jo's animal report

Although the teacher could not read what he had written, it was clear from the amount of writing he did that he knew a great deal about dragons. Bong Hee, his tutor, confirmed this, relating that he had gone into detail about the mythology of dragons in Korean history as well as their symbolism. We were dismayed to learn that the teacher had returned his work to do it again, because dragons are not "real" animals. Song Jo completed another report about tigers, but he did not care about tigers as much and, to Bong Hee, the work was inferior to the first report.

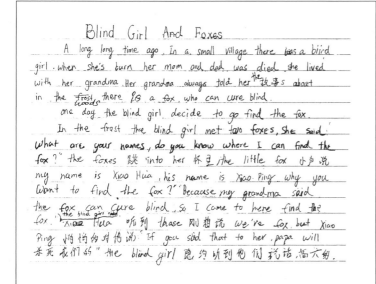

Figure 4.34 This was written by an eighth grader who was an accomplished student in her own language. When writing in English, she would occasionally insert a Chinese character in the middle of the text rather than lose her train of thought by stopping to search for the word she wanted.

CONCLUSION

Each student learns differently and struggles with different obstacles. When evaluating a student's progress, we must be able to see the big picture. We have to look at the context in which students are functioning and where their skills fall on the language continuum. Understanding these elements allows us to see many more of our students' abilities. Then, we can focus our planning and facilitate learning for each student. As teachers, we strive to provide the best environment for learning, and we want to be able to document all the progress that we see as accurately as possible. Knowing the broad picture is the starting point.

Diving for Pearls in their Shelves

HOW AND WHERE TO FIND INFORMATION

The family was camping at Naro Moru, at the base of Mt. Kenya, but for three days the mountain had been hidden, shrouded in mist. Then, one evening just before sunset, as they were taking a walk, Barb's father suddenly said, "Look!"

"Ohhh," said her sisters, in awe.

Barb turned and looked but saw nothing out of the ordinary. "What?"

"There!"

"Where?"

"There!" He took her face and pointed it in a new direction, and she looked hard but still could not see anything. "The mountain!" he exclaimed.

Then, she saw it, the sister mountain of Kilimanjaro, looming over them in the last light of day, so huge it filled the entire horizon. How could she have missed it? It was right there.

This chapter is about looking, about observation. But, like Barb and the mountain, unless you know where to look and what it is that you are looking at, you do not always see it. What is a mountain for some is invisible for those who do not have the framework for perceiving what their eyes are taking in.

What's in this Chapter

+ Steps you can take to learn about your students

+ Where to look for answers

+ How to plan and set up opportunities to collect information

+ How to analyze and interpret the information

To observe is more than simply to look. It is to see, by directing your attention carefully and analytically, and to *perceive*, by understanding what it is you are looking at. When you are observing, you are on the lookout for significant events, for qualitative leaps in understanding, for almost imperceptible inching forward toward mastery. Part of observation includes making judgments about what it is you are seeing and, thus, making decisions about what you will do next.

Besides looking, observing means listening, asking questions, and analyzing. Observing is not a passive activity. In fact, observation could be referred to as "snooping." According to Florio-Ruane (1990), eavesdropping, having informal conversations with students, listening for the "why of things, things people take for granted, those they choose to comment upon and the themes that recur in their talk," are all legitimate methods for finding what you want to know. Observation is important because it

+ is one way to form hypotheses or ideas.

+ is a means to answering specific questions.

+ provides a more realistic picture of behavior or events than do other methods of information gathering.

DEFINING WHAT YOU WANT TO KNOW

Two basic questions all teachers ask include: How effectively am I presenting the material in the curriculum? How is this student doing? To ascertain whether we are reaching our students, what the most effective reinforcement is, and which areas need to be reviewed, we need to know what our students know. But that question is so broad and unwieldy that it becomes unmanageable. We need to define more clearly what we want to find out. Cambourne (1988) has defined five broad categories of information we need to know about our ESL students.

+ The **strategies** they use as they read, write, and speak

+ The **level of explicit understanding** they have of the processes they can and should use when reading, writing, and communicating

+ Their **attitudes** toward reading and writing, conversation, and the English language

+ Their **interests** and backgrounds

+ The degree of **control** they display over language in all its forms and the content they are expected to master

Finding the Answers

Finding the answers and collecting information in usable form can be an overwhelming task. You do not want to gather just any information or you simply end up with barns full of paper that nobody wants to dig through. You want data that is telling and useful. You must decide where to look and at what. There are many methods of collecting information, but they fall under three general headings.

[handwritten margin note: Same things I look for in all my reading students]

[handwritten margin note: Schools are good for this]

1. Observing the student working

2. Talking with the student

3. Sampling student work

To get a balanced picture of a student, you want to be sure to collect enough information and ensure your observations come from a number of different contexts. Sampling only one area may give an incomplete profile of the student. Il-Hwa may write very sophisticated and thoughtful prose, demonstrating competent English abilities. However, she may not be able to participate in class discussions because her speaking skills are still limited. She may only participate on a limited basis in small-group work with her peers where the setting is less formal. Paco, on the other hand, may have trouble writing even the most basic sentences; to balance the weaknesses reflected in his writing samples, you need a method to record the tremendous progress he has made in his speaking skills and his insightful additions to class discussions.

The Quad

Researchers Anthony et al. (1991) developed a complex framework called "The Quad" (see figure 5.1) as a guide for knowing where to look to find answers to that all-important question of how students are doing. As we discussed in chapter 2, this framework encompasses all types of testing in an effort to counterbalance the effects of large-scale, high-stakes tests.

Observation of Process	Observation of Product
Students immersed in • Speaking • Listening • Reading • Writing	• Audiotapes • Selected pages from notebooks or journals • Reading logs • Writing folders • Group-work logs • Projects • Learning logs • Homework
Classroom Measures • Text-related activities • Teacher-made tests • Comprehension questions	**Decontextualized Measures** • Criterion-referenced tests • District exams • Provincial or state exams

Figure 5.1 The Quad

Routman (1991) notes that the two lower quadrants comprise the more traditional, *summative* means of evaluation, while the top two are *formative* and more dynamic; they are ongoing and can demonstrate cumulative growth.

We might also define these quadrants in terms of distance: the physical and temporal *distance* between the teacher and the learner; the distance between the teacher and the context within which the event took place; and the distance between the actual learning (or non-learning) that took place and when the measurement was taken. For instance, when you are observing your class in an activity, you can note who is succeeding and who is floundering, who is working diligently and who is goofing off, and you can intervene at any time. While listening to a student reading, you can see what strategies he is using to gain meaning and whether or not these strategies are effective. While students are engaged in writing, you can ask them how it is going, help them find the words they want, and grapple with them to find the best organization. You can listen to their speech and see how they are gaining proficiency through what they say, who they talk to, and how much or how little they can carry on through interaction or class discussion.

In a testing situation, however, you often cannot intervene, even though you can see a student struggling. In many testing situations, you do not see or know scores until much later. You are not privy to the method the student used to reach the answer he did—in most cases you can only see if he got it right or not. You have limited insight into all but the student's ability to answer the narrow range of questions of that particular test.

The categories in the Quad are not as clearly delineated as they would seem, largely because what students say about what they have written and read are just as important as what they have actually done. We have found that trying to pick apart each of the categories in the Quad might create more confusion. We suggest you not worry a great deal about which category the group project on Native North Americans belongs to, but be sure to take the observations you made into consideration. Samples of work can be the subject of conferences and interviews, and written products can be returned to again for continued polishing and revision, as we will demonstrate in our discussion that follows.

We did not attempt to exhaustively answer to each category in the Quad, and you should not feel obligated to do so either. They are suggestions of where to look for evidence of learning and what to ask your students about their learning. With these in mind, we can look at each student and gain insight into his strengths and weaknesses.

OBSERVATION OF PROCESS

Observing learning while it is taking place is part of your main role as a teacher. The processes you observe are the *hows, whens, wheres,* and *whys* of what happens within the context of an average school day, when students are immersed in their tasks of learning. Goodman and Goodman (1988) point out:

> ...*evaluation provides the most significant information if it occurs continuously and simultaneously with the experiences in which the learning is taking place...Teachers who observe the development of language and knowledge in children in different settings become aware of important milestones in children's development that tests cannot reveal.*

When you are observing the processes of learning—while students are reading, writing, working out math problems, conducting experiments, collaborating on a project, or working alone—you are closest to the event, and you can respond, react, intervene, or participate in the learning. It is now that you can most readily see the learning take place. Observing processes is a natural part of your day.

Speaking and Listening: What Do Students Know?

According to Barrs et al., (1989), there are two main dimensions of talk—social and cognitive—and talk, above all, is about interaction.

> *It is to do with interaction between people. It is the principal means of making contact with others, and building relationships. It is also to do with interaction between ideas—[students] hear new ideas, put forward new ideas, and develop new ideas through talking with others.*

As second-language learners become more orally proficient in English, they grow in their linguistic, functional, textual, and socio-cultural capabilities. They also grow in their ability to use English to gain knowledge in the content areas.

Students come to us already skilled users of language. They know how to manipulate language for their own purposes: to wheedle the promise of a treat out of their parents, to make a joke, to weave fantasies or engage in imaginative play, to learn something new and tell others what they have learned. They are simply adding another language system to the skills they have already learned.

Omark (1981) points out that context is particularly important in considering a learner's oral proficiency. He writes that a student "may be silent in the classroom, quiet on the playground with new peers, talkative at home, and boisterous on the streets." He goes on to stress the importance of watching the student in more than one setting. In addition, the social relationships of the student affect what he says. On the playground, for example, relationships based on dominance prevail, and students on the lower end of the hierarchy may be more passive and much quieter. In the classroom, your presence as teacher can have a profound affect on what and how much is said. It is often helpful to have several adults watching and giving their input on how a particular student is functioning.

For instance, Yoichiro was sullen and unresponsive in class, talking in his own language while the teacher was trying to conduct a lesson and refusing to do the work on the grounds that he did not understand. He only answered in monosyllables to the aide. His mother reported that at home he was disrespectful to the point of being abusive. On the playground, he was clearly a leader, bossing a group of smaller boys around, declaring what the play would be for the day, and holding a kingly sway over all activities.

By watching the processes of students acquiring language, you can see most clearly into the five categories Cambourne (1988) defined: strategies, level of explicit understanding, attitudes, interests, and control.

Strategies

These are the means a language user employs to get his point across in a conversational or learning setting. For example, Juan communicates most effectively with his friend Ricardo, whose English is better, and who helps by negotiating a lot of meaning in Spanish. Juan, however, has a very effective strategy for getting help in completing an English sentence with a non-Spanish-speaking person. He will mumble through a sentence until he comes to an English word he knows, say that word, mumble some more, then wait for his listener to fill in the gaps. It is not Spanish, it is not English. For example:

Juan: *Mumblemumblemumble* counselor *mumblemumblemumble.*
Barb: Oh, you need to see the counselor?
Juan (*relief shows on face*): **Yes.**

Level of explicit understanding (metacognition)

Every language user has strategies he uses to get his point across. Users are very often aware of their own strategies and the choices they have available to them. Even very young children learn that "pwease," a big smile, and large soulful eyes can get them what they want faster than whining. Four-year-olds will try out strategies such as commanding, "You have to buy that for me because I'm the boss," or bargaining, "If I show you what's in my pocket, I don't have to wear my helmet," or acting like Sam, who said to the store salesperson, "This isn't really a truck under my shirt, I just ate a lot for lunch."

This "knowing about knowing" is called *meta-awareness or metacognition*—becoming conscious of your thought processes so that you can control them when suitable. Knowing that you have these strategies available to you, you can use them consciously in listening, or speaking, or reading. Metacognition can be revealed in a student's speech through

- Experimenting with forms or styles a student has not quite mastered yet. For example, Valeria was very sociable, and wanted to be part of the action at all times. When she first arrived, she learned chunks and phrases of language such as "Can I play?" and "It's not your turn," that enabled her to participate immediately, even though she could not articulate the meaning of each word apart from the whole. Later, as her proficiency progressed, she would pretend she was queen, and say queenly things, such as, "I command you to bring me my pencil."

- Self-correcting oral errors. Carlos was slowly sorting out tenses. He knew *ed* endings but was working through irregular verbs. He said, "I buyed...I bought it at K-Mart yesterday." Nick told his mother, "I want to hold Ben Daddy's hand. Ben Daddy hands. Ben's Daddy hand. Ben's Daddy's hand."

Attitudes

These can be attitudes toward the target language or attitudes about learning language in general. Blia, a sixteen-year-old Hmong girl, came to Mary's ESL class with very little English or classroom experience. She lacked literacy in both Hmong and English. She struggled with her lessons and the going was slow for reading and writing.

Yet Blia was making tremendous strides in her speaking abilities. She was already great friends with several of her teachers at school. The other Hmong students in the class relied on her to help communicate their questions and problems. Blia was a natural negotiator and instinctively knew where the gaps were when Mary was having problems getting a lesson across. "Oh, Teacher, they don't look to you now because they feel shy about talking this lesson." Then she would chatter away in Hmong to the other students, and, eventually, they would nod their heads and say, "uh, uh, uh." Blia would then turn to Mary and say, "It's okay. They not be shy tomorrow." When Mary needed to clarify a concept or explain an issue to the rest of the class, she made sure Blia was around.

Interests and background

Alva resisted learning. He would do anything to avoid schoolwork. Then, Mary discovered that he loved sports and gambling. Alva knew all the stats on every baseball player on his favorite team, so Mary decided to use this information to her advantage. Together with Alva, she used sporting events such as the World Series to create math charts on averages, statistics, and language focus. And, when the Winter Olympics were underway, she seized the opportunity. Mary and Alva made predictions about who would place in the events and which countries had the best shot at the most medals. Alva also had to write essays explaining what would happen if this or that athlete was injured or disqualified. He was wholly engaged in these activities and developed his language skills by haranguing his teacher over who looked best in this event or who he thought was just a lucky shot.

Control

This refers not only to control over vocabulary and syntax, but also to control over the types of language used in the different domains of life. Learners of a language often acquire the BICS (basic interpersonal communication skills) first but take much longer to master the kinds of language one uses in a school situation and the demands that language makes on its user.

For example, six little boys were sitting with the teacher who was asking them "yes and no" questions. Because the teacher was familiar with the boys, she could read between the lines of their answers to see what they actually knew.

> Teacher: Does it snow in winter?
> Chang: **Yes, we do.**

Chang had been through one winter and, although he understood the concept of snow, his control of English grammar was limited, and he often used formulaic answers.

> Teacher: Does she have a hat?
> Choua: **Yes, she doos.**

Choua's answer showed a good grasp of English and grammatical forms. He knew that an s-ending showed third person singular. He had not mastered the finer points of irregular forms and pronunciation yet.

> Mark: **Yes, she doesn't.**

Mark knew the correct answer but had not learned the difference between does and doesn't and gave a formulaic answer.

> Teacher: Does he have his shoes on?
> Alem: **Yes, he is.**

The answer was no. Alem did not have a clue, and simply gave a sentence he had heard before in the course of the lesson.

> Ben: **No, he's doesn't.**

Ben answered this question correctly but, like Choua, had yet to refine the nitpicky points of grammar, and added an *s*-ending to both the pronoun and the verb, showing a good ear for English grammar.

Speaking and Listening: Determining What Students Know

Understanding how ESL students gain control over their speaking and listening skills will help you to see the steps they make toward fluency and competence. Even nonverbal communication demonstrates some degree of understanding.

Since all provinces and states (and some districts) now have their own standards, here is where you can use them to focus your observation. It does not matter whether you decide which standard to watch for first or you just listen and collect information, referring to the standards afterwards. And it does not have to be as random as this may sound. If you know at which level your student is operating, you can focus on (or refer to) the standards applicable for that level.

If, for instance, according to the WIDA levels, Wilson is a level 1 (he can follow simple directions, participate in social contexts, and use spoken English in daily activities), you would not expect him to be analyzing the style of a particular author. He may be able to say "go to bathroom" and "I don't understand," which falls under the Michigan English Language Proficiency standard S.1: using "spoken language for daily activities," and you can use this opportunity to refine your knowledge of his competencies. He may surprise you.

Gathering and using information about your students involves four very important steps: planning, collecting, analyzing, and interpreting information. Here, we will show you how to take these steps within the framework of the Quad.

Planning: setting up your system

Create an individual file for each student, a repository of work samples and observations such as anecdotes. It is then a fairly straightforward task to jot down each student's use of language in a way that is easily retrieved.

Collecting: where to look

Listen in on conversations in different settings and contexts. You can check for comprehension, fluency, vocabulary development, pronunciation, and grammar. Choose activities that are routine and embedded in your daily schedule. It is easier to collect information when it is part of what you are already doing than to set aside a specific time for each student. Natural samples are more likely to be realistic than if you are prompting.

You can, however, give students a specific task and instructions that will allow them to demonstrate their proficiency. For speaking and listening, it is fairly simple to elicit the structure you want. For instance, in the Michigan State Board of Education English *Language Proficiency Standards for K-12 Schools*, the goal for level L.1.1.b in listening is to "follow simple two-step oral directions to complete a task in English." A demonstration of this would be to say, "Push in your chair and stand up."

Jot down examples of students' use of language. For each observation, record the date, the context, and the setting. If observing for a specific standard, record in your notes the actual standard for which you are watching, as opposed to just the reference number (for example, level L.1.1.b). Otherwise, when analyzing later, you will be running back and forth between the standards and your notes to determine what each number means.

Analyzing

Review your notes. What does this tell you about where your student is functioning? Is this an emerging skill, or is it solidly in place with your student already moving on to another, more sophisticated and challenging level?

Interpreting

Use the information you have gathered to plan further instruction, give feedback to your students, document student growth over the school year, and collaborate with other teachers. What interventions or strategies can you use to achieve an unmet benchmark? What contexts or situations can you set up to give this student the exposure he needs to move forward? For example, could Salvador benefit from being in a group with more verbal students?

Jonathon was a level 1. The third graders were doing a science experiment involving solids and liquids. Jonathon showed comprehension when someone said, "It disappeared," and replied loudly, "Unh uh!" Here, he challenged someone's statement of fact.

Andreas, struggling to find the right vocabulary, simply asked, using the words he knew: "Chicken husband. What is?"

Reading: What Do Students Know?

Whether students come to school knowing how to read in their first language or are illiterate, they are already, as noted earlier, skilled language users. They know how to project, speculate, and predict—all skills they need to read fluently. To help them become good readers in English, we can build on these skills and evaluate their reading based on what they can say and do *while* they are reading.

Strategies

If we define reading as getting meaning from print, then strategies are the methods a reader uses to achieve this meaning. Johnston (1992) writes:

> A child reading a book comes across a word he doesn't recognize. Reading suddenly shifts from recognition to reasoning. Some strategy needs to be used to render the word recognizable. Perhaps he will relate it to a different word he does know, or use some of his knowledge of the relationships between letters and sounds. Perhaps he will read on and come back to figure it out, or ask a neighbor.

Good readers have a variety of strategies they use whenever they come to a word they do not recognize or a passage they do not understand. Paris, Wasik, and Turner (1991) state that "strategic readers are not characterized by the volume of tactics that they use but rather by the selection of appropriate strategies that fit the particular text, purpose and occasion."

As teachers, we can note the strategies students use, and help them learn additional or better ones as they become increasingly independent readers. Nilakhone, a third grader, could call out words but could not remember what she had read. Through observation and conversation, the teacher discovered that her goal in reading was not necessarily to make sense but to read correctly. So, he taught her the strategy of continuously asking oneself, does this make sense? One day, he observed she was reading a three-paragraph passage. She was just into the third paragraph when she came to a confusing word. She stopped, looked at the words around it, but could not figure it out. She began reading the entire passage again from the beginning. This might not have been the fastest strategy, but it showed that she was aware she needed to understand the passage. Her comprehension had broken down, and she now had several strategies with which she could try to pick up the thread.

Tonio had very few strategies available to him besides guessing at the word based on the first letter. His most effective strategy was to hesitate at every new word and look up at the teacher with a big pleading smile, trying to get her to say the word for him.

Understanding of process (metatextual awareness)

Readers also need to know which strategy is going to help in any particular situation. For instance, when Angel was confronted with the unfamiliar word *neighborhood*, she could use any number of strategies—sounding it out, guessing, asking someone, skipping the word—to work through it. If her only strategy was sounding out the word, she would be limited in her abilities to obtain meaning, because the word *neighborhood* is particularly unsuited to using phonics to decipher. Explicit understanding of the options she had and knowing which one would work best in any given situation served her well. Asking her outright what she thought she could do when she encountered a word she did not recognize would give you insight into her understanding of what her options were.

Attitudes

Feelings, attitudes, and dispositions also play a critical role in becoming an independent reader. This includes a student's beliefs about himself, his attitude toward learning, how persistent he is, and how much personal responsibility he is willing to take in working toward a goal. Most readers are very aware of how well or how poorly they read. In Ms. Lang's class, the fact that the "Robins" are the good readers while the "Bluebirds" are the strugglers and stragglers will never be a secret to students. Readers can often *become* disabled simply because they think they already are. It is important to be aware of a student's attitudes toward the act of reading and of himself as a reader. The statements "I can't read very well" or "I hate to write" are red flags that need to be taken as seriously as a child stating, "I'm a failure" or "I'm a bad boy."

Interests and background

The importance of a student's pleasure and interest in reading topics and in authors has been well documented over the years. Barrs et al. (1989) write:

> If children are to develop as readers there must be personal involvement in reading. The pleasures of reading often begin as shared pleasures and arise from reading with an adult. When a child experiences the emotional satisfaction of involvement in a story, s/he is likely to want to read more.

Encouraging independence and involvement in reading entails urging students to choose their own books as often as possible, even if this means reading the same ones over and over. Interest and participation in reading can influence how much a student gets out of a book. While Pam and Lan loved *To Kill a Mockingbird* and were moved by the experience of reading it, Naoki, who was only interested in facts and did not enjoy fiction, was bored to tears and found the reading, discussion, and related projects excruciating. Keeping an eye on what texts a student chooses to read, having students keep reading records, and conducting interest inventories are all ways to understand a student's reading interests.

Background knowledge is also particularly critical in learning to read for second language learners. When students from other countries are placed in content classes like history, science, or literature, they often lack the fundamental concepts—things that we take for granted—to understand the texts, even if they can understand the words. For instance, an ESL text Barb was using for an intermediate-level class included Shirley Jackson's story "The Lottery." The students had no clue what the story meant. They did not know what a lottery was, and even after Barb painstakingly explained the concept, the story had little impact. The text also contained a chapter from the book *Cheaper by the Dozen*. The humor went entirely over students' heads, and while Barb was chuckling away, they were moping through the story, not enjoying it in the least. The lesson was a dud.

Control

There is no such thing as achieving perfection in reading. Learning to read is a lifelong pursuit. Barb can read difficult linguistics texts with ease, but is a terrible cook because she cannot read recipes—she is always skimming for the main point. There are always new concepts, new ideas, new areas to explore. Learners who come to school with little or no knowledge about print just have further to go. In the next chapter, we provide checklists and examples of anecdotes about readers gaining control. You can also see developing control in

+ Growing confidence or independence in choice of texts. This may involve students grappling with genres and tasks apparently beyond their capabilities

+ Self-correcting (or not self-correcting) of miscues when reading

Here is John's reading of a portion of *The Boxcar Children*. The miscues, in bold, are above the text as it actually appeared. The self-corrected mistakes are marked with a "(c)".

repleed   **Adams**

Come any time, replied Mr. Beach, starting back. The Aldens

say (c)

noticed that Mrs. Beach had not said a word.

As the Beach family went into their new house Violet said,

other   **Violet**

"I have an idea." The others looked at her because Violet's ideas

ask   tried

were always good. She said, "Mrs. Beach will be too tired to get

super (c)   **super** (c)

supper, so let's send their supper over to them.

Reading aloud to determine strategies is always followed by a retelling, which is also a critical part of understanding a reader, his abilities, and his control over the act of reading. Many readers need to be prompted with questions to help them both understand the stories they read and retell them. This process is vital to determining what they know. After reading from *The Boxcar Children*, John's teacher interviewed him about his understanding of the text.

[handwritten: Explain DRESS]

Teacher: Can you tell me what you remember from that part of the story?

John: **They were meeting at the beach.**

Teacher: What else?

John: **Benny and Jessie were staying at home...**

Teacher: What's the excitement in this part?

John: **The new neighbor came in.**

Teacher: Where did they come in?

John: **To the empty house.**

Teacher: What else happened?

John: **Um...Violet asked "Who are the new neighbors?" Um...she ran upstairs into Mr. Andy room.**

Teacher: What did they decide to do?

John: **Um, cook supper?**

Teacher: Why?

John: **Because, um, the new neighbor didn't have food.**

[handwritten: That would be a significant error then because it affects meaning]

John's retelling confirms that his correction of *supper* for *super* meant he understood that part; however, his lack of correction of *tried for tired* and his subsequent retelling showed that he did not understand why the characters in the story cooked supper for the neighbors. The need for the teacher to continuously question him, and John's short responses, showed that he remembered only basic concepts with few supporting details. John was a very slow, word-for-word reader. A thorough analysis of his miscues and his retelling revealed that he scored very low in comprehension. He had problems attending to the surrounding context both before and following the words on which he miscued. Knowing these things, the teacher was able to plan a program for John that focused on predicting situations and words, using surrounding text to identify words and concepts within a story.

In contrast to John's retelling, Thanousay, another student John's age, read the same text and said:

The part, um, I liked the part is when, um, they making pie, making, um, supper for their next neighbor is they name is Mr. Beach. They got four, four children, think so, and, um, and they didn't know yet when they gonna move in they first time. They um, um, you know, the house near the beach was old, no one had stayed there for long time, no one had moved in, but then a new neighbor had moved to a new, to um, next door neighborhood so they want to be a friend with them. Benny and they want to give some food to give to them to, um, if they tired, they could eat it.

This retelling reveals a much deeper understanding of the story. Thanousay was able to bring out all the main points with supporting details, without prompting from the teacher.

Reading: Determining What Students Know

To demonstrate how you can establish what your students' reading skills are, we guide you again through the four steps of planning, collecting, analyzing, and interpreting information within the framework of the Quad. The goal here is to gather information that is useful both for planning your instruction and for gauging where your student is at the moment.

Planning

→ entrance task

Choose a specific setting or routine activity that requires students to read. If you are accustomed—or required—to do running records, this process will be simple to implement, and you might even kill two birds with one stone. If not, it will take some practice. You can observe students during their designated silent reading time. Other times to observe include

+ students reading in formal and informal situations
+ students reading independently, in small groups
+ students reading aloud in pairs

Collecting

Document your students reading, record the date, their comments, and any discussion that happens while they are reading. It is best to try to record every word. What you want to achieve is specific information to which you can return when you have time to analyze. When you are reviewing your notes, entries like "retold accurately with all the details" or "retold with indifference" are no more helpful than "faked the ending and the details—had not really read it." You want to be able to see and demonstrate progress, with some degree of accuracy—and after any number of other lessons, bad days, and crises have wiped this particular observation from your memory. This takes some practice, but it is worth it in the end.

Analyzing

When you review your notes/running records, cross-reference them with your state/provincial/district standards. Look for developmental trends and patterns. What does this tell you about where your student is functioning? Is this an emerging skill or is it solidly in place with your student moving on to another, more sophisticated and challenging level? What strategies is this reader using? In which strategies is he weak?

Interpreting

What are the implications of what you have observed? What sorts of intervention or teacher direction does your student need? Where does he show growth? Where is he stalling? What is the next step for this student? Use this information to plan instruction, give feedback to your students, document student growth over the school year, collaborate with other teachers, and confer with parents.

To follow are examples of several students reading. For the sake of brevity, we have not attempted to include all levels but rather to present a cross section of students. The methods vary simply because we were tinkering and learning as we went. Choose what works best for you, or use these ideas as a springboard for your own type of reading assessment.

Mai Lor, a fifth grader, was tested for reading using a story from the Flynt-Cooter (1998) battery of reading assessments. She tested at a level 4 when reading the sentences for initial passage selection. She read:

New _____
New Clothes

        youga   m…(c)   **don't**
Bobby was the youngest member of his family. He didn't like being

   yugli   **sta (c) latin**   **telwish**
the youngest because he couldn't stay up late and watch television.

        dwi   **war had**   **cwitchi**
Most of all, he disliked having to wear hand-me-down clothes from his brother.

                         say   **try**
One day Bobby went to his mother and said, "Mom, I'm tired of

    Bry   cosen   **cosen**
wearing Brad's clothes. Why can't I have some more new clothes this school year?"

                                 every
His mother replied, "Bobby, you know we can't afford to buy even

    news chowsen   **chowchi**
more new clothes. You should be happy with the new clothes we

      bogen   **Bord chowchen**
have already bought. Besides, most of Brad's clothes are just like new.

Story retelling:

> About Bobby. Bobby want to he new school ... Bobby took care of bed with Susie for four weeks. Mom took him to the mall. Bobby got to pay out a new pants and a new shirt.

Analysis

Most of Mai Lor's errors were mispronunciations, which disrupted meaning severely. She substituted nonsense words for words she did not know ("youga" and "yugli" for *youngest*; "cosen," "chowchi," "chowsen" for *clothes*). Nineteen of the twenty-two errors disrupted the meaning. Further questioning would have revealed whether or not she knew subsequent story details, such as that Bobby earned money himself to buy some new clothes. The test administrator should have done this but did not. Mai Lor's retelling, although very sparse, was partially correct. Bobby took over his siblings' chores for four weeks and then went to the mall to buy his own school clothes.

Mai Lor's sight-word vocabulary had gaps. Although the word *youngest* was not central to the story, the word *clothes* was. She obviously did not understand the term *hand-me-downs*. As she continued through the reading, however, even though she mispronounced *clothes* to the end, she did understand that Bobby wanted to buy them because, in her retelling, she used the words *pants* and *shirt*.

Mai Lor is a word caller. She relies on phonics as her number-one strategy. She plows onward without stopping to ask herself, does this make sense?

Interpretation

Mai Lor needed more practice reading, at an easier level, in order to build her vocabulary, fluency, and confidence. She would benefit from explicit instruction in additional and more effective strategies to gain meaning from what she was reading. Listening to books on tape, guided reading, and discussing meaning would also help. The level of intervention required was moderate and focused.

Odette had met most of the standards for speaking and listening. She had achieved a level 4 in oral proficiency, and she was very verbal. Her reading skills, however, were very low. She was given a fourth-grade reading test from the National Association of Educational Progress (NAEP) about Sybil Ludington's ride, in which Sybil rides on her horse, Star, to warn neighboring villagers of the approaching redcoats.

Story retelling:

> Sybil...if they lost that star they will be in war or something.

Analysis

Odette's ability to retell the story was poor; she did not demonstrate comprehension of the main idea of the story beyond a vague notion that there would be a war. Odette was like Mai Lor in that she did not stop to ask herself whether or not what she was saying made sense. She blundered on through passages, plopping nonsense words in place of words she did not know and making leaps in analysis.

Interpretation

Finding texts in Odette's primary language was impractical if not impossible. Odette needed strategy lessons about how to get meaning from context and how to ask the right questions. (As it turns out, Odette had never been taught any phonics word-recognition skills. When given a couple of quick lessons in what consonants and vowels sound like and how they blend, she had a better base for attacking words. That helped somewhat, and gave her one more tool in her stock of strategies.) Guided reading, even at this higher level, was to help, as well as lots of high interest, easy reading. Pairing her with stronger classmates worked well because she was a very social person who liked to talk. The level of intervention required was moderate to high.

Andreas was a level 3 in oral proficiency. He was fluent in several other languages and was adept at having conversations, even with limited vocabulary resources. Andreas read the same passage about Sybil Ludington's ride.

Story retelling:

> He father is in the house and British right field are in about 2000 redcoats and her father is for a short time in his house, so Sybil is very good on the horse. She has teaching other person for the horse. Father say, "you can go because you are special." She know her father need to stay. The author is telling how much danger.

Analysis

Andreas's retelling was much more complete, indicating he understood more of the story than Odette did. Although he did not know much of the vocabulary and he got confused about many of the details, he was able to pull out pieces of the basic meaning of the passage.

Interpretation

Andreas did not need basic lessons in strategies like Odette did. However, the issues you face with the Andreas's of the world are just as complex. Many of the strategies he had did not work when his background knowledge was not enough. It was impractical to spend a great deal of time explaining the background of the Revolutionary War simply to get through that particular reading since that war was not part of the curriculum. Andreas's challenges had more to do with time and exposure. A lot of enrichment in vocabulary and background building was to help. Reading stories at a lower level would build his fluency and vocabulary. He could also have been given videos to fill in the gaps, such as *The Patriot*. Nowadays, it is easy enough to find videos dubbed into foreign languages. The level of intervention required was moderate and focused.

OBSERVATION OF PRODUCT

Writing

Observing written work in a variety of forms allows you to see what a student can produce and how he has grown and developed over a period of time. In this case, collecting and observing go hand in hand. The beauty of this quadrant is that you can examine products in quiet reflection outside the classroom, but you also have the opportunity to return to the student with any questions you have about his production, and then observe him as he reflects, responds, and revises. When you can look at written products outside the context of the situation in which they were produced, you can identify the control a writer has over both the conventions of writing in any language and the punctuation, form, style, and cohesion demanded by writing.

Writing: What Do Students Know?

Learning to write is similar to learning to read. As Barrs et al. (1989) point out, it is "a journey from dependence to independence. Initially a child needs the help and support of another person...support which can be gradually withdrawn and the child takes over more and more of the process."

Strategies

Similar to with reading, the more strategies a writer has available, the more likely he will be able to solve problems. Johnston (1992) points out certain constraints on strategy use.

+ **The strategies a student has available.** Does a writer who is stuck know that he can find the word in a thesaurus; ask a buddy or a teacher; approximate the word; use an easier word; leave a space and go on? Or, does he simply bog down waiting for the word to come to him?

+ **The knowledge he has relevant to the topic.** Has he been asked to write about a subject with which he is intimately familiar (such as the flight from his country), or something beyond the realm of his experience (such as getting a bill passed through Congress)?

+ **The goals he is trying to accomplish.** Is the goal to get every word spelled correctly, to get ideas out, or is it to develop fluency without worrying about spelling?

+ **Situational constraints.** This includes deadlines, having an audience, having a dictionary handy, and so on.

+ **The student's perceptions of the cause of a problem.** Can he figure out why he is having a problem and how to fix it? Or, does he need direct intervention or guidance in how to continue?

We add another constraint: the language a second-language learner has available to express his meaning adequately. For example, Hide had trouble explaining the theme in *The Glass Menagerie*. He could give plot information, and understood the story, but he did not have the English vocabulary to encompass the abstract concepts of the theme.

Understanding of process: metacognition

Understanding what is involved in the process of getting thoughts down on paper, of working through drafts, of knowing how to organize, and of knowing what needs changing is, as with reading, an ever-evolving skill. Explicit understanding can be revealed through

- **Self/peer-editing.** One teacher used the process approach to writing, whereby students worked through several drafts of an assignment. When the final draft was due, she passed out bottles of correction fluid with the instructions that this was last-chance editing time. Students were asked to correct all grammar, punctuation, and spelling so that all papers would come in perfect and error-free. Armed with their handbooks, students went over their partners' papers with fine-toothed combs and debated about structure and spelling.

- **Critical appraisals of own work.** Michael, who was active and athletic on the playground, got frustrated when trying to write and would tell his teacher to do it, that he could not. He would pick up his pen, make several scribbles, and give up. His fine-motor skills were very limited at this point.

  Gordon, whose command of spoken English was outstanding and who was deft enough in the language to display his wry wit, handed in an essay that was barely a paragraph long, much shorter and less developed than those from other, less proficient students and off-topic enough to concern the teacher. Here is a portion:

  > **Reflecting on my life (which is quite long: oh! I am eighteen years old, an old man) I think that the very first event that has caused the chain of others, without which nothing would have happened to me, is my birth. Unfortunately I don't remember that event. Because of that I cannot tell you in detail how it was. The only thing I can definitely say about it is that it happened approximately at eight o'clock in the evening.**

  When his teacher conferred with him, he hesitated and resisted revising it, telling her he thought it was fine. When it came time to hand in the final draft, he simply turned in the first draft, having done nothing to it.

Attitudes

As with reading, writers can become disabled and helpless simply because they believe they have nothing to say, that they are lousy writers, or because they distrust the teacher. They will not reveal their inadequacies on paper to be bloodied, ridiculed, or punished. Many reach high school or even college fearing and loathing writing, because they have been pummeled so often. ME

Students who know they will be penalized for misspellings, comma splices, or fragments will be cautious writers who will not venture beyond what they know to try anything new. For instance, Mary recalls a college linguistics class in which students were required to write their final papers in Black English Vernacular (BEV). The professor found all papers to be unacceptable and handed them back, then posted the rules for the vernacular with the instructions to rewrite their essays according to these rules. The students complied, but the essays were reduced from in-depth analyses to simple-sentence statements of fact; they had such difficulty applying the rules of the dialect that they stuck to the known, unwilling to risk being penalized for mistakes in grammar. Good exercise for teachers

Students who are encouraged to stretch their verbal wings will try new things, be creative, even attempt to be funny or outrageous. But if students are given stringent parameters, the opposite can happen.

132

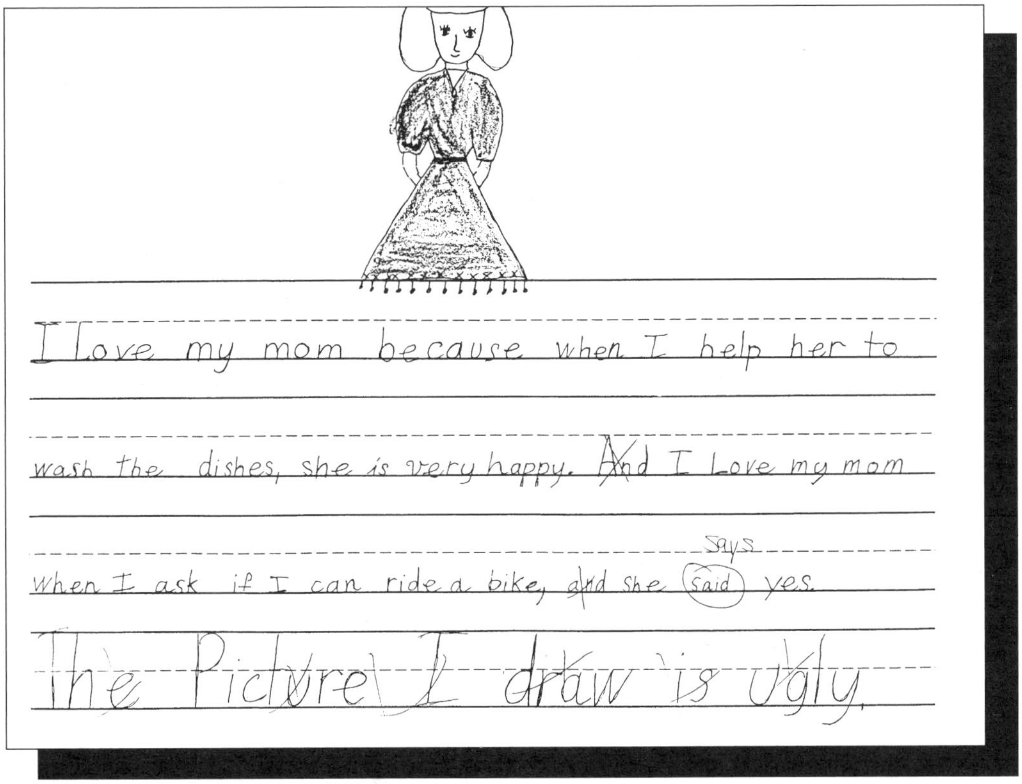

Figure 5.2 Sandy's analysis of her drawing is very sad. Rather than simply crossing out Sandy's comments, perhaps the teacher could have encouraged her drawing.

Interests and background

Writing teachers know that engaging the writer is a very important issue. Often, students will produce dull, stilted, uninteresting prose when asked to write on a topic about which they could not care less, but will produce fresh, vivid images when writing something about which they care. For example, Phoebe generally wrote very structured prose and took few risks with her writing, preferring to stick to safe prose that had few mistakes. She was excited about one particular assignment, however, and wrote:

> If I were a bird I would fly to my lover whenever, and also I can see everything beneath of me after sit on the top of the building. And I wish to go in the forest. I will talk with another birds about men in there, because they fly anywhere, maybe they know many things. About honest men, richmen, poormen, children...But especially I wish to know men's mind. We can see everything that we apeard in front of my eyes. But we never see one's mind. It is very difficult that we judge one's mind. Anyhow, birds look like very freely and feel easy to fly But it is only apeared in surface. They feel pain, hunger, loneliness...too. Birds are not necessarily happy. Finally, if I were a bird, that is ony for three days, for three days, I will have many experiences and much emotion. That is enough. And then I will thank what I was born a man to my God.

Phoebe's organization is meandering, and she gets off-topic, but her enthusiasm for the entire idea carries her far beyond what she was previously able to produce.

Control

The following examples of written work, including writing about reading, demonstrate what products can reveal to the teacher. This collection of work, produced over a period of time, demonstrates Carmela's explosive growth in conventions, skills, and proficiency.

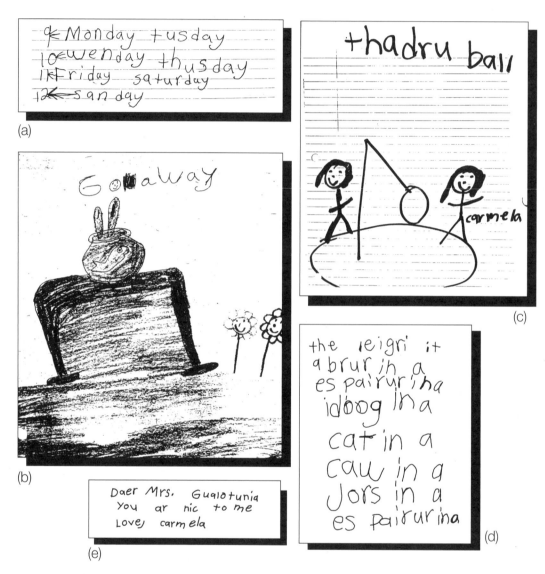

Figure 5.3 (a) The errors in this sample demonstrate that Carmela was working from memory using sound-letter principles. (b) Carmela's "book report" on *The Cat in the Hat*. (c) Carmela was supposed to meet her tutor on the playground. She drew a map telling the teacher that she would meet her by the tetherball court. (d) The tutor read "I Know an Old Lady" to the group. This is Carmela's retelling. She was very excited, and by this time was beginning to take risks with her writing, trying to spell words on her own. Several of her words are in Spanish; others (*cow* and *horse*) demonstrate her knowledge of Spanish spelling principles. (e) This sample reveals that Carmela knew a great deal about the standard format for letters. She used appropriate punctuation. Her spelling was very close to standard.

Carmela's artifacts reveal her strategies (copying and using her knowledge of English and Spanish to write sentences), her control over forms in a letter, and her increasing control over written English. As students like Carmela gain control over written forms, they are able to further develop their writing skills.

Carmela's writing folder was a collection of writing produced over time. It can also be instructive to collect all work produced from rough draft to the finished product on a select piece of writing (see figure 5.4). This allows you to see how much a student knows at the outset, which strategies help him improve, and how much growth he shows during the process. Keeping several samples, or having students choose a select number for inclusion in their portfolios for grading, is one way to really get a picture of the writer's evolution. As Nancie Atwell (1998) points out, "writing growth is seldom a linear progress"; each piece can demonstrate improvement over the last.

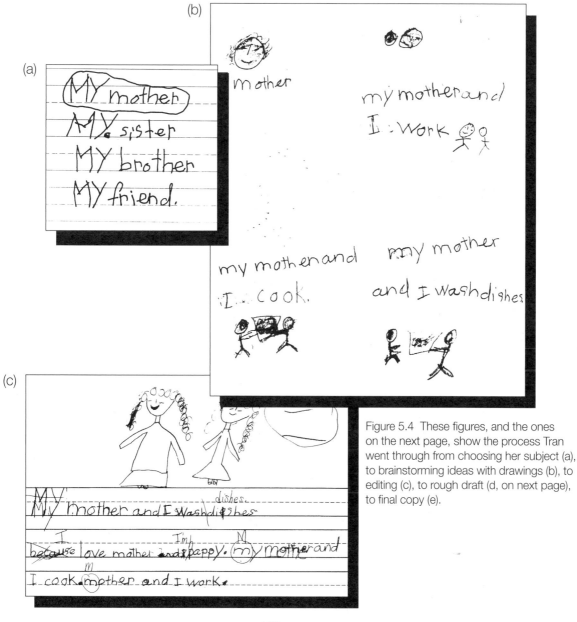

Figure 5.4 These figures, and the ones on the next page, show the process Tran went through from choosing her subject (a), to brainstorming ideas with drawings (b), to editing (c), to rough draft (d, on next page), to final copy (e).

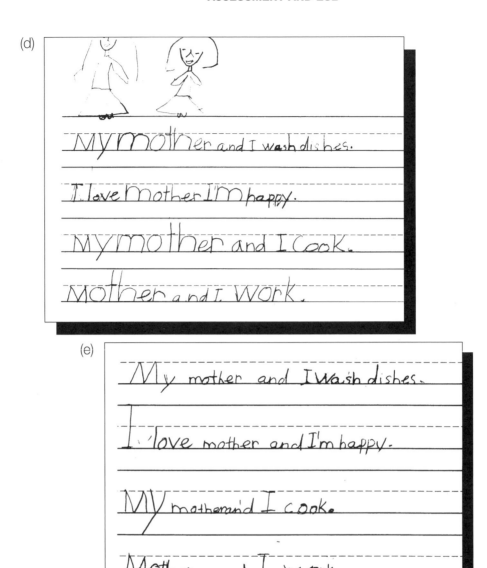

(d)

My mother and I wash dishes.

I love mother I'm happy.

My mother and I cook.

Mother and I work.

(e)

My mother and I wash dishes.

I love mother and I'm happy.

My mother and I cook.

Mother and I work.

Writing: Determining What Students Know

Again, we guide you through the planning, collecting, analysis, and interpretation of information to facilitate future teaching and for evaluating how your student is doing.

Planning

Decide what to collect. Now that writing across the curriculum is commonplace, finding writing samples is easy. Some states require that the samples you collect are representative of what your learner can produce independently. The trick is to collect items that give you maximum insight into the student's present level of functioning.

Collecting

Remember to record the date and assignment description for each artifact you collect.

Analysis

Look for developmental trends and patterns as well as specific benchmarks. What does this tell you about where your student is functioning? Is this a budding skill or is it already well developed with your student progressing to another, more complex and demanding level? What has improved since the last artifact was collected?

Interpretation

What are the implications of what you are observing? What sorts of intervention or direction does the student need? Where does he show development? What are his limitations? What is the next step for this student? Use this information to plan instruction, give feedback to your students, document student growth over the school year, collaborate with other teachers, and confer with parents.

José, a third-grade student, wrote:

> **mi fra I si** (*my favorite animal is*)
> **Acnec** (*snake*)
> **mi ascnec is cuo** (*my snec is cool*)
> **I ple wef mi asnec** (*I play with my snake*)
> **My snec is preco** (*pretty cool*)
> **Mi snec is year 8** (*My snake is 8 years old*)

Analysis

José was beginning to show attention to letter-sound correspondences in his writing. This artifact represents a significant leap for him. Before this, he would not write on his own, preferring to copy everything.

Interpretation

One could have fretted about how far José was behind his age-mates, but he was making progress. He had a solid understanding of which letters made which sounds, and he was ready to move toward standardizing his spelling without losing his enthusiasm. This type of frame sentence gave him a structure upon which to build.

José needed much one-on-one work to catch up to his peers. Time would help him as his exposure to English increased. He needed people to continue reading to and with him in both English and Spanish as well as to write about or label pictures he had drawn. Having him start a word bank would make him accountable for the correct spelling of certain words. He could also be asked to write stories with a partner or a tutor. The level of intervention required was high and focused.

Here is Yung Tae, writing about his experiences in Korean schools:

> **The new wild directness which in the graduates is delivered from the roster. Hyep2 years vocal chord schools it keeps a period rain for additional post international normal subjects tanks commission, the mirror image college religion department head, total students slice raw fish election commission The Toe it sprouts, su the processed marive products**

Analysis

The toe it sprouts? No one could begin to guess what this meant. It was typical of Yung Tae's writing—dense, turgid. This was probably from the web-based translation program BabelFish. He probably wrote it in Korean and then plugged it straight into the program. What was worse, he was so slow to answer orally that no one was willing to take the time to ask him to comment.

Interpretation

Yung Tae needed practice writing without the translation crutch. His resistance to writing independently might have been because he was overwhelmed at not knowing what to say in English. Pre-writing activities would really help Yung Tae. He needed to map out what he was going to write so that he had the basic vocabulary there and the task would not be so overwhelming. A writing plan would help him organize his thoughts before he wrote. He needed to make multiple revisions to his writing, focusing first on untangling what he had meant to write from what he had actually written. In an assignment such as this, perhaps giving him specific questions, rather than the nebulous "write about school in Korea" would have helped.

Here is another product by Yung Tae. This was a fun assignment in response to a series of pictures about a bank robbery. Students were to write a detailed story about the events.

> **On Friday front bank stand two robbers. They name pam and Sam. They were parking a buy ways van and put on hoods. The left hands have guns and right hands have bundle. They go in bank and everybody hearing it. Pam a loudly asked him "now hand over and lie." Everybody was scared. Robbers snatch to policeman guns. Pam tall to staff, put on a higher place a cashbox. Staffs take the money out in cashbox and hand over it. The staff hand the money over 50 hundred million. Suddenly spring up the problem. Robbers haven't enough a bundle. Each other saw them. Pam talked him. What's the problem? Maybe your thinks a paper envelope. each other saw on face in eye. And then Your are fools**
>
> **As a result. Robbers moving a change position bundle.**

Analysis

Yung Tae obviously enjoyed the assignment and put a great deal of effort into writing it. It demonstrated a higher level of proficiency than his previous writing did.

Interpretation

After comparing and reflecting on both assignments, it became apparent that Yung Tae's second product was better than his first for several reasons: the second one was linked to a visual, and there was a great deal of discussion about the pictures beforehand (in which Yung Tae did not participate, but listened); there was much modeling of possible answers, and he was allowed to use his imagination; he enjoyed this assignment more than the first one; and, Yung Tae handed in the assignment two days late (not okay) after all his classmates had read their stories aloud. Strategies to explore included more active pre-writing, talking about options, possibly extended time, and a chance to listen to others' stories as models for his own. The level of intervention required was moderate to high.

Yat Sang had the same bank-robbery assignment as Yung Tae:

> A bank on the 200 Fountain Street have been stolen over 3,000,000 dollars early this morning. First, they drove a white van to the bank and two people run into the bank with their weapon. They both have balaclavas so no people see the real face. Then a black jacket man threatened the manager for money and at the same time the alarm was ringing. Another robber quickly took all the money into his huge bag. After that, a man who hold the weapon told all the people put their hands up or lied on the floor. When the other one finished collecting the money, he run out the bank and started the engine. They looked like easy to escaped by all bank security.

Analysis

Yat Sang also provided a detailed description of the bank robbery with more varied sentence structure and vocabulary. He, too, enjoyed this assignment.

Interpretation

Yat Sang was cruising along at a level that allowed him to function in the regular classroom. He still needed ESL instruction, assignments that were less intense than mainstream work to build his fluency and fine-tune his mistakes. Always working at a higher level did not allow him to step back and observe what he was doing or see what he needed to work on. Light-hearted assignments like this allowed him to stretch his creativity and gain confidence. When he was working on assignments in the mainstream classes, Yat Sang needed one-on-one time. Scheduling some conference time before big assignments would help him sort through what he needed to do and in what order. The level of intervention required was moderate and focused.

Yong Min was an intermediate (level 4) writer, a quiet student who had a delightful sense of humor and a willingness to try anything. Here is a portion of a story he wrote about an argument between two men:

> Her brother approach him and he said to him "what did you say my sister?" When Patterson heard that words, he get angry very much, so he speak ill of him and he flourish his arms. Some people came in crowds. Someone called the police office. For a while, policeman arrived that place.

Analysis

Yong Min was obviously using his electronic dictionary, too. He was not as dependent on it as Yung Tae was, and so his toes did not sprout. He produced phrases akin to music that is slightly off-key but which added a zip to his writing that we do not often see in students whose primary language is English.

Interpretation

This assignment was a step up from the frame sentences we have shown before. Students were given a story and asked to substitute words, phrases, and characters while keeping both the story structure and the sentence structure virtually the same. The beauty of this assignment was that students had a framework on which to hang their own ideas, and even though much of the work was the same, the story was their own. This type of assignment worked well for Yong Min and others who did not have the framework for structuring essays or stories that we take for granted with English-speaking students. The level of intervention required was moderate and focused.

Maria was a seventh-grade bilingual student. This (figure 5.5) was supposed to be a limerick. The class had studied limericks and was given a frame on which to hang their own limericks.

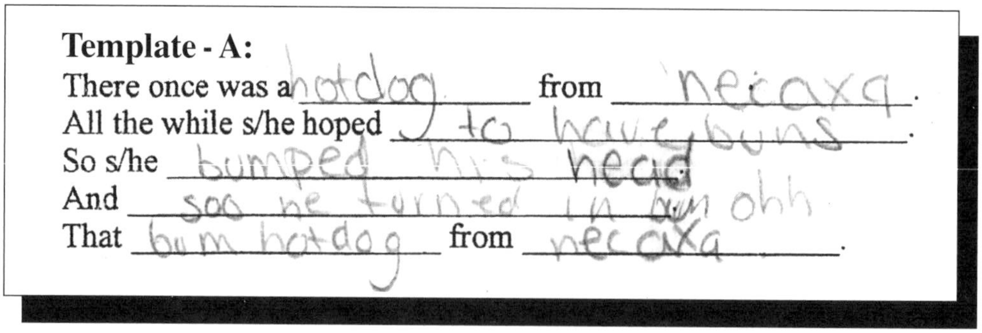

Template - A:
There once was a ~~hotdog~~ from ~~necaxa~~.
All the while s/he hoped ~~to have buns~~
So s/he ~~bumped his head~~
And ~~soo he turned in an ohh~~.
That ~~bum hotdog~~ from ~~necaxa~~.

Figure 5.5 Maria's limerick

Analysis

Hmm. Somebody was not listening to the instructions.

Interpretation

Maria was goofing off too much. Her teacher needed to make sure she was paying attention and doing what she was supposed to be doing. The level of intervention required was moderate.

Lark's assignment was written for a mainstream English class:

> Family is the most peaceful place for growing. It also a stage that the children learning everything. When the children open eyes to see this world, the family is the start stop. They try to enjoy the environment of seeing, speaking and listening. They also can cry anytime, and do what they want to do. The family always takes care of them without any condition. The family influents the children to think, to do, and to taste during their growing. The family is the good place for the children draw the rich and colorful childhood. It is the first important step in life.

Analysis

Several of the not-quite-on-target word choices were simply the result of not enough time logged. Lark may always write with this "foreign accent." Her writing and meaning were clear, her sentence structure sophisticated and varied. Most of her forms—infinitives and gerunds—were correct.

Interpretation

Lark's English was good enough that it only needed fine-tuning. At this stage, it did not always help to just point out the errors. It was better to work with her and discuss options, if possible. For instance, discussing what her intent was with the phrase "the family is the start stop" would not only help her to broaden her horizons, but also help her clarify her thoughts. The level of intervention required was low to moderate, but focused.

More Ways to Assess Writing Development

Journals, reading logs, written story retellings, and book reports are four more types of product that can help you assess students' writing progress.

Journals

Journal writing is ideal for gaining fluency, for practicing getting ideas on paper, for articulating thoughts and feelings, and for exploring language and concepts. Many students resist writing in journals because they feel they have nothing to write—moreover, they do not know how. They are leery of exposing their lack of knowledge. They are also afraid they will get nailed for their errors. (For this reason, journals should not be corrected, nor should they be used to point out grammatical deficiencies.)

It takes effort and commitment to get and keep journals going. Students have to be encouraged to use journals and should be allowed to copy books, magazines, and such, until they feel confident enough to express their own ideas. Dialogue journals help overcome this problem. Having real readers respond to their ideas—to content and not to form—gives readers confidence that they have something to say that is worth reading.

Over time, journals can reveal significant growth. For instance, here are some selections from high-school-student TJ's journal, written over the course of two years:

September, year one
My firsh day come to school confuse

December, year one
I like to listen the music because, the music make me fill happy and sad. sometime I go with my family we listen to the radio in the car. It is make my heart blocken. because I love the song.

April, year one
If I be come the president of U.S.A. I with give people job, education, also I with help the person that don't have money. I want that family go to training job to help there own family.

September, year two
The first think I like in school is have lot friend. The second thing I like is do something fun in school. Like rewarding all go to gym and do something

that all students do together. I like to do some outside like playing football with teacher and play something that we want to play.

December, year two

If I were a president of the United States, I would do some thing good for all the people like to make school for children and make jobs for people. And if people don't have food to eat, I would give money to government to buy food and give to them...And I would help people that have no jobs... In school the teacher can hit the kids so the kid would not run away from your house or school.

June, year two

Yesterday I went to see the Russian dancers at Washington High School. Dancers that I saw yesterday were very good because I get to see something good like jump in the air and spin around for long time with out dizzy. I like ...one part that four girl dancers with a candle because when they dancers it was so smooth and soft. Also one girl she scream so loud it all most wake my ear can not hear for 5 second. That all I can think for now! Thank you for the tacket. I really enjoy the show.

!The End

Analysis

TJ progressed from a single sentence to a wonderful, detailed description of a dance performance. He used some basic past-tense but mostly present-tense constructions. His descriptions were charming and detailed with good organization. Overall, the spelling was correct with just a few errors.

Interpretation

TJ was improving and needed continued support in language development. The level of intervention required was moderate and focused.

Reading Logs

Keeping track of everything students are doing individually can become a real problem. Having them keep logs of their reading is one of the simplest ways to keep a record of their abilities, interests, and progress. This log is simply a place for the student to list the materials he has read during sustained silent reading, and eventually becomes a profile of the reader. Debra Goodman (1992) writes:

> *How much reading is she doing? Is he having trouble finding books to read? Is she sampling different genres? What kinds of books is he interested in? What book is she able to read on her own?*

One effective method of gaining more information about reading choices is to have the student rate each book—*C* for challenging, *E* for easy, or *JR* for just right.

A reading log provides an easy reference for you, for readers, and for parents. It gives the student a sense of accomplishment, and it gives parents and other stakeholders a clear representation of what the student is accomplishing.

Written Story Retellings and Book Reports

Requiring students to produce a book report for every book they read may discourage them from reporting the full extent of their reading, notes Goodman (1992). However, you may decide to have students select one book a month to share in class or about which to write a report or demonstrate understanding in some other way.

Figure 5.6 shows a kindergarten child's response to the story "The Princess and the Pea." She included all the story elements: the castle, the princess sleeping on top of piles of mattresses, and the pea. She clearly understood and enjoyed the story.

Figure 5.6 Kindergarten student's book report

Here is an eighth grader's book report:

> The title of my book is *The Monster in the Third Dresser Drawer*. The author is Janice Lee Smith. The page number is 86 the characters is the monster and Adam Joshua. The setting is when Adam Joshua go to bed. The plot was when Adam Joshua go to bed and the monster come out of the third dresser drawer everyday at night when morning comes the monster go back to the third dresser drawer everynight the monster come out and play with the toys and scary him all the day of the week and for the hole night. At the end of the store Adam Joshua has a baby sister to sleep with.

Analysis

This student demonstrated a clear understanding of the story. Although the report had grammatical errors, it would have been pointless and inappropriate to correct them, as this was not the focus of the assignment. If the report was to be presented to the class, revising, correcting, and polishing would be in order.

When evaluating book reports, it is not always fruitful to grade each one separately, or even at all. They are instructive in the students' understanding of the story, and show students' burgeoning control over both comprehension of texts and ability to articulate what they read. Looking at reports over time is more productive than sitting down to give each single report a grade.

Interpretation

This student needed continued work with easier-level reading assignments. He also needed to be encouraged to write in a way that allowed him to describe both what happened in the book and how he felt about what he had read. Using the Language Experience Approach (LEA) would help develop his vocabulary. The level of intervention required was moderate and focused.

Howard Gardner's multiple intelligences theory (1993) has a great deal to offer second-language teachers. Many of our students who have not achieved high levels of proficiency naturally, access other intelligences to make themselves understood. For example, drawing is a way for students to demonstrate their understanding of a story and to extend their knowledge of English and their writing and speaking skills, as in Andreas's assignment, below.

Open Mind

In the Open Mind, illustrate your thoughts and feelings about the trial from the perspective of one of the characters. Show what was going on in the character's mind using graphic symbols and images. You may also use single words and phrases.

Figure 5.7 Andreas's picture of Scout (*To Kill a Mockingbird*) and comments

Explain the meaning of the pictures, drawings, symbols, and /or images that you illustrated in the "Open Mind" and why you chose to include them.

> I painted three faces in one becouse they have diferent colours, years old, know leges but they have the same heart, desire and sakrifice's spirit. They are Attikes, Tom and Scout.

Analysis

Andreas, a serious and talented artist as well as a deeply intuitive person, was able to capture, in resonant pictures, his grasp of the story *To Kill a Mockingbird*, of Scout's personality, and of how she mirrored her father.

Interpretation

The description Andreas gave of his art was clear. Although he made some mistakes in his writing, he was still able to communicate his thoughts. He needed to broaden his vocabulary and continue working with more complex sentences. The level of intervention required was moderate and focused.

Response Journals

Having students respond to reading is a very important part of their comprehension of the text. Many non-English-speaking students—particularly at the high-school level—are shy and quiet, unsure of their language capabilities and unwilling to talk in class. They are also unfamiliar with many of the cultural references and implicit assumptions made in texts. Thus, they sit at the back of the classroom and wait for others to expound on what they perceive in the story.

Response journals are a superb way of promoting independent thinking, fluency in writing, and of extracting meaning from texts. Bartholomae and Petrosky (1986) write:

> *Our comprehension of texts, whether literary or not, is more an act of composition (for understanding is composing) than of information retrieval... the best possible representation of our understanding of texts begins with certain kinds of compositions, not multiple choice tests or written free responses.*

Reading, responding, and composing are aspects of understanding, and journals are a way for the reader to express and explain, in his own way, what he understood from the text. When responses are part of the reading assignment, then the reader has a chance to explore his own vision of the story or text and articulate it before he has heard what others have to say. These journals, according to Petrosky, can be judged by the usual standards: "adequacy of elaboration, coherence, clarity, and aptness of illustration."

Some sample questions that can be used to elicit and guide responses, are

- What did you notice while you were reading the text?
- What did you think and how do you feel about what you noticed?
- What events or ideas from your own life connect to what you read in the book?

Such simple questions can elicit sometimes poetic and heart-rending responses from students. For instance, in response to the book *Sarah, Plain and Tall*, one reader wrote:

> **What can we expect is in the future? What are we going to do and to have? It is so difficult to give an exact answer because this is life. Sometimes life presents lots of unexpected things and problems. I think that everybody has had some dreams about their future at youth. But some did not always come**

true. I think that Sarah had her own dreams about her future too. But her fate turned on having to leave her home. At first sight it looks like I have the same situation, but that is not correct. And we have different kinds of challenges in our life. It is not easy to get used to a new life. You cannot forget everything from the past. "There are always things to miss, not matter where you are," said Maggie.

Another student, responding to *To Kill a Mockingbird*, commented:

> We are used to saying "hello" or "hi" to people who we meet on the street. We say "happy birthday" to someone who's having birthday. We can wish to each other a good day, good evening, good luck...But what could we wish people whose life is hanging by a thread? What could we wish a person like Tom Robinson, who has a black skin and who lived at the time of Negro discrimination? Many people like Tom have been penalized for things they didn't do. In my country people are discriminated against because of their nationality. My mother has been in this situation too. She lost her job because she was Armenian in Azerbaijan. Because of this it's easy for me to understand discrimination.

These were both students who had struggled through the books, felt they understood little, and missed a great deal of the word-by-word, point-by-point understanding. But their grasps of the stories themselves were solid. Moreover, these are the sorts of reactions to which one would probably never be privy if responses to books were elicited solely from class discussions or quizzes.

TRADITIONAL ASSESSMENT TOOLS

Many schools and teachers continue to use a variety of traditional assessment tools, including tests, homework, and comprehension questions in their assessment of students.

Tests

Tests are a hoop all students must jump through. Often administered at the end of a lesson, a test can be a summative assessment that measures how much the student has learned. Tests rarely reveal students' strategies, attitudes, interests, or explicit understandings of processes; they mainly reveal control over language and content matter. Because a student's performance on a test so often has nothing to do with his competence in the subject matter, we believe it is not a good idea to use tests as the sole measure of learning or the only resource for making educational decisions.

On the next page is a world history test, which all students in one district were required to take. (Note that the test was printed with the errors in the second and third sentences.)

If the sentence states a fact, write A in the space. If the sentence states an opinion, write B.

_____ *The lot of the serf was a sorry one.*

_____ *Florence is more beautiful and 540 years older than you Venice.*

_____ *We have round about us 30000 estates, owned by noblemen and merchants, citizens and crafts men.*

_____ *The lord's wife, the lady of the household, had important duties to perform.*

_____ *Castles often had dark, dirty, and damp dungeons where captured prisoners were held for ransom.*

This test demands knowledge of complex English grammatical structures, what castles and community life were like, and idioms such as "a sorry one." From the student's completed test, the teacher cannot tell whether he really knew the answer, copied his neighbor's, or guessed. He may even have known a great deal about the Middle Ages, but the way the test was worded may have thrown him off.

In another example, a test was given to seventh graders after an extensive unit on Australia, during which they had watched several movies including *Kangaroo Jack*, *The Rabbit Proof Fence*, and several documentaries about animals unique to the continent. To the right is an example of one test-taker's answer sheet. She received an *F* on the test. If this had been the most important grade for the unit or semester, she likely would have failed.

Angelica was probably being obstinate. The teacher knew from experience that Angelica did know the answers, because she had enjoyed the movies and had participated in class discussions. This is impossible to tell from the test alone.

There are times when it is appropriate to use tests. As Hamayan (1985) points

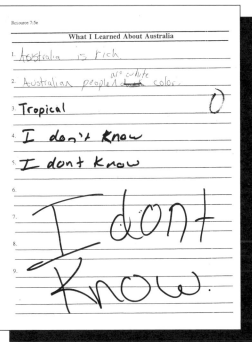

Figure 5.8 Angelica's answers from the Australia test

out, "tests do not allow for much individualization because they consist of one or more standard tasks that all students are expected to respond to in more or less the same way." This can be an advantage at times, because it gives you systematic, uniform feedback about the entire class.

Hamayan notes that it is important to consider how much and what kinds of language skills the student needs to take the test. If the test is to assess how much content the student has mastered, you can select tasks that use relatively simple language or allow the student to use his home language or methods other than language to demonstrate his knowledge.

Here are some more examples from the test on Australia. It was an open-ended test, which asked students to record "ten things I learned about Australia." It did not quantify knowledge as would a traditional test that asks closed questions. Rather than asking specific facts, it allowed students to relate what they remembered.

Enrique

> **Echidnas and platypus are the only mammals that are able to lay eggs**

Analysis

Enrique's sentence is complex, and his facts are correct. He was extremely interested in his project about echidnas and learned a great deal about them and, tangentially, about Australia.

Interpretation

Enrique understood the concepts and the language and could function in a mainstream classroom with ease. The level of intervention required was moderate.

José

> **Como los kanuros bebn en diferentes partes en Australia**
> (*Well, kangaroos live in different parts of Australia*)
>
> **Y los dingos son diferentes porque se paresen alos perros**
> (*And dingos are different because they seem like dogs*)
>
> **Y tambien el kookaburra se paresen a los animals que los de Mexico nomas que tienen diferentes nombre**
> (*And also, the kookaburra seems like animals from Mexico except it has a different name.*)

Analysis

It is clear that José, a level 1 who read and wrote at a very low level in Spanish, learned a great deal during this unit, even though it was presented entirely in English. It was immaterial that he wrote his answers in Spanish. His understanding of the content is what was important.

Interpretation

Time and exposure would help José. The important thing was to have expectations. Continuing to working with him in English would, in time, bring about response from him in English. For now, José needed to be encouraged to participate in any way he could. The level of intervention required was high and focused.

Ezekiel

> The Australia most of the lands is desert and mountan

Isabella

> I learn that is too much species of animal
> I learn the Taxmania fox no exit more

Analysis

Both Ezekiel and Isabella were level 2s in English but were functioning at grade level in Spanish. Ezekiel readily admitted (to his doting mother's chagrin) that he was a lazy speller.

Interpretation

Both Ezekiel and Isabella could be encouraged to continue their Spanish and to read in the content areas as much as possible in Spanish. Isabella was a serious and dedicated student; Ezekiel preferred to horse around with his friends. It was important to push Ezekiel forward, not allowing him to get away with his poor spelling and rotten penmanship. The level of intervention required was moderate to high, and focused.

Josefina

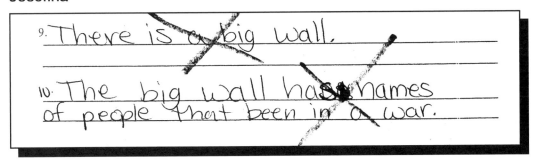

Figure 5.9 Josefina's answers from the Australia test

Analysis

Josefina's answer is not about Australia; she is thinking of the Great Wall of China and the Vietnam War Memorial, both of which she had also studied. She must have been dreaming. She knew better.

Interpretation

Josefina needed to be engaged. She worked best with one-on-one help to keep her focused on the task at hand. The level of intervention required was moderate and focused.

Pedro

> The kangoroos put they bebis they put them is a bag they have in they stomok
> Digos are liks dog put they are little diffents

Analysis

Pedro was a puzzle. He spent most of his day in special ed and paid little attention in class, but his answers revealed that he had learned many things during this lesson.

Interpretation

In the past, mainstream teachers had few expectations for Pedro and had given the bulk of the responsibility to the special-ed teacher. It seemed that when Pedro was accountable for something, he could, in fact, do the work. The level of intervention required was moderate to high, and focused.

If there is content-obligatory language involved—such that the student cannot learn the content without learning the vocabulary, too—you must find ways to integrate the two. For example, Tong had to take a test for his earth-science class. He could answer most of the questions with words, but for a more complex answer, he drew a diagram.

For a laboratory test, a science teacher presented students with items that they had to identify. They had to master the content-obligatory language to pass the test, but they did not have to read extensive text to demonstrate their knowledge. When the same teacher was testing students in their health class, she had them respond to a question such as, "Your brother cut his wrist and he is bleeding hard. What do you do?" The student could demonstrate what he should do on himself or on the dummy.

English-language learners can also demonstrate what they have learned about content and language through regular assignments. The assignments we discuss here were not writing for the sake of writing but, rather, writing for the goal of extending knowledge.

For instance, in a study of India, a class of seventh graders learned about arranged marriages. They examined actual newspaper ads for prospective brides and grooms and then wrote their own ads. They used writing to have fun, practice persuasive writing, and explore the notion of what it might be like to put themselves "on the market" for a suitable mate.

Both Elise's and Georgia's primary language was English.

Elise

> **If You Are Cute Come This Way!**
> I am 5 feet and 3 inches tall. I come from a rich family and loving. I am looking for someone who is beter then me (look) has a great job and make up to $5000 a month. I'm smart, fun funny. I'm looking for a man with cute eyes, cute hair, is nice to women and loves his mother.

Georgia

> I am a student at Harvert Law school, highly educated seeking to find a highly educated perfurable black or Hispanic man, must be at least 6' nice smile nice big lips and nice teeth. And nice house.

These two girls were right on target. José (next page), however, did not quite understand that he was supposed to advertise himself. He had the right idea—describing the qualities he would look for in a wife—but his answer reveals that he needed more explanation.

José

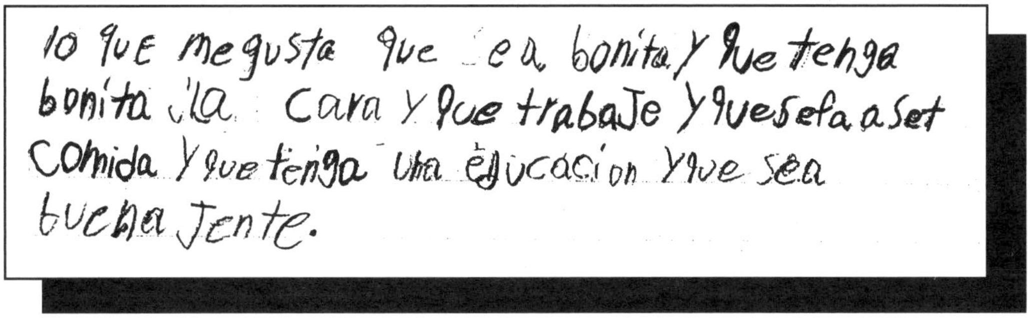

> lo 9uE me gusta 9ue sea bonita Y 9ue tenga bonita la cara Y 9ue trabaJe Y 9uesefa a Ser Comida Y 9ue tenga una éducacion Y 9ue sea buena Jente.

Figure 5.10 José's newspaper ad. Translation: "I like it when they're pretty and have a pretty face and work, and know how to cook and have an education and are good people."

In another example, students had read the short story "All Summer in a Day," by Ray Bradbury. The story is set on the planet Venus, where it rains continuously except for one hour of sunshine every seven years. One girl, Margot, actually remembers the sun and pines for it; the other children hate her because she is different, and they shove her into a closet just before the sun comes out. They go outside to play and only remember her after the rain has started to fall again. The assignment (courtesy of Carol Booth Olson, *The Reading/ Writing Connection: Strategies for Teaching and Learning in the Secondary Classroom*, 2007) was to write a letter as Margot five to ten years after the incident, telling her classmates where she is, what she is doing, and what she learned from that terrible incident.

Here is an exemplary letter written by a seventh-grade student whose primary language was English; it can be useful to compare an ESL student's work to that of a mainstream student in order to gauge how far the former needs to go.

Dear Classmates

It's me Margot. I now live on earth. There is sunshine everyday in every room. I'm so happy to be here. I'm now a Brain Surgeon. I've lived her for many years and no rain yet. I'm writing because I want to know why you pushed me in the closet. Especially when you know I really wanted to see the sunshine. All I can think about is what you did to me. All I remember about that day was you didn't believe me about the sun and you looked me in the closet. I think that you did this to me because you were scared of what would happen if the sun came out. When you locked me in the closet it rally hut me. You know how much I believed in the sun coming out. I was so happy when I heard the rain stop falling.

I learned not to trust anyone. I learned that if you know something and other people don't believe you don't tell them. They will try to prevent you from doing the thing or seeing it. It is disturbing to know that another human being could do that to you. They just crush your dreams like that. I would have never done that to you. I would have just let you believe what you want to.

Here are more examples of the same assignment written by seventh graders from a low-income school.

Ezekiel

Dear: Class mates,

I am in Mexico city and that is not for you now. Thank's that I move from Venes and thant's to Mrs. J I am a great architect. And I learnt that you were a bad influence on me and I hope I never see you again.

Sincerely:

Analysis

Ezekiel was cruising along again without taking the time or effort to fix errors. However, even though his handwriting was rudimentary and his spelling was terrible, he demonstrated that he understood the story very well. To make this a better paper he needed to elaborate, to show why he had become an architect and what exactly was the bad influence they had had on him. He also needed to correct the spelling and mechanical errors.

Interpretation

Ezekiel needed to strengthen his ability to communicate his thoughts. He also needed one-on-one help with vocabulary. The level of intervention required was moderate and focused.

Eduardo

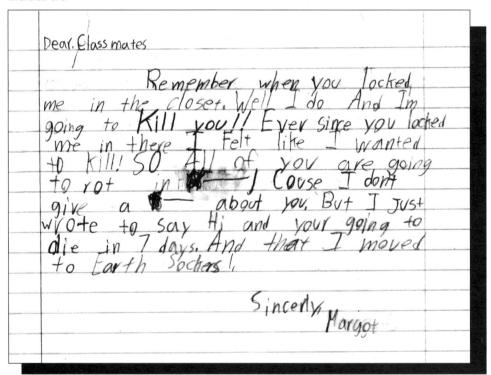

Figure 5.11 Eduardo's letter-from-Margot assignment

Analysis

In spite of the many errors, Eduardo's assignment is very strong. It is filled with emotion, pain, and vengeance. The writer rubs it in that he, as Margot, now lives on Earth, while they do not. In many ways, this work is as strong as that of the mainstream student, even if it is lacking some essential components to fulfill the assignment.

Interpretation

Eduardo needed to expand his skills. He enjoyed being creative and needed help developing his ideas. The level of intervention required was moderate and focused.

Luis

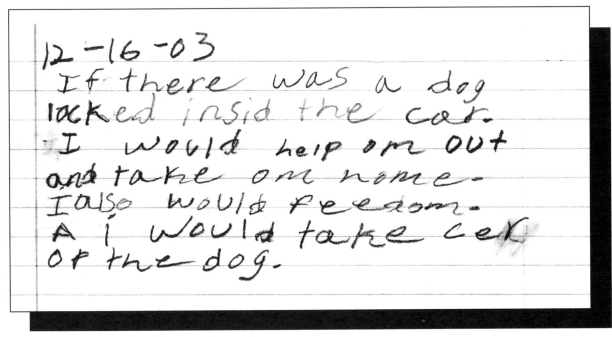

Figure 5.12 Luis's letter-from-Margot assignment

Analysis

Luis did not even address the issue. He was completely off topic.

Interpretation

Luis wanted to goof off in class and would slap together his assignments just to turn something in. He needed one-on-one attention to help him keep his mind on his work. The level of intervention required was moderate and focused.

José

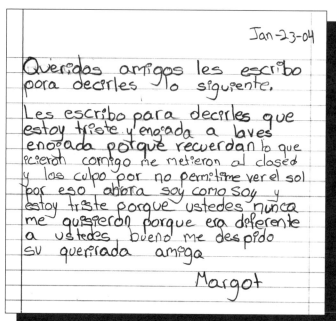

Jan-23-04

Queridos amigos les escribo para decirles lo siguiente.

Les escribo para decirles que estoy triste y enojada a laves enojada porque recuerdan lo que icieron comigo me metieron al closed y los culpo por no permitime ver el sol por eso ahora soy como soy y estoy triste porque ustedes nunca me quisieron porque era diferente a ustedes, bueno me despido su querirada amiga

Margot

Figure 5.13 José's letter-from-Margot assignment. Translation: "Dear friends, I write you to tell you the following. / I am writing to you to tell you that I am sad and angry at the same time. Angry because they remember what they did to me. They put me in a closet and I blame them for not letting me see the sun."

Analysis

José was on track this time. It is clear that he understood the story as well as the assignment, and he fulfilled the basic expectations for it. He needed reminding that this was a letter, and he should have been speaking to his classmates. One-on-one conferencing with the teacher, to do more brainstorming, would have helped him explore the possibilities.

Interpretation

It was important to continue expecting José to participate. He needed a lot of one-on-one attention in order to understand what he needed to do. He also needed teachers to be tolerant of his work in Spanish and to help him develop his vocabulary in English. The intervention level required was high and focused.

Homework

The problem with homework is that you can never be sure who completed it or who had input. Homework is removed in both time and space and precludes a teacher from looking over the shoulder of a student and seeing what is wrong. But teachers still assign it and parents—and even some students— still expect it.

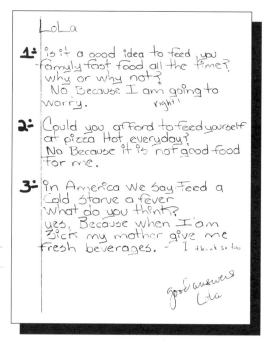

Lola

1: Is it a good idea to feed you familiy fast food all the time? why or why not?
No Because I am going to worry. right!

2: Could you afford to feed yourself at pizza Hot everyday?
No Because it is not good food for me.

3: In America we say Feed a Cold Starve a fever. What do you think?
yes, Because when I am sick my mother give me fresh beverages. – I think so too

good answers Lola

Figure 5.14 Lola's homework: exploring the verb *feed*

154

For example, a class of very traditional students asked for homework in English grammar. They were given an exercise on one irregular verb per day. As shown in figure 5.14, the teacher went through the verb forms and then asked questions; students got to practice the forms as well as their writing skills.

Comprehension Questions

These are simply checks to see if the student has understood the assignment. They can be as formal as a written quiz or as informal as asking students to draw or write down three things they learned from the lesson.

they eat the rice three times a day – breakfast, lunch, and dinner.
In Laos they plant in May some baskets and parts of houses are made of rice plants.

RIA

Figure 5.15 Ria's summary of what she learned from a presentation on rice

Figure 5.16 This eighth-grader's drawing demonstrates his understanding of the horrors of slavery.

The following assignment had high-school students display their understanding of the problems faced by the contemporary farmer by writing a letter to their congressman. Here are two of the results:

> **Dear ladies and Gentlmen,**
>
> **I'm most graceful to write this letter to you at the congressman this time.**
>
> **I'm very need your help me and my family this year. On these year we don't had enough money to pay my tax. Then we don't have enough money to buy food to my family eat this year. Therefore, please can you low the price to all the farmer. Please can you solve this problem is soon is prosble. Then, please low all of the price to a very low prices, to all the people.**
>
> **Thank you! very much.**
>
> **Sincerely**

Dear Congressman,

I have problems about my farm this year a lot of insect distral my corn, my corn can't grow every well, so I need help from you, see how much you can help me solve my problem, and how much you can give me the posonous or thing to help my farm, now I am going to poor because I can't buy fertilizer, posonous, seeds clothing, machinery tools or everything to protect my farm from the companies. The companies are sold the thing so expensive, therefore I have no money to buy it and pay for the railroads to go to the store or back home, and I have no enough credit, or loans, borrow money from the banks, the bank charged high rate of interest too. So I hope you would help me for sure this year by regulating the company and giving some loan.

Your farmer

Teachers inexperienced in working with English learners are often overwhelmed by the errors, and focus on the grammatical problems. It is critical to look past the errors and respond to the content itself. The previous two letters revealed a great deal of understanding about the issues at hand—high prices for inputs and low returns on crops produced. Both students wrote compelling letters that also showed their ability to grapple with audience, purpose, and style.

DECONTEXTUALIZED MEASURES

Standardized tests are administered outside the context of the classroom. Although test makers and legislators have attempted to align standardized tests with the curriculum as well as with state/provincial/federal standards, Anthony et al. (1991) write that, for the most part, they do not "originate in the instructional context" of our classes, and their content and purposes are removed from our control. Thus, their applicability and appropriateness also lie outside the domain of the classroom.

We discussed standardized testing in chapter 2, and we made our position on them clear. They are a fact of life in the careers of most students, however. Whether we like it or not, these tests will be part of each student's academic record.

CONCLUSION

Teachers must develop a variety of ways in which to view their students' progress. We have a wide range of student behavior to observe and record, and we need an equally broad range of data collection methods. Trying to accomplish this for thirty or more students can be a true challenge. Be realistic in your attempts. Do not try to change all your assessment methods in one year. This approach to assessment is a process. You can adapt your current techniques as you feel comfortable. We believe you will find the outcome is worth the effort.

6

The Santa Maria, the Pimpas, the
Ninny Sailing with Baflaf's Dog

RECORDING YOUR OBSERVATIONS THROUGH CHECKLISTS, RUBRICS, ANECDOTES, AND CONFERENCES

Part of Mary's job as curricular support for technology at a high school in northern California is to provide support for the ESL students with whom she works. This can mean anything from clarifying the history packet questions Keiko needs to answer, to correcting the spelling in Pancho's English assignment, to discussing and challenging the advanced students with their literature assignments.

Kim, one of Mary's brightest students, worked extremely hard on a literature essay in which she was asked to describe the elements of alienation in F. Scott Fitzgerald's *The Great Gatsby*. Kim did a magnificent job. She used the right quotes, and she was able to appropriately bring into the essay her own experiences of wanting to fit in. When Mary reviewed Kim's paper, she felt Kim's English teacher would be quite proud.

Two weeks later, to Mary's surprise, Kim announced that she was getting a *D* in her English class—the result of receiving a *D* on her *Great Gatsby* essay. Mary was dumbfounded. After meeting with the teacher, she discovered that the problem was not in the paper's content but that Kim had not turned it in on time. The essay—which accounted for two-thirds of the overall grade in the class—was automatically downgraded by fifty percent.

Mary had kept notes about Kim's progress as well as a checklist of when her assignments were due. Her records showed that Kim had completed the paper well in advance of its due date. Moreover, after reviewing her notes more thoroughly, Mary could see a pattern of self-destructive behavior in the student. The classroom teachers did not have this information. All they knew was that Kim either missed assignments completely or turned them in late. Because of her own notes and record keeping, Mary knew something more was going on—Kim had done the work but was sabotaging herself for some reason. With checklists and notes in hand, Mary headed for the counselor's office to get help dealing with the problem.

What's in this Chapter

+ Four methods of recording observations: checklists, rubrics, anecdotes, and conferences
+ Advantages and disadvantages for each method
+ Guidelines for the development of each method

HOW TO RECORD YOUR OBSERVATIONS

Observing and gathering data are two different tasks. While observing is a natural part of your day, collecting data is not as easy, because it often has to be done on the run. You do not always have the luxury of sitting down and looking at concrete pieces of evidence. Therefore, data-collection methods must be simple, efficient, and they must not interfere with your first priority: teaching. Happily, in a classroom where you have built-in opportunities for student interaction and collaboration, collection can be accomplished in concert with the methods we discussed in chapter 5.

+ Through observation of process: writing down your observations of the learner in the form of checklists, rubrics, and anecdotes
+ Through observation of product: looking at samples of what the learner has produced
+ Through interviews and conferences: talking to the learner about what he is doing and what he thinks about it

Checklists

Checklists are matrices organized to monitor specific skills, behaviors, attitudes, traits, and accomplishments of individual or all students in the class. They are also record-keeping devices that help you keep track of who has mastered certain skills and who needs to work on them. Checklists encompass features that you determine you want to assess in students.

Advantages of checklists

+ They are a quick and easy way to observe, focus on, and record specific skills and behaviors.

+ Creating checklists helps you to think through and clarify what is important about certain processes and products.

+ They can be useful for summary purposes.

+ They provide a simple, graphic display of what a student knows or has accomplished, and can clearly demonstrate to stakeholders which concepts or skills have been learned.

+ They act as reminders for note-taking and observation purposes.

+ They can show you and your students which areas need work—before it is too late.

Disadvantages of checklists

+ They can be very limiting, and can act as blinders, caution Anthony et al. (1991). When you are only looking for certain things, you may miss other significant qualitative leaps that a student has taken, which are not as readily apparent.

+ They do not provide a rich context for understanding behaviors. They are simply lists.

+ They "lend themselves to misreading by other people" (Johnston, 1992), because scanning quickly for items that are *not* checked off focuses on deficits rather than on things that have been mastered.

+ They can be time-consuming to construct. That said, it can be difficult to use someone else's checklist if the creator has a different agenda or different values. Turbill and Cambourne (1997) note that trying to use a checklist someone else has devised can be frustrating, because the originator's focus may be different from your own. Many teachers are happier using checklists they have developed themselves.

+ It is easy to become trapped by what is included on the checklist and to believe that everything must be mastered in order for the student to be deemed proficient or to move on to another level.

On the next page is a checklist that is aligned with the Michigan state standards for ESL. As a snapshot of a student's competence, it is terrific. It is important, however, to use checklists for evaluating overall growth and not to focus on minutiae. A student need not achieve success in every single area in order to be considered eligible for the next level.

Name **Ashraf** Date _____

English Language Proficiency Level Checklist

Level 1A	Level 1B	Level 2	Level 3	Level 4
☐ Interrupted schooling (1 year +/-)	☐ No understanding of English	☐ Can comprehend short conversations on simple topics, relying on familiar structures and utterances	☐ Understands standard speech in most settings with some repetition and rewording	☑ Language skills are adequate for most day-to-day communication needs, although occasional structural and lexical errors occur ~ *(syntactical)*
☐ Interrupted schooling (2 yrs +)	☐ Limited understanding of English	☐ Sustains conversation by using repetition, gestures, and other non-verbal cues	☑ Understands main ideas and relevant details of extended discussions or presentations	☐ May have difficulty using and understanding idioms, figures of speech, and words with multiple meanings
☐ Pre- or semi-literate in native language	☐ Rarely uses English for communication	☐ Reads and understands basic narrative text and authentic materials	☑ Draws on a wide range of language forms, vocabulary, idioms, and structures	☐ Communicates in English in unfamiliar settings, but has occasional difficulty with complex structures and abstract academic concepts
☐ Academic performance significantly below grade level	☐ Responds nonverbally to simple commands, statements and questions	☐ Uses contextual and visual cues to derive meaning from texts that contain unfamiliar words, expressions, and structures	☐ Comprehends nuances but depends on repetition or rephrasing	☐ Reads a wide range of texts with considerable fluency and can locate specific facts within the texts; however, students cannot understand text in which concepts are presented in a de-conceptualized manner with complex structures and abstract academic concepts
☐ Needs more time to adjust to school & cultural environment	☐ Beginning to imitate verbalization of others using single words or simple phrases	☑ Comprehends passages written in basic sentence patterns but guesses at meaning of more complex materials	☐ Oral communication is adequate in most settings	
☐ Cannot participate meaningfully in testing	☐ Starting to construct meaning from non-print features of text (pictures, illustrations, maps, tables)	☑ Begins to make informed guesses about meaning from context	☐ Can comprehend the content of many texts independently, but requires support with academic content areas	☐ Reads independently, but may have occasional comprehension problems
☐ Arrived less than 30 days ago	☐ Starting to construct meaning from words, but construction is incomplete	☑ Begins to identify main idea and supporting details in written passages	☐ Able to read many literature selections for pleasure	☐ Produces written text independently for personal and academic purposes
☐ Doesn't know English alphabet	☑ Able to generate simple written text, but with many non-conventional features (invented spelling, grammatical inaccuracies)	☐ Can produce simple writing using basic vocabulary and common language structures	☐ Separates main ideas from supporting ideas	☐ Structures, vocabulary, and overall organization approximates the writing of native speakers of English
	☐ English reflects features from native language		☐ Uses context of a passage and prior knowledge to increase comprehension	☑ Errors persist in one or more of the English language domains (listening, speaking, reading, and writing)
			☐ Writes multi-paragraph compositions, personal & business letters, and creative passages	
			☐ Shows good control of grammar structures, but with some errors	
			☐ Expresses complex ideas with wide range of vocabulary, idioms, and grammar structures	

Figure 6.1 Ashraf illustrates many students, because his acquisition of English proficiency is not even. He is very fluent verbally, but he is not so proficient in reading, and even less so in writing.

Use checklists to help you think through the evaluation purposes they serve. If you are using one that someone else created, take the time to make adaptations to suit your own situation. Using a form without thinking it through or modifying it deprives you of the benefit of involving yourself in the process. Checklists are worth the effort to create because, if properly conceived and used, they can yield a great deal of information. For example, Mary devised the checklist shown in figure 6.2 to record a child's oral language mastery.

Language Function Checklist

Student's name_____ Date _____

Age_____ Grade _____

F	S	N	BEHAVIOR/ABILITY	CONTEXT/COMMENTS
			Demonstrates comprehension nonverbally	
			Uses physical motion to communicate (pushing, pulling, etc.)	
			Listens and attends to the work at hand	
			One-word response	
			Uses English in an informal conversation	
			Makes a request "I want…" or "I need…"	
			Talks about himself/herself	
			Participates in formal classroom discussion within small group	
			Understands and answers questions about material presented through discussion	
			Volunteers additional information in the class discussion	
			Asks for additional information privately	
			Asks for additional information within the group	
			Presents a dissenting point of view	
			Uses language to communicate sadness	
			Uses imaginative language, e.g., "If I were a bird, I would fly home to my country."	
			Uses language to be funny	
			Uses language sarcastically	
			Uses language to show anger	
			Uses authoritative language, e.g., "You must…"	
			Uses language to anticipate a future event	
			Communicates using indirect coding, e.g., "You must be tired of correcting all our papers," meaning, "Don't give us so much homework."	
			Other:	

F – Frequently   S – Seldom   N – Never

Figure 6.2 Language Function Checklist (reproducible master in appendix B)

You can also make checklists for the vocabulary students know upon arrival or have learned during a specified amount of time. Figure 6.3 (next page) is a student vocabulary checklist that can be used as a progress indicator.

Student Vocabulary Checklist

Teacher_____ Student _____

Grade_____

Have student identify English Vocabulary. Use check marks to note those words the student knows. Leave others blank.

1. Colors
   - ☐ red
   - ☐ blue
   - ☐ green
   - ☐ yellow
   - ☐ white
   - ☐ orange
   - ☐ black
   - ☐ purple
   - ☐ brown

2. Numbers—Kindergarten
   - ☐ 1
   - ☐ 3
   - ☐ 5
   - ☐ 7
   - ☐ 9
   - ☐ 2
   - ☐ 4
   - ☐ 6
   - ☐ 8
   - ☐ 10

   Grades 1-3, as above plus
   - ☐ 11
   - ☐ 13
   - ☐ 15
   - ☐ 17
   - ☐ 19
   - ☐ 12
   - ☐ 14
   - ☐ 16
   - ☐ 18
   - ☐ 20

3. Shapes
   - ☐ circle
   - ☐ square
   - ☐ triangle
   - ☐ rectangle

4. Alphabet (present in random order)
   - ☐ A
   - ☐ G
   - ☐ M
   - ☐ S
   - ☐ Y
   - ☐ B
   - ☐ H
   - ☐ N
   - ☐ T
   - ☐ Z
   - ☐ C
   - ☐ I
   - ☐ O
   - ☐ U
   - ☐ D
   - ☐ J
   - ☐ P
   - ☐ V
   - ☐ E
   - ☐ K
   - ☐ Q
   - ☐ W
   - ☐ F
   - ☐ L
   - ☐ R
   - ☐ X

5. Holiday names
   - ☐ Easter
   - ☐ Halloween
   - ☐ Valentine's Day
   - ☐ New Year's Day
   - ☐ Christmas
   - ☐ Thanksgiving

6. Personal information
   - ☐ name
   - ☐ age
   - ☐ address
   - ☐ phone number

7. Body parts
   - ☐ eye
   - ☐ nose
   - ☐ cheek
   - ☐ mouth
   - ☐ neck
   - ☐ chest
   - ☐ shoulder
   - ☐ arm
   - ☐ hand
   - ☐ stomach
   - ☐ leg
   - ☐ knee
   - ☐ foot
   - ☐ finger

8. Spatial orientation
   - ☐ left
   - ☐ right
   - ☐ in front of
   - ☐ out
   - ☐ over
   - ☐ above
   - ☐ beside
   - ☐ behind
   - ☐ in
   - ☐ near
   - ☐ far

1

Figure 6.3 Student Vocabulary Checklist (Note: only half of checklist shown here; reproducible master of full checklist in appendix B)

Developing your own checklist

There are many ways of putting together a checklist to suit your own purposes. Here are five steps for developing one.

1. To determine what the student knows, select the tasks or skills you want to observe. For example:

   - ◆ Reading
   - ◆ Talking
   - ◆ Writing
   - ◆ Collaborating
   - ◆ Editing
   - ◆ Doing experiments
   - ◆ Computing
   - ◆ Graphing
   - ◆ Problem solving
   - ◆ Socializing

Checklist for Assessing Emerging Readers

Student's name _____ **Date** _____

Age _____ **Grade** _____

	Not yet	Emerging	Yes
Listens to story but is not looking at pages			
Tries to read environmental print			
Demonstrates book-handling knowledge (right side up)			
Watches pictures as story is read aloud			
Makes up words for picture			
Demonstrates directionality of written language (left to right, page order)			
Pretends to read			
Recognizes some words from a dictated story			
Participates in reading by supplying rhyming words and some predictable text			
Memorizes text, and pretends to read story			
Looks at words and tracks words when reading or is being read to from a familiar story			
Recognizes words in a new context			
Reads word-for-word			
Reads familiar stories fluently			
Reads familiar stories haltingly			
Uses context clues, phonic analysis, sentence structure to read new words and passages			
Reads easy books fluently			
Chooses to read independently			
Reads fluently			

Figure 6.4
Checklist for Assessing
Emerging Readers
(reproducible master
in appendix B)

2. Select the setting in which you want to observe your students.

+ In class
+ On the playground
+ In the hallway
+ In the gym
+ In the science lab
+ In the computer lab
+ Individually
+ In groups (pairs, small groups, large groups)
+ With older students
+ With younger students

3. Determine the specific achievements to include in each checklist.

4. Design the rating scale. According to Jett-Simpson (1997), the best checklists for documenting growth indicate dates and degrees (for example, "degree of independence a child has reached in literacy") rather than simply showing items to check off in yes/no categories. Examples of rating scales include

    +   Frequently, sometimes, not yet

    +   Yes, somewhat, not yet

    +   Yes, no, not observed

    +   Usually, occasionally, working on it, never

    +   Not yet, beginning, developing, independent

    +   Happy face (☺), neutral face (☺), sad face (☹) (for very young children)

5. Leave space for comments.

Rubrics

The development of rubrics marked an important step in helping teachers and students to define quality and focus on what is important in work being produced, as well as in grading. A rubric is a clear and concise scoring guide that helps the user assess performance. It clearly defines mastery for a given skill or task, as well as providing varying degrees of mastery through points on a scale. A rubric includes criteria for what you consider to be "excellent," "good," "fair," and "poor" in terms of the given skill or task. For example, if you assign a 5 to exemplary performance, the rubric for this score would describe the features that correspond to excellent performance. Those features would necessarily represent a higher quality than would be represented by a 4 or a 3. A 4 on the scale would show clearly both what a student has achieved and what is lacking.

Rubrics are very much like checklists. In fact, there is a great deal of overlap, so much so that we have seen rubric-checklists. Do not sweat the difference.

Advantages of rubrics

+   They help clarify your expectations.

+   They help you define, in concrete terms, what quality is.

+   If constructed properly, they remove much of the guesswork and ambiguity from grading. Each time you look at a product, you can clearly see what you have decided is exemplary, and on which points a student has not measured up.

+   For each body of work, students know, up front, what is expected of them; when they are assessed on it, they know exactly where they did well or where they missed the mark.

+   They are flexible enough to accommodate learners with a range of abilities.

+ Students can take responsibility for their own work, instead of repeatedly asking you whether they are done yet; they can also assess and revise their own work, because they know where they need to improve.

+ They offer a concrete place to begin a discussion about how to improve work and where a student needs to focus his efforts in revising and reworking.

+ Copies of rubrics can be attached to student work; when you meet with parents, you can explain what went into the assignment of a grade.

+ Numerous outstanding rubrics have already been created for you, particularly for writing, with the 6+1 Trait® writing assessment model (a framework for assessing writing that has carefully developed rubrics for each of the seven characteristics of good writing). Below is the Northwest Regional Educational Laboratory's (NWREL) 6+1 Trait® Writing Scoring Continuum, an example of a *good* rubric. Resources like RubiStar <http://rubistar.4teachers.org/index.php> also help you construct rubrics quite easily by yourself.

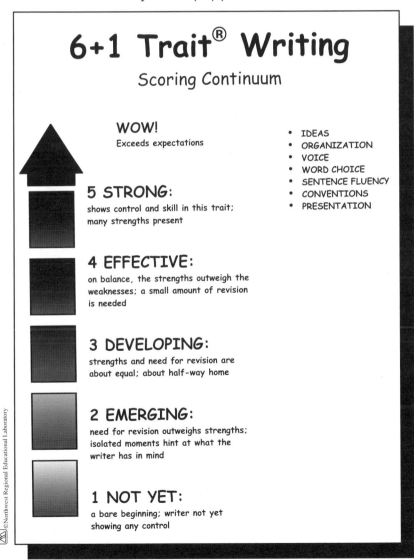

6+1 Trait® Writing
Scoring Continuum

WOW!
Exceeds expectations

5 STRONG:
shows control and skill in this trait; many strengths present

4 EFFECTIVE:
on balance, the strengths outweigh the weaknesses; a small amount of revision is needed

3 DEVELOPING:
strengths and need for revision are about equal; about half-way home

2 EMERGING:
need for revision outweighs strengths; isolated moments hint at what the writer has in mind

1 NOT YET:
a bare beginning; writer not yet showing any control

- IDEAS
- ORGANIZATION
- VOICE
- WORD CHOICE
- SENTENCE FLUENCY
- CONVENTIONS
- PRESENTATION

©Northwest Regional Educational Laboratory

Figure 6.5 The NWREL 6+1 Trait® Writing rubric identifies the seven characteristics of good writing and provides a scoring continuum, which you can use to steer students in the right direction.

Disadvantages of rubrics

+ The problems with grading and grade inflation do not disappear when you use rubrics, as has been claimed.
+ They can be very time-consuming to develop and to train students in their use.
+ They can be time-consuming when using for grading purposes.
+ They are sometimes poorly designed, with improper weighting of elements or scores.

On the next two pages are more of the letter-from-Margot assignments that we presented in chapter 5. They help illustrate the various levels of achievement into which students can fall. Students may shine in one area and fall short in another. You can use the near-misses to show them where they need to improve and what they can do to make their writing clearer and more powerful.

To evaluate students' work, we used the 6+1 Trait® writing rubric shown on the previous page (visit <http://www.nwrel.org/assessment/pdfRubrics/6plus1traits.PDF>). We also used the rubric specifically designed by Carol Booth Olson for the letter-from-Margot assignment, which is presented in *The Reading/Writing Connection* (2007) and the book's companion website. Below are the characteristics of a 6 ("superior") paper outlined by Booth Olson (note that although it is very specific to this assignment, this scoring rubric is, in our opinion, another example of a *good* rubric. We include the entire scoring rubric as appendix A3 on page 270-272; you can also download it from the companion website to *The Reading/Writing Connection* at <http://wps.ablongman.com/ab_olson_readwrite_2/0,11768,3060221-,00.html>):

Superior

The **6** paper is clearly superior: well-written, insightful, carefully organized, and technically correct. The 6 paper does most or all of the following well:

+ Is written in standard letter form: greeting, body, closing
+ Assumes the persona of Margot and impressively writes in her voice
+ Begins by reminding classmates of who the writer is
+ Clearly describes Margot's present situation including where she lives now and what she is doing
+ Thoughtfully explains why Margot is writing
+ Reviews in detail what happened on the day the sun came out
+ Uses concrete evidence from the text to make the letter specific
+ Offers perceptive insights into why the children treated her as they did
+ Explores the children's final act of cruelty and analyzes in depth how it affected Margot
+ Concludes by articulately and thoughtfully expressing what she learned
+ Uses rich, descriptive language to paint a vivid picture for the reader, including similes and/or metaphors
+ Contains few, if any, errors in the conventions of written English[1]

---

[1] From Olson, Carol Booth *Reading/Writing Connection, The*, 2/e. Published by Allyn and Bacon, Boston, MA. Copyright © 2007 by Pearson Education. Reprinted by permission of the publisher.

The work sample below is by Arturo, a bilingual seventh grader who was raised in the
United States and spoke English in school and Spanish at home.

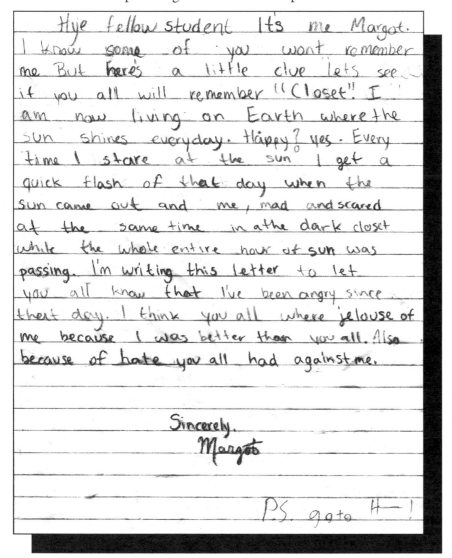

Hye fellow student It's me Margot.
I know some of you wont remember
me But here's a little clue lets see
if you all will remember "Closet". I
am now living on Earth where the
sun shines everyday. Happy? yes. Every
time I stare at the sun I get a
quick flash of that day when the
sun came out and me, mad and scared
at the same time in athe dark closet
while the whole entire hour of sun was
passing. I'm writing this letter to let
you all know that I've been angry since
that day. I think you all where jelouse of
me because I was better than you all. Also
because of hate you all had against me.

Sincerely.
Margot

P.S. go to H—!

Figure 6.6 Arturo's letter-from-Margot assignment

This was a great start. The voice was strong and angry. Arturo's letter exhibited the
following:

+ It was honest, appealing, and written from the heart, creating a vivid impression in
  the reader's mind.

+ Arturo assumed the persona of Margot and wrote believably in her voice.

+ His word choices, particularly his use of the word closet, were fresh, even striking.

+ He used vivid details.

+ He offered some insight into why the children had treated her as they had.

+ It was written in standard-letter form.

However, the letter was largely superficial and generalized. He had quit before going into any detail about the incident. In order to make the letter stronger, Arturo needed to explore, in-depth, Margot's classmates' final act of cruelty and analyze the effect it had on her. He needed to use even more colorful language and concrete evidence from the text, as well as clean up the errors.

Carlos was another bilingual student who spoke accentless English. He was a reluctant writer, though, who would rather fool around than try hard. This was one of his better efforts:

> **Hi Do you remember me I am margo Do you Rmember when you put me in the closet but now the more I think about it I am going to make you pay I am going to make you suffer I am going to put you in a closet to**
>
> **Sincerely margo**

For a first draft, Carlos had accomplished the bare bones of the assignment. He did demonstrate that he understood the story very well. Other strengths included an evident voice and understanding of how Margot must have felt. As well, Carlos assumed Margot's persona and reminded the classmates of who she was. But he did not review what had happened, offer plausible reasons why they had locked her in the closet, describe the effect it had had on her, or explain what she had learned from it. Carlos, too, needed to explore using descriptive and vivid language to paint a powerful picture.

Criteria for designing rubrics

+ They should be clearly written, specific, and understandable to students.
+ The descriptors must be suitable so they can tell us what we want to know.
+ They should include all elements worth evaluating and not leave out any worthwhile factors.
+ They should be explicit enough so students know what they need to do to achieve success.
+ The features you are grading (by means of the rubric) should be worth grading, not focusing on trivia.
+ The weighting should be proper (see next page).

Developing your own rubric

1. Decide on which areas of an assignment you want to assess students (for example, for a presentation, clarity of expression, content, flow).
2. Decide what shows mastery, what is acceptable, what is less than satisfactory, what is poor, and what should receive no credit.
3. Make sure the language is positive, even at the beginning levels, so that students can think about themselves and their work in positive terms.
4. Review for clarity, specificity, and thoroughness.
5. Check for importance of different factors you have included.

The importance of proper weighting

The biggest problem with rubrics can be a very serious one—the improper weighting of collective scores. We have seen many poorly designed rubrics. For example, here is a rubric designed by an administrator who imposed a science research paper on seventh- and eighth-grade students.

Science Research Paper Rubric
Paper Due:

Traits	5	4	3	2	1
References Cited	Has seven or more references	Has six references	Has five references	Has three to four references	Has one to two references
Length of Paper	Has more than seven pages.	Has six to seven pages	Has more than four pages but less than six	Has three to four pages	Has two pages or less—maybe it is just a long paragraph?
Format of Paper	The finished paper is word processed and could be published in a Science journal it looks so good!	The finished paper is word processed and formatted correctly.	The finished paper looks somewhat like the example and is word processed.	The finished paper is not word processed and the format is somewhat correct.	Can't tell if the paper is done.
Conventions	Wow! There are **no** spelling errors and **no** grammar errors!	Oops! Found an error!	Hey! There are less than 3 spelling errors and less than 3 grammar errors but more than one.	Looks pretty good but there are 3 – 5 spelling and grammar errors	Not sure if the spellcheck feature works (6 or more errors in spelling and in grammar.).
Sentence Fluency	All sentences are complete and easy to understand. They are masterpieces!	Really good but still needs a little work in sentence fluency.	A few sentences are fragments or run-ons.	The paper is a little disjointed and doesn't flow smoothly.	It's hard to tell where one thought begins and another one starts!
Content and Ideas	The paper is extremely clear and focused. Accurate, precise details are used to support the main topics, resources are cited for credible support.	The writer has defined the topic, more than half the time the details and support are clear and relevant, 1 or 2 resources are cited as credible support	The writer has defined the topic but development is basic or general, support is attempted but not very supportive, ideas are clear but not detailed or always supported.	The paper hints at the topic, support is incidental or confusing, no real details are there, the content is pretty broad.	The paper might not even be a science paper! Looks like the writer is still looking for a topic and doing some brainstorming

Students need to be taught how to use rubrics for feedback purposes. Teachers should use the writing process and the rubric to continue to give students feedback until the student's research paper is successfully done. All students should be able to succeed!

* Seventh and Eighth Grade*

Figure 6.7
An example of a poor rubric, for a science research paper

The problem is that the rubric weighted everything equally. But neither the number of sources for the paper used nor its length (number of pages) is anywhere near as important as the content of the paper or how well it was organized.

On the following page is another rubric. Appearance (dress) and adherence to time limits are weighted equally with content. This is nonsense.

Students will be evaluated on	Possible points	Points earned
Content	2	
Organization/structure	2	
Style/presentation/appearance (dress)	2	
Use of visual aids	2	
Adherence to time limits	2	
Total points	10	

Figure 6.8 Rubric

It is very important to think through which characteristics of quality you consider to be the most important.

Anecdotes

Anecdotes are focused narratives. They are both a method of observing and a means of keeping records of ongoing incidents involving the learner. According to Cohen and Stern (1970), anecdotal records can help you do three things.

1. Test hunches about reasons for a student's behavior or learning style
2. Identify what conditions may be reinforcing behavior
3. Gain feedback about what students have learned from a particular lesson or presentation

Advantages of anecdotes

- They include the context and the richness that checklists lack.
- They provide an efficient method of collecting what you deem to be pertinent.
- Over time, they can reveal changes, patterns of behavior, growth, progress, improvement.
- They can function as ammunition if you have a student whose behavior is consistently inappropriate. If you have documented, in detail and over time, the student's behavior (and your attempted interventions) and how it has negatively impacted classroom dynamics, learning, and other students' behavior, you can use the anecdotes as leverage for change. Simply complaining without documentation will get you nowhere.
- Although using anecdotes for all students can be impractical (particularly at the secondary level when a teacher may have a hundred or more students), they are useful with individual students who need special attention and observation.

Joe, 17, was a student whose social skills were as limited as his English. While waiting to see the counselor, he sat in the only available chair, leaving his elderly mother to stand. He sat too close to his classmates, and they disliked him intensely. He constantly needed rides because he would not take the bus alone. Once, when in a teacher's car, he shouted obscenities out the window at several of his classmates. He sometimes appeared only twice a week for classes and often seemed under the influence of drugs. No amount of counseling seemed to change or improve his attitude—until a chance remark by his mother revealed that the family was in this country so that Joe could escape mandatory military service. After talking with his mother about the conditions of their visas, the counselor was able to reassure Joe that he did not have to return to his country. This improved his attitude and proficiency remarkably.

Anecdotes were useful for tracking Joe's enhanced behavior. In response to a request from the counselor, Joe's teacher kept a log and made the following observations:

> *February 15, History, first hour*
> Joe appeared. He had bathed. He smiled and said hello. He sat at his desk, moving it close to Sonia. When asked to move his seat back, he did.

> *February 22, History, first hour*
> Observed working in pairs on activity on Bronze Age. Found some information in books. First time he revealed he could read or extract information from a text.

> *February 28, History, first hour*
> Joe brought in a book from his country that showed actual artifacts found of Bronze Age tools. He managed to explain some pictures, and beamed when several students asked questions.

Disadvantages of anecdotes

The disadvantages of using anecdotes to record observations have more to do with the logistics and the skill it takes to record usable information than with the concept itself.

- It takes persistence and practice to make them concise enough so that you do not get bogged down.
- It takes practice to include information that will be telling and revealing to you or to another stakeholder days or weeks after an event happened.
- It takes thought in order to see and perceive which behaviors are salient to what is happening in the student.
- You have to organize your classroom so that you have time to stand back, watch, and record while students are working independently.
- Trying to record anecdotes for every student can be overwhelming if you do not make the process efficient.
- They tend to lose their practicality at the secondary level. If you teach over a hundred students a day, finding time to fit anecdotes into your day can be prohibitive.

Developing a structure for recording anecdotes

1. Establish a system. One method that works for many teachers is to divide a large sheet of paper into small squares, affix the sheet to a clipboard, and jot down comments about an individual student in each square. You can also use a sheet of sticky address labels, one label for each student. Post-it notes are another useful alternative.

2. Write down an anecdote about your observation as soon as possible after it occurs.

3. Describe an event as explicitly as possible.

4. Identify the basic action(s) and what was said, and include the response or reactions of other people.

5. Include setting, time of day, and context within which the event or interaction took place.

6. Report with objective language rather than evaluate with value-laden language. Instead of writing, "His behavior was intolerable," write, "While the other students were working on their group skits, James took a bottle of Elmer's glue and dumped it onto the rug. As he went out the door when the bell rang, he emptied the shavings from the pencil sharpener onto it." Transcribe the anecdote from the paper or label into a more permanent record at a later time.

Anecdotes about reading

Anecdotes about the process of reading can demonstrate how a reader has progressed over time. The following transcript shows a tutor's notes about a thirteen year old who was reading at a second-grade level:

> **Student Name: Choua**
>
> *October 6*
> **Material:** *The Alphabet Book*
> Read aloud a Richard Scarry book to Choua. Choua enjoyed listening to the story, and smiled and laughed at Scarry's humorous pictures. We discussed various animals. When asked, "Which ones have you seen?" she was able to answer with farm animal names such as *chickens, cows, horses,* as well as *mice, dogs, cats.* "Do animals really wear clothes?" Choua laughed and said no very loudly. Her spoken vocabulary is good, and she can understand much better than she can read.
>
> *October 8*
> **Material:** *Birds Fly, Bears Don't*
> I read the story aloud first. Then Choua read the story. She read as fast as she could and as quietly as possible. When asked to retell the story, she couldn't. I read her each paragraph at a normal pace, pausing to explain words or point to pictures to help her understand. When the story was finished, Choua was able to answer questions and retell story.

October 18

Material: *Birds Fly, Bears Don't*

I read the story aloud, and Choua chimed in on words she knew. When, again, she read on her own, she rushed through without pausing and had a hard time retelling what she had read. I read it aloud to her again, then we choral read the story a second time. I deliberately slowed down so she could hear the cadences and process the phrases. Then we talked about the words she didn't understand or couldn't read. When she read it aloud on her own, she didn't stumble.

October 21

Material: *Clifford at the Circus*

Choua encountered some new words like *didn't, wasn't,* and *I'm* that were hard for her to understand or sound out. Her strategy for the contractions was to ignore the meaning. I suspect this is because she doesn't know why they were there or what they mean. After we discussed that a contraction is really two words put together and specifically which words were put together, she began saying the endings and understood them.

November 22

Material: *Birds Fly, Bears Don't*

I'm noticing a large difference in her reading. She doesn't rush through words that she doesn't know. She has slowed down quite a bit, reading in a more measured and fluent way, phrase to phrase, not word to word, speeding up and jumbling words together when she isn't sure. We still go over it together after she reads, to make sure she understands it.

November 27

Material: *The Foot Book*

We read this story the same way, me first, then her. She read very easily. She's made a lot of progress.

December 10

Material: *Birds Fly, Bear's Don't*

Choua again read from *Bird's Fly, Bear's Don't*. She likes this story and chooses it with a smile. She likes to read all of the pages now, so I don't trade with her. She is getting better at understanding, but still often speeds through, slurring the words she doesn't know. I thought we had this story down, but sometimes she goes back to the same old strategies. I think we're going to keep coming back to this story, and read it together until she's got it almost from memory.

Anecdotes about writing

Steve was a small boy enrolled in an extended-day kindergarten. He had been born in the United States to preliterate parents and into a home with no books, pencils, or crayons. He seemed to make no connection between print and meaning, and showed no interest in pencil-and-paper tasks. In February, the teacher noticed he was showing an interest in writing. These are her notes:

February 12

The children were cutting out and coloring valentines. Steve picked out a red crayon and, holding the crayon clumsily, laboriously colored a heart.

February 21

Steve has continued to show interest in coloring. Today he drew, for the first time, a face that looked like a face, with eyes and a mouth.

March 3

Steve held the pen correctly for the first time.

March 8

Steve wrote his name.

March 10

Steve likes to make shapes with pipe cleaners. He then asks what that letter is and what animal begins with that sound.

Figure 6.9 An early drawing of Steve's. Squiggles at top and middle right are the combination of "letters" he consistently uses to represent his name, even though the *s* is the only letter present in his name.

April 3

Steve goes to the wall where there are simple faces showing all the emotions, looks at one carefully, and returns to his desk to draw it from memory. It is very accurate.

Sometimes, just snippets written in your notebook become revealing over a period of time. For example:

Carmen was looking under the letter *J* in her dictionary to figure out how to spell *dress*.

and

Bao asked, "How do you spell *apana*, with an *a* or an *o*?" When the teacher looked puzzled, she continued, "Like once apana time."

Conferences

Another way of learning about your students is to sit down, talk to, and listen to them. Florio-Ruane (1990) advises that interviews should never be the sole source of information because people—especially second-language learners—cannot or will not always tell you all that they know. They might tell you what they think you want to hear. Often students, especially middle-schoolers, will try to fake it. If you can find answers to questions by a method other than an interview, do so; save the interview for finding out thoughts, feelings, memories, values—things you cannot ordinarily see or pick up by just listening or through casual conversation. Burke (1992) suggests using interviews and conferences to collect feedback and reactions to

+ books

+ students' work (projects, research papers, scientific experiments, pieces of writing)

+ films or videos

+ field trips

+ assemblies or guest speakers

You can also conduct interviews with individuals to

+ check for fluency and grammar

+ review portfolios

+ discuss grades

+ check for comprehension

Conferences can either be short and informal—carried on throughout the day or the class period as you move through the classroom, or more formal—a set time is allotted for the student to meet with you about a specific agenda or a set of questions. At the secondary level, you can use the time when students are doing assigned work. Some teachers assign Sustained Silent Reading for part of the class a few times a week in order to meet with individual students. Keep a folder with all students' names and a space for recording details of a simple conference in order to practically and easily work your way down the class list, a few students at a time.

Conferencing is more than simply sitting down and talking with a student. As Johnston (1992) points out:

> *If an interview is to provide useful information, it is important for the student to do most of the talking. This seems reasonably obvious, but in my experience teachers...often have the greatest difficulty keeping quiet...In general, the more you listen, the more you learn (and often the more the student learns about himself). If the dialogue sounds stilted, like a test, then it probably was a test, and any information gained will be about as useful as if it had been gathered on a test.*

His advice is to "strive for opening the mind and closing the mouth."

Advantages of conferences

+ You can gather information that you sometimes cannot find any other way.

+ ESL students, in particular, are often more verbal speaking than they are writing. With a considerate and supportive audience, they can often reveal what they know better than they could with paper and pencil.

+ They can give you insight into a student's awareness of their strategies and why they do things the way they do. For instance, Annie was writing and illustrating a report on Paul Bunyan, but abandoned it midway. When asked why, her answer was simple: she could not draw an ox.

+ Rather than simply finding a blank answer on a questionnaire, you can see where and when comprehension of a question breaks down and intervene.

Disadvantages of conferences

+ The logistics to finding the time to sit down and talk with each student can be tough, particularly at the secondary level and especially if you have thirty others with a tendency to horse around when you are not looking.

+ Unless students are comfortable and trained in the process, they may dismiss it or clam up.

+ Students may feed you what they think you want to hear rather than give honest answers. Or, they may read into a question something other than what you intended.

Developing a system for conferencing with students

1. Select a time when other students are occupied in a self-guided project and do not need your help or attention.

2. Establish rules with the classroom so that quiet discussions can take place. If students are constantly interrupting, then you cannot devote your attention to the student with whom you are conferencing; your thoughts, your concentration, and the interview will be disrupted and disjointed.

3. Do not ask questions to which you already know the answers or to which the answers are available from tests or your grade book. Ask open-ended questions about what the student thinks, what his interpretation means, and why.

4. Strive to balance the power differences between yourself and the student so that you are not the knower or the keeper of all the knowledge. Let the student be the expert.

5. Keep it short.

Booth Olson (2007) gives some pointers, too.

+ Do not ask yes-or-no, one-word, or fill-in-the-blank questions. Instead, ask open-ended questions, beginning with words or phrases such as *why*, *how*, or *to what extent*.

+ Practice wait-time so your students have an opportunity to generate thoughtful responses.

+ Respond as a fellow learner rather than as an inquisitor.

+ Practice accepting responses like, "that's a thought," "I understand," and, possibly, "I felt that way, too."

+ Ask for clarification. Research shows that clarifying helps contribute to students' development of their own metacognition.

Writing conferences

Although written work is essentially a product, you can gain insight into a learner's writing process by questioning him. A writing conference is one of the most effective tools you can use to help improve writing skills for both students who are fluent in English and for those who are not.

There are two kinds of writing conferences: those that take place while the student is writing, and those that occur after the first draft, to help with the revision process. For the latter, keep the conference focused: do not overwhelm the student with too many things to revise. Concentrate on one or two important points, and work on those. For writing-in-progress conferences, Nancie Atwell (1998) suggests circulating quietly among writers at work and asking them how it is going, giving them feedback, and listening. She advises to keep these conferences short, too—not more than a minute or two. Ask a writer to tell you about his piece. Longer conferences that involve trouble-shooting an entire piece at a time can lead to a student becoming dependent on you to solve his problems rather than learning to solve them on his own.

Developing a system for conducting a writing conference with students

1. Sit next to the writer, and let him hold his own writing.

2. Read as a reader—someone who is genuinely interested and wants to know more—not as a judge.

3. Begin by referring to a major strength of the writing. Focus on the positive: "I can tell you did a lot of research," or "You have a strong thesis statement."

4. Build on what the student has done, finding things to commend. Do not dampen his enthusiasm or crush an already shaky ego by finding fault.

5. Resist making vague judgments such as, "This is good." Give specific feedback on parts that are particularly effective. For instance, when Freddy writes, "It was like standing under a waterfall," point out that the image really helped you see what he was trying to convey.

6. Ask questions such as (Reid, 1993)

   How did you choose this topic?

   What is this writing piece about?

   Who is your intended audience?

   If you were to add information here, how would you do it?

   How do you feel about your writing so far?

   What do you like best about your writing?

7. Focus on the writer, and give him responsibility for making decisions. Reid (1993) cautions that students who are in most need of help are often the least successful at getting it, because they are unable to take charge and negotiate meaning. In countries where the belief is that the teacher is "master," teaching means telling students what to do. Training beginning authors, especially ESL students, to think for themselves and to have confidence to take authorial control takes a great deal of time and effort.

Here is an interview Mary had with Enrique halfway through the school year:

Mary: How are your assignments going so far this year?

Enrique: **Well, this year is a little better than last year. I feel like I know what I'm supposed to do.**

Mary: You are working on an assignment about the hero's journey. How is that going?

Enrique: **This paper is easier for me because I don't have to look for information. I understand this one the best of all the other papers we did. I know the ideas we talk about in class. I like better writing about things I already know about like basketball. I know this a lot because I play it everyday. I don't have to think for so long about what to write, so I don't get stuck.**

Mary: What things are difficult for you when you have to do a written assignment?

Enrique: **I don't like to write about history. The textbook is too hard and I don't always understand what they want me to write about. I just sit there and look at my paper. I hate punctuation stuff. I don't understand the quotations, where to put them, and when to stop putting them. I sometimes get confused about question marks. I also hate spelling. I try to sound out the words, but I either misplace the letters or I don't put them in right. I try spell check, but sometimes I don't know which word to choose.**

Mary: Can you see where you are improving?

Enrique: **I can write longer than I used to. My ideas are getting a little better and I am learning about brainstorming to get more ideas to put in the paper. That helps a little. I just want to get better grades. So I will keep trying.**

Sometimes, it is difficult to figure out what a beginning writer is trying to say in his writing. Simply asking him to read his writing aloud reveals his thoughts or even his logic. For instance, kindergartner Alexi was writing a book about the sense of touch. He pasted a paper doily onto the page and then dictated, "It feels like paint." Mystified, the teacher asked what he meant. He reached out and ran his fingers down the bumpy, textured wall. "Like paint," he repeated. Then he pasted a cotton ball onto the page. "It feels gloopy." "Oh yeah?" asked the teacher carefully (if dubiously.) "Yeah, gloopy, sloopy, loopy." She realized Alexi was fed up with thinking hard and was just playing around with sounds.

CONCLUSION

When recording your observations of what and how well a student is doing, traditional checkmark or letter-grade systems are not very revealing, especially in the upper grades when you have several classes and many students. There are, however, many other ways of recording your observations of a student's performance. One of the most important aspects of each of the four methods we discussed is the process of deciding what to look for, what is important to find out about each student. The clarity in values and priorities that often goes hand-in-hand with the creation and completion of any of these observation-recording tools can be as worthwhile as the checklists, rubrics, anecdotes, and conferences.

EXITING

Franco was bored. He had been faking it in his sheltered English class, pretending he did not understand and could do much less than he really could so that he would not have to work very hard. Then he started acting up because the material was too easy. The other students were functioning at a much lower level than he was, and he could breeze through assignments in a third of the time. This left him with plenty of opportunity to make the teacher's life miserable by pestering the other students, talking out of turn, and distracting everybody.

Perhaps it was time to exit Franco from the sheltered program into the mainstream. Franco was much more advanced than the rest of his peers and had been successfully mainstreamed for gym and geometry. His ESL teacher knew he would be able to comprehend most of the material in the content classes. But was he really ready? Could he make the leap from what was required in his sheltered classes to what regular teachers demand of their students?

What's in this Chapter

+ A definition of full English proficiency

+ How to determine when a student no longer needs second-language programs

+ Criteria for exiting students

On the following page is Franco's grade-eleven presentation on Thai architecture. It had clearly been cut and pasted from the Internet.

> In Thailand, scholars and laymen alike, consider architecture to be one, if not the most important of all the arts. Thai architecture is a blend of different influences, styles and methods. Down the ages, these have been adapted and improved upon by various cultures and kingdoms, and as a result, Thai architectural style is both unique and very memorable.

This strategy—copying straight from the Internet on the assumption that the information he found had no errors—worked for him, temporarily. Franco's writing gave the impression that he was a level 5 and was proficient enough to be considered for exiting. But all it really demonstrated was his ability to manipulate the system—at least for a short time. The strategy backfired when he was given a writing prompt but no access to a computer.

> I'm living America now but there are some problems such as food, weather, friend, noise…etc. Basicly, this town isn't really comfortable place to live. So what or where is the best living area.
>
> First, nobody doesn't want too cold. If I were around north pole, I couldn't stay one month. Second, nobody want too hote like a place where is frequently over 150. Third, nobody want too rainy or snowy.
>
> Thus, there are many conditions we can list. However, there are many people live in place where is so difficult to live. In fact, some people live around north pole, On the other hand, some live in Sahara desert. In spite of both of those are very hard place to live and they are living. Therefore actually the living area has different and it must have own advantage such as food, future. Thus it is not important that lank those luct the importance might be to adapt those circumstance.

"This is unacceptable," announced the English teacher when she and Franco's ESL teacher reviewed the writing together. "I wouldn't accept this from a third grader."

Franco was not ready to be exited. If the ESL teacher had relied on his phoney homework assignment and his oral proficiency, he might have been able to fake it for a while longer—but he would not have been able to keep his head above water in a mainstream English class.

Ready or Not?

Knowing when a student no longer needs services and is ready for the mainstream is difficult and, for many teachers, the decision is fraught with anxiety. Can your student function without help in a classroom with peers who have spoken English all their lives?

It is easy to say a student can be exited when he has achieved a level 5 in English proficiency: when he can understand and speak both conversational and academic English well, and is near proficiency in reading, writing, and the content area skills expected at his grade level.

It is also easy to say, it depends. And it *does* depend. Your student might be very fluent in spoken English and capable of handling himself well in math, science, and other courses. But he might still need monitoring. He may continue to need help with background information. And he will likely write with a "foreign accent" (clear traces of his native language in syntax and word choices) for a great deal of his career, if not always, which may or may not bother teachers.

DEFINING FULLY ENGLISH PROFICIENT (FEP)

We defined *proficiency* in chapter 3. Now, we need to ask, what does it mean to be proficient enough to be on a par with classmates whose primary language is English? It has been a long and slow uphill climb for educators and administrators to recognize that it takes more than oral fluency to succeed in the regular classroom.

The Council of Chief State School Officers (CCSSO), an independent organization of public officials in the United States, which provides leadership, advocacy, and technical assistance on major educational issues, proposed the following definition for fully-English proficient (1992):

> *A fully English-proficient (FEP) student is able to use English to ask questions, to understand teachers and reading materials, to test ideas, and to challenge what is being asked in the classroom. Four language skills contribute to proficiency, as follows:*
>
> + *Reading: the ability to comprehend and interpret text at the age- and grade-appropriate level.*
>
> + *Listening: The ability to understand the language of the teacher and instruction, comprehend and extract information, and follow the instructional discourse through which teachers provide information.*
>
> + *Writing: the ability to produce written text with content and format, fulfilling classroom assignments at the age- and grade-appropriate level.*
>
> + *Speaking: the ability to use oral language appropriately and effectively in learning activities (such as peer tutoring, collaborative learning activities and question/answer sessions) within the classroom and in social interactions within the school.*

This seems fairly straightforward, but it is actually more complicated than it appears, for several reasons.

+ Linquanti (2001) states that, "part of the difficulty in defining 'proficient' lies in specifying *for what purposes*, since, to a great extent, language performance must be considered in the context of the particular language tasks to be performed, the subject matter or topic, the audience or interlocutors…and the setting (Bachman et al., 1998)." In the context of the school experience, a student might use language to clarify, to investigate, to justify, or to elaborate, depending on the subject or task. These functions are much more complex and sophisticated than simply holding a conversation with a peer, or even a teacher.

- Functioning and succeeding in the mainstream is not just an academic issue, but also a social and a linguistic issue. Patricia Duff (2001) wrote that "to become fully integrated into the mainstream curriculum, these newcomers must learn to adapt to the linguistic, sociocultural, discursive, and academic norms and practices in content areas." She examined the lives of secondary ESL students who were struggling to adapt to mainstream content classes in a Canadian school. Duff concluded that many of these students were marginalized because, although they were deemed proficient, they had not acquired the more subtle nuances of the language that would allow them to function smoothly in the mainstream.

- Acquisition is uneven. A student may function well in math and lag in English and social studies.

- Age and grade appropriateness are not clearly defined. Is proficiency measured against the best student, the most average student, or the one who is barely keeping his head above water?

We would rather err on the side of conservative, holding a student longer than maybe we should, rather than pushing him to compete in a mainstream classroom, because:

- Even though he may be fluent in English, a student may exit an ESL program with inadequate general knowledge and background vocabulary. He may then "flounder... expending much effort with little gain because the language level of the coursework is so far beyond [him] that [he] can understand little and cannot use bilingual materials to help [himself]" (Dufrensne, 1993).

- A student may pass mainstream content classes without truly understanding the material and may then be unprepared to deal with more difficult academic or work-related tasks.

- A student may become jaded or disaffected due to continual frustration. This could eventually lead him to drop out—and become a prime candidate for various social problems (gangs, substance abuse, and so on).

- Mainstream teachers can become frustrated with the taxing effort of communicating with the student and the additional work it entails. They may then end up either ignoring the ESL student or spending an excess of time with him in remediation, thereby spending less time with mainstream students.

- Students who are exited too early often either struggle in classes that are over their heads or stagnate in ones that have little academic substance.

GUIDELINES FOR EXITING DECISIONS

Exiting decisions should never be the job of one person, but, rather, the job of a team of teachers. The decision should be based on a number of factors; some districts have "trigger criteria." You may be mandated to test ESL students each year or each semester; eventually, your students may reach a level on the test at which they are no longer eligible for services.

When deciding whether or not a student is ready to be exited, you need to ask, what knowledge, skills and attitudes does this student need to succeed in, for example, grade nine? Does his work look like that of a typical ninth grader? If not, it is best to reconsider.

Here are more questions to ask yourself when you are considering exiting a student (adapted from Hargett, 1998):

- Can the student participate in the oral language of a mainstream classroom?
  The tasks you assign for assessing this must simulate the oral language of a mainstream classroom.

- Can the student read and write English at levels similar to his or her mainstream grade mates? What are the grade-level expectations?
  The tasks you assign to make your judgment should require the student to read and write something at that level.

- What specific aspects of English does the student still lack?
  The tasks on which you base your assessment should pinpoint specific areas, such as vocabulary, background knowledge, and so on.

We examine each of these questions in more detail through specific examples.

Can my student participate in the oral language of a mainstream classroom?

Paul's oral comprehension seemed to be on par with his peers. However, the mainstream class into which he was moved presented severe problems. Paul's sixth-grade science teacher used the lecture method exclusively. He wrote an outline on the board and expected students to copy it and then take notes based on the lecture. Although Paul had learned the same content as the other students and he knew the material, he could not keep up with either the pace or the format of the lectures. He began to flounder. In order for Paul to succeed in that classroom, he needed to be part of a study group, he needed a buddy with whom to compare notes, and, perhaps, he needed to audio-record class lectures. Alternatively, he needed to be moved into a different class where the teacher used more hands-on teaching methods.

Can my student read and write English at levels similar to his mainstream grade-mates?

Guillermo was funny, friendly, and frustrated in the ESL classroom. His oral proficiency was high, and he was convinced that he could function in the mainstream class. But here is an example of his writing:

> Stereotypes
>
> Stereotypes are usually to description person, object, but not really true. In my life, I met many people like be always the best, is natural best, in my opinion sometimes is not true because I prefert be a good student or excellent worker but not tell something if not true.
>
> Example: I am the best students at the school. (it's not true) Because some people are more intelligent then me.

Guillermo's grammar was rudimentary. Although his comprehension of the issues was in place, his control of English structure was not sufficient for him to navigate the demands of a high-school English class without substantial support, intervention, and accommodations. He was not ready to be exited.

On the other hand, Wai Yan wrote:

> Some people I met, when they know I'm a Chinese then they'll ask, "Do you eat cats or dogs?" Of course, I don't feel good being ask a question like that. Many people have the impression that Chinese people eat cats or dogs. But not EVERY Chinese. Yeah, I'm pretty sure there's some parts of China where you can find people eat cats, but NOT everywhere in China and not everyone.

His writing was fluent, even colloquial. His sentences were complex and correct. Wai Yan could write on a topic in depth and with ease.

What specific aspects of English does my student still lack?

Edward and Mike were both mainstreamed for most of their classes without assistance or modifications to assignments. They were given the following question in their English class to provoke thought prior to reading *To Kill a Mockingbird*: Is prejudice universal? Edward was from Azerbaijan. He wrote:

> Yes, it is. Because I think that the main idea is a nationalixm. White hate black and black hate white. You will ask: but why it is universal? Because nationalixm is one of the global problems in our days. This problem existed always and it continue it's existence. And here I righted about nationalism is a global problem. And global—this is a key work. Global means belonging to everybody to all contryes, to all the world. Yes, it exist in Russia to! I am a victim to! In my country there is a big nationalism. There is an oppression.... Some "white" Russians who came from Belarus or Ukraine hait me and they say somethink like: "Oh, you came here from your south coutry what are you doing here?" And I can't tell nothink because some poeople do not believe me that I am a real Russian. Sometimes I sad somethink like this:
>
> 'Let do not talk about this." Some times I laffing at this people inside, but engrary it herts and is hert's realy strong. And after every this even I fill so bed, I don't fill me a ful person.

Mike was Russian but had grown up in Sweden. He wrote:

> Prejudice is something that exists everywhere. There are two types of prejudice I think. One is the prejudice that is dictated by the society. Not everyone agrees on that. The second type is personal prejudice. This type forms in an individual's consciousness as a consequence of that person's experiences or points of view. In Sweden the biggest prejudice is against people from abroad. That's because this country lived as a closed society for years. They got used to their own people and they sometimes don't

accept anyone else. They have a hard time adjusting to somebody with different habits, language and religion. They call these people "svartskalle"— that means "blackhead.

Both boys could write at a level similar to their peers. Both clearly understood the question and were able write at length and stay on topic. Their sentences were complex, their writing clear and cogent. Edward's writing contained more grammatical errors than Mike's, and he needed more time to consolidate his skills, with assistance in grammar. Keeping him in sheltered classes on the basis of his productive capacities would not help him to move forward. Mike was able to hold his own. *BUT*

However, both boys needed a great deal of help getting through *To Kill a Mockingbird*, particularly with the cultural and historical background including: the dialect, the background of the South, the legacy of the Civil War, and the American judicial system. They did not know how a jury functions. They did not know that only those who could read and write and who owned land were allowed to vote, or that women did not serve on juries. They missed the significance of several key turning points, such as the tense scene between Atticus and Mr. Cunningham on the steps of the courthouse. Much of the dialogue went straight over their heads. They could not be turned loose to read and discuss the book on their own.

In another example, students were instructed to write about the past semester using certain forms designed to elicit their knowledge of English grammar. Kazuhiko wrote:

> *I should have…***a more English.**
> *One of the main things I did…***good job.**
> *I could have…***sandwich more.**
> *I need to…***soft drink.**

Kazu clearly needed to work more on his grammar forms.

Yong Min had learned more. He wrote:

> *I learned…***way to live in America.**
> *I should have…***some money.**
> *When I…***came here, first time, I don't know anything.**
> *I could have…***saved many time, If I study hard.**
> *It's important to…***study hard, because past time doesn't come again.**
> *I used to…***play vidio games…but now I…go to a gym.**

Yong Min was on his way to mastery of the forms. He still made mistakes, but these were errors in the intricacies of the forms, not in his comprehension of what they meant.

Odette wrote:

> *I have had…***trouble with English.**
> *I used to…***speak English badly…but now I…speak well.**
> *It's important to…***learne English because it's my second language.**

Odette's mastery of grammar was much higher. She made few mistakes, primarily spelling errors.

It is important to note, again, that this test is but one of the many areas from which you should collect information about a student's capacity. It would be remiss to assume that a simple test like this one could offer enough information about whether or not a student could function without assistance.

Not an Either/Or Issue

The issue of exiting is somewhat easier to handle if we stop thinking of it as an either/or situation. We must perceive the process not as a withdrawal of support but, rather, as a gradual increase of skills that allows a student to function on his own. The Council of Chief State School Officers' Advisory Committee (1992) states that "services for LEP students should represent a continuum of appropriate programs, not be dichotomous (i.e., provided or not based on entry or exit requirements)."

We understand all too well that too many students reach an intermediate level and are left on their own simply because there are too many needy students at the lower levels and not enough time. But whenever possible, it is so important to thoughtfully consider the options for exiting students and not simply releasing them because of budget, time, and space constraints. Students need the opportunity to work their way naturally through, and out of, the support system you have built.

Making the Decision Based on Multiple Indicators

To successfully make the decision about whether or not to exit a student, you need to assess a variety of skills and abilities. Here, we show how two third graders were evaluated in order to determine if they could function alone in a mainstream classroom:

Pana had entered kindergarten preliterate and speaking no English. There was no bilingual Hmong program, so she received ESL pull-out help. Nara received bilingual instruction in Spanish and English. The school suddenly received an influx of African refugees. With more students than Cheri, the ESL teacher, could manage, she was under pressure to completely mainstream the more proficient students.

Oral proficiency

Both Pana and Nara were lively, talkative, and verbally proficient, neither one with any trace of an accent. They had both been coming to ESL for extra work in reading. Cheri and Sara, the mainstream teacher, compared notes on a number of students, including these two.

The performance definitions for the TESOL *English Language Proficiency Standards for K-12 Schools* state that at the given level, the English-language learner must be able to process, understand, produce, or use

+ the technical language of the content areas

+ a variety of sentence lengths of varying linguistic complexity in extended oral or written discourse, including stories, essays, or reports

- oral or written language approaching similarity to that of proficient English peers when presented with grade level material

In November, the class studied chemical reactions. Sara gave oral instructions very slowly and clearly, waiting for students to accomplish each step before moving to the next. Both girls were able to follow the instructions, could predict the results, and could provide oral and written rationales for their predictions. Both girls could also interpret the results of the experiment they had conducted. And both could retell the "volcano incident," where Sara had added vinegar to baking soda and the mixture had erupted all over the desk and onto the floor.

Cheri and Sara concluded that both girls had achieved enough proficiency in oral English to function without help in the classroom.

Written proficiency

The traits of a level 5 writer include

- Growing independence in using writing for a wide range of purposes (expressive, informational, imaginative, and so on)

- Awareness of different audiences and beginnings of text shaping for a reader

- More consistent ability to punctuate texts for meaning

- In writing, increasing attention to visual patterns in spelling

Sara had kept nearly all of the girls' writing from the year. To the right and on the following page are letters written by each girl. Pana's letter (figure 7.1) shows her strong awareness of voice and audience. She uses a delightful conversational tone.

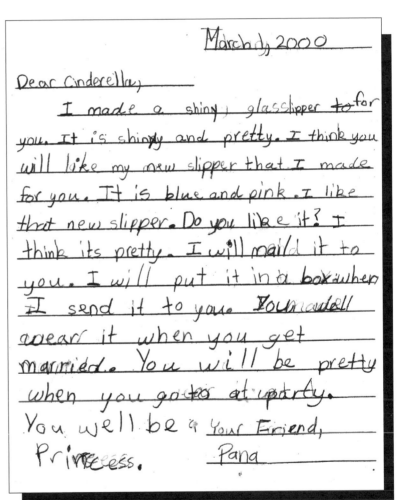

Figure 7.1 Pana's letter to Cinderella

189

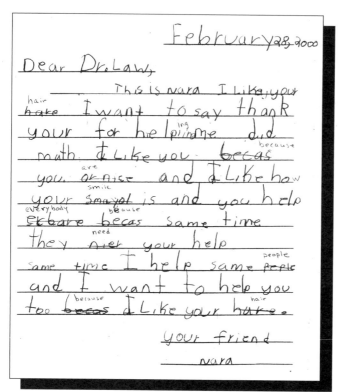

February 28, 2000

Dear Dr. Law,

     This is Nara I Like your

hair

~~hake~~ I want to say thank

              ing

your for hel piinme did

                      because

math. I like you. becas

    are

you. oknise and I Like how

       smile

your smayot is and you help

everybody   because

~~Ekbare~~ becas same time

    need

they niet your help

                   people

same time I help same pepte

and I want to help you

   because   hair

too ~~becas~~ I Like your hake.

            your friend

                nara

Figure 7.2 Nara's letter to Dr. Law

Nara's letter (figure 7.2) also shows her voice and awareness of audience. Her spelling is not as strong, and her penmanship demonstrates emergence, rather than mastery, of the demands of third-grade writing.

Reading proficiency

According to the Learning Record Assessment System™, a level 5 reader

- Is a capable reader who now approaches familiar texts with confidence but still needs support with unfamiliar materials
- Is beginning to draw inferences from books and stories
- Reads independently
- Chooses to read silently

Each girl was asked to choose a book to demonstrate her reading. Pana chose the picture book *Keep the Lamp Burning, Abbie.* She read the story aloud with little prompting and could retell what it was about, showing that she was not just calling out the words. She demonstrated that she was a strong reader, able to read confidently and independently from a text of her own choosing.

Nara read the picture book *Arthur's Birthday.* She was not as strong a reader. She could read for meaning, but she needed help with some of the words. She used the strategy of sounding out words but was not as strong with other strategies like predicting from context. She had not yet made the transition to silent reading.

Sara and Cheri were less confident of Nara's ability to function without assistance in the classroom than they were of Pana's ability, and, normally, they would have kept Nara longer.

But with seven new, level-1 third graders still adjusting to the classroom and to school, they were tempted to exit both girls. Because their energy and attention was required elsewhere, they decided to go against their instincts, and they did exit both girls.

This decision was put to the test when the third graders took a multiple-choice test about the solar system. The results were dismal. Only three second graders in the entire class, including Pana, achieved more than fifty percent. The highest score was seventy percent.

To review the test, Sara read the questions aloud to students. Now, most students did considerably better, and Sara could see where they had gone astray. For example, look at the following question:

What is the brightest light in the night sky?
a) The sun
b) Stars
c) The moon
d) The planets

Most students answered "The sun." When Sara pointed out the words "night sky," they were able to answer correctly. They also knew the answer to the question, "What is Venus?" and that the Big Dipper and the Little Dipper were constellations. They did know the concepts.

From this exercise, Cheri and Sara concluded that although Pana was on target, if not ahead of her grade with her reading, and Nara was gaining confidence, they still struggled with reading technical text. But they were not alone: the entire class needed instruction in this area.

Cheri and Sara concluded that both Pana and Nara were able to function in the classroom with oral language, writing, and general reading. However, they both needed continued assistance with reading in the content areas. Cheri rearranged her schedule so that she could continue to keep an eye on the two girls in case they started to flounder. It was not a solution about which they were completely confident, but they agreed to try it out for a while. In the end, both Pana and Nara did well in the classroom. Pana continued to be a stronger student than Nara, but both girls performed acceptably. Cheri and Sara were satisfied with the decision they had made.

Our second example begins with Mary, who worked as an ESL support teacher at an intermediate school, and Tong, a new sixth-grade student from Taiwan. Tong had tested NEP, and most of his responses to her questions on the first day were "yes," "no," and "I don't know." But within a year, Tong had made substantial progress. By seventh grade, he was functioning with some ESL support, and by grade eight, he was on his own.

Writing proficiency

On the next page is Tong's first writing sample from September of sixth grade. The assignment, called "The day I was born," was part of a large autobiography project. Tong was asked to write an essay that included information about the date and place of his birth, the town in which he was born, what was going on in the world when he was born, who was president, and so on.

Figure 7.3 Tong's first attempt at "The day I was born" assignment

From this writing, Mary learned that Tong knew English script, he could use capitals as well as lowercase letters, he could print in English, and he had a beginning vocabulary in English. He also got the gist of the assignment and could attempt basic answers to some of the questions. Mary also learned that writing at any length about multiple items was beyond Tong's abilities just yet. To succeed, he needed the assignment to be modified—broken down into workable pieces. His mainstream teacher, Anita, agreed that he could have the whole year to chip away at the project.

Tong worked on the second draft of his autobiography assignment in November. He was able to correct errors when Mary read the paper out loud to him.

By December, Tong had made enough progress to work independently. Although at first, he had been overwhelmed and he hated writing first drafts, as time passed, he could do shorter assignments with less direction.

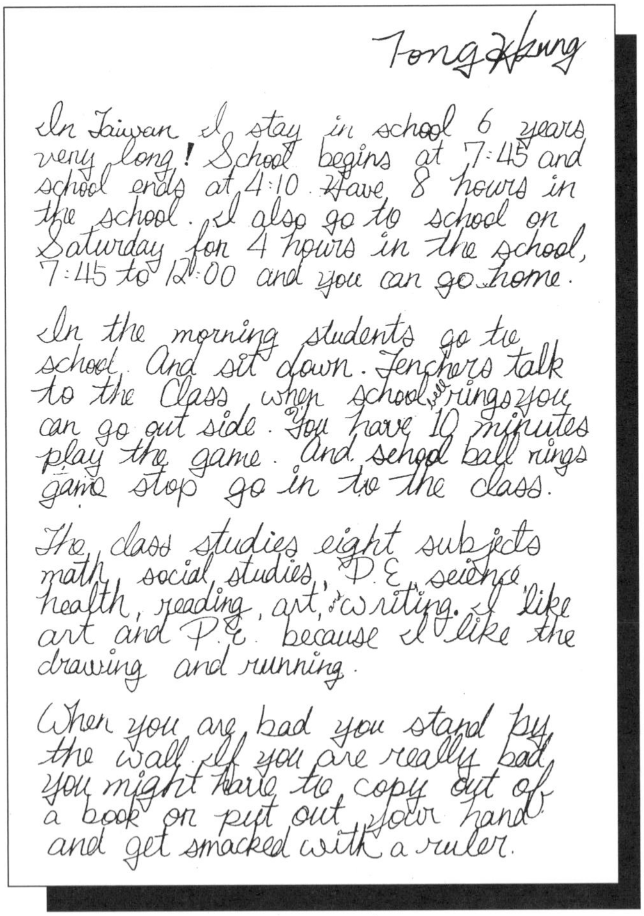

Tong Hung

In Taiwan I stay in school 6 years very long! School begins at 7:45 and school ends at 4:10. Have 8 hours in the school. I also go to school on Saturday for 4 hours in the school, 7:45 to 12:00 and you can go home.

In the morning students go to school. And sit down. Teachers talk to the class when school rings you can go out side. You have 10 minutes play the game. And school ball rings game stop go in to the class.

The class studies eight subjects math, social studies, P.E. science health, reading, art, writing. I like art and P.E. because I like the drawing and running.

When you are bad you stand by the wall. If you are really bad, you might have to copy out of a book on put out your hand and get smacked with a ruler.

Figure 7.4 Tong's second draft

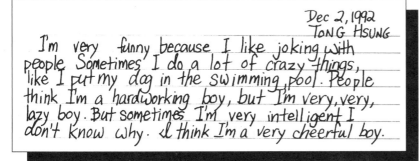

> Nov. 19, 1992
> Tong Hsung
>
> When I look in the mirror, I see a boy. The boy looks like average, thin, and young. The boy is twelve years old. The boy has black hair, black eyes, face like monkey and the boy has glasses. The boy's name is Tong Hsung.

> Dec 2, 1992
> TONG HSUNG
>
> I'm very funny because I like joking with people. Sometimes I do a lot of crazy things, like I put my dog in the swimming pool. People think I'm a hardworking boy, but I'm very, very, lazy boy. But sometimes I'm very intelligent I don't know why. I think I'm a very cheerful boy.

Figure 7.5 Tong wrote these at home with no help from Mary.

Tong did very well on the assignment despite its short length. He managed to communicate what he was like, even with limited English. This told Mary that he could work independently, and he had learned to function within the assignment constraints.

Reading proficiency

As Mary and Tong worked on assignments, she took an informal assessment of his reading skills. When he worked on his science assignments, she observed that he was very good at skimming for the answer. He wanted to fill in the blanks and complete the work as quickly as possible so he would not have to do it for homework. He would learn the target word to look for and then find the word in the text. Most of the time, he found the answer he needed. As Mary assessed Tong's oral reading abilities, she saw the same savvy strategies he used for speaking.

Oral proficiency

Tong's oral skills were better than his written and reading skills. He could communicate effectively with his peers about eating lunch together or playing basketball at break, and as Mary watched him flick the hats off of his friends' heads and laugh at them, she was sure he knew more than he was letting on.

By late February, Anita indicated that he was beginning to volunteer short answers in class. In March, he gave an oral report in class that he had prepared with Mary. He liked being with his friends and working on classroom activities, not being pulled out of class.

Mary and Anita decided Tong should remain in class for science and for all group activities; Mary pulled him out of class less frequently to help with the content that was less accessible, such as in social studies or with more complex science projects. He still needed help with writing assignments, not so much for comprehension but for vocabulary and structure. He was becoming more capable of editing his own work.

By late March, Tong was able to take most quizzes on his own and read texts independently with limited support. He could also skim for answers on open-book tests. Mary wanted him to be in the classroom more, but Anita, who was very structured and did not like deviations from her outlined approach to the lessons, was reluctant to have him full time. Unfortunately for Mary, but happily for Tong, Mary came down with pneumonia and was out for a month. As a result, Tong was placed in his classroom fulltime. By May, he only needed support for more complex tasks like end-of-unit tests or big essays that required planning.

Figure 7.6 shows Tong's rough draft of the last entry to his autobiography assignment. He completed this as a homework assignment, with no help from Mary. Notice that he used the English alphabet to write the names of Taiwan's president and vice president. He was also able to provide details about his own name, his favorite toy, and what Taiwan was like. He had come a long way.

Mary met with Anita and the school principal, and together they devised a plan for Tong's seventh-grade year. They decided to place him in a combined social studies/English class with Mary as push-in ESL support for those classes; he would also receive one period of individual pull-out support for help with homework and content work including content-specific vocabulary and background information.

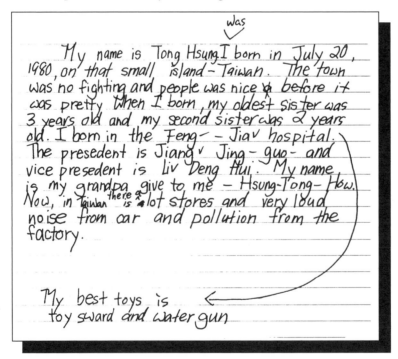

Figure 7.6 Tong's completed autobiography assignment shows real control.

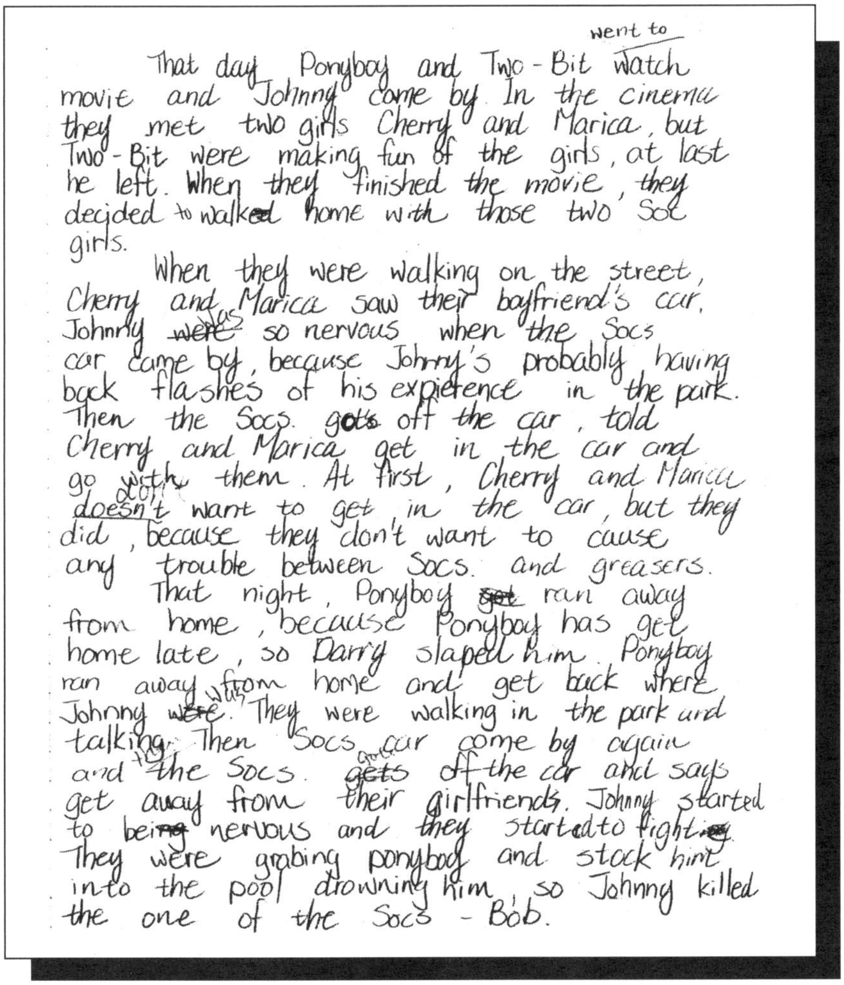

That day Ponyboy and Two-Bit went to watch movie and Johnny come by. In the cinema they met two girls Cherry and Marica, but Two-Bit were making fun of the girls, at last he left. When they finished the movie, they decided to walked home with those two Soc girls.

When they were walking on the street, Cherry and Marica saw their boyfriend's car. Johnny were as so nervous when the Socs car came by, because Johnny's probably having back flashes of his expierence in the park. Then the Socs. gots off the car, told Cherry and Marica get in the car and go with them. At first, Cherry and Marica doesn't want to get in the car, but they did, because they don't want to cause any trouble between Socs. and greasers.

That night, Ponyboy get ran away from home, because Ponyboy has get home late, so Darry slaped him. Ponyboy ran away from home and get back where Johnny were. They were walking in the park and talking. Then Socs car come by again and the Socs. gets of the car and says get away from their girlfriends. Johnny started to being nervous and they startedto fighting. They were grabing ponyboy and stock him into the pool drowning him, so Johnny killed the one of the Socs - Bob.

Figure 7.7 Tong's *The Outsiders* chapter summary

In seventh grade, Tong performed well in class and had little problem speaking to teachers or interacting with peers. He volunteered answers or asked questions when he needed to. He still required help with essay writing because he struggled with the format and with thesis statements. But as Tong became more familiar with the writing routine, Mary gave him less prompting and let him work on his own.

Mary also worked with Tong on expanding answers that were not just copied from a text. She tried to help him improve his text-reading skills and gave him practice in skimming for the main points. For a Beowulf assignment, Mary had Tong skim for the warrior's physical descriptions and heroic qualities. Then he had to answer questions requiring him to expand the information.

As the year progressed, Mary and Tong's routine focused on working with whatever novel the English class was studying. They developed Tong's essay-writing skills including writing thesis statements, support sentences, and conclusions. Above is a second draft of a summary he wrote for a chapter of S. E. Hinton's *The Outsiders*.

Mary could see that Tong understood the details of the chapter, which he had read on his own. His vocabulary had continued to expand, he was improving on providing details, and he could use transitions from one paragraph to another. He was having some problems with the more complex issues of past tense but, overall, his English continued to improve.

By May, Tong was studying for tests on his own with limited support from Mary. He still needed some help with essay writing, but he understood how to structure a good essay, and he had passed his writing competency for that year. Mary met with his teaching team and they reviewed his written work and his participation in class. They all felt he could manage fulltime in a regular class for grade eight. He would be continuing with the same English teacher and would have access to support should he struggle on any assignments. His independent nature and outgoing personality were strong indicators that he would have a good eighth-grade year.

Then What?

It is not enough to talk about exiting *from*; we also must discuss what students are exiting *to*. It is often advisable to exit a student in stages and not just "cold turkey" into a mainstream English-only classroom. Even level-5 students need continued support from bilingual or ESL teachers to fill in the gaps or to translate when the student has questions.

At the secondary level, if you have a sheltered or Specially Designed Academic Instruction in English (SDAIE) program, you can exit students course by course. Franco, for instance, was mainstreamed first in gym and geometry, then in science, then in history, and, finally, in English, with grammar support and coaching in the writing process. Again, we must reiterate that acquisition is uneven. Students may function well in math and lag in English and social studies. Exiting a student wholesale from ESL support is not in his best interests.

Post Exit

Exited students should continue to be monitored for two full years to ensure their success in the regular program, receiving language development and other types of support where needed. An important component of language assistance programs should be that students can be reclassified yet continue receiving (or resume receipt of) language development services, if needed, in the mainstream classroom.

CONCLUSION

Because of the many variables that influence success in the mainstream classroom, the complexity of what constitutes proficiency, and the vast differences between students, exiting should be approached cautiously. We disagree with the idea that test scores can determine eligibility for exit—that once a student attains a certain score, he can no longer receive language development support. Exiting should be a careful review on a case-by-case basis, with the opportunity to revise decisions remaining a viable option.

The Final Nail in the Coffee
GRADES

José and Anna were concerned and conscientious parents who wanted their daughter, Luisa, to succeed in school. They helped her with her schoolwork as best they could with their limited English. Luisa's report card, shown to the right, was a blow to them. Luisa, too, felt discouraged.

Luisa's parents had a lot of questions: How did Luisa's teacher, Mr. Mansfield, decide on these grades? What criteria did he use? Was Luisa being compared to her other English-speaking classmates? What did a C in reading actually mean? What did she need to learn to improve in arithmetic? He wrote that she was "doing well but [was] capable of much more"—in geography? English? Where? What exactly did "doing well" or "much more" mean? And what did a grade of S (missing from the key) signify?

What's in this Chapter

+ Who the stakeholders are
+ The thorny issue of grading ESL students
+ Setting standards for grades that can include ESL students

GRADES 4 - 5 - 6 REPORT CARD

Dear Parents,

This report is a record of your child's achievement in basic skills, study habits, and citizenship. Close contact between parents and the schools is important to provide the best learning opportunities for your child.

We encourage you to meet with the teacher, visit classrooms, and participate in school activities.

Teacher's comments: *Luisa is doing well, but is capable of much more. I enjoy having her in class and I look for more of her best work this next quarter.*

Pupil *Luisa Fernandez* Grade *4* School Year
School *Cedar Valley* Teacher *Mr. Mansfield*

REPORT PERIOD SUBJECTS	GRADE	BELOW GRADE LEVEL
READING	C	
with understanding		
uses skills accurately		
LANGUAGE *written*	C	
SPELLING weekly lesson *Contracts*	C+	
OTHER SUBJECTS *Tuesday homework*	S	
ARITHMETIC	D+	
fundamentals		
reasoning		
HISTORY	C	
GEOGRAPHY	S	
SCIENCE	C+	
HEALTH	S	
FOREIGN LANGUAGE		

SUBJECTS REPORT PERIOD	FIRST
PHYSICAL EDUCATION	S
HANDWRITING	S
ART	S
MUSIC vocal	S
instrumental	
CITIZENSHIP	
obeys school rules	B
courteous/considerate of others	B
respects property of others	B
assumes responsibility	B
STUDY HABITS	S
listens and follows direction	✓
does neat and careful work	S
completes work on time	✓
uses time and materials wisely	
ATTENDANCE RECORD	
Days present	43
Days absent	

KEY: A: Superior   B: Good   C: Average
D: Passing   F: Failure   ✓ : Needs improvement

Figure 8.1 Luisa's report card

my mom had didit that she didn't learn to read until 6 grade or so now!

Harris was loud and obnoxious, he would boom, "I hate this!" in the middle of an assignment—and Barb loved him. His first dialect was Hawaiian pidgin, no ESL program was available to him, and English as a Second Dialect (ESD) had not been invented yet. He was placed in a low-achieving seventh-grade class of nonstandard English speakers, with a number of NEP students who received no special help. The books they used were twenty years out of print. There were no pencils and few other classroom materials.

Harris did not hand in assignments, so the grade book had large gaps that made his average spiral downward. But, when he was engaged, such as when the class created a newspaper, he worked harder than anyone. He helped Hung Than, who was just off the boat from Vietnam, he planned the newspaper layout, and he bullied the others in his group to finish. He even cut other classes to sit in on Barb's class two and three times a day, crawling in through the window in the back of the room.

Giving Harris a *D*, based on what he had turned in, was such a hardship that Barb gave him a *C* based on his effort. And she wished there was a place on the report card where she could let others know what a great kid he was—to identify what such an ornery, irrepressible, likable boy was really capable of doing, instead of pushing him further down the road to failure or second-class citizenship.

++++++

Boris had forgotten to bring his book to class, so he ducked out to retrieve it from his locker. The result was a major altercation with his teacher about leaving the classroom without permission. Always the hothead, Boris left again to cool off. Now, he was threatened with suspension. He shrugged and said he did not care. His teacher directed him to copy the class rules 100 times before he could do his group presentation. Boris refused on the grounds that he was not learning anything by writing lines. So his teacher disallowed him from doing his group report, and he received an *F* on it—even though he had worked very hard on it.

By the time Dad arrived on the scene, Boris was in the office with his teacher, the vice-principal and the principal, who had moved beyond haranguing him about leaving the classroom and were threatening that he would end up in prison if he continued to do only as he wanted. Dad's main concern was that a behavioral issue was being factored into an academic one. What did a behavioral transgression have to do with his grade on a project?

These troubling scenarios reveal how tangled and messy the issue of grading can be. Everybody loathes grades (unless you're an *A* student and are placidly sure about how well you are doing). Teachers dislike giving them. Students hate getting them. If you have ever been tempted to (or actually did) hide your report card from your parents, or you have experienced that sinking feeling when you are sure you failed an exam, you know how painful and threatening grades can be. To have your entire effort—or, worse, to have your entire personhood—summed up by a neat row of letters is, in many ways, limiting, dismal, and defeating. Which is why we keep revisiting the issue of grades, and why waves of reform keep washing up against the banks of tradition.

Many schools and districts have overhauled their reporting systems time and time again. Barb's children spent their elementary years at a wonderful school where they were evaluated according to their own personal growth—not against others. Grades did not count. There was no competition, but simply a reporting of what they had achieved. It was exhausting and time consuming, and teachers were often at a loss for what to say; it was difficult to articulate, in narrative form and in any useful detail, over and over again, what thirty different kids could do. It was easier simply to check off what students did know, or which skills they needed to develop.

Teachers from the school were given an extra day off just for writing the narratives for the report cards. And *still* Barb wanted to know, "how are my kids doing in relation to the others?" It was a natural question to ask.

Because each method proved to be unsatisfactory, the school had to keep revising the grading system. Generally, when ambitious schools do deviate from tradition, they eventually return to the old *ABC* system simply because it is easier, and parents understand it. We all think we know what an *A* is, and we all certainly know what an *F* is.

When Barb's kids moved on to more traditional schools where grades mattered, the transition was rough and they sometimes stumbled. It can be even rougher for ESL students when they enter the mainstream, or if there are few resources allowing for special programs and they are in the mainstream from the beginning.

WHY WE GRADE

Grades are a fact of life in schools. But what role do they play? What *should* they do? Gullickson (2003) states that "evaluations of students should promote sound educational principles, fulfillment of institutional missions and effective student work, so that educational needs of students are served." This means that the primary purpose of grades is to guide students in achieving the goals set out for them, and to provide understanding of students' progress in relation to those goals. In this sense, grades are reasonable.

The Stakeholders, and What They Need to Know

Luisa's report card was standard for the district, but it was too vague to be of help to the primary stakeholders. Harris's report card only reflected a portion of what he could do. Boris was getting a poor grade for something that had nothing to do with learning

ENGLISH LANGUAGE ARTS	Trim. 1	Trim. 2	Trim. 3
Speaking and Listening			
Speaks for a variety of purposes and adapts the topic to the purpose, audience, occasion	X		
Plays a variety of roles in group discussions	X		
Listens attentively and contributes appropriately in discussions/conversations	X		
Makes eye contact when speaking			
Identifies important information from a speaker's message	X		
Reading			
Applies a wide range of strategies to read a variety of works both fiction and non-fiction	P		
Relates events, ideas, and characters in text to his / her own life	X		
Acquires and organizes information from reference books, magazines, texts, media			
Reads for a variety of purposes	X		
Reads self-selected materials for personal enjoyment	P		
Recognizes when a text is intended to influence			
	X		

Marking Code

Benchmarks listed for each subject area are addressed during the Intermediate Level Years (Gr. 5 & 6). Many of them are ongoing and will be worked on throughout your child's educational career with accomplishment at different times and at different levels of understanding for individual students. See narrative for individualized progress comments.

X	=	Presented this trimester
P	=	Shared at Portfolio Conference
C	=	See Comment Section
"Blank"	=	Not presented this trimester

Individual Progress Narrative

Trimester 1

Reading/Language Arts Our read-aloud, *Harris and Me* began a review of how to read fiction. All students have read at least one piece, and most have written at least one. Reading and writing are emphasized in other subjects as well. A piece on each student's positive attributes and one thing they would like to improve was required. Other reading and writing was self-selected. The expectation for writing was eight to ten pages of final copies. Nick is very fluent and has good comprehension skills. He has completed several books, none of which were challenging. His writing shows good mechanics and spelling, but staying on task is a constant struggle. He did not meet basic expectations. He will be expected to use various prewriting strategies next trimester to help correct this.

Figure 8.2 Part of Barb's son's report card, which simply identifies what was presented that term. It is a faulty design, because, of course, there is always a difference between what is taught and what is learned.

199

the content of the course. Because he was in high school, the stakes were even higher. But the students are not the only ones who have a stake in their grades. Other stakeholders include

+ Parents
+ Administrators
+ Teachers (mainstream, next year's)
+ ESL teachers or aides

Each stakeholder wants—and has a right—to know what, and how well, a student is doing. What each one wants to know, however, might be different.

+ Parents want to know what, and how well, their children are doing so they can help them, encourage them, and begin intervention if things are going off track.

+ Administrators (including principals, board members, legislators, state and provincial department of education staff members, and superintendents), concerned with accountability and programs, want data to help plan and budget for resources. They make important instructional and policy decisions based on information about student achievement. Anthony et al. (1991) write, "administrators need to know in general terms whether present programs are working satisfactorily. If not, they must ask what changes should be made." Because they need to see things in broad terms, bound as they are to representing large numbers of people, they are often obliged to use standardized and decontextualized measures that do not take into account individual teachers and students.

Teachers want to know what their students have or have not learned. You need to plan your instruction. You need to communicate your judgments to other stakeholders. You need to describe, in unambiguous terms, the "worth, merit, or value" (Scriven, 1974, in Davis, 1993) of your students' work. Next year's teachers want to know what Luisa has accomplished, and how well, so they can meet her at her level. Counselors want to know how Harris has done so they can make a reasonable academic plan for him. Mainstream teachers want to know what ESL teachers have covered in their lessons, and vice versa.

+ Luisa, Harris, and Boris want to know so they can feel good about themselves, understand what they have accomplished and on what they need to work, and have a concrete record of what they have mastered so that when they move on, they can demonstrate what skills they have.

+ Boris also needs a record of this academic achievements that is free from the overlay of concerns with behavioral issues.

Most will agree that grades are assigned to provide feedback to the stakeholders, or the users of data, as Stiggins (1991) refers to them. Stiggins states that users must understand "the decisions they make, how those decisions relate to effective teaching and learning, and what kinds of data can inform their decision making." He continues that if the decisions they make "are made well, students benefit. If they are made poorly, students suffer. But those decisions can only be as sound as the data on which they are based."

[Handwritten marginal note: I don't always like looking at grades because it gives me a prejudgement before I meet the student. example—Quentin]

THE CHALLENGES OF GRADING

The difficulties in grading lie in the following areas:

+ What the experts tell teachers to evaluate often conflicts with what they do evaluate. Grades are frequently a jumble of criteria, including mastery, behavior, encouragement, motivation, or recognition. *I do evaluate behavior in the form of participation points*

+ Evaluation involves a value system. Often, parameters are imposed by school or district policy: the final exam must equal no less than ten percent of a student's overall grade, for instance. But it is you, the teacher, who puts the value into the evaluation system. It is you who builds in the fudge room for effort or boosts a grade because a student is showing improvement. Some teachers are outcome-based, interested in how much growth the student has shown. Others rely on cooperative learning. Others still are interested in norm-referenced criteria, which compare each student's score to other students at the same grade level. An *A* or a *C* means different things to each of them. It gets worse when teachers are forced to factor in things that are misconceived or contrary to their own philosophy or set of values.

Here is a portion of the mandated final English exam for grade six, which Barb was forced to use when she taught at Lied Middle School in Las Vegas:

Think about the writing process. Choose the best answer to the following questions.

49. How many traits are there in Trait Analysis?

   A. 3   B. 4   C. 5   D. 6

50. The names of the traits are:

   A. introduction, overall, value, composition

   B. ideas, organization, voice, convention

   C. ideals, originality, voice, construction

   D. none of the above

51. What score do you have to earn in each trait to pass the proficiency test?

   A. 5.0   B. 4.0   C. 3.0   D. 2.0

Figure 8.3 Mandated final English exam from Lied Middle School

Grading the test was easy. Barb simply zipped them through the Scantron machine, which produced a score and a percentage for each student. But it revealed almost nothing about a student's mastery of English. Knowing how many traits there are in trait analysis has nothing to do with whether or not a student is able to write an organized, coherent, interesting essay. Even the better students in Barb's classes barely scored eighty percent.

To follow is the spelling portion of the same test, in which students had to identify the correctly spelled word for each question. Note that for question 98, the *correct* answer, *subcommittee*, is not even an option!

96.	a. bandgo	97.	a. supernatural	98.	a. subcommitte
	b. bango		b. supernaturile		b. subcommitte
	c. banjoe		c. supernacheral		c. sub comittee
	d. banjo		d. supernateral		d. subcomittee

Figure 8.4 Spelling portion of mandated final English exam from Lied Middle School

After slogging through the test with her first three classes, watching her sixth graders agonize for two hours over something that was so totally contrary to anything current research promoted for teaching reading and writing, Barb changed tactics. Knowing her accelerated class (which took grades very seriously) would be distraught over their inability to answer the questions with any degree of certainty, and that her Rogue's Gallery of boys (all of whom had come from prison, were in "opportunity camp," or were headed for prison) would rebel against the exam, she just shut the door; the whole class did the exam together, and they all got the same mark. Did she risk getting fired? Yes. Did it make any difference in their learning? No. Did it make a difference in their attitude? Absolutely.

The issue of grading gets even muddier when we add English learners like Luisa, Harris, and Boris, into the equation. Often, they know the content, but their grasp of English is either so rudimentary or so imperfect that their ability to articulate or demonstrate what they know gets derailed in the process. Hills (1991) writes:

> *If we start with the assumption that grades should be meaningful and that they should communicate meaningfully the academic achievement of individual students in the content explicitly being taught, then...grades should not be used for disciplinary purposes. If a grade is altered as a way of inflicting punishment, it no longer accurately reflects academic achievement, and its proper meaning is destroyed.*

Not only is he correct, but using grades to inflict punishment does not work. You can motivate students with good, or boosted, grades, but not the other way around. "Grades have some value as rewards," writes Guskey (1996), "but they have absolutely no value as punishment." Have you ever threatened an eighth grader that you will give him an *F* if he does not behave? If you have reached that juncture, he does not care. One more *F* is not going to make any difference. Grades do not make good leverage, only good bridges.

We do not ascribe to what Boris's teacher did. However, as we get older and meaner, we have taken a more realistic approach. We recognize that part of success is being responsible, taking charge of our learning, and doing things the way they are supposed to be done in the "real world." Lateness is not acceptable for business proposals, or for making credit card and utility payments. If you show up late for work every day, sooner or later you will get fired. But what is more important—turning in an assignment on time or learning something from it, late or not? And how much should the lateness count?

Eighties' activists like Frank Smith advocated eradicating grading and evaluation altogether. He writes (1988):

202

Grades are the sole reason that most school activities are undertaken, requiring or enticing students to engage in tasks they would never otherwise go near. And grades degrade undertakings that could otherwise be worthwhile in their own right.

In the nineties, when interest in authentic assessment was soaring, articles such as Seeley's ("The Mismatch between Assessment and Grading," 1994) were optimistic about moving from a "testing culture…to an assessment culture." Sadly, this has not happened. We are still firmly entrenched in the old ways.

In 2005, World Net Daily reported that schools in Florida had moved to a 1-, 2-, 3- grading system for each subject and skill on the grounds that "the letter grade system can be an obsession with students and parents and doesn't reflect how a student is really learning." Thus, a 1 meant a student was working a year or more below grade level, a 2 indicated he was working less than a year below grade level, and a 3 meant he was is working at or above grade level.

But these are still grades. The numbers do not give any further explanation or detail about achievement levels. Thousands of miles away, Utah mandated a return to letter grades. The seesawing continues.

Eradicating grades altogether might be a worthy goal, but their existence is a reality, at least for the time being. Schools are not about to abandon them, and they are something that our ESL students are subject to. What then, are we to do?

Questions to Consider When Grading

For Barb, one of the great things about teaching ESL at the elementary level was not having to give grades. It was great just to be able to see students' progress without the pressure and the hassle of trying to pin a grade on the work.

Then, as a junior professor teaching both lower-level composition and upper-level linguistics university courses, after the luxury of years of not having to give grades at all, Barb was extremely uncomfortable with the idea. She would read a stack of papers and think, "Well, this one is pretty good," then, "Gee, that's better than the first." Then, she would read one that did not quite follow the assignment instructions but was so fresh and vivid that she did not know what to do. What was an *A*? How was it better than a *B*? In graduate school, a *C* had been an unacceptable grade. So what did that make a *D*, and who deserved one?

After Barb's first lecture course, the chairman of the department said she had given too many high grades. After some hesitation, Barb explained that several of the students had not done well on the tests, so she had given them the opportunity to work on extra-credit assignments to make up for their low grades and bring up their averages. He seemed dumbfounded and told her that not many teachers would be willing to put in the extra time to do that. No more was said about the high scores.

Even more challenging for Barb, when she taught at the adult level, was the issue of grading ESL students. In her beginning literacy class, there was a huge range in both English proficiency and experience with schooling. Some students were more proficient and competent readers and writers, as well as more studious, than others who had barely begun to read and write. Was an *A* in beginning literacy equivalent to an *A* in a mainstream course? Take, for instance, Kao's essay, laboriously typed into the computer:

> **My top mountain**
>
> **Black mountain is a taller and famous mountain.**
>
> **Near my village when I was a childhood everyone spend one week in the summer to climb on the top and stayed. At there they were have many kind of bird their are singing very different sound. When I hear that bird singing my hart got lonely and I missing the honey girl looked down there are many villages the wind brow up all leaves dried below me. Upper there are green leaves on me. It was only the dirt road their haven't car haven't traffic they are some rode the horses very often all people took walk by foot.**
>
> **I love that mountain very much.**

This was the most Kao had ever produced and was truly his best effort. There was so much good in the writing: Kao had managed to capture his feelings for that particular spot, he included descriptive details, and he showed why it meant a great deal to him. And yet, for the average English-speaking tenth grader, or even the average eighth grader, this would not be acceptable because it was not the quality or quantity one expects from an English speaking fifteen-year-old. Should Kao have been graded against the standard for a tenth grader, which he was, or as a tenth-grade beginner doing his best in an ESL class?

After working as a grader of standardized tests and having graded thousands upon thousands of tests, Barb reached the conclusion that the knowledge and mastery of content was often present in the low-income and second-language kids. What was missing was the fluency of articulation, the mastery of words, and the finer points of language. But is mastery of content not the bottom line? We think it is.

A FRAMEWORK FOR GRADING

We cannot tell you how or what to grade. This is something you must decide for yourself. In addition, many variables will change what you do and the grades you give. However, there are some things you can do to give you structure for making the decisions.

+ Grade only a carefully selected, minimum amount of work; do not grade everything. Choose to grade an item because it is a student's best work or because it is most representative of the student's work.

+ Grade what you think is important for students to be learning. If learning to make reading an integral part of their lives is important, find a way to grade it.

+ Grade both process and product in student work. Students frequently make progress in the processes of reading and writing before the learning shows up in their products.

+ Carefully define and communicate to students what you will grade in their work. In chapter 6, we gave examples of rubrics. How a student meets the varying levels of expectations can be used for his grade.

- Involve students in the grading process. If we want to develop a student's ability to critique his own work, we must provide opportunities for him to learn how to do so. Students need practice and guidance in this, or they may suggest grades and be surprised and dismayed by what they actually receive.

Some teachers have students choose what they will be graded on at the end of the semester. This takes a great deal of training and attention. Students are not generally accustomed to that sort of responsibility. A student will often choose an item for grading because it means something to him, or because he worked hard on it—but not because it represents quality work. Students often have unrealistic ideas about what constitutes, and what should be factored into, a grade.

— example ??

Defining Our Values

Irmscher (1978) writes:

> *Evaluation implies values, but many teachers evaluate without defining them or just feel frustrated they can't quantify the values they hold. Without clearly defined values, it is impossible to make consistent judgments and discriminations. What most characteristically happens when...teachers read student papers, or for that matter, when students read each other's papers...is that they find fault. Comment emphasizes what is wrong and not what is right... [focusing] on the limitations of the prose; the strengths are taken for granted.*

Even with the troublesome issue of grades, the focus can be on what has been done right, with an emphasis on improvement, not punishment. For Barb, this helped to clarify what to consider an *A* and what made a *B* different from a *C*.

Concerning non-English or non-standard dialect speakers, Irmscher says (1978):

> *The writing of these students can be atypical in many ways. In content, it may be mature and perceptive, although lacking in formal control. In language it may be vigorous, although lacking in consistency of tone and usage. In style, it may be moving, although fragmentary and error-ridden. Often the psychological barriers to writing are so strong that special emphasis must be given to encouragement, whenever and wherever possible.*

The idea of a student demonstrating competence in any given subject is a productive way to perceive the issue of grades. Grades can, and should, be a positive force in a student's progress. Competence can be demonstrated in spite of a lack of proficiency—if one can look beyond the errors to the essence of what is important and focus on the learning that is taking place. *I wish more teachers feel this way especially @ secondary level*

Reexamining the concept of the bell curve, Rhodes and Shanklin (1992) point out:

> *A normal curve, after all, operates under the assumption that some students cannot learn what we teach. Of course, it's usually the same students who are at the bottom of the bell curve; they learn to expect that they cannot improve their grades because someone has to be at the bottom.*

The bell curve philosophy denies the fact that all students can demonstrate competence and can improve. It is, as Bloom et al. (1981) write:

> *The distribution most appropriate to chance and random activity. Education is a purposeful activity, and we seek to have the students learn what we have to teach. If we are effective, the distribution of achievement should be very different from the normal curve. In fact, we may even insist that our efforts are unsuccessful to the extent that the distribution of achievement approximates the normal distribution.*

Rhodes and Shanklin (1992) suggest, "instead of grading a student in comparison to other students, we can grade against a set of criteria, or against a student's own past performance and what we know we can expect next developmentally."

How would you grade these writers?

To follow are some case examples to consider for grading. Figure 8.5 is third-grader Nara's letter to Rapunzel. She was considered a low level 2, but she was clearly interested in the topic and displayed not only comprehension of the story, but creativity and a lively sense of humor.

Here is part of grade-twelve student Tomás's essay (the rest can be found on page 213):

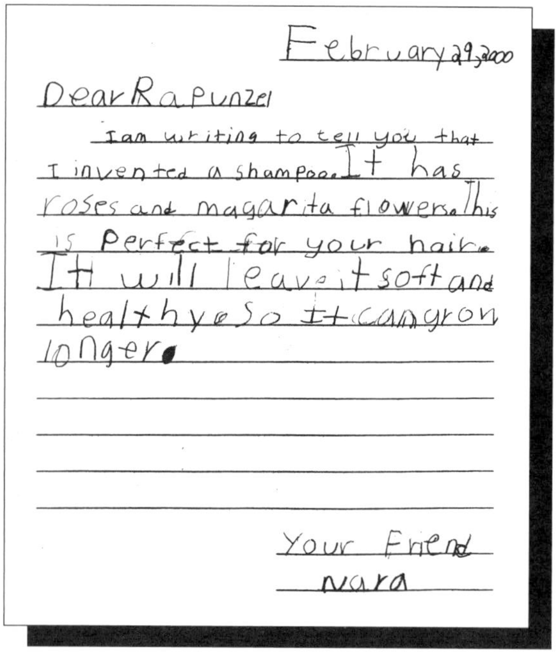

February 29, 2000

Dear Rapunzel

I am writing to tell you that I invented a shampoo. It has roses and magarita flowers. This is perfect for your hair. It will leave it soft and healthy. So it can grow longer.

Your Friend
nara

Figure 8.5 Nara's letter to Rapunzel

My important thing is my car. I have a 1970 red 250 Chevy Nova, the interior color is red and black, it has a old engineer but with my special care it is till raning. When a first got this Nova it was trash, the body pinte, the engeen, tires, everthing was destroyed. My Chevy Nova is important to my because, I made a new look to this car, is like if I had gived life to something but not only that, also because it was my first car and it was a gift from my brother, this car it has ben from my older brother to me and I am planing to pass it to my next brother that is important to me red Chevy Nova.

My car it has been there for my when a feel sad or lonlly I like to go to my special place which is my car, I like to talk to him or in some way expres my feelng to him some times waching him or others times licining to the radio with him.

Tomás was graded against other twelfth graders, with the same criteria used for English speakers. He failed. Is this fair? Based on what you see in his writing example, was he competent in English? The biggest problem with this essay was his spelling. Once you remove the errors, you can see the essay's good points. He addressed the topic and did not deviate from it. He developed his idea, gave details to support it, and he stayed within the framework of the assignment. He also showed his interest in the topic. But the interference can be like white noise, and it is easy to let it block a sense of what has been accomplished. If his spelling was not so bad, would you have a different opinion of Tomás's essay?

This essay was part of Tomás's first attempt at passing the English competency test. If he did not pass, then no matter how well he had done in his classes in school, he would not have graduated. He could actually write better than the example shows, but he was hamstrung by the rules of the test. He was given a limited amount of time in which to take the test, and no dictionary. The high stakes could have cost him his diploma—on a test that did not reflect what he knew and could do. The poor spelling held as much weight as the content, idea development, and style elements.

Grade-twelve ESL student, Daniel, wrote the following:

> **I hated the first day in school because that's when we brought the small weapons of mass destruction. Every student brought his or her cane and teachers would pile them in a corner of the teachers' staff room. It was a miracle to me if a day passed and I was not caned. Mr. X was my teacher. He was a tall guy, very energetic, with muscles all over his body. He was built like a linebacker, and I had a feeling that caning students made him the man he was, strong. He caned not only because we made mistakes but because he liked to.**

Daniel's descriptions were precise, lively, even riveting. He helped the reader to actually see his teacher and his actions. The problem Daniel had encountered in the past was that his writing was so good he had been accused of plagiarizing. He had reached the point where he was not only articulate, he was playing with the language in ways many English speakers cannot. He managed to evade an *F* here because the writing was so original it could not possibly have been copied from someone else. It rated a WOW! He got an *A*.

To follow are several columns from newspapers written by seventh graders. The assignment (courtesy of Carol Booth Olson, from *The Reading/Writing Connection*, *2007*) was based on the picture book *Cloudy with a Chance of Meatballs*, by Judi Barrett. Students were asked to create the front page of a newspaper from their own imaginary town. Compare the different pieces with the first one (right), which was written by Monique, whose primary language was English.

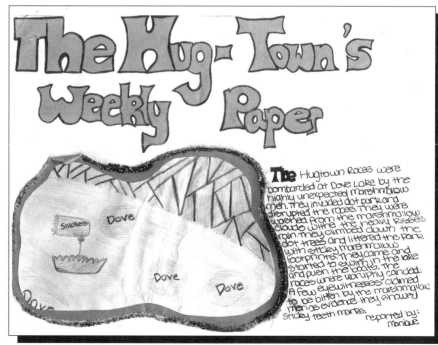

Figure 8.6 Monique's newspaper assignment

Wilson (right) was a level 5 who had been mainstreamed. He had reached a level where he could play with the language, using both humor and a Southern accent. As in Monique's piece, within the confines of the assignment you can see imagination and originality.

Ezekiel was a level 2 who chose to write in Spanish:

> **La Lluvia de Gomitas en el Pueblo de Macaroni!!**
>
> **Noticia el Pueblo de macaroni esta sido atacado por meteoios de gomas y las ciudadanas estan peliando contra la arenaza que los asecha – y de sesperados secuen asu vitimo recursos pero les fallo peso no se rindieron y smasias a eso pudieron sat**
>
> *(Gumdrop rain in Macaroni land!!*
>
> *Notice: Macaroni land is being attacked by gumdrop meteors and the citizens are fighting the hailstorm that entraps them and, desperate, use their last resources, but were unsuccessful. they did not give up[indecipherable] to that they were able to [indecipherable])*

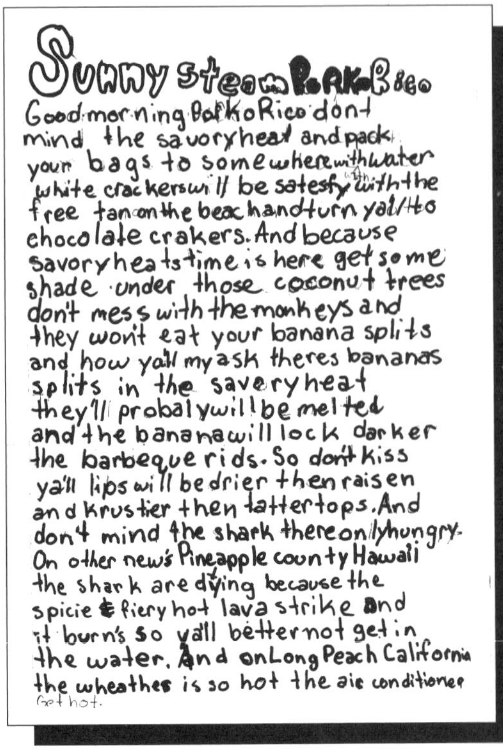
Sunny Steam [illegible]
Good morning [illegible] Rico don't mind the savory heat and pack your bags to somewhere with water white crackers will be satesfy with the free tan on the beach and turn yall to chocolate crakers. And because savory heats time is here get some shade under those coconut trees don't mess with the monkeys and they won't eat your banana splits and how yall my ask theres bananas splits in the savery heat they'll probaly will be melted and the banana will lock darker the barbeque rids. So don't kiss ya'll lips will be drier then raisen and krustier then tattertops. And don't mind the shark there only hungry. On other new's Pineapple county Hawaii the shark are dying because the spicie fiery hot lava strike and it burn's so yall better not get in the water. And on Long Peach California the wheather is so hot the air conditioner get hot.

Figure 8.7 Wilson's newspaper assignment

Although Ezekiel had addressed the assignment, it was difficult to translate because it was written in poor Spanish, with weak spelling and syntax. His sloppiness impeded the reader from understanding what he had tried to say. Putting a grade on it was difficult without a rubric.

Establishing a Scale for Grading

There are many grading scales available on the Internet. We like the grading policy below, adopted by Indiana University, because it is clear.

A	=	Outstanding achievement. Unusually complete command of the course content; exceptionally high level of scholarship.
A–	=	Excellent achievement. Very thorough command of course content; very high level of scholarship.
B+	=	Very good achievement. Thorough command of course material.
B	=	Good achievement. Solid, acceptable performance.
B–	=	Fair achievement. Acceptable performance.
C+	=	Not wholly satisfactory achievement. Marginal performance on some aspects of the course requirements.
C	=	Marginal achievement. Minimally acceptable performance on course assignments.
C–	=	Unsatisfactory achievement. Inadequate knowledge of course content.

Figure 8.8 Indiana University grading policy

Student achievement refers to full command of course materials, to creativity that far surpasses course expectations. An *A* can be an *A* for any class, and suggestion or demonstration of competence can transcend language. In spite of an incomplete control of the language, a student can demonstrate

- his depth and breadth of understanding of the content
- the amount of grappling he has done with the ideas
- his control over subject matter
- an awareness of the parameters and the subtleties of the topic
- an ability to organize

When reviewing the following examples, consider the scale adopted by Indiana University.

Lark, a grade-11 partially mainstreamed ESL student, wrote this essay for a social studies class:

> **Family is the quiet and comfortable port in life. When people tired flying, they choose to stay at home. They are not young any more, and they got a lot of experience outside. They start to return nature and think their life. They will choose the family as the last stop in life. They will recall the picture of their whole life, enjoy sunset, and be joy everything in the family. From Chinese proverb "A family with an old person has a living treasure of gold. Family is the angle in life. She always stays there and opens for you anytime. Family is the first port and the last port that give you happy, sedateness, and peace in your life.**

Lark's writing is peppered with missing prepositions and articles as well as a verb-tense error. It takes a little thought to work through the essay, and yet it is totally readable, even beautiful. If the teacher chose to see through the errors, she could see the maturity and insight that Irmscher discusses. Lark's writing warranted a high *B*, or even an *A*, depending on how much weight the teacher gave to the errors.

Figure 8.9 (right) shows Lan's response to the book *To Kill a Mockingbird*. While there are grammatical errors, Lan demonstrated a depth of understanding of the book that goes beyond what most teachers could hope for.

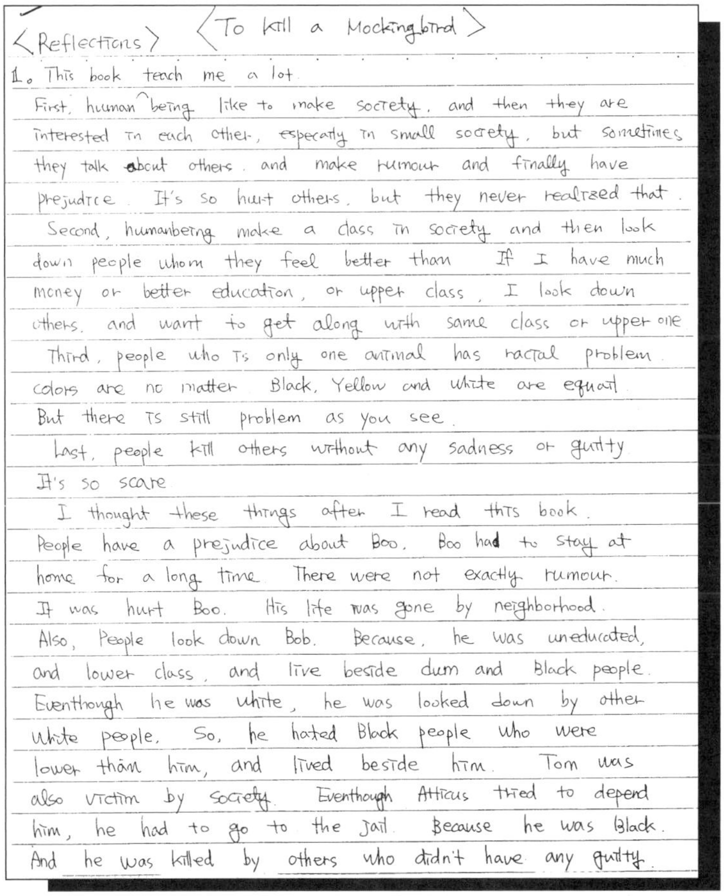
<Reflections> <To kill a Mockingbird>
1. This book teach me a lot.
First, human being like to make society, and then they are interested in each other, especially in small society, but sometimes they talk about others. and make rumour and finally have prejudice. It's so hurt others, but they never realized that.
Second, humanbeing make a class in society and then look down people whom they feel better than. If I have much money or better education, or upper class, I look down others. and want to get along with same class or upper one
Third, people who is only one animal has racial problem. colors are no matter. Black, Yellow and White are equal.
But there is still problem as you see.
Last, people kill others without any sadness or guilty. It's so scare.
I thought these things after I read this book.
People have a prejudice about Boo. Boo had to stay at home for a long time. There were not exactly rumour. It was hurt Boo. His life was gone by neighborhood.
Also, People look down Bob. Because, he was uneducated, and lower class, and live beside dum and Black people. Eventhough he was white, he was looked down by other white people. So, he hated Black people who were lower than him, and lived beside him. Tom was also victim by society. Eventhough Atticus tried to depend him, he had to go to the jail. Because he was Black. And he was killed by others who didn't have any guilty.

Figure 8.9 Lan's response to *To Kill a Mockingbird*

In *The More-Than-Just-Surviving Handbook* we discussed criteria for grading tests.

+ Did the student understand the question?

+ Did he answer the question?

+ How well did he develop his thoughts?

+ How thoroughly did he present his case?

+ Is he performing to the best of his abilities given language competency, or is he just goofing off?

A seventh-grade beginning literacy class read a Hmong folk tale about the first farmer. One of the questions was, "How long did the farmer wait? Why?" Here are some of the responses:

> **Seven. Because he lazy.**
>
> **Seven. So the corn could grow big.**
>
> **Seven. He waits so many day because he want to get rest and sleep.**
>
> **Seven. He's lazy and want the weeds grow bigger. So he doesn't have to come alot of days.**
>
> **Seven. Because he wait until the corn grew and ready for eat then he only take them home and one thing he was lazy man.**

All students' answers were correct. However, they had previously discussed the fact that the farmer was lazy. The additional inference from at least two of the students—that he wanted to wait for the weeds to grow higher so he would not have to come as often or work as hard—was made on their own, and it revealed an added depth of understanding.

The teacher awarded two points for each correct answer. She could have given extra credit for the inferences, but she did not. This was her choice, and her values and standards may differ from yours or ours. Standards and grading reflect the individual objectives, priorities, tastes, and philosophies of a teacher. We cannot set the standards for every teacher or every course, nor can, or should, we establish absolute standards. According to Belanoff (1991), the inability of teachers to agree on grading systems and standards is "a sign of strength, of the life and vitality of words and the exchange of words [because] texts reflect life and the multitude of tastes and standards in real life."

Another class of seventh graders was asked to list ten things they had learned about Australia. The class of inner-city kids consisted of both ESL and English-speaking students. Here, we include a range of answers to show that, in spite of weak spelling and answers that may be less complete than others, students can still show learning. Of course, if you look only at the errors then you miss the point.

Both Georgia and Monette were English-speaking students:

> **The sugar glider eats sap from accasia tress and they are grayish blue Wallaroos live in Australia and they eat grass and shrubs (Georgia)**

> **I learned that aberichinineis live in Australia** (Monette)

Monette's spelling was off the mark but readable.

Wilson was bilingual and mainstreamed:

> **Dingoes are domesticated animals and dingoes eat meat.**

> **Playpus lay eggs but their still mammal and they have bad eyesite so they use the bill.**

Wilson had an error of fact: dingoes are not domesticated. How many points should have been deducted?

Marcus was a level-4 student:

> **It is like a desert. Abergeinese are from Astrilia.**

> **I has red sand.**

> **It has 10 of the most dadyest snakes in the world.**

> **They always worm there.**

Marcus understood the facts and wrote complete sentences and correct facts. Should he have been held to ESL standards where spelling is overlooked *or* should he have been compared to his English-speaking classmates, because he is a level 4?

Crystal was another English speaker:

> **That kangoo grow 6 ft tall and they have pouches.**

> **Kangroos run vary fast and it vary hot there**

> **It at the bottom of the earth.**

This example shows how some of the higher-level ESL students do better and write more than some of the lower-level English-speaking students. How would you take that into account?

José was a level 1, not yet able to write in English:

> **que 101 animales sen diferentes qualos de otros paises**

> *(that 101 animals are different than those of other countries)*

> **Porque los animals cumen diferentes comidas**

> *(Because animals eat different food)*

> **En Australia lost son diferente que otras partes**

> *(Australia has parts that are different than other part)*

Also a level-1 speaker, José chose to write in Spanish. The other students repeatedly said that he did not know any English, but the lesson was conducted entirely in English, and he still managed to get his facts right and to communicate them. *that is because it is easier to listen and understand before being able to speak*

Here is Ezekiel again, a Spanish-speaking level 2:

> Once of the weirds animals in Australia is the love pus.

> Australia is the smoles continent is the words, but haves the most weird animals

In spite of his abysmal spelling, Ezekiel did get his facts right.

Isabella had come from Mexico at the beginning of the year with no prior English experience:

> I learn the lyrebird only can have one egg a the time around agust

> I learn the Australia is a Island and is the more bigger

> I learn about the lyrebird eat only incepts.

Six months later, Isabella's proficiency had developed enough to write very clearly, with accurate facts in English.

Mitigating Factors

There are many mitigating factors that must be taken into account when grading. For example, much as we dislike the idea, grades must also reflect the standards of the institution.

A student who challenged Barb intellectually was Bob, a retired military career man who was taking the university course in upper-level linguistics that she was teaching. The class of potential ESL teachers was discussing the challenges of grading students fairly. Bob suggested the following hierarchical view of grading. It has some very interesting ideas to consider:

1. *Purpose of the work*

2. *Execution of the work*

    a. *Grasp of the idea being expressed*

    b. *Flow of supporting information, management of the idea*

    c. *Resolution of the idea*

3. *Mechanics of the delivery*

    a. *Choice of supporting vocabulary*

    b. *Packaging of word groups*

4. *Fundamental language skills*

    a. *Sentence structure and punctuation*

    b. *Appropriate word structure*

    c. *Spelling*

    d. *Penmanship and neatness*

5. *Standards of the institution*

6. *Demonstrated effort of the student*

7. *Extenuation and mitigation*

   a. *age and linguistic background of the student*

   b. *time available to finish the project*

   c. *mental and physical state of the student*

   d. *cultural and social standards of the student*

Bob acknowledged everything that we, as teachers, take into account when grading a student's work. Whether we like it or not (or are willing to admit it or not), when a student becomes a person and not a number, who he is—his emotional, intellectual, cultural, ethnic, and moral makeup—influences the grade we give to him. Is it not reasonable to admit that this happens? What we now must ask is, can we, and should we, be allowing this to happen?

Again, we cannot tell you how to grade. As with standards, these issues must be resolved at the local level, because each district, each school, each classroom has its own challenges and unique makeup.

Here is the rest of Tomás' essay. Which factors should be used to grade him? How much should each factor be weighted?

> My Chevy it has ben a great help to me and it has made a great difference in my life. It helps me to get from home to school and from school to work if a did not had my car I would not be able to work. I remember one time when my car was very important to my and I was proud to have my car. When my parents came from Mexico, the P/U truck were they came on it berly got home and they did not had another car to go to work of even to go to the store, my chevy Nova was the only one who was running so we use my car to go to work, store and other places. The red Chevy Nova made a great difference in my life not only because it was helpful but because it made my feel that I was helpful to, I help my parent to get to their jobs and help them in a hard time. That is why my car is important to me. It made a difference in my life.

On the following page, we present some test answers. It is worth considering how you would grade these particular answers.

3. If you were Jewish and forced to wear the symbol, would you wear it? Yes or No. Explain why you said yes or no.

I can still be part of my religion but had not to wear the star; I just didn't let anybody know Beside the German put me in concentration camp if they see me wear the star where I don't want to be.

4. What is a concentration camp? Give me an example of something that happened there.

Concentration Camp - Place where the German put Jewish in. There the people were served little and bad food. they had to work and the German kalt the Jewish women take their cloth and go to shower room.

5. Write a conversation that Anne and her Daddy would have.

Anne: Can I bring my cat with me?
Mr. Frank: No, we did had food to the cat and they only so much stuff that we had to bring with us.
Anne: I guess you right daddy.
Mr. Frank: Is that ok with you that we couldn't bring the cat with us?
Anne: yes, but I'll miss the cat!
Mr. Frank: I know, that just the way thing work out - Sorry.
Anne: Itok. Thank daddy.

3. If you were Jewish and forced to wear the symbol, would you wear it? Yes or no. Explain why you said (yes) or no.

because I am very belive my god so I wuld like to wear it. If I don't want Mr. Hitler see I can put the symbol inside the shirt.

4. What is a concentration camp? Give me an example of something that happened there.

The concentration camp is Mr. Hitler take the jewish people come to stay in this camp. the jewish in this camp this hurries and get sick in the camp.

5. Write a conversation that Anne and her Daddy would have.

Anne = Daddy can you tell me something?
Daddy = yes, what is your question Anne
Anne = Why Mr. Hitler hate jewish people?
Daddy = because he is belive another god but is not jewish just why he hate jewish people.

Figure 8.10 This test was administered in a sheltered high-school social studies class.

3. If you were Jewish and forced to wear the symbol, would you wear it? Yes or No. Explain why you said yes or no.

yes becuas I not wear than got kill Than I have to wear.

4. What is a concentration camp? Give me an example of something that happened there.

The Hitler don't like junish people.

They no priwol on the bed than they have ever thing are dirty in the concentration camp.

5. Write a conversation that Anne and her Daddy would have.

Anne: Daddy do you has a book for me to read? yes I has one.
do you like it?
Anne: yes I very like
Daddy: ok you can take it

Figure 8.11 Here is how one group of fifth graders retold, in writing, a story they had just heard. They included all salient points of the story. Is this an A?

Loan, Thuan, Dan, Anhi

I look around and I go anywhere and I lost. I felt frightened.

first I saw mapie gave me a flute; I saw the beavers building the dam and the make music slapity, slap, slap; he saw robin singing Ina lalalala, tralalala, tralala

and he saw a bullfrog sitting in the marsh broak, broak, broak then he saw racoon sitting in the tree and Hary said

Have you seen my mother racoon said

Yes, I saw your mother looking for you. Just stay in one place and played music your mother came to see who making music.

214

Modifying Grades

If you decide to modify grades, to which students does this apply—just the beginners, the intermediate students too, or all students? If you decide to modify for beginners only, where is the cut-off point?

I think it is on a case by case basis

Strickland (1990) writes that modified grading systems should maintain as many characteristics of the regular grading system as possible. This brings us back to the concept of base-line competencies (see chapter 1, page 17). Strickland states that the same grading indicators, such as *A, B, C*, should be used whenever possible to ensure continuity, instead of moving to a different system, such as check, check-plus, check-minus.

Modifying grading systems may include the following:

+ Adjusting the amount of time available for completion of tests and assignments (For many ESL students, reading the test and understanding the questions can take up to half of the class period. They run out of time to complete their answers or do the work.)

+ Administering tests orally rather than in written form

+ Using an interpreter during testing

+ Modifying the format of a test from narrative to short answer

+ Altering course requirements to focus on the most important ones and deleting less critical requirements

+ Additional reports that interpret grades

CONCLUSION

Grading is a challenge that will not go away. We feel that Rhodes and Shanklin (1992) give the best advice when it comes to grading: base your criteria on what your students are capable of doing and producing at that particular age, level of proficiency, and literacy level. We must grade to students' competence within the demands and content of the course or grade level. If a student meets or exceeds the standards within those conditions, he receives an *A*. After all, the fundamental goal for grading reading and writing should be—no surprises here—mastery of content; to improve reading and writing skills.

Lunching Several Measures

PRESENTING THE INFORMATION TO STAKEHOLDERS

A school in Mindamon, a small, Midwestern town, opened its doors the first day of school to find 103 non-English-speaking students on its doorstep. Over the summer, the local packing plant had recruited overseas and south of the border and had imported a large number of families. Somehow, they had forgotten to inform the schools, and teachers and administrators were left to scramble. The town had never experienced the challenge of non-English-speaking students before, and the appearance of this crowd sent everyone into a panic.

With help from the local university, somehow, students were tested and placed, and gradually the flurry died down. However, no one had any idea what to do about grading and record keeping. It was clear that the old, standard report cards would not work and that student files needed additional information. They decided to investigate additional methods of reporting and began a slow overhaul of their system. In light of the fact that districts were now required to disaggregate their data—test results needed to be sorted by groups of students: economically disadvantaged; racial and ethnic minorities; those with disabilities; or those with limited English—and that they needed to demonstrate that they were meeting the needs of all students, this was a particularly pressing issue.

What's in this Chapter

+ How to systematize information about students
+ How to present the data in usable form
+ How to hold conferences with stakeholders

SYSTEMATIZING INFORMATION

Reporting-System Objectives

Designing a system for reporting the appropriate information to each stakeholder can be overwhelming from the outset. How do we fashion a system that gives each stakeholder a clear picture of how a student is doing? To begin, a reporting system should

+ Recognize, acknowledge, and give credit by differing methods (report cards, grades, and so on) for what students have achieved and experienced in a range of contexts

+ Increase students' awareness of their strengths and weaknesses, and provide encouragement and opportunities to enhance motivation and personal development

+ Help schools support the development of students' diverse talents and skills

+ Provide a summary document of a student's qualities and achievements that can be used by others (Burgess, 1993)

This is a tall order and will not be achieved overnight or without struggle. But we have to begin somewhere.

To design a successful reporting system, some key issues must first be resolved.

+ What information is useful to report to stakeholders?

+ How will the information be gathered?

+ How will the information be used?

+ How will the information be judged?

Steps for Compiling Information

1. Establish your system

Mindamon began by creating a file for each student in which to keep the data the teachers would accumulate. This also got them thinking about the students whose work would fill the folders. At this stage, the folders were not portfolios—selected collections of student work chosen specifically as assessment samples. They were merely files designed to hold relevant information about a student.

2. Decide who the audiences are for the files

The Mindamon school district had to decide who the file was for.

+ The mainstream teacher, for monitoring progress

+ The part-time ESL teacher

+ The administration

+ Next year's mainstream teacher

+ The students themselves

The question of accessibility raised other issues.

+ Who would have access to the file?

+ At the end of the school year, how much of the contents would stay in the classroom?

+ How much of the contents would go home with the student?

+ How much of the contents would remain in the file to follow the student into the next year? *this is always difficult because I hate clutter*

Different audiences need different information. Winograd (1994) points out:

> Assessment can be tailored to its stakeholders by recognizing that assessment data serves different audiences with differing agendas. With more specific information available, the stakeholders can make their decisions based on the accumulated data they need: administrators can determine if programs are successful or other forms of support are indicated; teachers can better shape their teaching; parents can gain specific insight into their children's progress as learners; and students can focus on where they have succeeded and what areas need attention.

Mindamon decided to create three subfolders for each student: the mainstream teacher's folder, the ESL teacher's folder, and the cumulative folder. The two teachers' folders—the working folders—represented the first level of work, an ongoing collection of student work. The cumulative folder represented selections from the two working folders.

3. Define the purposes of the student file

It is crucial to shape the data and keep the folder from becoming simply a pile of papers that has no form or meaning to anyone. Its purposes, therefore, must be clearly defined. What best illustrates the type of instruction and learning taking place? You must decide whether anecdotes, writing samples, reading records, checklists, or other methods will best demonstrate competency for a particular audience. This step goes hand-in-hand with defining the audiences. Hebert (2001) writes that in an effort to counterbalance standardized test scores (or even to prove them wrong), teachers often feel compelled to put only a student's best work into his portfolio. This is something you have to decide for yourself: do you include only the best work, work that gives an accurate picture of what a student can accomplish over a range of tasks, or something else? For ESL students, for example, Mindamon teachers felt it was important that data

+ demonstrate growth and gains over time

+ demonstrate mastery of skills and content

+ provide an authentic and concrete picture of students' capabilities

+ help students become self-reflective

+ provide concrete support for bringing about change

+ shift the focus from negative indicators to those of positive achievement

4. Decide which areas of the quad you will use to show progress and mastery

The Mindamon ESL and classroom teachers had to decide on which areas of the Quad (see page 117) to concentrate. They felt it was better to start slowly and build as they got accustomed to this kind of collecting and reporting.

To follow is a sample table of contents for a complete student file. Choose from this list according to your individual needs, available time, and feasibility. Do not feel obligated to include everything; select what is right for you. You may decide to divide the files according to the Quad: process, product, classroom measures, decontextualized measures (mandated tests and exams). It is important not to become too rigid about what goes into them.

+ Cover sheet
+ Contents list
+ Student personal data/attendance record
+ Placement records
+ Assessment of reading comprehension (running records)
+ List of books read
+ Student reading and writing surveys
+ Student work samples
+ Tests
+ Standardized test scores
+ Checklist of skills learned
+ Student progress reports: objectives taught/met
+ Areas needing work
+ Student profiles from previous grades
+ Dated-entry record of parent contact
+ Parent-teacher conference reports
+ Self-evaluation

The teachers at Mindamon chose to include the following in each of the three subfolders:

The mainstream teacher's folder

This included student work done in the mainstream classroom, charting progress in reading, writing, language arts, and in content areas. The elementary and secondary language-arts teachers decided to begin by collecting the following from each student:

+ A reading log
+ Four writing samples, one from each quarter of the school year
+ A running record for reading
+ A record of student conferences
+ Benchmarks for the grade level and indicators of which ones had been reached

The ESL teacher's folder

This included student work done during ESL time, charting progress in English proficiency. The file included

+ Checklists of vocabulary learned

+ Writing samples

+ Work samples from the themes covered

+ ESL standards checklists and records of which ones had been mastered

The cumulative folder

This folder included the information the school kept in its cumulative record as well as a student portfolio. The latter, assembled at the end of the year by the mainstream and ESL teachers, demonstrated mastery of skills and content, and showed what the student had accomplished during that year so that the next year's teacher knew where to begin. The cumulative folder stayed with the school or was sent with the student if he moved. The cumulative folder included

+ Student personal-information records

+ Home-language survey

+ Additional assessment reports

+ Data such as grades

+ Standardized placement test scores

+ A student portfolio including

    + Vocabulary checklist

    + Narrative reports of semester progress

    + Reading inventory

    + Student work samples, including one written sample that included a rough and a final draft

    + Parent-teacher conference report

5. Decide how each piece of evidence will be used

Evidence in the folder might be used

+ to retain or pass a student ~~reccomendations~~

+ to assign grades

+ for reclassifying a student

+ to show growth

+ to demonstrate mastery of standards

6. Decide how to present the data

Mindamon teachers knew that data had to be valuable to the stakeholders, so they tried to determine at what point data loses its meaning. They discovered that there are many ways to put collected information into clear and readable form for interested audiences, including through narratives, checklists, portfolios comprised of work samples, student self-evaluations, and so on. We explain this in the next few pages.

7. Decide how to evaluate folder contents

You need to ask

+ Has this student met, or made progress toward, his goals?

+ Does this evidence document that progress?

+ If not, what clearer or better evidence will document mastery and progress?

PRESENTING THE DATA TO THE STAKEHOLDERS

In chapters 5 and 6, we discussed three ways of collecting information about students: observing the student at work, talking with the student, and sampling the student's work. We discussed the use of anecdotes, rubrics, checklists, and conferences, as well as looking, in a focused way, at student processes and product. Now, the data has to be arranged in a way that the other stakeholders can understand. This means looking at the collection of information—the anecdotes, the writing folders, the reading logs—and selecting the ones that are the most telling. It also means capturing the information in readable form.

Folders can get out of hand in a hurry, becoming huge bins of information bulging with papers, samples, and anecdotes that no one wants to wade through. Sooner or later, someone has to do some weeding and sorting, coalescing the information for both presentation to the stakeholders and for the cumulative file. There are three primary ways to do this.

1. Narratives provide summaries of student progress.

2. Checklists put, into graphic form, what the student knows and how well he knows it, focusing on specific markers in skill development or content area mastery.

3. Portfolios reveal both growth and mastery and are best suited for showing progress over a longer period of time.

Narratives *— this is what I bring to TCP} 504's etc. written from my notes*

Narratives are used by many elementary teachers to describe student progress, adding notes from their anecdotal records on a regular basis. When you use narratives along with a grading and/or report-card system, it rounds out the picture of the student. For instance, after reviewing her notes about an eight-year-old student, one teacher wrote this on her progress report:

> *November*

> **Anna is adjusting to the third grade. She participates in classroom discussions and volunteers to read.**

January

Anna had a difficult time with the time and money units and could use extra help at home. We have started multiplication and Anna could use help at home to learn her facts.

March

Anna is a very hard worker. She always stays on task. As her English becomes better, she will use better sentence structure. Anna always wants to do her best. Anna needs to work on telling time and place value—ten more, ten less.

June

Anna has been a pleasure to have in class. She is a good learner. Be sure to go to the library a lot over the summer. It will help Anna be a better reader in fourth grade. Have a safe and happy summer. I have enjoyed working with Anna. She is a nice girl. Anna is a hard worker.

It is important for the teacher to find positive things to say. In the above example, the extra information in the affective areas was valuable, because it helped the parents feel good about what their child was doing right. The extra note to Anna also helped her to feel good about herself. The teacher also let the parents know specifically where Anna needed to work harder and how they could help her at home.

Many schools use narratives exclusively. To be effective—especially when they are the only means of reporting—narratives must be

- concise and specific

- geared and useful to the audiences reading them, offering a clear idea of what to do next with the student

- indicative of the student's strengths and weaknesses

Davies et al. (1992) suggest ways of making narrative reports specific and effective.

- Have a collection of evidence upon which to base your observations

- Support what you say with samples of classroom activity. For example

  Tien is making real strides with her listening and speaking skills. She is beginning to raise her hand to ask a question during group discussion.

- Include quotations from students' work. For example (italicized words were copied straight from the text):

  Chun is making good progress in his language skills. He can write his assignments on his own more and more. I notice when he gets stuck trying to find a word for what he wants to say, he finds a phrase that is close to what he wants out of the books and inserts it into the text. Even if the syntax is awkward, he can get his point across. For example, on the erosion assignment, Chun wrote, "Wind is one of main force erosion. It move only *small rock particles. Abrasion and deflation help wind erode the land.* Also help erode mountain too."

+ Use quotations from students. For example:

> Maria is much more relaxed in her conversation this year. She has all but mastered conversational English, even to the point of using the popular slang of her peers who use the phrase "I'm all" (the word *all* functioning as a verb) tacked onto another phrase. For example, "Barb told me this homework was easy but, I'm all, 'sure it was a piece of cake'." As Maria explained her disagreement with her brother, she said, "Tonio is so lazy he won't do anything and, I'm all, 'What do you want, I can't do everything for you'."

The following narrative was on the right track but didn't give enough information:

> Tou is very ambitious to do and complete just about anything. He doesn't have a problem being creative at all. His striving for perfection, such as in spelling, sometimes keeps him from advancing. Overall he's doing well, but sometimes lacks certain cultural knowledge due to his own culture.

This narrative could have been improved by citing examples of Tou's creativity, while examples of cultural knowledge he was lacking could have helped both the mainstream teacher and his parents work with him to fill in the gaps.

The following narrative is better, but still missed the mark:

> Diana has been developing number base. She can tell if numbers are greater or less, that numbers have a sequence, and that there is an order when writing them. She continues to recognize patterns not only with numbers and objects but also in her reading. Diana is a slow math worker. We have worked on solving one- and two-digit addition/subtraction problems. Diana understands the process and uses manipulatives to help solve the problem. Subtraction is much harder for Diana to understand and we are practicing only one-digit problems with that.

This report was frustrating for Diana's mother, because it was not specific enough. It did not tell Diana's mother whether or not Diana was working at the level she should for a first grader. And the tone suggested that the teacher was really reaching for something nice to say about the student.

At the time, Diana had been complaining that she hated school and had continually tried to invent reasons to stay home. Because she had always loved school, this set off alarm bells for Diana's mother. So she did what good teachers do: she watched, listened, and asked questions. She learned that Diana was so slow completing her work that she never got any free time. The other children teased her about this, and it had become such a source of anguish that she did not want to go to school. At home, Diana would cry when she tried to do worksheets. Her mother discovered that she knew how to add 1, 0, and the same digit to itself, but beyond that she had to count on her fingers. Subtraction was extra hard. Once, when trying to figure out 5 − 4, she counted out five fingers on one hand and four fingers on the other; then, she counted down four and came up with the answer 5. It was clear that she was not grasping the basic principles.

Diana's mother told the teacher what she had noticed. Knowing what Diana did and did not understand helped both mother and teacher determine how to help her—both at school and at home.

The following narrative provides concise, specific information:

> **Ahmer is improving in math. He has shown that he is very capable in adding two-, three-, and four-digit numbers. He handles regrouping well. He can carry and borrow in addition and subtraction. For the math assignments, Ahmer worked independently. During problem solving Ahmer worked with a partner or small group. I am beginning to use story problems in class, and in this area, Ahmer is having a difficult time. I feel he does not understand the language of the problem and thus has a hard time with the problem solving itself. This type of problem also shows up in science and in social studies.**
>
> **Ahmer does well in classroom discussions, but when it comes to reading independently, doing idea maps or similar activities, he struggles. He did not do well on the science test, and for future tests his ESL teacher will have him take it with her so he will be evaluated on his content knowledge, not his language ability. Ahmer is a likable little boy who gets along well with his fellow students. He is artistic and is a reliable and hardworking student. Ahmer is a nice child and tries very hard to work to the best of his ability.**

In the upper-grade reporting systems, it is unrealistic to expect narratives to play more than a small role. Being saddled with narratives could be the proverbial last straw when trying to stay on top of the logistics of teaching more than 100 students in several classes. However, as discussed in chapter 8, grading is one of the most frustrating aspects of teaching. How many times have you looked at a C– or a *D*+ and thought, "There is so much more to this kid; how can I convey that with more than a letter grade that will just defeat him?" A couple of simple sentences would go a long way. Used in conjunction with checklists, portfolios, and videotapes, narratives can be invaluable to each of the stakeholders.

Checklists

We discussed checklists in chapter 6. However, we want to emphasize their usefulness for

ASSESSMENT OF LITERACY SKILLS

Name	Evaluator		Date
READING	**Emerging Skill**	**Developing Skill**	**Mastery of Skill**
AUTONOMY	1 2	3 4 5	6 7
* Enjoys listening to stories			
* Selects books independently to "read"			
* Brings book from home to read or share			
* Takes books home to read			
* Talks about what he/she read			
* "Read" favorite stories to others			
BOOK HANDLING SKILLS			
* Recognizes front of book			
* Holds book right side up			
* Turns pages one at a time			
* Identifies top			
* Identifies bottom			
* Runs fingers from left to right			
CONTEXTURALIZED PRINT			
* Recognizes common logos (e.g. McDonald's)			
* Reads common logos (e.g. McDonald's)			
* Comprehends common logos (e.g. McDonald's)			
* Recognizes generic product name (e.g. Crest = toothpaste)			
* Reads generic product name (e.g. Crest = toothpaste)			
* Comprehends generic product name (e.g. Crest = toothpaste)			
* Recognizes food product names (e.g. Cheerios)			
* Reads food product names (e.g. Cheerios)			
* Comprehends food product names (e.g. Cheerios)			
* Recognizes traffic signs (STOP)			
* Reads traffic signs (STOP)			
* Comprehends traffic signs (STOP)			
* Recognizes toy names/logos (e.g. Lego's)			
* Reads toy names/logos (e.g. Lego's)			
* Comprehends toy names/logos (e.g. Lego's)			
* Recognizes clothing labels/logos (e.g. alligator = swish logo = Nike)			
* Reads clothing labels/logos (e.g. alligator = swish logo = Nike)			
* Comprehends clothing labels/logos (e.g. alligator = swish logo = Nike)			
* Recognizes survival words (e.g. MEN, EXIT, PHONE)			
* Reads survival words (e.g. MEN, EXIT, PHONE)			
* Comprehends survival words (e.g. MEN, EXIT, PHONE)			

Figure 9.1 A checklist such as this is useful for reporting both formative and summative data.

reporting both formative and summative data. Figure 9.1 (previous page) is a good example of such a checklist. However it is used, a checklist must reflect your philosophy and your beliefs about what is important.

Portfolios

The number of publications about portfolios is staggering. Their promise and use as alternatives to standardized testing excited a great deal of interest in the early and mid-1990s. In those heady days, when alternative/authentic assessment seemed to be *the answer* to all our assessment woes, portfolios were at the forefront of the movement. In the intervening years, we have become more realistic about what portfolios can do and their place in the overall system of student evaluation. But, while portfolios have taken a back seat to standardized testing, they are still the most useful and revealing way of showing growth, mastery, and true pictures of where a student is functioning.

According to Hebert (2001), the significance of what portfolios can accomplish has not changed, but their use has not reached its full potential because "portfolios are sometimes made into what they shouldn't be." Defining portfolios as a collection of student work is what Solomon (2003) calls an "empty definition." Then, they become simply "a collection of almost anything for almost any purpose for almost anyone."

Hebert writes, "Teachers who are uneasy with standardized tests and single number characterizations of children's progress instinctively use portfolios in an attempt to prove their students' achievements." When we have a student, particularly an English-language learner, whose gifts and abilities are not reflected in his test scores, we naturally turn to collections of his work to demonstrate what he really can do.

Hebert believes that the notion of a portfolio reflecting the realities of a child's education, rather than only the high points, has been lost.

> *This shift in function from memory box to standardized test supplement is an impediment to the portfolio's usefulness. The first problem is the overriding expectation to serve as a qualitative companion to quantitative measure and has placed a huge burden of expectation on portfolios—an expectation that cannot be fulfilled appropriately.*

This is a caution we must hold in the forefronts of our minds. As one administrator noted, teachers can often be heard saying, "It's all right. I have his portfolio," as if that would override the test scores and the grades. It will not, and we cannot expect portfolios to fill in that large gap and satisfy everyone.

So what can we reasonably expect from portfolios? We agree with Paulson's (1991) definition of portfolio as

> *...a purposeful collection of student work that exhibits the student's efforts, progress, and achievement in one or more areas...the collection must include student participation in selecting contents, the criteria for judging merit, and evidence of student reflection.*

Some (French, 1992), include the word "chronological" in the definition, but we find this to be too limiting. At their best, portfolios take into account product, process, growth, achievement, and individual difference. They serve as the basis for examining effort, improvement, process, and achievement, and they support

- Alignment with the curriculum
- Student engagement in their own learning and evaluation
- Growth over time   *Not chronological?*

Collections of work can become portfolios with the addition of one ingredient: student input. The key difference between a portfolio and a folder of a student's work is the *student participation*. A fourth-grade teacher notes:

> *The real value as I see it is an ownership role that it puts the students in. They can take the initiative in their own interest, have some control over how they are seen, and be able to make decisions that affect them…A portfolio can reveal a student's growth and strengths in a way that standardized testing cannot. It can present a more complete and tangible picture of a student's academic and creative abilities.*

There are some drawbacks to portfolios.

- They take a great deal of thought to develop and implement. Teachers and schools must decide what place portfolios have in the grading scheme and what weight to assign their contents.

- They take time—time to learn how to use them; time to work through what to include; time to instruct students in their uses; time to reflect upon; time to retrieve from storage or to download, if digital.

- They take up space. Storing the collections can be unwieldy, overwhelming, and sometimes ludicrous, even when they are electronic. To be manageable, they must be tended regularly, weeding out the extraneous or no-longer-useful items.

- They take constant tending. Maintaining and revising them are all time-consuming.

- The onus for upkeep and maintenance is often put on students. This can backfire without constant supervision.

- Their long-term credibility is not always supported. It can be a tough sell to stakeholders that a pile of "stuff" is a better indicator of student achievement than a test score.

- If they are mandated, they can become rigid, inflexible, and lose their effectiveness altogether.

There is no single system (nor should there be) of standardizing what a portfolio is, what it should include, and what it reveals to the outside world. We have all seen the calamitous effects of trying to mandate changes at the government level. To mandate such a personal practice as what a portfolio should include, reveal, and rank could invite wholesale disaster. Simply stated, "There is no single correct portfolio" (Hebert, 2001).

There are three guiding questions to consider when designing a portfolio system.

1. **What is the purpose of the portfolio?** To showcase best work? To refute what standardized tests say? To demonstrate progress? To give students a chance to take ownership of their own learning? To teach self-reflection? It could be any of these or any combination of them.

2. **Who owns the portfolio?** Is it the student, the teacher, or the school?

3. **What should the contents of the portfolio be?** Who gets to decide? And who organizes this content?

We believe, as Resnick (1993) stated, that portfolios initiate a "thinking curriculum by stirring up a decision-making process." They oblige you to decide

- what student work is important, showing progress and mastery

- how your teaching will be affected by what the student has achieved or not achieved

- how your teaching can affect your students' work

- how students perceive what they are doing and learning

Advantages to portfolios

Portfolios

- capture and capitalize on what students *can* do, rather than on their errors or deficiencies

- are an ongoing part of instruction and evaluation

- inform instruction. Looking at what has been accomplished, you can see what needs to be revisited, what has been mastered, and where a student is along the continuum

- are multidimensional, including the cognitive, the affective, and the social

- provide for active, collaborative reflection by both you and your students

- are authentic. Students are assessed while they are involved in the learning

- tell a vivid story or history of a student's learning over time. They can show what a student can accomplish in ways that tests and report cards cannot

- give students ownership of their learning in ways that no other assessment tool can

- provide a structure for what is to be assessed

- act as models for other students of what is expected of them

- provide a structure for understanding grades and report cards, which can be meaningless to students and parents

- provide concrete access into conversations and interactions about learning

- respond to the individual needs of the students. All students learn in different ways and at different rates

- allow students to examine, and take an active part in, their own learning

Stages of usefulness of portfolios

Hebert (2001) discusses various stages of usefulness of portfolios. This can help you to determine what is valuable to schools and the parents of limited-English students.

Stage 1: No material presented

Fernando's dad, Mr. Rodriguez, came to the school for a parent-teacher conference. His English was minimal, so he relied on Fernando to translate. "So far, Fernando has 89 out of a possible 137 points. He got a 20 out of a possible 40 on his exam," Mr. Johnson told Mr. Rodriguez. He also said that Fernando did not participate in class discussions and that part of his grade was based on participation. Mr. Rodriguez did not have anything concrete to look at and had to take Mr. Johnson's word for the fact that Fernando was not living up to expectations.

Many non-English-speaking parents do not—and cannot—understand the whole picture. They may not know what the norms are for schooling in North America. They have no frame of reference, no context for what they are being told. And, in this case, they also have nothing to see, only words or numbers. This sort of conference is useless. All Mr. Rodriguez learned was that Fernando was not doing well—not why, not how, and certainly not how to help him improve.

Stage 2: Student work folders

Even a collection of "stuff" at the earliest stages can be useful and constitute a beginning. For instance, Barb had her seventh graders put all their work into folders. That was their responsibility. When a student complained about a 0 in the grade book, Barb would say, simply, "Show me what you have done."

These folders can be shown to parents for discussing what is happening with their child. During parent-teacher conferences, Barb could bring out the folders and show parents exactly what their child had completed, what was shoddy or incomplete work, what

he had put together in slapdash fashion, what he had labored over, and how much content he actually understood and was able to articulate. Parents like to see what is going on in the classroom. A student work folder keeps all the product in one place and can be dumped at the end of the marking period.

To the right is Elise's free-write to the prompt "That substitute was so strange!" The teacher could have shown this to Elise's mother and said, "Here is Elise's work. She is really doing well. Look at her vivid descriptions."

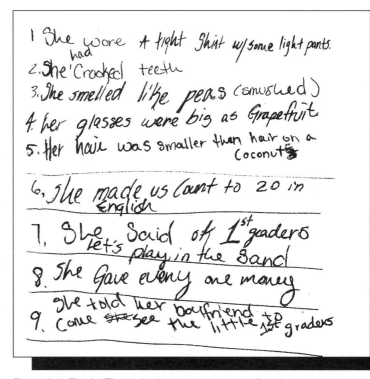

Figure 9.2 Elise's "That substitute was so strange!" assignment

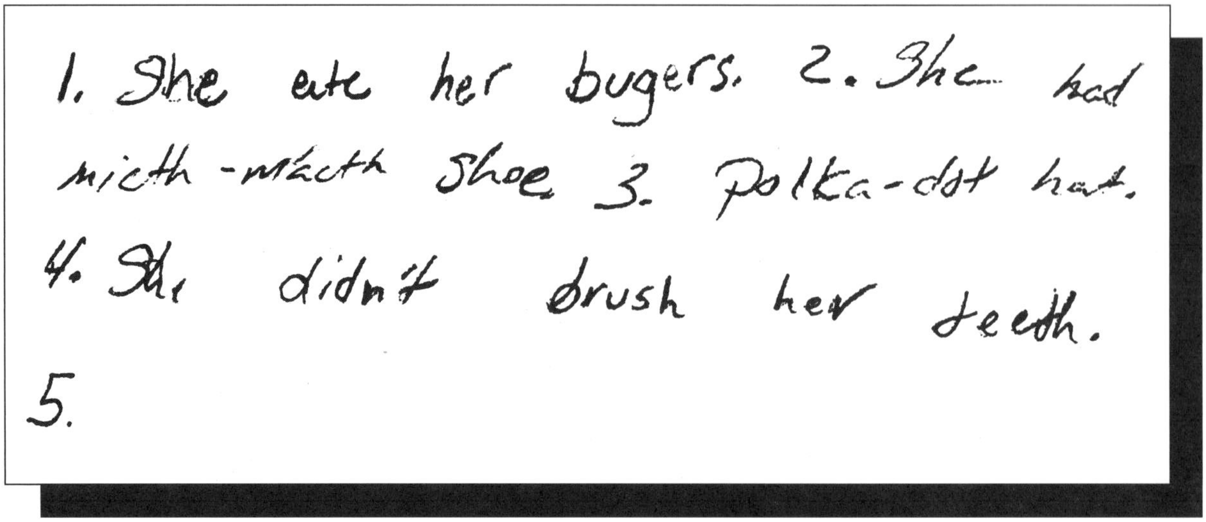
1. She ate her bugers. 2. She had micth-macth shoe 3. Polka-dot hat.
4. She didn't brush her teeth.
5.

Figure 9.3 Javon's "That substitute was so strange!" assignment

On the other hand, she could have shown the figure above (figure 9.3) to Javon's mother and said, "This is what Javon has done. This is not seventh-grade quality." She could then also have shown Javon's mother Elise's work and said, "Here is what a seventh grader can and should be doing."

At this stage, student reflection is not an integral part of the picture. But students like to look at their work. Whether or not reflection has been institutionalized in the process, they do have an opinion about it, and they certainly know what quality work is, what trash is, and whether they are demonstrating their learning or not.

Stage 3: Collections of selected student work

This stage of usefulness of a portfolio requires more thought and must contain pieces of work that reflect what the student is capable of doing. What goes in it depends on who will be looking at it.

On the opposite page are samples of Barb's daughter's writing, collected during her first semester in school. It is revealing to see what Kate knew about print and how she gained control over forms.

On page 232 are selections of José's writing over a period of time. Shown side by side, these graphic examples are very helpful in showing his progress in ways a narrative never would. In the first piece, José was just an emerging writer, and his letters were not clearly formed. In the second piece, José showed much more control over his writing. He was responding to frame sentences: "I was born in… My father's name is…" His spelling was, for the most part, correct because he was copying his teacher's writing. But when he did not pay careful attention, he went astray as in "Metico" and "mot nr's" (mother's). When asked to write his own thoughts, José made errors typical of a beginning writer, writing the consonants *n* and *w* for *now*, and sounding out *rock and roll*. Note how he wrote the *m*, in *music*, upside down. In the third piece, José was in third grade, and his writing had progressed further. He made one minor error in *would*, which he later corrected.

(a)

(b)

Figure 9.4 Kate's writing: (a) Barb wrote Kate's name on a piece of paper, and Kate copied it over and over again. (b) Kate wrote her name by heart. The uppercase and lowercase letters reveal that she knew her letters and probably included them all to make sure she got everything in. (c) By the middle of kindergarten, Kate could write her name competently.

(c)

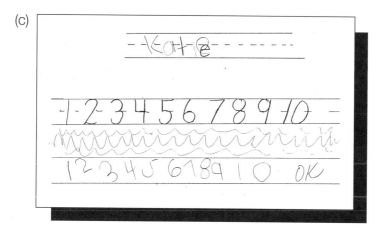

Stage 4: Progress portfolios and showcase or achievement portfolios

This stage of usefulness of a portfolio takes even more thought. With a goal to show growth over time, a progress portfolio includes samples collected at regular intervals, while a showcase portfolio shows selections of the student's best work. For both types, you either define who will be looking at the portfolio and then tailor its purpose and content accordingly, or you create the portfolio for a specific purpose, which the work will demonstrate.

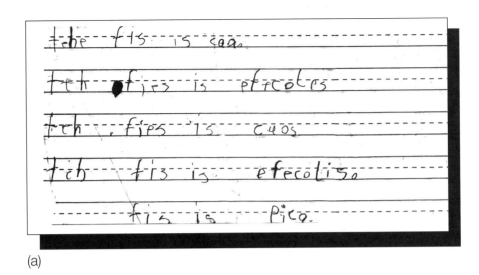

(a)

Figure 9.5 José (a) as an emerging writer (b) with more control (c) as a third grader

(b)

My name is Cose
I was born in Mexico.
My fathers' name is
Carlos, My mot nr's
name is Sara. I have
one broter.
    When I was little I li
d to suim I took
my friends
with me to the
circus. Nw I like
to titen to rouk
and roll wa sic.

(c)

February 28, 2000
Dear Dr. Law,
    I would like to read
with you. You help me to learn
words in English.
I like when we practice the
flash cards. I like when we
write about flowers.
Your f

your friends
José 9

232

Here is a generic example of what the contents list might look like for either a showcase or a progress portfolio:

+ A reading inventory

+ A running record or a summary/response to a grade-level text

+ Selected student work samples including

    + One piece written early in the year

    + One written research report including a rough draft and a final draft

+ A writing sample using an English-language scoring device (for example, the 6+1 Trait® Writing Assessment Scoring Guide)

+ Content achievement in English and/or primary language

+ Teacher observations

+ A parent-teacher conference report

+ Student self-evaluations

+ Grades

+ Teacher and/or parent recommendations

The ideal portfolio has students participating in the selection and analysis of its contents. Even at the lower grades, it is important for students to learn how to ask, where am I as a learner, and how do I get to the next step? (An example of self-analysis can be found on page 178 of chapter 6: Mary's interview with Enrique.) A student can analyze any of the following for inclusion in his portfolio:

+ A "best" piece of work

+ Written reflections, such as

    + A letter describing his personal and academic growth

    + Work he should do over or evaluation of a project that needs improvement

+ Goals: a statement outlining three goals for the following semester

Experimenting with portfolios, Barb created selection guidelines for her upper-level ESL class. First, she produced a checklist that included all the assignments students had completed that term. Then, she generated questions students had to answer when selecting pieces of work on which they wanted to be graded. Here is what it looked like:

1. *Fill out the assignment checklist, checking off all that you have completed and including a page number for each assignment. Hand in the entire set of assignments with the checklist.*

2. *Rate your writing. Which piece is the best? Which is the worst? How did you decide?*

3. *Make your own portfolio of work. Include the pieces of work on which you would like to be graded. Fill out the self-evaluation sheet for your portfolio.*

Portfolio Self-Evaluation

Name_____

1. What does your portfolio reveal about you as a reader?

    _____

2. What does your portfolio reveal about you as a writer?

    _____

3. What does your portfolio suggest your strengths are?

    _____

4. What does your portfolio suggest about how you have changed?

    _____

5. What do you think people will learn about you from your portfolio?

    _____

6. Select what you think is your best piece of writing from your portfolio.

    a. How does this piece compare with other items you've written this semester?

    _____

    b. How does this piece reflect your strengths in writing?

    _____

    c. How does this piece reflect any difficulties you are having in writing?

    _____

    d. Why did you choose this selection as best? What were your criteria?

    _____

    e. In reflecting on this piece of writing, what do you think you would do differently if you were writing it again?

    _____

7. How has your English improved over the past semester?

    _____

8. How can you document that improvement in your portfolio?

    _____

Figure 9.6 Portfolio Self-Evaluation form. Reproducible master in appendix B

Graves (1992) points out that "the portfolio movement has uncovered just how much help students need in order to learn how to evaluate their own work." Writers often know when their writing is good, he says, but it is hard for them to know why. We cannot expect students to know how to evaluate their work on their first try. This is especially true for many foreign students from traditional cultures who are simply recipients of the knowledge bestowed upon them by the "master," and do not take an active part in their own learning. The questions on the self-evaluation form to the left require much thought and reflection, and students' responses to them are an essential component of the portfolio. Figure 9.6 shows how one student completed it.

Having had little experience articulating what was good and why, this student struggled with the form and came up with vague, inadequate answers. Perhaps the questions were too ambitious for beginners, and Barb should have built up to them slowly. However, if students have difficulty on the first try or teachers fumble around trying to come up with the right questions and procedures, this does not mean the idea should be abandoned. Students need to be trained to look at their writing or their content work and judge for themselves what they have accomplished.

Sotir and Hadi wrote the mock newspaper article on the following page (figure 9.7) together after their class read the play, *Terra Nova*, about the fateful race to the South Pole during which the entire British team perished of cold and starvation. They selected the article as the portfolio piece about which they were most proud.

Portfolios should be designed to communicate clearly with the reader. As with anything meant for another set of eyes, each item needs an explanation. A stakeholder wants to know

+ what the expectation for the item was

+ what the context of the item is

+ how the item compares to what other students have produced

+ if the work shows improvement

+ what needs improvement with the piece of work

As your use of portfolios evolves, the contents can become more and more thoughtful and, as Hebert suggests, more student driven.

Learning to self-evaluate

Evaluating one's own work, as mentioned earlier, is a skill that takes time and effort. To follow are several different examples of self-evaluation formats used for different purposes. Figure 9.8 shows the work of a non-English-speaking fourth grader who completed a simple evaluation of her year at an English school in Paris.

To follow is what Jaesung wrote about his first semester in the U.S., answering the prompt "What I learned this semester." Jaesung was a level 5, and although he made some errors, his writing was clear, and he articulated himself very well:

> Since I came here, I've experienced both joy and sorrow and I've learned a lot of things. Actually, when I left my country, I was filled with restless expectation. So I thought if I go to U.S., I will experience only good thing. However, the result was different because I've experienced some bad thing. For example, I could experience to receive help a lot. When I asked someone's help, I felt happy to receive their help, but on the other hand I felt I become a useless person because I couldn't do anything by myself…
>
> We don't know a person's innermost feelings who needs help before we experience that. This is one thing that I've learned from here. I know that's not enough to be good experience in here, so I'm gong to try to do many things like helping handicapped person. That's my one of plans.

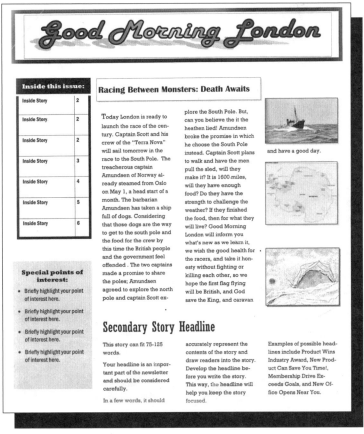

Figure 9.7 The portfolio piece about which Sotir and Hadi were most proud

Figure 9.8 A simple self-evaluation of a fourth-grade student

Evaluation of Presentation

Name *Stephan*

Other members of your group *Maria, Yuki, Miller*

1. What do you think was best about <u>your</u> presentation?

It was not an indifferent presentation

2. What would you change if you could do it over again?

nothing, madam

3. In terms of work, I did (choose one)

    _X_ about the same as everyone else

    ____ more than everyone else

    ____ less than everyone else

4. Explain <u>your</u> part of the work in preparing and in presenting.

I have done everything, the others have just shared the fruits of my work

5. The person(s) who did the most in our group was (were) *of course me*

6. Which group presentation do you think was the best and why?

I don't understand, what is the point of all these questions! Certainly our group's was the best

Figure 9.9 Stephan's evaluation of a group presentation

Figure 9.9 is an evaluation of a group presentation. In it, Stephan demonstrates his wry wit as well as his command of English.

Below, and on the following page, are three evaluations composed in picture form. In them, students are expressing what they enjoyed most about their summer camp experiences.

A word about transient families

Many families are transient, meaning they move often. Maintaining a basic educational record for a transient student, even an unofficial record, and giving it to him at the end of the school year, will help the receiving school know where and how to place him. You can send the student home with a basic portfolio that includes

- A copy of his report card
- A list of books he has read
- A writing sample
- A checklist of skills or content mastered

Figures 9.10, 9.11 Evaluations in picture form

Figure 9.12 Evaluation in picture form

It is also helpful to write a summary of your observations of this student as a learner for inclusion in his cumulative folder. Mary had a student who had fallen through the cracks throughout his educational career. Enrique was a good boy; he was likeable and willing to learn, and his family moved a lot. As a result, the learning challenges he had were never addressed.

By the time he was in tenth grade at the school where Mary worked as an ESL teacher, he was very far behind. He had a great deal of trouble reading, and, because he was an ESL student, it was always assumed that language was the issue. After working with him for a quarter of the year and observing his difficulties, Mary suspected there was more going on than language problems. She kept records and, at an individualized educational plan (IEP) meeting for Enrique, she requested additional testing for him along with other interventions, such as giving him more time for assignments and help reading content texts.

After some diagnostic tests and another quarter of careful observation by Mary, his classroom and special education teachers, and the school psychologist, it was determined that Enrique needed support for reading. With that as well as support for his English, Enrique made great strides.

Then it came time for Enrique to move out of the district. He had only two years of high school left, and Mary did not want him to fall through the cracks again. She recorded what she knew about Enrique so his new teachers could be successful in their work with him right from the start. Mary's report included the following:

+ He did best when given a specific checklist of the parts of an assignment that needed to be completed.

- If, before he wrote something, he was able to describe to someone what he needed to write in sufficient detail, he would finish the work.

- He needed support in reading content texts like history or psychology.

- He loved art and was very good at it.

- He had never considered college or other post-secondary education, because he did not know what options were available.

This information described Enrique's learning context. Of course, his new school would also have documents showing Enrique's special ed/ESL designations, but the description of who he was as a learner meant the new school would not have to reinvent the wheel when it came to what he needed to succeed.

MEETING WITH THE STAKEHOLDERS: HOLDING CONFERENCES

Conferences with Parents

Convincing non-English-speaking parents to attend conferences or even to come to the school can be a trial. However, it is wrong to assume that parents who do not visibly participate in their child's education do not care about it. A fundamental wish of many immigrant parents is for their children to have a better life than they have had. Many leave their home country and come to the United States or Canada for that very reason.

Realizing the dream is another matter. Often parents are disenfranchised. They may believe that they have no part in their child's education—that this is the domain of the teacher. They may believe they have nothing to contribute, especially if they are not literate. They may be shy. Their language may be a barrier.

But these obstacles do not preclude having meaningful communication with parents and certainly should not prevent you from trying. Conferences can be enormously revealing for both parties and, if it takes extra effort, the payoff is worth the time taken.

Davies et al. (1992) recommend holding conferences before, not after report cards come out, possibly a month after school has started. This gives you a chance to get to know your student somewhat, but it is not long enough to have formed set opinions. Early on, a parent's insight can help you learn a great deal about your student.

Before the conference: getting to know the parents

It is essential to establish communication with parents right from the outset. One way to get to know parents and their children is to ask them about their child. You might try sending home a questionnaire with questions such as

- What are your child's interests?

- What are your child's strengths?

- What are your child's limitations?

- Are there any things about your child that concern you?

- Is there anything you would like us to know about your child?

Getting the questionnaire to non-English-speaking parents can be nearly as challenging as having it returned. But using whatever means necessary to get the questionnaire translated and having the parents complete it is worth the effort. Parents know more about their child than anyone else and can offer insights that you may not have. Do this early, before you have had a chance to form hard and fast judgments about a student. Following this initial contact, you can set up a three-way conference to include teachers, parents, and the child.

Having participated in numerous successful three-way conferences, both as parents and as teachers, we are convinced of how very useful, revealing. and even touching they can be. Simply meeting with a teacher for ten minutes and looking at a grade sheet brings none of the richness, humanity, and joy that including a well-prepared and proud student, who has carefully selected work to show his parent, can bring.

Ten steps to holding an ESL conference with parents

1. **Be prepared**

   ♦ Find an interpreter, if necessary.

   ♦ Compile the student's portfolio. Make sure it is up to date and shows examples of both his mastery and strengths and his limitations, chosen with the conference in mind.

   ♦ Invite the student. Do *not* use your student as the interpreter if you have serious problems to discuss. This puts him in an extremely awkward, if not anxiety-ridden, position. He may not accurately relay the information between teacher and parent, which can only lead to more problems.

   ♦ Have a plan. Formulate specific questions to ask, know the issues on which you will focus, and prepare recommendations for the parent and student. Fill out a conference record, such as the one shown in figure 9.13, to help you think through what you will say to the parents. The form also compels you to think positively about the student, rather than focus simply on shortcomings.

2. **Make time**—for parents to review the work in their child's portfolio and to explore the room together with their child.

ESL Conference Record/Notes

Student _____ Date _____

Teacher _____

Parents or Guardians _____

Others in attendance _____

| Reasons for conference: |
| Overall classroom performance: |

| Areas of strength in language acquisitions: | Areas needing improvement in language skills: |
| Areas of strength in content: | Areas needing improvement in content: |

| Recommendations and goals: |

| Student will: | Teacher will: | Parent(s) will: |

| Comments: |

Figure 9.13 Use an ESL Conference Record both prior to the conference (to organize your thoughts) and during the conference (to record your notes and establish direction and goals). Reproducible master in appendix B

3. **Keep it simple.** Parents may not have had any experience with schools. Do not use overly technical words that they may not understand.

4. **Respect their culture, heritage, and language.** Parents may feel threatened because they are not literate in their own language. They may also have vastly different perceptions of a teacher's role.

5. **Keep a record of the conference.** Also, make sure you address all relevant issues.

6. **Look at the parents.** This might sound obvious, but, it is particularly important if you use an interpreter, to look at the parents while you are talking. Also, allow time for translation, and keep your attention on the interaction, even if you do not understand what is being said.

7. **Discuss both strengths and weaknesses.**

8. **If the student is not working at grade level, be sure that is explained.**

9. **If there is a problem, tell the parent, but offer a solution.** It is difficult for some parents to help their children with school work.

10. **Set goals together.** Map out a plan, giving each party specific goals to accomplish.

To follow are two case examples of ESL conferences with parents. In both cases, the parents' needs had a profound effect on the outcome and on a change of goals for the child.

Abir

Abir arrived from Egypt with no school records, so she was simply placed in the eighth grade. She did poorly in her initial assessment and was rated non-English proficient (NEP). She rarely completed any schoolwork and never turned in homework. She did not fare much better in ESL, usually answering "I don't know" to questions.

Abir was overweight and wore clothing that other students found to be loud and clashing. The boys quickly discovered they could goad her into violent outbursts: she would scream, slam locker doors, and chase them. She was absent at least twice a week; by the end of the second quarter, she had been absent nearly half the time. However, repeated phone calls to her house were never answered.

Finally, the school reached Abir's father, who agreed to come in for a conference. Her teachers had little or no written work to show him. At this point, however, they were more concerned about Abir's absenteeism and behavior than anything else and wanted to talk about that.

Abir had been invited to the conference, but she did not come. The ESL teacher, the counselor, and both team teachers were present. They stated their concerns politely, presented the father with Abir's absentee report, and showed him the curriculum and the subject matter she needed to learn if she was going to pass eighth grade.

Abir's father said the family was returning to Egypt at the end of the school year. Because both he and Abir's mother worked, they needed Abir at home to take care of the younger children. He did not care if she passed eighth grade here or not. Her future in Egypt was far more important. She was missing a year of school there and needed to pass some very difficult tests in her home language to progress through school and into a good college. Therefore, at home, they concentrated on her studies in Arabic.

The conference resulted in a change of perception for the teachers. Since Abir's father did not have any goals for her as far as English proficiency was concerned, the teachers set a few for themselves. They warned him about truancy, and their threats of reporting him to the authorities seemed to work because Abir's attendance improved. The teachers decided to try to make Abir's stay in the United States more pleasant. They arranged for her to have study time so she could bring her Arabic books to school. They set up additional time in the reading lab and the ESL room for her, and they drew up a plan for modifying grades so that the work she did turn in would count and the year would not be lost. To the right is the completed ESL conference record.

Amos

Five-year-old Amos arrived at the school at the end of January. He had tested NEP and did not respond to any questions on the standardized oral test. He was placed in kindergarten but was soon promoted to first grade, even though the ESL teacher felt his readiness skills were weak.

ESL Conference Record/Notes

Student __Abir__   Date _____

Teacher __Mrs. Crockett__

Parents or Guardians __Father__

Others in attendance __Team Teachers Mrs. Morley and Mr. Dyer__

Reasons for conference:
Abir's attendance has been very low. Has made no friends, and is prone to violent outbursts. Does not do any class work. Teachers are concerned about attitude, attendance, behavior

Overall classroom performance:
Very poor. Does not participate in class, either mainstream or ESL. Does not return homework.

Areas of strength in language acquisitions:	Areas needing improvement in language skills:
Teachers have had little chance to observe any language use.	

Areas of strength in content:	Areas needing improvement in content:
None	All.

Recommendations and goals:
Make this school year a profitable one for Abir. Modify goals & school agenda so that she can study her curriculum and still pass 8th grade.

Student will:	Teacher will:	Parent will:
Attend class every day. Turn in assignments.	Adapt lessons. Build in time for study of Egyptian curriculum at school. ↳ set up time in reading lab	make sure Abir is at school. Encourage English, Ensure homework completed. Send ↳ Egyptian curric. materials.

Comments:
Father seemed to be receptive to teachers' concerns. All parties agreed to meet again in one month.

Figure 9.14 Completed conference record following the meeting with Abir's father

On her report, she wrote that he needed continued ESL support and that he might need to repeat first grade.

Before the conference, Amos proudly showed his father around the room. He sat quietly on his father's lap during the conference, where they reviewed Amos's portfolio. The teacher presented the alphabet sheet Amos had received during his first month of school (see figure 9.15a) as well as a more recent one that Amos had completed confidently and without error. They also looked at some writing samples. The letter to the second-grade teacher was particularly revealing (figure 9.15b). Most of it had been copied; Amos had been unable to fill in his address and could not tell the teacher anything about himself. The final page showed much progress (figure 9.15c). Amos was moving along and demonstrating a good grasp of sound-letter correspondence in his spelling.

Amos had come a long way, but his teachers were still concerned that he was not ready for the demands of second grade. His problems were not simply language related; by the end of the school year, he still lagged far behind in skills and knowledge generally expected of a first grader. After carefully reviewing the work presented, Amos's father shared the teachers' concerns about Amos's reading level and his English proficiency. He requested that Amos be retained in the first grade. However, concerned about the hazards of retention, the teachers recommended that he be placed in a grade one-two split. That way, he could enter in grade one and, if he made sufficient gain, he could exit from grade two. Together, teachers and parent decided on the best solution.

(a)

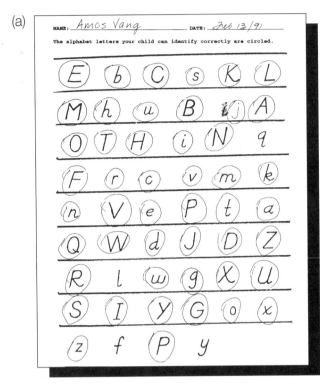

Figure 9.15 Samples from Amos's portfolio, including (a) an alphabet identification sheet, (b) a letter to the second-grade teacher, and (c) a later writing sample

(b)

(c)

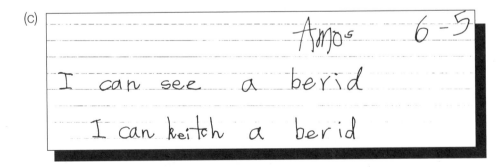

READING LANGUAGE ARTS CHECKLIST
FIRST GRADE

Name _Amos Vang_   School _Elm Vale_

Teacher _Connie Greene_

Key   Beg. = the student is just beginning to develop behavior
       Dev. = the student is developing the behavior
       Secure = the behavior is characteristic of the student
       Directions: Circle a descriptor on the continuum, or make a slash at
       the appropriate point.

	Date: X	Date: 5-91
Print Awareness & Conventions:		
1) Expects print to be meaningful	Not yet Dev. Secure	Not yet (Dev.) Secure
2) Recognizes letters of alphabet (upper and lower case)	Not yet Dev. Secure	Not yet (Dev.) Secure
3) Aware of letter-sound relationships	Not yet Dev. Secure	Not yet (Dev.) Secure
4) Understands directionality of lines of print and page sequences	Not yet Dev. Secure	Not yet (Dev.) Secure
Oral Reading:		
1) Joins in unison reading	Not yet Dev. Secure	Not yet (Dev.) Secure
2) Reads own dictated stories with fluency	Not yet Dev. Secure	Not yet (Dev.) Secure
3) Reads with expression	Not yet Dev. Secure	(Not yet) Dev. Secure
4) Self-corrects miscues that do not make sense	Not yet Dev. Secure	(Not yet) Dev. Secure
5) Knows common sight words	Not yet Dev. Secure	Not yet (Dev.) Secure
Reading Strategies/Comprehension:		
1) Uses prior knowledge to make predictions	Not yet Dev. Secure	(Not yet) Dev. Secure
2) Uses clues (pictures, meaning, word order, phonics) when reading	Not yet Dev. Secure	Not yet (Dev.) Secure
3) Uses strategies to correct difficulties (e.g., rereading, reading ahead, pausing to reflect)	Not yet Dev. Secure	(Not yet) Dev. Secure
4) Retells stories (heard or read) in appropriate sequence	Not yet Dev. Secure	Not yet (Dev.) Secure

Figure 9.16 This detailed checklist of skills and strategies was another important component of Amos's portfolio (note that only half of the checklist is shown here).

Conferences with Teachers

Teachers are critical stakeholders in a student's education. Communication among ESL teachers, mainstream teachers, and other service providers is especially critical, and time must be allotted for this. Because ESL teachers assume responsibility for the student's English, they also tend to assume responsibility for the student himself. This means they must also take responsibility for establishing meetings and ensuring that information is exchanged. Adamson et al. (1990) report that many teachers schedule a block of time every day to meet with other teachers; they arrange their schedules to facilitate that communication on an ongoing basis. There are several times during the year when ESL and mainstream teachers should meet.

* **At a student's first placement within the classroom.** It is only fair that a teacher receive advance warning when a new student is coming. At this meeting, it is important to discuss the student's proficiency levels, his English, his reading skills, and any other factors that might impact the teacher and the class.

* **For intermittent reviews concerning parent-teacher conferences.** Each school must decide who is responsible for parent-teacher conferences. In many schools, the ESL and mainstream teachers meet to plan what to present to the parent.

* **For progress reviews.** ESL teachers should not be focusing solely on English skills; they should also be teaching the curriculum. Conversely, classroom teachers should be teaching English, not simply leaving the responsibility of language acquisition to the ESL teacher. During this meeting, teachers should review the student's progress, coordinate instruction, and share ideas, impressions, concerns, and lesson plans.

* **When exiting a student from ESL into the mainstream.**

By discussing the following, the ESL teacher and the mainstream teacher can define instruction that the student needs:

* What is the student achieving in the regular classroom? The mainstream teacher reports on curriculum mastery.

* What is the student achieving in the ESL classroom? The ESL teacher reports on language gains.

* What does each teacher observe in the student?

* What should each teacher put into the student's portfolio, and how should they share the portfolios?

CONCLUSION

Demonstrating what students have mastered, where their weak points are, and where they need to go next has always been a difficult hurdle to overcome. But, as districts and schools have continued to struggle with the best approaches for change, important steps have emerged. One thing remains certain: before any reporting system can be successful—no matter what type of system is used—it must be clear who the data is for so that content can be organized with that audience in mind.

Converting Fahrenheit into Cellulose
STANDARDS

Barb attended a conference about the launching of standards that would anchor all educational endeavors thereafter in that discipline. At the end of the conference, when the audience was invited to ask questions, she stood up at the back and asked, "Now that we have standards in place, have we given any thought to what happens when students do not meet them?"

The moderator looked blankly at her for a moment and then abruptly concluded the meeting, leaving Barb wondering which foot she had put in her mouth this time, and what was wrong with that question.

Bad timing? Maybe. Premature question? No. Important? Absolutely. It is one of the most critical questions to ask, is it not? It is wonderful to have standards. Who wants their kid to go to a school with low standards? But how high is high? And when is high not so high? And who decides where the cutoff is between high and low? And what do we do about those kids who cannot get high enough?

If we put standards in place, it is imperative that we also ask, how do we make sure all students reach them and make doubly sure that we have programs in place to help kids achieve them? And, even before that, we must ask, what is the purpose of these standards, who are the standards for, and can they accomplish what they are meant to accomplish?

What's in this Chapter

+ What standards are

+ Why we have standards and what their purpose is

+ The pitfalls of standards

- Living with standards
- What standards ought to look like

When she was working as an associate professor, Barb's department at the university was informed by the state that, as part of a restructuring effort, it must become standards- and outcome-based. All courses were to be aligned with standards. All outcomes were to be determined and articulated. The education program at the university could no longer offer straight elementary or secondary credentials and needed to be overhauled. Students within the education program would have to undergo assessment before, during, and at the end of their course of study in order to determine how well prospective teachers were meeting the articulated education standards.

The faculty met for days and days, even on weekends—all on top of their regular load of teaching, service, and scholarship. They had no choice. If they did not make these changes, the state could shut down the entire program and take away their right to certify teachers. In the fall of 2001, an official from the state came to lead yet another all-day meeting. When Barb arrived at the meeting, the official was intoning at length how her department was two years behind schedule and would have to work double-time to have this restructuring in place by the deadline. Barb could not stand it any longer. She asked, "Is there any evidence to demonstrate that, after all this work, we will produce a better teacher?"

The answer? "Barb, it does not matter." What mattered was that the state had told them to do it.

Beg pardon?

Even more critical questions pop up. Where have our priorities gone? What is really important? Why are we doing this?

Despite others' agendas, an educator's main priority is to increase learning for students. Implementing arduous change that does not help to raise student achievement can be pretty hard for a teacher to take.

STANDARDS: WHAT THEY ARE AND WHY WE HAVE THEM

Clearly and simply, standards are expectations of what all students should know and be able to do. To say you have reached a given standard, you must be able to demonstrate that you have the knowledge, the skills, or the abilities at a specified level of competence. We have standards "to ensure that all students achieve the same levels of knowledge of content and expectations" (Carr, 2001). Governing bodies generally tout standards as a way of encouraging students to achieve a higher level of learning.

This sounds reasonable. Other people have standards to meet, too. We expect lifeguards to have demonstrated they are attentive, can swim out and reach a struggling swimmer in time, and know how to tow the swimmer safely to shore and, if necessary, resuscitate him. We have the right to expect that doctors know the difference between a spleen and an appendix or that school bus drivers are not likely to overturn in the ditch. All of the people on whom we depend have to demonstrate skills and meet standards of excellence. We also have the right to expect that the teachers with whom we entrust our kids know the content they are teaching and know how to deliver it in such a way that our kids not only learn it but love learning. And, we have the right to expect that what our kids are learning is worth learning.

In an ideal world, standards would be

- Public
- Shared across schools and districts
- High quality
- Balanced (one skill or subject does not outweigh other important areas of knowledge)
- Coherent
- Relevant
- A foundation onto which schools and teachers could build a deep and rich educational experience

This sounds simple and straightforward, but it is not. Nor is it necessarily realistic. We are not saying that we cannot hold our students to high standards, or that we would not want to. But is it realistic to expect that a non-English-speaking student, who arrives to our English-speaking country in the tenth grade with little or no schooling, has to meet all the standards for high school graduation or be denied? The reality for English-language learners is that many of them move often. They start school in October, return to their birth country in November, only to leave again in April. They arrive from war-torn countries with profoundly disrupted schooling and a great deal of emotional baggage. They have different educational standards in their home countries, and they acquire English at differing rates. None of these situations makes the implementation of standards easy.

The Pitfalls of Standards

In the years since we published the first edition of this book, many things have changed. In the 1990s, authentic assessment held great promise, and we were hopeful we could break the bonds of standardized testing and assess all students more fairly and accurately. Since then, accountability, outcome-based assessment, and standards have taken center stage while authentic assessment has been put on the back burner and failed, in many ways, to achieve the promise it held for teachers.

In this chapter, we raise more questions than we answer. But this is critical in order to untangle the mass of conflicting opinions about standards and try to figure out, in face of the fact that standards are not optional, what we are going to do about them.

Neill (2003) writes that the difficulties and disruptions caused by the federal government and its imposition of high-stakes testing would be worth enduring if "we could be reasonably sure that the test-driving changes would produce improved learning opportunities and outcomes." At this point in time, we can only be reasonably sure they are not. Even when the standards are well defined, there is no indication that achieving them will lead to success in life. In fact, quite the contrary is true: even those who do poorly on standardized tests can go on to succeed at college and in life.

In one district, the superintendent came to see the first-grade teachers. He was very concerned because test scores had gone down. His understanding was that teachers had done something wrong. The teachers pointed out that they were facing several serious challenges: they had only limited support for the severely disabled and the autistic students under their charge. They had lost hours of aide time, to the point where they had only one hour of aide support per week. They had parent volunteers who did not know how to support in the classroom. The school district had been operating under the common delusions that if you speak English, you can teach ESL, and if you can read and you are a parent, then your presence will be helpful in the classroom. In addition, they had funding to support only four of the twelve Title I (environmentally "at risk") children in their care.

In spite of all the challenges they recounted to the superintendent, and even though they were highly qualified and experienced teachers, they were still blamed for the drop in scores. The superintendent signed them up for beginning-level training in the Open Court reading program (a regimented and systematic phonics/decoding-based program) even though they had been teaching Open Court for years. It did not matter that the teachers did not like the program—the district used it because that was what was funded.

Nothing was done for the eight Title I students who were not receiving support. Their scores would likely drop even more, and the teachers would likely be blamed again. What a waste of everyone's time!

No Child Left Behind

The No Child Left Behind (NCLB) Act, President George W. Bush's education reform plan signed in 2002, substantially upped the ante for everyone in the United States. Today, NCLB is said to be based on stronger accountability for results, increased flexibility and local control, expanded options for parents, and an emphasis on teaching methods that have been proven to work (we beg to differ on those last three pillars, but that is for another book). Two fundamental (although fallacious) principles behind NCLB are: (1) high scores equal high standards (schools the president's kids attended), and (2) low scores equal low or no standards at all (poor schools in poverty-stricken areas). The implication is that teachers in the poor schools are lazy.

According to the government document, *No Child Left Behind: Standards and Assessment – Non Regulatory Guidance (2003):*

> *The cornerstone of any substantive education reform lies in the creation and application of rigorous academic standards…The No Child Let Behind Act has ushered in a new era in American public education, an era that begins with the premise that every child can learn and an era that demands that all children achieve to high standards, regardless of race, socioeconomic status or disability. Only by holding all students to high standards and believing that all children can learn, will every child in America excel and be able to live out his or her dreams.*

The reasons behind NCLB seemed well-intentioned: it championed accountability for all students, particularly minority and non-English-speaking students; it gave states more flexibility in how they spent federal dollars; it claimed to emphasize scientifically proven methods; and, it gave parents choices—if their child's school was underperforming, they could transfer him to a school that was performing better.

[handwritten margin note: No there is less assistance / support, etc.]

At first, teacher-advocate organizations like the National Education Association backed NCLB. However, it became clear that the act was just one more example of the federal government taking control of what had been, and should still be, the role of the states. Consequently, unions and advocate groups needed to fight hard to eliminate some of the worst parts of NCLB.

If meeting standards was not at the top of the agenda before the enactment of NCLB, it certainly became a priority afterwards. The United States Department of Education affirms that "all states and schools will have challenging and clear standards of achievement and accountability for all children, and effective strategies for reaching those standards" (1997). In response, all states developed their own model standards. Each district within a state could choose to adopt the state standards or develop a set of its own.

Several basic assumptions undergirded the original standard setting and testing programs that emerged following the enactment of NCLB (Meier, 2000; Freeman, 2003; McCaslin, 1996). Unfortunately, many of these assumptions were flawed.

+ **Goals:** It was possible and desirable to agree on a single definition of what constituted a well-educated eighteen-year-old and demand that every student and every school be held to the same definition.

+ **Authority:** The job of defining what "well-educated" meant was best left to the experts—politicians, industry leaders, educators. The fact that each state had a different definition meant that a single national standard needed to be instituted.

+ **Uniformity:** When local districts set up their own standards, they were often a hodgepodge, collected or developed higgledy-piggledy without reference to other areas of the curriculum or to other states. As a result, student achievement was frequently inconsistent, and students who moved often got a piecemeal education.

+ **Enforcement:** Sanctions needed to be standardized. It was important to remove decision-making about who failed and whether a school measured up from those closest to the student—teachers, parents, and school boards—who might be susceptible to local pressures. These were the people who had "become accustomed to low standards" (Meier, 2000).

+ **Equity:** The standards would lead to improvement in everyone's education and achievement, resulting in true equity in education, because it would force all schools, especially those with limited resources, to focus on the essentials.

+ **Effective learning:** These clear-cut expectations would be imposed by testing and accountability systems. Testing would lead to positive behavioral changes in both students and teachers, and punishing everyone involved for not meeting those standards would goad them into improvement.

+ **Motivation:** Being compared to more successful peers would motivate low performers to do better. Rewards and punishments led to greater effort. Shame and failure were powerful motivators.

Perhaps the most fundamental assumption behind all this standard-setting brouhaha was the notion that until the experts came around, nobody had any standards. In fact, some authors (Tucker and Codding, 1998) say it outright: "The U.S. has never had any standards at all." This is a load of hooey.

Following the enactment of NCLB in 2002, a firestorm of criticism and rebellion resulted in response to the draconian sanctions, the unrealistic expectations and timelines for change, and the enormous cost of testing. Schools and districts were angry because they were all judged alike, regardless of their population differences or economic difficulties. Economically challenged schools were threatened with closure if they did not perform, but they were not given the tools or funds to improve. Moreover, most ESL students were expected to take the standardized tests, even if they lacked understanding of the language or culture in which the test was administered. Their schools were to be held accountable for those scores.

Janelle Brown (2005) states:

> Twenty-one states have so far introduced some form of legislation opposing the NCLB, ranging from bills that would prohibit state money from being used to implement the act's requirements (Maine, New Hampshire, Vermont, and Wisconsin) to resolutions simply critical of it (Colorado, Connecticut, Hawaii, Maine, New Mexico, Utah, and Virginia) to a Maine law that will allow the state attorney general to file suit against the federal government if the act is proven to be inadequately funded.

As a result, the United States government has had to change many of its original requirements for standard setting and testing programs as well as the timelines in which they must happen. Unfortunately, the changes have only added to the confusion. For instance, when the government granted states local control for standard setting, it actually restricted them even more by imposing new flexibility for spending federal money and yet implementing very strict constraints for doing so. This, in effect, strangled states' abilities to meet the needs of their own students.

It reminds us of an old joke about communism: The government took over a shoe factory. To make the factory more efficient, it decided to make all shoes the same color. Then, to increase efficiency even more, it decided to make all shoes the same style. To further streamline things, it decided to make all shoes the same size. As a final coup de grace in an effort to achieve utmost efficiency, it decided to make shoes for the right foot only.

The enactors of NCLB seemed to be operating along the same lines. They forgot that, as Tip O'Neill (1987) put it, all politics is local. A remote, central government does not understand the limits and possibilities of the local situation. It cannot be flexible and creative in finding solutions to local problems. It cannot make decisions based on changing populations, changing needs, changing circumstances. But the government does make laws, and we have to live with them.

Living with Standards

Here is an example of a district-imposed response to the pressure of meeting the standards—imposed without input from those meant to implement it. A mid-sized district purchased—at enormous cost—a database of all the state's standards in each discipline. It then spent half the year trying to train teachers to use the software. The point of the database was to help instructors track each student's progress in mastering content standards. Theoretically, teachers could create tests and upload them to the database. Done correctly, the database would then keep track of standards reached and record the class's successes (or failures). The teacher could decide to re-teach and retest the material if sufficient progress was not accomplished and could download new test questions to help.

The rationale behind the software was to help teachers focus on the standards and record accurate and detailed information about students' performance. But there were problems with the software. It did not work well for essays or questions requiring short answers. One science teacher complained that only half the standards for her courses were in the database; where would she find the time to add the other half? Most important, teachers were not given the opportunity to decide if this effort would be helpful to them. It was simply purchased, and teachers were trained to use it.

What should standards look like?

In each American state, a task force of educators, parents, school-board members, and industry personnel developed a set of model academic standards describing the skills each student should have by the end of a certain grade. It also detailed what a student might be asked to do, and how well he must perform, to demonstrate that he has met those standards.

Most standards documents begin with very general, all-inclusive statements. Then, each subject area is divided into specific standards: content standards—what students should know and be able to do, performance standards—how students will show they have met the standards, and proficiency standards—how well students have learned the content. The content, performance, and proficiency standards are then broken down into general benchmarks, which describe progress toward the standards. Benchmarks are broken down further still into more specific, embedded concepts and skills.

There are two opposing camps that disagree about how standards should look. Camp one, which includes the American government, believes standards should be clear and specific, and should give teachers, students, and parents plenty of direction. When achievement objectives are inadequately defined, they cannot be grasped by students or teachers, nor can they be successfully taught or reliably assessed.

Camp two swings to the opposite side of the spectrum. Alfie Kohn (2001) writes:

> Most standards are highly specific. Often they consist of hundreds of detailed items, facts, and sub-skills that students have to know. Harold Howe II, the former U.S. Commissioner of Education, was once asked what national standards should be like if they had to be issued. He summarized a half a century's worth of wisdom in four words: 'As vague as possible.' The more narrow and rigid the requirements are the less responsive educators can be to what distinguishes one circumstance from another, or your child from mine.

It is easy to argue for either side. On the one hand, when the expectations are clear, you know where you stand. You can tell when you have met the standard and when you have fallen short of the mark. On the other hand, when there are too many standards and benchmarks, and the focus is increasingly refined, it is easy to get lost in the minutia.

One school outlined that a student in a beginning ESL class had satisfactorily met performance standards when he could

+ discriminate the letters of the alphabet
+ make use of sound/symbol relationships
+ apply prior knowledge to print
+ recognize meaning of common signs
+ recognize personal information text
+ read experiential stories
+ recognize gender-specific names
+ make use of world maps
+ make use of calendars

This led to even more questions: What if Xiong did not know *all* of the letters and sounds of the alphabet? Would he be held back? What if Dave did not know how to apply his prior knowledge to print, but he *did* know the letters? This is not a ridiculous discussion. We have seen it get to that point. And it gets nasty.

Every student is an individual, and learning follows neither a straight nor a tidy path. It is never discrete. Some kids pick it up quickly in one area, but not another. Trying to delineate hard and fast benchmarks just does not work.

Making sense of the standards

You might find yourself straddling the two standards camps when trying to determine how your students are doing. The ESL standards developed by TESOL a decade ago and revised in 2006 are purposefully broad; achieving more extensive goals takes time, so looking for evidence of one standard per lesson would not be feasible. On the other hand, most standards developed by individual states are organized into various levels of sub-standards; you could, in this case, observe ESL students for evidence of which standards they have met lesson by lesson.

For example, Ying Yan, a level-5 sophomore in a regular English class, had a "Burning Issues" assignment in which she was to write about an important, unresolved issue in the book *Fahrenheit 411*. Students had a set format to follow (the assignment had to be presented in the form of a brochure), and they had to cover certain elements of the unresolved issue. They also had to adhere to general essay rules, and the paper was to be two pages long (Ying Yan wrote three).

The TESOL ESL standard addressed in this assignment was goal 3 standard 3. Ying Yan also had to attain the state mainstream English standards addressed by the lesson, which included a general one involving literary response and analysis (standard 3.0), a reading-related one related to themes and issues (3.12) and, for writing, writing applications (2.0), expository composition (2.3), and the mechanics (1.0 through 1.5).

Ying Yan did not really meet the mechanics standards right off, but she did meet the other standards. She was making progress with the ESL standards but it was difficult to see in just one assignment. It was even more difficult not to trip over your feet trying to keep track of all the different standards in the different domains (TESOL, state, and district). It did not boil down to a simple checklist.

252

Why Standards Matter to ESL Students and Teachers

In spite of all its flaws, NCLB had some positive outcomes. It profoundly impacted education in ways that have benefited English-language learners. It has encouraged their full participation in schooling. Lawmakers have recognized what ESL and bilingual teachers have known for a long time: we have received less attention, less help, and less than adequate funding. By finally paying attention to how society allowed many of these students to slip through the cracks, the act has offered opportunity for change.

The act has also forced us to act on behalf of the English-language learners. They are now a rightful part of our community. It is everyone's business to see that they receive the same opportunities as the rest of us so that they can be held to the same standards and have the same options for the future.

TESOL's ESL standards, which have been in place since 1997, were revised in 2006 to address the substantial increase in numbers of ELLs across the United States as well as the passage of the NCLB Act. These standards represent a major step forward. They are carefully thought out, and the indicators offer plenty of leeway for designing methods that demonstrate whether or not your students have met them.

But many issues related to standards still need to be resolved.

- Even minimum standards are usually high stakes. To be considered both reasonable and rigorous, some students have to fail. But, in order to forestall the outcry of parents and other stakeholders, the cut scores have to be set so that fewer students actually fail. The upshot is that these types of standards do not represent challenging or even appropriate expectations for students.

- Standards involve quantifiable data. But, when assessing students, there is much more involved than just scientific data. Some of it is quantifiable; much of it is not.

- Standards presume equal access to education, and this is one of the most problematic issues. Brown (2001) writes:

> To establish standards as though all students have had access and opportunity to learn from a common curriculum is to deny the reality that exists in most schools. Standard setting must be enlightened in terms of fairness to the individual and honest in its representation of quality. In many, if not most schools, it is not possible for a single standard to represent an appropriate expectation of academic quality for the school and still be fair for all of the individuals in that school.

- The consequences of failure to meet the standards are high. Barb's own children attended an inner-city high school where ninety-five percent of students were cultural minorities. Kate's ninth-grade class was about 300 students. By graduation, that was down to 114. Somewhere along the line, two thirds of her class disappeared from the roster. Where did they end up?

- Scapegoating is a real hazard. The National Center for Fair and Open Testing asserts:

> ...demanding that...limited English proficient students reach "proficiency" on standardized tests sets those students and their teachers up for failure. Rather than provide resources so schools can offer the individualized approaches these

students need, NCLB claims that by holding them to the "same standards" they will magically rise to the occasion. But these are the groups disproportionately failing to meet targets. NCLB is causing many students to be scapegoated for dragging down average scores, tempting some schools to drive them out.

- Because tests are bound to fail a certain number of students, the assumption is that remediation will be in place for those who do fail. This means money. But the schools most in need of resources are the very schools from which resources are being taken away as punishment. The National Center for Fair and Open Testing (FairTest) notes that this is based on the "faulty premise that low test scores are caused primarily by inadequate or lazy public school teachers… [and that] strapped districts will see their budgets pinched further and be forced to lay off staff and cut back on services to students who most need extra help."

- No one has decided *whose* standards ultimately should be used. There are TESOL standards, there are state-imposed standards, there are district standards—which ones get followed? Who decides?

- How do the standards fit with what you are teaching? They can really strong-arm your curriculum to the point where you can no longer teach what you need to teach.

For instance, in one district, the high-school English teachers had successfully used novels in their classrooms for many years. Then, they were forced to change to a textbook, because they needed to meet the standards. The district bought the textbooks, which sat on the shelf while the teachers continued to use the novels. Thousands of dollars were wasted on textbooks because the decision, which came from the top, was one that teachers did not readily support.

CONCLUSION

Standards are gates. It is worth the time to investigate what exactly the standards demand from students (and from us), so we can help to open those gates for our students.

Our primary decisions for the future will be based on the following questions:

- What *are* our goals for our English-language learners? What are our goals for *all* students?

- What are the best ways to achieve the results?

- How will we measure the results of these goals?

- What needs to happen, when, how, by whom, and how much will it cost?

We must implement all the decisions that we make in ways that will make our lives and the lives of our students better. We owe it to our students to try. As Meier (2000) writes:

> *We need to make sure that students are well-educated in ways that validate who they are and what they perceive to be their own ends in our society, rather than shoving them into cookie-cutter molds decided for them by policy wonks in Washington, in Ottawa, and ministries of education throughout North America and beyond.*

Fight to the Spinach!

MAKING THE CHANGE

One school district was attempting to implement a comprehensive reading program as a foundation for all other learning. As part of the reading program, the district was also promoting best practices for teaching reading, writing, and in the content areas. Intensive staff development was mandated and teaching was monitored carefully. In Barb's school, the best practices were imposed without warning and with little explanation. The vice-principal announced that the middle-level team had to use word walls. The team complied, and Barb's class dutifully put words on the wall—vocabulary from the social studies and language arts units, Spanish/English cognates, and a beautiful display of numbers in five different languages.

No, that's not a word wall, Barb was told. Well, what is? The vice-principal could not elucidate, other than to say that what Barb was doing was not it.

Next, the team was told it had to do SSR. They began sustained silent reading. They were immediately corrected. It was not *sustained silent* reading, it was *self-selected* reading. What's the difference? Again, the VP could not explain—but they had to do it.

After that, they were told they had to implement centers—groups of students rotating from one activity to another during the time slot that had previously been SSR. The team put it off because of upcoming semester finals, the state standardized test (which would sprawl across three weeks), and the approaching new semester.

Then, the VP interrupted their team planning one morning, demanding a report on how the centers were going. When the team said they had not initiated them yet, she said the centers should have begun yesterday. The centers were up and running the next day, without adequate thought or proper planning. And, in the three weeks between the start of the semester and the resumption of the curriculum, the team managed all of one rotation.

The intense frustration and gnashing of teeth Barb experienced during that dreadful year is, unfortunately, not uncommon. In fact, it is case in point for how the American education system has always functioned. We have been yanked about by the newest fads, cyclical returning to old ways, and too much meddling from power brokers with no insight into what actually happens when the bell rings and you stand before a room full of students.

Something needs to change, and it cannot be more change for the sake of change.

What's in this Chapter

+ How to effect assessment changes in your school and district
+ How and where to begin the process
+ How to involve your stakeholders
+ How to collaborate with your colleagues

WORKING FOR CHANGE

The Elements of Change

Change rarely occurs by happenstance. In any given realm, there are various forces at work, both independently and in concert, that can alter the status quo. *Vision, capacity, ownership,* and *support* are the bases for transforming our schools, according to Spady and Marshall (1991). Solomon (2003) adds the variable of *time* as possibly the most critical factor in this process of change. We add *history* and *voice* to that list.

Vision

According to Spady and Marshall (1991), a view of what we want in the future helps us decide what we need to do in the present. We have to look beyond our resistance to standardized testing, accountability, and narrowing of the curriculum to a concept of what we actually want our schools and our assessment methods to look like. We also need to look beyond the limited discussion of what standardized testing cannot do to what balanced assessment can do.

The concept of vision, however, needs to be qualified. According to Goodson (1993), a vision must represent the voices of those for whom the vision is intended. Currently, the voices pushing the agenda for assessment are not the teachers or the students' but, rather, the politicians and the business sector.

For it to be accepted, the vision of change proposed must also be convincing, Goodson notes. This is where the efforts of teachers and other advocates of alternative assessment tend to fail. Rarely do we present a united front. Teachers are notoriously resistant to change. We are often reactive instead of proactive, and we fight through noncompliance and sabotage. We are too busy in the classroom to fight our own battles, and we allow ourselves to be belittled by a public who, nevertheless, relies on us to do some of the most crucial work in our society.

Capacity

The capacity we have for change depends on many things. We have invested long hours into learning our craft. We have many responsibilities during and after school. We have our own core beliefs. Often, we are operating at maximum capacity; any more change is too much, so it does not happen.

It helps to have people who share your vision at the helm. There is little chance for change if those in charge do not believe in or understand it, or if they are just trying to implement it because someone told them to.

Ownership

It is difficult to feel ownership for changes over which we have no control. If change is to happen, we have to believe in it. We have to change ourselves and our practices to make it reality. We must be able to see the benefits it can bring in order to make it worth the enormous effort it will take.

Support

Program changes in education are frequently abandoned after only a few years due to loss of funding, change of political focus, or changes at the administrative level. New programs promoted by political views will shift with the political winds. Others will be discarded to make room for new ones when the administration in a school or district changes. And so it goes.

It can be difficult to gather reinforcement for change when it is so frequent and willy-nilly. What is consistently missing is support: a person (administrator, teacher, or other) who oversees the new program and maintains its focus and vision. The support person can train, observe, and facilitate the changes in the classroom as well as adjust the program to meet the specific needs of the site. But, when change is imposed from above, the vision is not at the school level and is often doomed to wither on the vine.

Time

Transforming our schools takes time. When trying to implement a new program, such processes as training, assessing of its effectiveness, and adjusting to it all take time. Unfortunately, time is often considered to be too much of a luxury and is the one element schools are not given. As Solomon (2003) says:

> *Time has always been a significant but underestimated variable in our efforts to improve schools. In many cases, our impatience, while in the process of change, takes over without regard either for the chaos and uncertainty, or for the power of the vast and different forces that need to be understood and dealt with before order can come.*

History

People often think of change as building something new. But change is usually built on an older foundation. Solomon writes that "just as visions project into the future, history looks at the past." We cannot implement an entire new system of assessment without examining carefully what we are doing now as well as what we did in the past. We need to look at the failure of the whole-language movement, the foundering of alternative assessment in the mid-1990s, the return again and again to phonics and "back-to-basics," and learn from those mistakes.

Voice

Aside from the federal government, the loudest voice in the education-system change process in the past decade has come from the business sector, who has demanded that education be reshaped to fit the business model. All students are Fords. Each model must have the same chassis, the same windows, the same headlights. We will then roll them all down the assembly line, with quality controllers standing by at every turn, ready to fire anyone who makes a mistake while each teacher adds her bolt, drops in a hose, or sprays with paint.

Teachers know this is nonsense. We are reassured that educators across North America, Europe, and elsewhere do not buy into this baloney. But our voices have not been strong enough to be heard over the loudest voice: test scores. We need to start shouting.

Steps Toward Change

1. Decide

Do not accept the status quo in a district, state, or nation where test scores hold sway. As Kohn (2004) writes, the attitude that "standards and tests are here to stay and we might as well get used to them" is defeatist and leads to inaction. He continues:

> *Real children in real classrooms suffer from this kind of defeatism, which can quickly become a self-fulfilling prophecy; assume something is inevitable and it becomes so precisely because we have decided not to challenge it…What we are facing is not a force of nature but a force of politics and political decisions that can be questioned, challenged, and ultimately reversed.*

We have attempted to provide a discussion of what exists now and a vision for what could be. If we hold to that vision and resist pressure from outside forces who do not know what goes on in the classroom, then the next step is possible.

2. Do your homework

Take advantage of professional-development opportunities. Collect articles and books that advocate balanced assessment. Check out websites such as:

+ Whole Schooling Consortium: <www.wholeschooling.net>

+ Rouge Forum: <www.pipeline.com/~rgibson/rouge_forum>

+ FairTest: the National Center for Fair and Open Testing: <http://fairtest.org>

+ Alfie Kohn website: <http://alfiekohn.org/index.html>

If we do not do our own homework, someone will mandate the change for us and we will be running to catch up.

3. Become an agent of change

Assessment and grading, like access and equal opportunity, are political issues. We need to fight on all fronts. Lobbying for ways to demonstrate students' real capabilities, instead of reducing them to numbers, grades, and statistics, is essential. According to Rhodes and Shanklin (1992), this means "identifying like-minded colleagues. Find people who think like you do, and get together." States, provinces, and districts have already discovered the perils of mandating change that teachers are not ready to implement. Broadfoot (1990) writes,

> *No amount of external coercion will make teachers change the affective relationships in their classrooms, or shoulder the heavy burden of a fundamental reconsideration of their teaching approach. Where teachers are so committed, however, the impact on the range and quality of pupils' learning, and on teachers' morale, has been shown to be considerable.*

Change must come from the bottom with support from the top. Clearly and concretely define the change you want to pursue. Educate all stakeholders about the assessment process you are taking so they understand what you are doing, why you are doing it, and that the assessment is accurate and valid and reflects the student information you are seeking.

4. Challenge yourself

Simply begin. Try something: Add an item to your folder. Design a checklist. Modify one you have seen in this book or somewhere else.

5. Approach the people involved

Elsewhere, parents and teachers have collaborated and have successfully lobbied for change; it can work in your district or school, too. Present research and your intentions to the administration and to other teachers to garner their support.

6. Introduce the process of change slowly

Start small. Choose an activity that is manageable. When you have tweaked it enough to achieve success, move on to something more challenging. But do not try too much at first. Be reasonable and methodical.

7. Establish a comfortable pace for change

Change is a long process, which cannot happen overnight. When we try to change too fast, we often abandon the effort and return to old ways. In addition, we risk negative reactions from administrators or parents who are comfortable with the old ways, and who may complain loudly enough to thwart your efforts.

8. Act as a buffer

As an agent of change, also think of yourself functioning like a shock absorber for those whom the change will affect. Kohn (2004) recommends, "whatever your position on the food chain of American education, one of your primary obligations is to be a buffer—to absorb as much pressure as possible from those above you without passing it on to those below."

9. Be test savvy and politically astute

It is one thing to teach to the test; it is quite another to be aware of how it can impact students and how to negotiate those traps. It is still another thing to be proactive and effective change makers. Teachers can be our own worst enemies; sometimes, we let others make decisions for us because we are just too busy. A university colleague of Barb's had become so dismayed over the absurdity happening at the English/education department level that she refused to attend the meetings. Barb had to convince her to attend, because if she did not vote, she would have to accept whatever folly the others decided. Calkins et al. (1998) write, "We need to initiate and actively participate in discussions of what else we could be doing with our teaching, so that our voices will be the lead voices in these conversations." This includes joining organizations like TESOL at the national or state level, not leaving the decisions to others, and commenting and critiquing when versions of standards cross our desks.

COLLABORATION

As ESL teachers, we are often tempted to think of English-language learners as ours, and ours alone, taking responsibility for all aspects of their learning. Our tendency is to shut our doors and do what we think is best for students without working in partnership with other teachers.

But collaboration, especially in ESL, is critical. Collaboration means seeking support of administration and parents. It means teachers working together to implement change in the system of assessment. It means coordinating the curriculum. It means support staff—like ESL teachers—complementing the mainstream curriculum by using content from the regular classroom as the basis for their instruction.

Collaboration often does not happen, however, for the following reasons:

+ There is not time. Teachers feel there are too many other skills that need to be taught. We become overloaded with standard upon standard and the burden of time constraints for learning English, and then we scramble to get everything completed in time. Who has time left to collaborate with others—except in whispers during in-services or faculty meetings?

+ There is little communication between teachers. Everyone assumes someone else will take care of the issues. Coordinating instruction seems to be a remote luxury.

+ Mainstream teachers do not feel competent handling issues of ESL students. In our years as ESL teachers, we have noted that many classroom teachers are reluctant to accept responsibility, because they feel that they do not know enough.

Pugachi et al. (1990) write that the success of collaboration depends on

> *...a mutual and reciprocal process between teachers and specialists...Parity is an essential aspect of successful collaboration. Mutual respect cannot be taken for granted. Although the issue of parity is raised...little direction is offered concerning the kinds of assistance classroom teachers can bring.*

Resolving the Problems

There are ways to overcome negative attitudes, lack of time, and lack of resources. Flynn (1992) makes these recommendations for building a collaborative service model.

- **Build in time to communicate.** Flynn (1992) writes, "The most important factor in establishing a collaborative relationship among teachers is communication." Teachers need time to establish trust within their teams and share expertise, to discuss instructional strategies and align curricula, to establish organization models and classroom expectations, to outline lessons and designate responsibilities, to plan assessments and evaluate student performance. Build this time in

  - at meetings
  - through shared prep time
  - by providing a substitute teacher once each month
  - by having a team member take over while others meet
  - by scheduling planning time during staff-development release days
  - by a combination of methods

  When time for planning is not built into the week, then implementing shared service becomes problematic. Scheduling planning time is essential.

- **Consider classroom placement when forming ESL instructional groups.** When students are pulled by grade level from several different classrooms or by proficiency level from several different grades, the possibility of melding content with language becomes virtually impossible.

- **Limit the range of grade levels with whom an ESL teacher works.** This is the ideal. However, if there are several ESL teachers in one school, it is appropriate to allocate several grades and several mainstream teachers to each.

- **Encourage ESL teachers to use the mainstream curriculum as their guide for instruction.** Reading, writing, speaking, listening, and grammar can and should all be taught within the framework of the core curriculum. Mainstream teachers can exercise their knowledge and skills to help the ESL teacher meld content with language.

- **Schedule ESL support services carefully.** This ensures that students receiving support do not miss vital instruction in their mainstream classrooms. Students are often pulled from class during science or math—the very subjects at which many students can most naturally succeed.

- **Have ESL teachers maintain their roles as advocate for their students.** Always be there for your students. Be the expert who focuses on their needs for the majority of the day.

Collaboration at the Secondary Level

Specific issues concerning pull-out and sheltered classes must be addressed at the secondary level. It is essential that secondary students learn both English and academic skills as rapidly as possible. Collaboration between content-area and ESL teachers is an important component of service delivery. ESL teachers can meet this challenge by

+ obtaining copies of the textbook(s) for each class

+ asking the content-area teacher for copies of the syllabus and course objectives

+ reviewing the major content standards that the teacher plans to emphasize that year

+ conferring on which base-line competencies students need to succeed, and working on those in the ESL time that you have

+ establishing a file of study guides

+ collecting lower-level, simpler texts in the subjects being taught in content-area classes

+ meeting regularly with content-area teachers to talk about students in their classes

+ making use of alignments to the curriculum made by previous mainstream and ESL teachers

+ begging, borrowing, or stealing lesson plans and other gems with which other teachers have had success

The rigid structure and departmentalization of secondary schools has been a problem in implementing effective ESL programming. Berman and Weiler (1992) state:

> *...by default, schools [have] relied on department chairs to schedule courses for LEP students. This practice [has] meant that faculty with no particular commitment to, or knowledge of, the academic needs of LEP students [have] made crucial decisions about course availability.*

The result: access to content has been limited and uneven, not necessarily by design but often by neglect.

WHAT KINDS OF CHANGE DO WE WANT?

Back in 1975, Allan Ornstein asked:

> *Will the advocates of accountability be found out? Will we come to realize that it is useless and unfair to hold teachers accountable for something they have little control over? Will the people and politicians admit that we cannot deliver on most of our promises to equalize education; that each student brings to school different equipment to learn?*

It has not happened yet, but we keep hoping.

Myers (2003) writes that "no expense has been spared to put politically correct policies and guidelines on paper with respect to equity for linguistically disadvantaged students… However, the walk doesn't match the talk."

Some of the most pressing things we need to change (aside from classrooms no bigger than broom closets, inadequate textbooks, unreasonable class sizes, and such) include

+ **Local control.** The "all brakes and no motors" (Tucker and Codding, 1998) version of education has to change. Whether any change is positive or negative depends on what happens at the local level. Secada (1998) writes:

  > *Putting a local stamp on the standards movement not only gives educators a sense of ownership, but provides an opportunity for them to engage in a type of reflection and study that is not encouraged by the present system. We don't learn unless we do it ourselves.*

  Assessment is a human issue: accurate and fair decisions about students and their learning can only be based on human contact, by those who know the students, their situations, the local context, and the environment in which they all function. We know our students best. We know who they are and what they need. We need to take control again of deciding how and what we are going to teach. We need to be able to allocate resources ourselves, depending on who comes in the door.

+ **Flexibility.** We need the flexibility to keep students who require more time to learn what we believe they need to learn. Harklau (1999) says flexibility is a key factor in teaching language-minority students effectively. The needs of exchange students from upper-class homes in the Far East are much different from those of refugee students whose schooling has been profoundly disrupted. Everything from programs to instructional strategies needs to be adjustable. Solomon (2003) writes:

  > *Clear statements of standards and expectations do not preclude the attention to student and contextual differences, as long as there is reasonable flexibility in the methods for reaching them, appropriate provisions for the different needs, and alternate and reasonable measures. There is nothing wrong with the goal of being above the standard, and individual schools can have such goals. I want to know where I am going, but I want the freedom to choose my own best path.*

  We need to be able to ask, how does this work for my students and, if it is not working, what can we do to fix it? That cannot be decided at the national, state, or provincial level. It needs to be decided on site, by the teachers involved.

+ **Appropriate tests.** In the classroom, we can administer tests that respond to our students' needs, we can change them when we need to, we can review the results and then either backtrack or move forward. It is not unreasonable to lobby for tests that also allow us to do this at a higher level. If we are going to have tests, they should be *good* tests that assess material students have actually learned. These tests should assess what is worth learning, or teachers will focus only on the things students need in order to pass and forget the things that are truly valuable in life and in school.

- **Bridges to success.** Somehow, we must build bridges across the gulf between the haves and the not-yets. Brown (in Cizek, 2001) writes:

  > *It is intellectually and morally dishonest to raise the bar for all students to a level that is currently being reached by only a relative few, unless governments at all levels are willing to undertake an unprecedented effort to reduce class sizes, put a qualified teacher in every classroom and upgrade school facilities.*

- **Appropriate standards.** The standards movement will not go away. As with tests, we can work to make certain the standards imposed on our students are worth working for and are attainable and reasonable. TESOL, the National Council of Teachers of English (NCTE), and the International Reading Association (IRA) are working intently toward this end. Just having standards is not enough. The standards have to provide direction toward what is worth learning and not confine teachers such that they focus on the small details and forget the big picture.

CONCLUSION

Lobbying for and working toward equitable forms of assessment at your school can be a positive experience and an opportunity to forge stronger ties among all individuals involved in the educational process. We can increase our capacity to change by building on past successes and using them to leverage more positive change.

Standardized testing will continue, as Kohn asserts, only as long as parents and teachers allow it. In the meantime, we must continue to explore and activate other forms of assessment that draw accurate and fair pictures of our students. They deserve nothing less.

APPENDIX A

A1. Grading Guidelines for Writing

A2: Language Acquisition Development Table

A3: Scoring Rubric for *A Letter from Margot: "All Summer in a Day"* (Booth Olson, 2007)

APPENDIX A1: GRADING GUIDELINES FOR WRITING

The following grading guidelines were developed by William Irmscher (from Irmscher, W. *Teaching Expository Writing*. New York, NY: Holt, Rinehart, and Winston, 1979). They can be adapted to content areas.

A – Demonstrates Unusual Competence[1]

1. An ability to avoid the obvious and thus gain insights that are personal and often illuminating

2. A capacity to develop ideas flexibly and fluently, yet with control and purpose

3. A special concern for the *bon mot*, even if it entails coining a word that the language does not provide

4. An ability to use punctuation rhetorically, using it for effect as well as clarity

5. A willingness to be inventive with words and structures to produce a clearly identifiable style, even though at times the efforts may be too deliberate or fall short of the writer's intentions

B – Demonstrates Competence

1. An ability to absorb ideas and experience and to interpret these meaningfully in a context of the writer's own conception

2. A capacity to develop an idea with a clear sense of order

3. A capacity to draw upon words adequate to express the writer's own thoughts and feelings

4. An ability to use mechanics as an integral part of the meaning and effect of the prose

5. A capacity to consider alternative ways of expression as a means for making stylistic choices possible

C – Suggests Competence

1. A tendency to depend on the self-evident and the cliché for the writer to write uninformative discourse

2. A tendency either to make the organization obvious or to write aimlessly without a plan

3. A limitation in the range of words and thus a dependence on the clichés and colloquialisms most available

4. An ability to use mechanics correctly or incorrectly in proportion to the plainness or complexity of the style

---

1. An *A* does not necessarily mean perfection. An *A* assignment can have more mistakes, according to Irmscher, than a traditional *B* assignment. "There may be less control, less patience with detail, greater daring; and hence, upon occasion, greater bathos. The *A*-writer risks more and thus gains more or loses more depending upon the sense of the venture." The *A* presentation or the *A* portfolio may not be perfect, but it shows a depth and grasp of subject matter that other competent works do not demonstrate. Competence can be demonstrated or suggested in myriad ways throughout the curriculum, whether the student has perfect command of the language or not.

5. A general unawareness of choices that affect style and thus an inability to control the effects a writer may seek

D – Suggests or Demonstrates Incompetence

1. A tendency to exploit the obvious either because of lack of understanding, inability to read, failure to grapple with a topic, or, in many cases, lack of interest. The substance of essays, therefore, ranges from superficial to barren

2. A tendency to wander aimlessly because of a lack of overall conception or, in some instances, to have a semblance of form without the development that makes parts a whole

3. A tendency to play safe with words, using ones the writer ordinarily speaks or the ones the writer can spell. These tendencies place obvious limits upon the writer to vary the expression

4. A frequent inability to make careful distinctions between periods, commas, and semicolons, although some writers in these categories can write correct sentences if they keep structures simple. The incidence of error, however, is high

5. Either a tendency to write highly convoluted sentences that are close to the rapid associations of our thoughts before we straighten them out or a tendency to play safe by avoiding the sentence elements that invite error

APPENDIX A2: LANGUAGE ACQUISITION DEVELOPMENT TABLE

THEORETICAL STAGES	CHARACTERISTICS	BEHAVIOR
1. Silence Does not speak	• Student quietly takes it all in • Lasts anywhere from a few minutes to a few months	• Student shows no understanding of English • Shrugs or looks blank • Usually makes no attempts to participate in any activities
2. Nonverbal Indications of Understanding	• Student uses no English except for a word or two • Does not respond verbally but does respond physically to instructions or requests • Understands only slow, simple speech; requires repetitions • Progresses to one-word responses in English or responses in own language	• Student understands simple sentences but only uses isolated words or expressions • Responds with gestures such as nodding and pointing • Often attempts to respond when spoken to first but has little repertoire on which to build • Progresses to one-word answers such as "yes" and "no"
3. Chunking Uses unanalyzed chunks of language that perform an important social function: For example: "It's my turn", "What's your name?", "Can I play?"	• Student understands simplified speech with repetitions and rephrasing • Produces some common English words and phrases • Understands more than can produce	• Student attempts to participate in classroom activities and social activities • Converses in English with help • Responds with more than simple words • Understands at least parts of lesson • Follows simple directions
4. Interlanguage The speech of the learner has characteristics of both the first and the second language	• Student understands adult speech but requires repetitions and rephrasing • Speech may be hesitant because of rephrasing and groping for words • Uses some complex structures • Over-generalizes rules of grammar • Has difficulty with choice of verb tense, verb-tense consistency, and subject/verb agreement • Vocabulary is adequate for carrying on basic conversation; some word usage difficulties • Uses "interim grammar": one part one language, one part another (usually vocabulary of new language on top of grammar of first language). For example: "They in school and home's live", "My friend likes the books to read."	• Student relies on English-speaking partner to scaffold conversations and fill in blanks he cannot produce himself • Often intersperses primary language into sentences when unsure of English word

THEORETICAL STAGES	CHARACTERISTICS	BEHAVIOR
5. Gaining Control in English	<ul><li>Student understands most adult speech except some advanced structures</li><li>Speech may be nonnative in evenness</li><li>An accent may be present</li><li>Demonstrates a high degree of proficiency</li><li>Controls most basic grammatical structures with occasional error in syntax</li><li>Some errors in young learners may be seen as developmental</li><li>Vocabulary is varied</li></ul>	<ul><li>Student understands and speaks English well but needs assistance in reading and writing in English to achieve at grade-appropriate level</li><li>Can participate with some minor assistance</li></ul>
6. Fluent Speaker	<ul><li>Understands everything expected of a native speaker of the same age</li><li>Speech is effortless and native-like; however, an accent may be present</li><li>Expresses ideas creatively, having mastered a broad range of syntactic features</li><li>Vocabulary is as accurate as that of a native speaker of the same age</li><li>Uses different varieties of language depending upon the situation (code-switching)</li></ul>	<ul><li>Achieves at appropriate level</li><li>Requires little mental editing</li><li>Thinks in English</li><li>Requires little or no help in any facet of English</li><li>Can participate fully in all aspects of classes</li></ul>

APPENDIX A3: SCORING RUBRIC FOR *A LETTER FROM MARGOT: "ALL SUMMER IN A DAY"*

Superior

The **6** paper is clearly superior: well-written, insightful, carefully organized, and technically correct. The 6 paper does most or all of the following well:

+ Is written in standard letter form: greeting, body, closing
+ Assumes the persona of Margot and impressively writes in her voice
+ Begins by reminding classmates of who the writer is
+ Clearly describes Margot's present situation including where she lives now and what she is doing
+ Thoughtfully explains why Margot is writing
+ Reviews in detail what happened on the day the sun came out
+ Uses concrete evidence from the text to make the letter specific
+ Offers perceptive insights into why the children treated her as they did
+ Explores the children's final act of cruelty and analyzes in depth how it affected Margot
+ Concludes by articulately and thoughtfully expressing what she learned
+ Uses rich, descriptive language to paint a vivid picture for the reader, including similes and/or metaphors
+ Contains few, if any, errors in the conventions of written English

Commendable

The **5** paper is a strong paper that addresses all of the aspects of the assignment well. It is a thinner version of the 6 paper—still impressive and interesting but less well handled in terms of insight, organization or language. The 5 paper does most or all of the following well:

+ Is written in standard letter form: greeting, body, closing
+ Assumes the persona of Margot and believably writes in her voice
+ Begins by reminding classmates of who the writer is
+ Explains why Margot is writing
+ Describes Margot's present situation including where she lives now and what she is doing
+ Uses some concrete evidence from the text to make the letter specific
+ Offers some insights into why the children treated her as they did
+ Explores the children's final act of cruelty and offers some analysis of how it affected Margot

- Concludes by clearly expressing what she learned
- Uses some rich, descriptive language to paint a picture for the reader and at least one simile or metaphor
- Contains few errors in the conventions of written English and none that interfere with the writer's message

Adequate

The **4** paper is a solid paper that meets most of the criteria of the assignment but does so in less depth than a 6 or 5 paper. A 4 paper may exhibit some or all of the following:

- Is written in standard letter form: greeting, body, closing
- Assumes the persona of Margot and writes in her voice but less believably than a 6 or 5 paper
- Begins by reminding classmates of who the writer is
- Briefly refers to Margot's present situation including where she lives now and what she is doing
- Explains why Margot is writing but explanation may be superficial
- Reviews what happened on the day the sun came out
- Uses less concrete evidence from the text than a 6 or 5 paper so the letter is more general
- Offers a plausible reason (or reasons) why the children treated her as they did but it is less insightful than 6 or 5 paper
- Explores the children's final act of cruelty but does not analyze how it affected Margot in enough depth
- Concludes by expressing what she learned but less thoughtfully than in a 6 or 5 paper
- Uses some descriptive language to paint a picture for the reader. May not include a simile or metaphor
- Contains some errors in the conventions of written English but none that interfere with the writer's message

Barely Adequate

The **3** paper is a lower-half paper that superficially addresses some requirements of the prompt but is weak in insight, organization and language. A 3 paper may exhibit some or all of the following:

- May not be written in standard letter form: greeting, body, closing
- Attempts to assume the persona of Margot but does not write in her voice believably
- May fail to remind classmates of who the writer is
- Briefly describes Margot's present situation including where she lives now but may not address what she is doing

- Fails to explain why Margot is writing or does so in a superficial fashion
- Reviews what happened on the day the sun came out to the exclusion of why or how
- Uses little, if any, concrete evidence from the text to make the letter specific
- Offers a superficial reason why the children treated her as they did or fails to address the children's motives
- Mentions the children's final act of cruelty and but does not explore or analyze how it affected Margot
- Fails to express what she learned or does so superficially
- Uses little, if any, descriptive language to paint a picture for the reader
- Contains many errors in the conventions of written English—some of which may interfere with the writer's message

Inadequate

The **2** paper is an insufficient attempt to write to the prompt. It has all of the weaknesses of the 3 paper but they are compounded by disorganization and a lack of understanding of the story. A 2 paper:

- Is not written standard letter form: greeting, body, closing
- Does not assume the persona of Margot
- Fails to explain who Margot is or why she's writing
- Relies solely on superficial plot summary
- Uses no concrete evidence from the text
- Fails to consider why the children treated her as they did or misunderstands their motives
- Contains many errors in the conventions of written English that interfere with the writer's message

No Evidence of Achievement

A **1** paper fails to address the prompt or writes so little so poorly that it cannot be understood by the reader

APPENDIX B

Reproducible Masters*

Primary-Language Literacy Questionnaire

Language Function Checklist (figure 6.2)

Student Vocabulary Checklist (figure 6.3)

Checklist for Assessing Emerging Readers (figure 6.4)

Portfolio Self-Evaluation (figure 9.6)

ESL Conference Record Notes (figure 9.13)

*Figures in this section may be reproduced for classroom use.

Primary-Language Literacy Questionnaire

Student's name_____ **Date**_____ **Age** _____

Primary language_____

Interviewee's name_____ Relationship to student _____

1. How many years of formal education has the student completed in _____?
   country of origin

   Number of years completed _____

2. What language was used for instruction? _____

3. How long has it been since the student received instruction in the primary language?_____

4. Did your child attend school in another country while en route to the United States/Canada?

   ☐ No ☐ Yes

   If yes, which country?_____ How long? _____

   Language instruction _____

5. Does your child read books in his/her own language at home?   ☐ No ☐ Yes

6. How well does your child read compared to other children of his/her age?

   ☐ very well ☐ the same as ☐ not as well ☐ cannot read ☐ don't know

7. Does your child write to friends or relatives?   ☐ No ☐ Yes

   In what language? _____

8. How well does your child write compared to other children his/her age?

   ☐ very well ☐ the same as ☐ not as well ☐ cannot read ☐ don't know

Language Function Checklist

Student's name _____ Date _____

Age _____ Grade _____

F	S	N	BEHAVIOR/ABILITY	CONTEXT/COMMENTS
			Demonstrates comprehension nonverbally	
			Uses physical motion to communicate (pushing, pulling, etc.)	
			Listens and attends to the work at hand	
			One-word response	
			Uses English in an informal conversation	
			Makes a request "I want..." or "I need..."	
			Talks about himself/herself	
			Participates in formal classroom discussion within small group	
			Understands and answers questions about material presented through discussion	
			Volunteers additional information in the class discussion	
			Asks for additional information privately	
			Asks for additional information within the group	
			Presents a dissenting point of view	
			Uses language to communicate sadness	
			Uses imaginative language, e.g., "If I were a bird, I would fly home to my country."	
			Uses language to be funny	
			Uses language sarcastically	
			Uses language to show anger	
			Uses authoritative language, e.g., "You must..."	
			Uses language to anticipate a future event	
			Communicates using indirect coding, e.g., "You must be tired of correcting all our papers," meaning, "Don't give us so much homework."	
			Other:	

F – Frequently   S – Seldom   N – Never

Figure 6.2 (page 161): Language Function Checklist

From: *Assessment and ESL: An Alternative Approach*, Portage & Main Press. By Barbara Law and Mary Eckes © 2007. May be reproduced for classroom use.

From: *Assessment and ESL: An Alternative Approach*, Portage & Main Press. By Barbara Law and Mary Eckes © 2007. May be reproduced for classroom use.

Student Vocabulary Checklist

Teacher_____ **Student** _____

Grade_____

Have student identify English Vocabulary. Use check marks to note those words the student knows.
Leave others blank.

1. Colors
   - ☐ red
   - ☐ blue
   - ☐ green
   - ☐ yellow
   - ☐ white
   - ☐ orange
   - ☐ black
   - ☐ purple
   - ☐ brown

2. Numbers—Kindergarten
   - ☐ 1
   - ☐ 3
   - ☐ 5
   - ☐ 7
   - ☐ 9
   - ☐ 2
   - ☐ 4
   - ☐ 6
   - ☐ 8
   - ☐ 10

   Grades 1-3, as above plus
   - ☐ 11
   - ☐ 13
   - ☐ 15
   - ☐ 17
   - ☐ 19
   - ☐ 12
   - ☐ 14
   - ☐ 16
   - ☐ 18
   - ☐ 20

3. Shapes
   - ☐ circle
   - ☐ square
   - ☐ triangle
   - ☐ rectangle

4. Alphabet (present in random order)
   - ☐ A
   - ☐ G
   - ☐ M
   - ☐ S
   - ☐ Y
   - ☐ B
   - ☐ H
   - ☐ N
   - ☐ T
   - ☐ Z
   - ☐ C
   - ☐ I
   - ☐ O
   - ☐ U
   - ☐ D
   - ☐ J
   - ☐ P
   - ☐ V
   - ☐ E
   - ☐ K
   - ☐ Q
   - ☐ W
   - ☐ F
   - ☐ L
   - ☐ R
   - ☐ X

5. Holiday names
   - ☐ Easter
   - ☐ Halloween
   - ☐ Valentine's Day
   - ☐ New Year's Day
   - ☐ Christmas
   - ☐ Thanksgiving

6. Personal information
   - ☐ name
   - ☐ age
   - ☐ address
   - ☐ phone number

7. Body parts
   - ☐ eye
   - ☐ nose
   - ☐ cheek
   - ☐ mouth
   - ☐ neck
   - ☐ chest
   - ☐ shoulder
   - ☐ arm
   - ☐ hand
   - ☐ stomach
   - ☐ leg
   - ☐ knee
   - ☐ foot
   - ☐ finger

8. Spatial orientation
   - ☐ left
   - ☐ right
   - ☐ in front of
   - ☐ out
   - ☐ over
   - ☐ above
   - ☐ beside
   - ☐ behind
   - ☐ in
   - ☐ near
   - ☐ far

1

Figure 6.3 (page 162): Student Vocabulary Checklist, page 1

9. School vocabulary

☐ recess	☐ hall	☐ washroom	☐ auditorium
☐ playground	☐ locker	☐ office	☐ lunch
☐ teacher	☐ lunchroom	☐ principal	☐ secretary
☐ tardy slip	☐ school	☐ science	☐ phys. ed
☐ math	☐ school bus	☐ language arts	☐ drinking fountain

10. Classroom words

☐ desk	☐ books	☐ paper	☐ blackboard	☐ table
☐ crayons	☐ notebook	☐ pencil	☐ glue	☐ window
☐ chalk	☐ clock	☐ eraser	☐ page	☐ chair
☐ rug	☐ scissors	☐ seat	☐ wastebasket	

11. Clothing

☐ coat	☐ dress	☐ jacket	☐ hat
☐ gym shoes	☐ mittens	☐ pants	☐ shirt
☐ shoes	☐ skirt	☐ socks	☐ sweater

12. Safety terms

☐ stop	☐ go	☐ walk	☐ don't walk

13. Time

☐ morning	☐ noon	☐ night	☐ afternoon	☐ next week
☐ tomorrow	☐ yesterday	☐ year	☐ month	

14. Other vocabulary

☐ first	☐ last	☐ big	☐ little
☐ small	☐ smaller		

15. Money

☐ penny	☐ nickel	☐ dime	☐ quarter
☐ cent	☐ cost	☐ dollar	

16. Transportation

☐ bus	☐ car	☐ truck	☐ plane

17. Everyday directions

☐ wait	☐ copy	☐ sit down	☐ stand up	☐ sit on the floor
☐ come here	☐ line up	☐ pick up	☐ open book	
☐ touch	☐ cut out	☐ raise your hand	☐ wash your hands	

18. Home words

☐ address	☐ brother	☐ sister	☐ father	☐ table
☐ mother	☐ home	☐ sofa	☐ chair	☐ bed

2

Figure 6.3: Student Vocabulary Checklist, page 2

Checklist for Assessing Emerging Readers

Student's name_____ Date _____

Age_____ Grade _____

	Not yet	Emerging	Yes
Listens to story but is not looking at pages			
Tries to read environmental print			
Demonstrates book-handling knowledge (right side up)			
Watches pictures as story is read aloud			
Makes up words for picture			
Demonstrates directionality of written language (left to right, page order)			
Pretends to read			
Recognizes some words from a dictated story			
Participates in reading by supplying rhyming words and some predictable text			
Memorizes text, and pretends to read story			
Looks at words and tracks words when reading or is being read to from a familiar story			
Recognizes words in a new context			
Reads word-for-word			
Reads familiar stories fluently			
Reads familiar stories haltingly			
Uses context clues, phonic analysis, sentence structure to read new words and passages			
Reads easy books fluently			
Chooses to read independently			
Reads fluently			

From: Assessment and ESL: An Alternative Approach, Portage & Main Press. By Barbara Law and Mary Eckes © 2007. May be reproduced for classroom use.

Figure 6.4 (page 163): Checklist for Assessing Emerging Readers

Portfolio Self-Evaluation

Name _____

1. What does your portfolio reveal about you as a reader?

   _____

2. What does your portfolio reveal about you as a writer?

   _____

3. What does your portfolio suggest your strengths are?

   _____

4. What does your portfolio suggest about how you have changed?

   _____

5. What do you think people will learn about you from your portfolio?

   _____

6. Select what you think is your best piece of writing from your portfolio.

   a. How does this piece compare with other items you've written this semester?

   _____

   b. How does this piece reflect your strengths in writing?

   _____

   c. How does this piece reflect any difficulties you are having in writing?

   _____

   d. Why did you choose this selection as best? What were your criteria?

   _____

   e. In reflecting on this piece of writing, what do you think you would do differently if you were writing it again?

   _____

7. How has your English improved over the past semester?

   _____

8. How can you document that improvement in your portfolio?

   _____

From: *Assessment and ESL: An Alternative Approach*, Portage & Main Press. By Barbara Law and Mary Eckes © 2007. May be reproduced for classroom use.

Figure 9.6 (page 234): Portfolio Self-Evaluation

ESL Conference Record/Notes

Student _____ **Date** _____

Teacher _____

Parents or Guardians _____

Others in attendance _____

Reasons for conference:

Overall classroom performance:

Areas of strength in language acquisitions:	Areas needing improvement in language skills:

Areas of strength in content:	Areas needing improvement in content:

Recommendations and goals:		

Student will:	Teacher will:	Parent(s) will:

Comments:

From: *Assessment and ESL: An Alternative Approach*, Portage & Main Press. By Barbara Law and Mary Eckes © 2007. May be reproduced for classroom use.

Figure 9.13 (page 239): ESL Conference Record/Notes

GLOSSARY OF TERMS

Accountability: The practice of holding teachers, schools, and districts responsible for the quality of education they provide, and the expectation that they will report the annual progress reflected in the standardized tests administered.

Adequate Yearly Progress (AYP): Students and schools are required to meet certain state-determined levels of improvement each year, measured by annual mandatory standardized tests. In theory, all students should improve until everyone in the world is functioning at 100% all the time and in all subjects. If schools do not meet AYP, they can be subject to increasing scrutiny and sanctions that sometimes result in dismissals, restructuring, or sending students to for-profit, charter schools.

Assessment: Evaluation based on a collection of information about what a student knows and can do. The data is collected at different times, in different contexts, in a variety of ways, using various methods.

BICS (Basic Interpersonal Communication Skills): The skills involved in everyday communication—listening, speaking, carrying on basic conversation, understanding speakers—and in getting one's basic needs met.

Chapter I: A federally funded program in the United States that seeks to provide direct reading instruction to identified students.

Evaluation: The process of making inferences about student data collected.

FEP (Fully English Proficient): This characterizes students able to participate fully in regular, mainstream classroom activities. ESL students are usually designated FEP after scoring beyond a designated percentile on a standardized proficiency test. The designation does not necessarily mean the student can perform successfully in the content area, however. Many FEP students struggle with the cognitive academic language in the content areas and may continue to need support.

Language Assessment Scale (LAS): A test used to determine a student's English proficiency compared to that of a fluent speaker.

LEA (Language Experience Approach): A method of promoting reading whereby the teacher begins with the experiences students bring to class (or experience together as a class), and then develops oral and written activities around these experiences. The teacher helps students use their own words to write stories, which are then used in a variety of ways.

Learning Record Assessment System™: A system of K-12 student evaluation, developed in California in the mid-1990s, which uses various sources of both student work and teacher-observation records to monitor and develop student learning.

LEP (Limited English Proficient): This characterizes students who understand some English but are not fluent enough to compete academically with English-speaking peers.

Miscue: A deviation from the text. Such errors are natural to the process of learning to read, and it is through monitoring for meaning that the reader makes corrections. These errors are made while the reader is attending to the four-language cuing system (semantics, syntax, graphophonics, and pragmatics). The most crucial aspect of this type of error is whether the miscue results in a loss of meaning or simply reveals that the reader is imposing meaning (for example, where text reads, "he ran through the forest," the student reads, "he ran through the trees").

NCLB (No Child Left Behind Act): American legislation geared toward closing the achievement gap among schools and districts and making schools more accountable for the quality of education they provide.

NEP (Non-English Proficient): Speaks little or no English.

NES (Non-English Speaking): Speaks no English.

Open entry: A program that allows students to enter or leave at any point in the instruction year.

Portfolio: A meaningful collection of student work that presents the student's efforts, progress, and achievement to the stakeholders. The student often plays an active role in the creating, evaluation, and maintenance of his portfolio.

Proficiency: Having a thorough level of competency or skill in comprehension, speaking, reading, or writing.

Pull-out: LEP students who are pulled out of the classroom to learn to be proficient in English but who otherwise take content classes in English with English-speaking students.

Push-in: When ESL teachers are pushed-into the content classroom to teach the content lesson to both LEP and English-speaking students.

Reporting: Communicating student achievement and progress to the stakeholders. This involves two steps: putting the information into usable form, and conveying the information effectively to the stakeholders.

Rubric: A set of guidelines for giving scores, which clearly defines mastery for given skills or tasks as well as varying degrees of mastery through points on a scale.

Sheltered English: A method of modified instruction where content is presented to LEP students in English that is understandable to them. (In California, this is referred to as SDAIE or Specially Designed Academic Instruction in English.)

Standardized test: Commercially designed and produced tests given on single occasions. They are frequently timed, are one-dimensional, and often consist of multiple-choice and short-answer questions. The results compare students' knowledge against a set core of knowledge and skills that have been deemed essential for students of a given level to know.

Standards: Broad statements of what students should know and be able to achieve at certain points in their schooling

Title I: Under the Elementary and Secondary Education Act of 1965, reauthorized by the No Child Left Behind Act (2002), this American legislation focuses on improving academic achievement of disadvantaged or environmentally at-risk students.

Title VII: Also known as the Bilingual Education Act, this American policy, enacted in 1968, provides funding for special ESL programs and services for non-English-speaking or limited-English-speaking students.

Validity: The accuracy with which any test or means of assessment measures what it says it is going to measure.

BIBLIOGRAPHY

Abedi, J. "The No Child Left Behind Act and English Language Learners: Assessment and Accountability Issues." *Educational Researcher* 33, 1 (January-February 2004): 4-14.

Acker-Hocevar, M., and D. Touchton. "How Principals Level the Playing Field of Accountability in Florida's High Poverty/Low-Performing Schools: The Intersection of High-Stakes Testing and Effects of Poverty on Teaching and Learning." *International Journal of Educational Reform* 11, 4 (2002): 106-124.

Adamson, D. et al. "Five Ways to Bridge the Resource Room-to-Regular-Classroom Gap." *Teaching Exceptional Children* 22, 2 (Winter 1990): 74-77.

Airasian, P. *Classroom Assessment*, 3rd ed. New York, NY: McGraw Hill, 1997.

Alvarez, M. "Psychoeducational Assessment of Language Minority Children: Current Perspectives and Future Trends." In *Bilingual Education and English as a Second Language: A Research Handbook, 1988-1990*, edited by A. Ambert. New York, NY: Garland, 1991.

Anthony, R. et al. *Evaluating Literacy: A Perspective for Change*. Portsmouth, NH: Heinemann, 1991.

Atwell, N. *In the Middle: New Understandings about Writing, Reading, and Learning*, 2nd ed. Portsmouth, NH: Boynton/Cook-Heinemann, 1998.

Au, K. *Literacy Instruction in Multicultural Settings*. Fort Worth, TX: Harcourt Brace College Publishers, 1993.

Baker, K. "Bilingual Education's 20-year Failure to Provide Civil Rights Protection for Language-Minority Students." In *Children at Risk: Poverty, Minority Status, and Other Issues in Educational Equity*, edited by A. Barona and E. Garcia. Washington, DC: National Association of School Psychologists, 1990.

Barrell, J. *Teaching for Thoughtfulness: Classroom Strategies to Enhance Intellectual Development.* New York, NY: Longman, 1991.

Barrs, M., et al. *The Primary Language Record: Handbook for Teachers.* London, UK: Centre for Language in Primary Education, 1989.

Bartholomae, D., and A. Petrosky (eds). *Facts, Artifacts and Counterfacts: Theory and Method for a Reading and Writing Course.* Upper Montclair, NJ: Boynton/Cook, 1986.

Belanoff, P., and M. Dickson. *Portfolio Grading: Process and Product.* Portsmouth, NH: Heinemann, 1991.

Berman and Weiler Associates. *Meeting the Challenge of Language Diversity: An Evaluation of Programs for Pupils with Limited English Proficiency.* Sacramento, CA: California State Department of Education, Program Evaluation and Research Division, 1992.

Black, P., and D. Wiliam. "Inside the Black Box: Raising Standards through Classroom Assessment." *Phi Delta Kappan* 80, 2 (October 1998): 139-144; 146-148.

Bloom, B. et al. *Evaluation to Improve Learning.* New York, NY: McGraw Hill, 1981.

Boggs, S. et al. *Speaking, Relating and Learning: A Study of Hawaiian Children at Home and at School.* Norwood, NJ: Ablex, 1985.

Bouffler, C. *Literacy Evaluation: Issues and Practicalities.* Portsmouth, NH: Heinemann, 1992.

Brandt, M. "When Are Writing Portfolios Powerful?" *The Kamehameha Journal of Education* 4 (Spring 1993): 97-104.

Braun, C. *Looking, Listening, and Learning: Observing and Assessing Young Readers.* Winnipeg, MB: Peguis, 1993.

Broadfoot, P. *Toward Profiles of Achievement: Developments in Europe.* Washington, DC: Taylor and Francis, 1990.

Brown, J. "It's Revolting: School Districts Rebel against the Education Mandate." *Edutopia* (November 2005): 43-44.

Brown, W. "Social, Educational and Political Complexities of Standard Setting." In *Setting Performance Standards: Concepts, Methods, and Perspectives*, edited by G. Cizek. Mahwah, NJ: Lawrence Erlbaum, 2001.

Burgess, R. (ed). *Educational Research and Evaluation: For Policy and Practice?* Washington, DC: Falmer Press, 1993.

Burke, K. *Authentic Assessment.* Thousand Oaks, CA: Corwin/Sage, 2005.

Calkins, L. et al. *A Teacher's Guide to Standardized Reading Tests: Knowledge Is Power.* Portsmouth, NH: Heinemann, 1998.

Cambourne, B. *The Whole Story: Natural Learning and the Acquisition of Literacy in the Classroom.* Auckland, NZ: Ashton Scholastic, 1988.

Carr, J., and D. Harris. *Succeeding with Standards: Linking Curriculum, Assessment and Action Planning.* Alexandria, VA: Association for Supervision and Curriculum Development (ASCD), 2001. Center for Language in Learning. "Learning Record Assessment System™," El Cajon, CA: 1994.

Cizek, G. (ed). *Setting Performance Standards: Concepts, Methods and Perspectives.* See Brown, W.

Clay, M. *An Observation Survey of Literacy Achievement.* Portsmouth, NH: Heinemann, 1993.

———. *Becoming Literate: The Construction of Inner Control.* Auckland, NZ: Heinemann, 1991.

———. *Stones: The Concepts About Print Test.* Auckland, NZ: Heinemann, 1979.

———. *What Did I Write?* Auckland, NZ: Heinemann, 1975.

Coballes-Vega, C., and B. Salend. "Guidelines for Assessing Migrant Handicapped Students." *Diagnostique* 13, 2-4 (Win-Spr-Sum 1988): 64-75.

Cohen, D. et al. *Observing and Recording the Behavior of Young Children.* New York, NY: Teachers College Press, 1997.

Council of Chief State School Officers (CCSSO). "Summary of Recommendations and Policy Implications for Improving the Assessment and Monitoring of Students with Limited English Proficiency." Washington, DC: CCSSO, 1992.

Covey, S. *The Seven Habits of Highly Effective People.* New York, NY: Simon and Schuster, 1989.

Crawford, J. "No Child Left Behind: Misguided Approach to School Accountability for English Language Learners." Paper presented at the Forum on Ideas to Improve the NCLB Accountability Provisions for Students with Disabilities and English Language Learners, NABE (National Association for Bilingual Education), Washington, DC, September 14, 2004.

Cummins, J. *Empowering Minority Students.* Sacramento, CA: California Association for Bilingual Education, 1989.

———. "The Role of Primary Language Development in Promoting Educational Success for Language Minority Students." In *Schooling and Language Minority Students: A Theoretical Framework,* developed by Office of Bilingual Bicultural Education, California State Department of Education. Los Angeles, CA: Evaluation, Dissemination, and Assessment Center, California State University, 1981.

Cunningham, P. *Phonics They Use: Words for Reading and Writing,* 3rd ed. New York, NY: Longman, 2000.

Cunningham, P. et al. *Guided Reading The Four-Blocks Way: The Four Blocks Literacy Model Book Series.* Greensboro, NC: Carson-Dellosa, 2000.

Davies, A. et al. *Together Is Better: Collaborative Assessment, Evaluation and Reporting.* Winnipeg, MB: Peguis, 1992.

Del Vecchio, A. *Handbook of English Language Proficiency Tests.* Albuquerque, NM: Evaluation Assistance Center–Western Region, New Mexico Highlands University, 1995.

Doake, D. "Reading-Like Behavior: Its Role in Learning to Read," In *Observing the Language Learner*, edited by A. Jaggar and M. Smith-Burke. Newark, DE: International Reading Association, 1985.

Duff, P. "Language, Literacy, Content, and (Pop) Culture: Challenges for ESL Students in Mainstream Courses." *Canadian Modern Language Review* 58, 1 (September 2001): 103-32.

Dufresne, J. "Mainstreaming LEP Students: The Case of the Hmong." *MinneTESOL Journal* 11 (1993): 95-122.

Dulay, H. et al. *Language Two:* New York, NY: Oxford University Press, 1982.

Durkin, D. *Children Who Read Early: Two Longitudinal Studies.* New York, NY: Teachers College Press, 1966.

Elley, W. (1989). "Vocabulary Acquisition from Listening to Stories." *Reading Research Quarterly* 24 (1988-1989): 174-187.

Erickson, F., and G. Mohatt. "Cultural Organization of Participation Structures in Two Classrooms of Indian Students." In *Doing the Ethnography of Schooling: Educational Anthropology in Action*, edited by G. Spindler. New York, NY: Holt, Rinehart, and Winston (1982).

Estrin, E., and S. Nelson-Barber. "Issues in Cross Cultural Assessment: American Indian and Alaska Native Students." Knowledge Brief 12, Far West Lab for Educational Resource and Development, San Francisco, CA, 1995.

FairTest: National Center for Fair and Open Testing. "No Child Left Behind After Three Years: An Ongoing Track Record of Failure (FairTest Fact Sheet). <http://www.fairtest.org/facts/NCLB_Year3_Fact.html>.

Falk, B. *The Heart of the Matter: Using Standards and Assessment to Learn*, Portsmouth, NH: Heinemann, 2000.

Ferreiro, E., and A. Teberosky. *Literacy before Schooling.* Exeter, NH: Heinemann, 1982.

Florio-Ruane, S. "Creating Your Own Case Studies: A Guide for Early Field Experience." *Teacher Education Quarterly* 17, 1 (Winter 1990): 29-41.

Fitzgerald, J. "Literacy and Students Who Are Learning English as a Second Language." *The Reading Teacher* 46, 8 (May 1993): 638-645.

Flynn, H. "A Collaborative Model of Service for LEP Students." Master's thesis, Hamline University, 1992.

Flynt, E., and R. Cooter. *Flynt-Cooter Reading Inventory for the Classroom*, 3rd ed. Upper Saddle River, NJ: Merrill, 1998.

Forester, A., and M. Reinhard. *The Learners' Way: Brain-Based Learning in Action*, 2nd edition. Winnipeg, MB: Portage & Main Press, 2000.

Fountas, I., and G. Pinnell. *Guiding Readers and Writers Grades 3-6: Teaching Comprehension, Genre and Content Literacy.* Portsmouth, NH: Heinemann, 2001.

Fradd, S., and W. Tikunoff, (eds). *Bilingual Education and Bilingual Special Education: A Guide for Administrators.* Boston, MA: Little Brown, 1987.

Fradd, S., and J. Weismantel. *Meeting the Needs of Culturally and Linguistically Different Students: A Handbook for Educators.* Boston, MA: Little Brown, 1989.

Freeman, N. "Keeping Assessment Authentic in an Era of High Stakes Testing and Accountability." *Childhood Education* (Association for Childhood Education International) 79 (January 2003): 331-4.

French, R. "Portfolio Assessment and LEP Students." Proceedings of the Second National Research Symposium on Limited English Proficient Student Issues: Focus on Evaluation and Measurement, Office of Bilingual Education and Minority Languages Affairs (OBEMLA), 1992. <http://www.ncela.gwu.edu/pubs/symposia/second/vol1/portfolio.htm>.

Galda, L. et al. *Language, Literacy and the Child.* Fort Worth, TX: Harcourt Brace Jovanovich, 1993.

Gardner, H. *Multiple Intelligences: The Theory in Practice.* New York, NY: Basic Books, 1993.

Genesee, F. *Learning through Two Languages: Studies of Immersion and Bilingual Education.* Cambridge, MA: Newbury House, 1987.

Genishi, C., and A. Dyson. *Language Assessment in the Early Years.* Norwood, NJ: Ablex, 1984.

Gentry, J. "An Analysis of Developmental Spelling in GNYS AT WRK." *The Reading Teacher* 36 (1982): 192-200.

Gibbons, P. *Learning to Learn in a Second Language.* Portsmouth, NH: Heinemann, 1993.

Gomez, M. et al. "Reassessing Portfolio Assessment: Rhetoric and Reality." *Language Arts* 68 (December 1991): 620-628.

Goodman, D. "Evaluation, Reporting, and Grading." In *The Whole Language Catalog Supplement on Authentic Assessment*, K. Goodman, et al. Desoto, TX: SRA Macmillan/McGraw Hill, 1992.

Goodman, K. et al. *The Whole Language Catalog: Supplement on Authentic Assessment.* See Goodman, D.

———. *The Whole Language Evaluation Book.* Portsmouth, NH: Heinemann, 1988.

Goodman, Y., and C. Burke. *The Reading Miscue Inventory.* New York, NY: Macmillan, 1972.

Goodson, I. *School Subjects and Curriculum Change.* Washington, DC: Falmer Press, 1993.

Gould, R. "The Development, Validation and Applicability of 'The Program Evaluation Standards: How to Assess Evaluations of Educational Programs'," report commissioned by the Joint Committee on Standards for Education Evaluation, August 1995 (ERIC# ED403314).

Graves, D., and B. Sunstein, (eds). *Portfolio Portraits.* Portsmouth, NH: Heinemann, 1992.

Gullickson, A. *The Student Evaluation Standards: How to Improve Evaluations of Students*. Thousand Oaks, CA: Corwin, 2003.

Gumperz, J., and D. Hymes, (eds). *The Ethnography of Communication*. Washington, DC: American Anthropological Association, 1964.

Guskey, T. "Defining the Differences Between Outcome-Based Education and Mastery Learning." *The School Administrator* 51, 8 (September 1994): 34-37.

––––––. "Reporting on Student Learning: Lessons from the Past–Prescriptions for the Future." In *Communicating Student Learning: The 1996 ASCD Yearbook*, edited by T. Guskey. Alexandria, VA: Association of Supervision and Curriculum Development.

Hakuta, K., and A. Beatty, (eds). *Testing English Language Learners in U.S. Schools: Report and Workshop Summary*. Washington, DC: National Academy Press, 2000.

Hamayan, E. *The Identification and Assessment of Language Minority Students: A Handbook for Educators*. Arlington Heights, IL: Illinois Resource Center, 1985.

Hamayan, E., and J. Damico, (eds). *Limiting Bias in the Assessment of Bilingual Students*. Austin, TX: Pro-Ed, 1991.

Handscombe, J. "Putting it All Together." In *Educating Second Language Children: The Whole Child, The Whole Curriculum, The Whole Community*, edited by F. Genessee. New York, NY: Cambridge University Press, 1994.

Hargett, G. "Assessment in ESL and Bilingual Education (A Hot Topics Paper)." Northwest Regional Comprehensive Center (NWREL), Region X, August, 1998. <http://www.nwrac.org/pub/hot/assessment.html>.

Harklau, L. et al., (eds). *Generation 1.5 Meets College Composition: Issues in the Teaching of Writing to U.S.-Educated Learners of ESL*. Mahwah, NJ: L. Erlbaum Associates, 1999.

Hayes-Brown, Z. "Linguistic and Communicative Assessment of Bilingual Children." In *Placement Procedures in Bilingual Education*, edited by Charlene Rivera. Clevedon, Avon, England: Multilingual Matters, 1984.

Heath, S. *Ways With Words: Language, Life and Work in Communities and Classrooms*. Cambridgeshire, England: Cambridge University Press, 1983.

Hebert, E. *The Power of Portfolios: What Children Can Teach Us about Learning and Assessment*. San Francisco, CA: Jossey-Bass, 2001.

Hillocks, G. *The Testing Trap: How State Writing Assessments Control Learning*. New York, NY: Teachers College Press, 2002.

Hills, J. "Apathy Concerning Grading and Testing." *Phi Delta Kappan* (March 1991): 540-545.

––––––. *Measurement and Evaluation in the Classroom* 2nd ed. Columbus, OH: Merrill, 1981.

Hymes, D. "The Ethnography of Speaking." In *Anthropology and Human Behavior*, edited by T. Gladwin and W. Sturtevant. Washington, DC: Anthropology Society of Washington, 1965.

Imhoff, G., (ed). *Learning in Two Languages: From Conflict to Consensus in the Reorganization of Schools*. New Brunswick, NJ: Transaction Publishers, 1990.

Irmscher, W. *Teaching Expository Writing.* New York, NY: Holt, Rinehart and Winston, 1979.

Johnson, D., and B. Johnson. *High Stakes: Children, Testing and Failure in American Schools.* Lanham, MD: Rowman & Littlefield, 2002.

Johnston, P. *The Constructive Evaluation of Literate Activity.* White Plains, NY: Longman, 1992.

Jongsma, K. "Questions and Answers: Portfolio Assessment." *The Reading Teacher* (December 1989): 264-265.

Kalantzis, M. et al. *Cultures of Schooling: Pedagogies for Cultural Difference and Social Access.* London, UK: Falmer Press, 1990.

Kane M. "So Much Remains the Same: Conception and Status of Validation in Setting Standards." In *Setting Performance Standards: Concepts, Methods, and Perspectives.* See Brown, W.

Kohn, A. "Beware of the Standards, Not Just the Tests." In *What Does It Mean to Be Well Educated? And More Essays on Standards, Grading, and Other Follies.* Boston, MA: Beacon Press, 2004.

———. "Practical Strategies to Save Our Schools," 2004 (downloaded July 21, 2006). <http://www.alfiekohn.org/standards/strategies.htm>.

———. "Why Students Lose When Tougher Standards Win" (interview). *Educational Leadership* (September 1999). <http://www.alfiekohn.org/articles.htm#null>.

———. "Grading: The Issue Is Not How But Why," In *What to Look for in a Classroom… and Other Essays.* San Francisco, CA: Jossey-Bass, 1998.

Krashen, S., and T. Terrell. *The Natural Approach: Language Acquisition in the Classroom.* San Francisco, CA: Alemany Press, 1983.

Lachat, Mary Ann. "What Policy Makers Need to Know about Assessment Reform for English Language Learners." Washington, DC: Office of Educational Research and Improvement (ED), 1999-2000 (ERIC# ED446137).

Lamme, L., and C. Hysmith. "One School's Adventure into Portfolio Assessment." *Language Arts* 68 (1991): 629-640.

Landerholm, E. "The Transdisciplinary Team Approach in Infant Intervention Programs." *Teaching Exceptional Children* (Winter 1990): 66-70.

Law, B., and M. Eckes. *The More-Than-Just-Surviving Handbook: ESL for Every Classroom Teacher.* Winnipeg, MB: Peguis, 1990.

Leeman, E. "Evaluating Language Assessment Tests: Some Practical Considerations." In *Communication Assessment of the Bilingual Bicultural Child,* edited by J. Good Erickson and D. Omark. Baltimore, MD: University Park Press, 1981.

Leslie, L. *Authentic Literacy Assessment: An Ecological Approach.* New York, NY: Longman, 1997.

Linn, R. *Accountability: Responsibility and Reasonable Expectations,* CSE Report 601. LA, California: National Center for Research on Evaluation, Standards, and Student Testing, Graduate School of Education & Information Studies, University of California, (2003).

Linquanti, R. "The Redesignation Dilemma: Challenges and Choices in Fostering Meaningful Accountability for English Learners" (Policy Report). Santa Barbara, CA: University of California Linguistic Minority Research Institute, 2001.

Loacker, G. et al. "Assessment in Higher Education: To Serve the Learner." In *Assessment in American Higher Education*, edited by C. Adelman. Washington, DC: Office of Educational Research and Improvement, U.S. Department of Education, 1986.

Los Angeles County Office of Education, Division of Curriculum Programs and Instructional Technologies. "Bilingual Education: What Does the Research Really Say?" Los Angeles, CA, 1992.

Maeroff, G. "Assessing Alternative Assessment." *Phi Delta Kappan* (December 1991): 272-281.

Malherbe, E. *The Bilingual School*. Johannesburg, South Africa: Rostra, 1943.

Manning, M., and G. Manning. "How to Assess the Spelling Levels of Young Children." In *The Whole Language Catalog*, K. Goodman et al. Santa Rosa, CA: American School Publishers, 1991.

Mathews, J. "Assessment: From Computer Management to Portfolio Assessment." *The Reading Teacher* (February 1990): 420-421.

McCaslin, M. "The Problem of Problem Representation: The Summit's Conception of Student." *Educational Researcher* 25, 8, (Nov. 1996): 13-15.

Meier, D. (compiled by). *Will Standards Save Public Education?* Boston, MA: Beacon Press, 2000.

Meisels, S. et al. "The Work Sampling System: Reliability and Validity of a Performance Assessment for Young Children." *Early Childhood Research Quarterly* 10, 3 (September 1995): 277-96.

Merina, A. "When Bad Things Happen to Good Ideas." *NEA Today* 12, 3 (October 1993): 4-5.

Meyer, C. "What's the Difference between Authentic and Performance Assessment?" *Educational Leadership* 49, 8 (May 1992): 39-40.

Meyers, M. *Myths and Delusions: The State of ESL in Large Canadian School Boards*. Toronto, ON: MainStreams Publications, 2003.

Michigan State Board of Education. *Michigan English Language Proficiency Standards for K-12 Schools*. Lansing, MI: Michigan Department of Education, April, 2004.

Mitchell, R. *Testing for Learning: How New Approaches to Evaluation Can Improve American Schools*. New York, NY: Free Press, 1992.

Moblo, T. "High Stakes Tests Unfairly Judge Students and Schools," *The Detroit News* (ID: det20761780), Feburary 2, 2006.

Morrow, L., and L. Gambrell. "Literature-Based Reading Instruction." In *Handbook of Reading Research*, Volume 3, edited by M. Kamil et al. Mahwah, NJ: Erlbaum, 2000.

Murphy, S. "Writing Portfolios: Implications for Linguistically Diverse Students." Plenary Address, CaTESOL State Conference, April 5, 1992.

National Council of Teachers of English (NCTE). "On Urging Reconsideration of High Stakes Testing" (Position Statement). Milwaukee, WI: NCTE Annual Business Meeting, 2000, <http://www.ncte.org/about/over/positions/category/assess/107357.htm>.

National Education Association, "Balanced Assessment: The Key to Accountability and Improved Student Learning" (Student Assessment Series). Washington, DC, 2003, <http://www.nea.org/accountability/images/balanced.pdf>.

Navarette, C. et al. "Informal Assessment in Educational Evaluation: Implications for Bilingual Education Programs." Washington, DC: National Clearinghouse for Bilingual Education, 1990.

Neill, D., and N. Medina. "Standardized Testing: Harmful to Educational Health." *Phi Delta Kappan* 70, 9 (May 1989): 688-97.

Neill, M. "Leaving Children Behind: How No Child Left Behind Will Fail Our Children." *Phi Delta Kappan* 85, 3 (Nov. 2003): 225-28.

Neill, M. et al. "Failing Our Children: How 'No Child Left Behind' Undermines Quality and Equity in Education." FairTest: National Center for Fair and Open Testing, 2004, <http://epsl.asu.edu/epru/articles/EPRU-0405-62-OWI.pdf>.

Newbold, B. "The Faceless Mandates of NCLB. In My View." *Kappa Delta Pi Record* 41, 1 (Fall 2004): 7-9.

North York Board of Education, Curriculum and Instructional Services. *Reception, Assessment, Placement and Monitoring of ESL/ESD Students in Secondary Schools.* Toronto, ON, 1994.

Northwest Regional Educational Laboratory (NWREL). "6+1 Trait® Writing Scoring Continuum," <http://www.nwrel.org/assessment/pdfRubrics/6plus1traits.PDF>.

Nuttall, E. "A Critical Look at Testing and Evaluation from a Cross-Cultural Perspective." In *Education of Cultural and Linguistically Different Exceptional Children*, edited by P. Chin. Reston, VA: ERIC Clearinghouse on Handicapped and Gifted Children/Council for Exceptional Children, 1984.

Olson, C. Booth. *The Reading/Writing Connection: Strategies for Teaching and Learning in the Secondary Classroom*, second edition. Boston, MA: Allyn and Bacon, 2007.

———. The Reading/Writing Connection Companion Website, chapter 3, <http://wps.ablongman.com/ab_olson_readwrite_2/0,11768,3060221-,00html>.

Olsen, L. *Crossing the Schoolhouse Border: Immigrant Youth in California Public Schools.* San Francisco, CA: California Tomorrow, 1988.

Omark, D. "Pragmatic and Ethological Techniques for the Observational Assessment of Children's Communicative Abilities." In *Communication Assessment of the Bilingual, Bicultural Child: Issues and Guidelines.* Baltimore, MD: University Park Press, 1981.

O'Neill, T. *Man of the House: The Life and Political Memoirs of Speaker Tip O'Neill.* Boston, MA: G.K. Hall, 1987.

Orfield, G., and M. Kornhaber (eds). *Raising Standards or Raising Barriers? Inequality and High-Stakes Testing in Public Education.* New York, NY: Century Foundation, 2001.

Ornstein, A. "The Politics of Accountability." *The Education Forum* 41 (1976): 61-68.

Paris, S. et al. "The Development of Strategic Readers." In *Handbook of Reading Research*, Volume 2, edited by R. M. Barr, et al. New York, NY: Longman, 1991.

Paulson, L. et al. "What Makes a Portfolio a Portfolio?" *Educational Leadership*, 48, 5 (February 1991): 60-63.

Peña, S. "Identifying and Placing the Limited English Proficient Student." In *Placement of Students in Bilingual Education Programs: Education and Policy Issues*, edited by C. Rivera. Avon, England: Multililingual Matters, 1984.

Perkins, D. *Smart Schools: From Training Memories to Educating Minds*. New York, NY: Free Press, 1992.

Phelps, R. "The Extent and Character of System-Wide Student Testing in the United States." *Educational Assessment*, 4, 2 (1997): 89-121.

Popham, W. "All about Accountability/Swords with Blunt Edges." *Educational Leadership*, 62, 4 (December 2004-January 2005): 86-87.

———. "Trouble with Testing: Why Standards-Based Assessment Doesn't Measure Up." *American School Board Journal* 190, 2 (Feb 2003): 14-17.

———. "Educational Mismeasurement: How High-Stakes Testing Can Harm Our Children (And What We Might Do About It)" (National Education Association, Teaching and Learning Series, 19). Los Angeles, CA: University of California, 2000.

Pugachi, M., and L. Johnson. "The Challenge of Implementing Collaboration between General and Special Education." *Exceptional Children* 56, 3 (1989): 232-35.

Ramirez, A. "Perspectives on Language Proficiency Assessment." In *Children at Risk: Poverty, Minority Status and Other Issues in Educational Equity*. See Baker.

Reid, J. *Teaching ESL Writing*. Englewood Cliffs, NJ: Regents/Prentice Hall, 1993.

Resnick, L., and D. Resnick. "Issues in Designing and Validating Portfolio Assessments. Project 2.3: Complex Performance Assessments: Expanding the Scope and Approaches to Assessment." Washington, DC: Office of Educational Research and Improvement, 1993 (ERIC# ED370967).

Rhoades, K., and G. Madaus. *Errors in Standardized Tests: A Systemic Problem*. Boston, MA: National Board on Educational Testing and Public Policy, Lynch School of Education, Boston College, 2003.

Rhodes, L., and N. Shanklin. *Windows into Literacy: Assessing Learners, K-8*. Portsmouth, NH: Heinemann, 1992.

Rivers and Associates. *Settlement Services for Immigrant Children: A Needs Assessment*. Report prepared for British Columbia Ministry of Education, Victoria, BC: 1991.

Routman, R. *Invitations: Changing as Teachers and Learners*. Portsmouth, NH: Heinemann, 1991.

Samuda, R. et al. *Assessment and Placement of Minority Students*. Toronto, ON: C. J. Hogrefe, 1989.

Scriven, M. unpublished manuscript, 1974, as cited in Davis, B. *Tools for Teaching*. San Francisco, CA: Jossey-Bass, 1993.

Secada, W. "Equity in the Standards Movement." In *Standards: From Policy to Practice*, edited by A. Lockwood. Thousand Oaks, CA: Corwin Press, 1998.

Seeley, M. "The Mismatch Between Assessment and Grading." *Educational Leadership* 52, 2 (Oct 1994): 4-6.

Shore, A. et al. "Guidelines for Policy Research on Educational Testing." NBETPP Statements 1, 4 (April 2000), <http://www.bc.edu/research/nbetpp/publications/v1n4.html>.

Shuy, R., and R. Fasold (eds). "Language Attitudes: Current Trends and Prospects." Washington, DC: School of Languages and Linguistics, Georgetown University, 1973.

Smith, F. *The Book of Learning and Forgetting*. New York, NY: Teachers College Press, 1998.

———. *Joining the Literacy Club: Further Essays into Education*. Portsmouth, NH: Heinemann, 1988.

Solomon, P. *The Assessment Bridge: Positive Ways to Link Tests to Learning, Standards and Curriculum Improvement*. Thousand Oaks, CA: Corwin, 2002.

Spady, W. "Organizing for Results: The Basis of Authentic Restructuring and Reform." *Educational Leadership* 46, 2 (Oct. 1988): 4-8.

Spady, W., and Marshall, K. "Beyond Traditional Outcome-Based Education." *Educational Leadership* 49, 2 (Oct. 1991): 67-72.

———. "Light, Not Heat, on OBE." *The American School Board Journal* 181, 11 (November 1994): 29-33.

Stahl, S. et al. "Learning Meaning Vocabulary through Listening: A Sixth-Grade Replication." In *Learner Factors/Teacher Factors: Issues in Literacy Research and Instruction: Fortieth Yearbook of the National Reading Conference*, edited by J. Zutell and S. McCormick. Chicago, IL: National Reading Conference, 1991.

Stayter, F., and P. Johnston. "Evaluating the Teaching and Learning of Literacy." In *Reading and Writing Together: New Perspectives for the Classroom*, edited by T. Shanahan. Norwood, MA: Christopher-Gordon, 1990.

Stiggins, R. "Assessment Literacy." *Phi Delta Kappan* 72, 7 (March 1991): 534-539.

Strickland, B., and A. Turnbull. *Developing and Implementing Individualized Education Programs*. Columbus, OH: Merrill Publishing, 1990.

Tannenbaum, J. "Practical Ideas on Alternative Assessment for ESL Students" (ERIC publication). Washington, DC: ERIC/CLL, 1996.

Teachers of English to Speakers of Other Languages, Inc (TESOL). *ESL Standards for Pre-K-12 Students*. Alexandria, VA: TESOL, 1997.

Teale, W. "Emergent Literacy: Reading and Writing Development in Early Childhood." In *Research in Literacy: Merging Perspectives. Thirty-Sixth Yearbook of the National Reading Conference*, edited by J. Readence and R. Baldwin. Rochester, NY: National Reading Conference, 1987.

Teale, W., and E. Sulzby (eds). *Emergent Literacy: Writing and Reading*. Norwood, NJ: Ablex, 1986.

Tierney, R. et al. *Portfolio Assessment in the Reading-Writing Classroom.* Norwood, MA: Christopher-Gordon, 1991.

Tucker, M. and J. Codding. *Standards for Our Schools: How to Set Them, Measure Them and Reach Them.* San Francisco, CA: Jossey-Bass, 1998.

Turbill, J., and B. Cambourne. *The Changing Face of Whole Language.* Newark, DE: International Reading Association, 1998.

Ulibarri, D. "Use of Achievement Tests with Non-Native-English-Speaking Language Minority Students." In *Children at Risk: Poverty, Minority Status and Other Issues in Educational Equity.* See Baker.

Underhill, N. *Testing Spoken Language: A Handbook of Oral Testing Techniques.* Cambridge, UK: Cambridge University Press, 1987.

United States Department of Education. "Alternate Achievement Standards for Students with the Most Significant Cognitive Disabilities; Non-Regulatory Guidance (No Child Left Behind)," August 2005. United States Department of Education, <http://www.ed.gov/policy/elsec/guid/altguidance.pdf>.

———. "Standards and Assessment: Non-Regulatory Guidance (No Child Left Behind)," March 2003. United States Department of Education, <http://www.ed.gov/policy/elsec/guid/saaguidance03.doc>.

———. *The No Child Left Behind Act of 2001* (Public Law 107–110, January 8, 2002, 115 Stat. 1425). Title IX–General Provisions, Part A–Definitions, Section 9101 (25).

———. *The Seven Priorities of the U.S. Department of Education,* July 1997. United States Department of Education, <http://www.ed.gov/updates/7priorities/index.html>.

———. *H.R.6: Improving America's Schools Act [IASA] of 1994.* United States Department of Education, <http://www.ed.gov/legislation/ESEA/toc.html>.

Valencia, S. "Assessment: Portfolio Assessment for Young Readers." *The Reading Teacher* 44, 9 (May 1991): 680-681.

———. "A Portfolio Approach to Classroom Reading Assessment: The Whys, Whats and Hows." *The Reading Teacher* 43 (January 1990): 338-340.

Valentin, T. "English as a Second Language: Get Ready for the Onslaught." *NASSP Bulletin* 76 (January 1993): 30-38.

Van Allen, R. *The Language-Experience Approach to Reading Instruction.* London, UK: Ginn, 1961.

Ventriglia, L. *Conversations of Miguel and Maria: How Children Learn English as a Second Language: Implications for Classroom Teaching.* Reading, MA: Addison-Wesley, 1982.

Weaver, C. *Reading Process and Practice: From Socio-Psycholinguistics to Whole Language.* Portsmouth NH: Heinemann, 1994.

Western States Benchmarking Consortium. "No Child Left Behind. Applying Tests of Common Sense (Critical Strategic Issues and a Recommendation)." March 15, 2004, <http://www.wsbenchmark.org/NCLB_position_paper.pdf>.

Wiener, Jocelyn, and Kim Minaugh. "Failing Districts Don't Add Up." *Sacramento Bee,* March 12, 2005, page A3, CA final edition.

Wiggins, G. "A True Test: Toward Authentic and Equitable Forms of Assessment." *Phi Delta Kappan* 70, 9 (1989): 703-713.

Winograd, P. et al. "Improving the Assessment of Literacy." *Reading Teacher* 45, 2 (October 1991): 108-16.

Wisconsin Department of Public Instruction (DPI). "A Parent's Guide to Standards and Assessment: An Overview for Parents of Wisconsin's Model Academic Standards and the Wisconsin Student Assessment System." <http://dpi.wi.gov/oea/pdf/testing. pdf#search=%22%22A%20Parent%E2%80%99s%20Guide%20to%20Standards %20and%20Assessment%20An%20Overview%20for%20Parents%20of%20 Wisconsin%E2%80%99s%20Model%20Academic%20Standards%22>.

Wisconsin State Reading Association. *Position Statement.* Madison, WI: 1990.

Wolf, D. et al. "To Use Their Minds Well: Investigating New Forms of Student Assessment." In *Review of Research in Education,* edited by G. Grant. Washington, DC: American Educational Research Association, 1991.

Wong F. "A Question for Early-Childhood Programs: English First or Families First?" *Education Week,* 10 (June 19, 1991): 32-34.

WorldNetDaily. "Letter Report Cards Dumped in Florida." May 11, 2005 (downloaded December 8, 2006). <http://www.worldnetdaily.com/news/article.asp?ARTICLE_ ID=44202>.

Worthen, B. "Critical Issues That Will Determine the Future of Alternative Assessment." *Phi Delta Kappan* 74, 6 (February 1993): 444-454.

———. "Is Your School Ready for Alternative Assessment?" *Phi Delta Kappan* 74, 6 (February 1993): 455-456.

Zanger, V. "Social and Cultural Dimensions of the Education of Language Minority Students." In *Bilingual Education and English as a Second Language: A Research Handbook,* edited by A. Ambert. New York, NY: Garland, 1991.

Zirkel, P. "A Method for Determining and Depicting Language Dominance." Paper presented at TESOL 1973, (ERIC# 234845), 1973.

INDEX

H

Hakuta and Beatty (2001), 24-25
Hamayan (1985), 147
Handscombe (1989), 61
Hargett (1998), 185
Harklau (1999), 263
Heath (1983), 83
Hebert (2001), 28, 34, 219, 226, 227, 228
Hillocks (2002), 29
Hills (1991), 202
Hinton, S.E., 195
Hymes, Dell (1965), 81

I

Idea Proficiency Test, 75
Infinitive. *See* Grammar
Information, stakeholders, 218-44
    compiling, 218-22
    objectives, 218
    presenting, 222
International Reading Association, 264
Interpreters, 44
IPT. *See* Idea Proficiency Test
IRA. *See* International Reading Association
Irmscher (1978), 205

J

Johnson and Johnson (2002), 23
Johnston (1992), 123,131, 159, 175
Journals, 141-42, 145-46

K

Kane (1994), 24
Kohn (1999), 35
Kohn (2001), 251
Kohn (2004), 258
Krashen and Terrell (1983), 85

L

Lachat (1999), 41
Language Assessment Scale, 62, 73
Language Assessment Survey, 33

Language Experience Approach, The, 144
Language Measurement and Assessment
    Instrument, 33
Language proficiency. *See* Oral proficiency
Language, interim, 111
LEA. *See* the Language Experience Approach
Learning
    continuum, 5, 38, 85-89
    facilitating, 2, 4-5. *See also* Student
LEP. *See* Limited-English Proficient
Limited-English Proficient, 23, 33, 43, 45, 188
    definition, 45-46
Linquanti (2001), 183
Listening proficiency, 87
Literacy
    assessing, 54-60, 80-81, 116-56
    context, 81-85
    copying, 92
    definition, 87-88
    drawing, 90
    emerging, 79-113
    home and, 54-56, 88-89
    home survey, 48-50, 54
    levels of development (reading), 98-110
    levels of development (writing), 89-98
    non-literacy, 54
    pre-literacy, 54
    print awareness, 63-66
    scribbling, 90
    spelling, invented, 93-98
    See also Grammar; Oral proficiency;
    Spelling; Talking
Little Red Riding Hood, 108-09
Logs. *See* Quad
Lon Po Po, 108-09

M

Manning and Manning (1992), 66, 68, 89, 91
McCaslin (1996), 249
Meier (2000), 249
Meisels *et al.* (1995), 6
Metacognition, 120, 131-32
Metatextual awareness, 124
Meyers (2003), 263

W